Charles Edward de Boos

A 'somewhat motley' life

Peter Crabb

First published by Busybird Publishing 2022

Copyright © 2022 Peter Crabb

ISBN
Print: 978-1-922691-73-6
Ebook: 978-1-922691-74-3

This work is copyright. Apart from any use permitted under the Copyright Act 1968, no part of this publication may be reproduced, stored in a retrieval system or transmitted in any form or by any means, electronic, mechanical, photocopying, recording or otherwise, without the prior written permission of Peter Crabb.

The information in this book is based on the author's experiences and opinions. The author and publisher disclaim responsibility for any adverse consequences, which may result from use of the information contained herein. Permission to use any external content has been sought by the author. Any breaches will be rectified in further editions of the book.

Cover Image: A most treasured possession. The front cover is a photograph of one side of the gold medal presented to Charles de Boos by the Chinese communities of the Braidwood district in March 1881. See Chapter 10. The reverse side of the medal is shown on the back cover.

Cover design: Busybird Publishing

Layout and typesetting: Busybird Publishing

Busybird Publishing
2/118 Para Road
Montmorency, Victoria
Australia 3094
www.busybird.com.au

*For Marilyn and her late sister Shirley,
great, great grand-daughters of Charles de Boos*

The Author

Dr Peter Crabb is an Honorary Senior Lecturer in the Fenner School of Environment and Society at The Australian National University, Canberra. He has taught at universities in Australia, Canada, and England, and has published extensively in the field of natural resource and environmental management. His focus has been on water resources in inter-jurisdictional river basins, especially the Murray-Darling Basin. Writing this biography has been a very different undertaking, taking him into new fields of study, especially the histories of the nineteenth century goldfields in Colonial New South Wales and Victoria and the work of the contemporary newspaper reporters. de Boos is an outstanding example of such people, but he was not alone, as indicated by published research on two others, Frederick Dalton and John Hux. And there is a link to the author's prime interest in environmental matters in the frequent reporting by de Boos of the damage done to land and water resources by gold mining and land clearing.

Table of Contents

Acknowledgements — 1

Introduction — 3

Chapter One — 4
Normandy and the early de Boos

Chapter Two — 18
The Huguenot Diaspora and the London Huguenots

Chapter Three — 26
The London de Boos: a fortunate Family

Chapter Four — 38
Leaving Home: School and the Carlist Wars

Chapter Five — 46
Early Years in Australia, 1839-1850: Sydney, the Hunter Valley, a Family

Chapter Six — 60
Melbourne, 1850-1856: Newspaper Reporter and Colonial Government Official

Chapter Seven — 88
A Reporter for *The Sydney Morning Herald*, 1856-1872

Chapter Eight — 132
Life and Family in Sydney, 1856-1875

Chapter Nine
An Official of the New South Wales Colonial Government, 1875-1889
144

Chapter Ten
The Temora Incidents: Setting the record straight
178

Chapter Eleven
His Family and Retirement
198

Chapter Twelve
The Writings of Charles de Boos
212

Chapter Thirteen
A Special Publication: Fifty Years Ago: an Australian tale
232

Chapter Fourteen
Charles de Boos the Writer
256

Chapter Fifteen
Charles de Boos
264

Appendices
269

References
301

Acknowledgements

This story of Charles de Boos comes with a warning: be very careful about succumbing to flattery! Quite some years ago, my wife Marilyn and her late sister, Shirley, were talking about their great-great-grandfather. Shirley had done some research in pre-internet and pre-digitisation days, but little was known about him. Then, out of the blue, Marilyn said to me: "You've done a lot of research. You're good at it. Why don't you do some family history?" I can't remember my reply, but being occupied with other ongoing research, I was barely even half-interested! A few more prods later, and I made a start on investigating the story of Charles de Boos. I was soon hooked.

A little later, Marilyn and I had a conversation over coffees at the National Library of Australia in Canberra with Victor Crittenden, who had done much to revive the fiction writings of de Boos through his Mulini Press.[1] He asked a subsequently much appreciated question: "Why don't you go beyond family history and write a biography?" Since that afternoon, Charles de Boos has, in one way or another, been an almost ever-present companion. It has been a journey of discovery. In this account, there is much that is new and myths have been put to rest. Hopefully, it will contribute to an important early Australian writer being given the recognition he deserves.

Other activities have meant that writing this biography has been spread over more than a decade. In that time, I have been helped by many people. I am grateful to every one of you. Some are mentioned at particular points in the text; others are too numerous to mention. As with much other recent research, this study could not have been done without the help of the National Library of Australia's 'Trove' website. It has made possible access to vast 'warehouses' of materials, real 'treasure troves'. In the early days of my research, I was given exceptional help by the staff in the Library's 'Newspapers and Family History' section. I can't name every staff member, but I must mention Colleen and Tessa. Those who use the National Library know that it and its staff are a 'National Treasure'. It is unfortunate that those who should be providing the Library with adequate funding continue to not do so.

---

1 - Clayton 2015.

Next to 'Trove', finding the Centre for Literary and Linguistic Computing at the University of Newcastle was good fortune beyond belief. Not only did Professor Hugh Craig make the Centre's facilities available to me, he enabled Dr Alexis Antonia to undertake considerable research on my behalf. Important parts of de Boos' story could not have been told without Lexie's work. I could not have had a better colleague and collaborator. Some of our initial work resulted in the serendipitous connection with Brendan Dalton, who was undertaking research on his ancestor, Frederick Dalton. The connection was a fruitful one for all of us.

My former colleague at the Fenner School of Environment and Society, The Australian National University, Clive Hilliker, very kindly provided the maps.

Finally, members of my family deserve a big thank you for their help and interest, especially my wife Marilyn and our daughter Ruth.

I would have liked to have been able to visit more of the places with which de Boos and his ancestors were associated: Le Pays de Caux in France, the Spitalfields district of London, the Fitzroy, the Oban and other diggings in New South Wales, and especially Milparinka. Resources of one kind and another did not permit, and then when it might have been possible, along came COVID-19 and its many travel restrictions. I would have liked to have found some de Boos family papers, but likely sources passed on just before and after my research commenced. There are many inadequacies, but this book is without doubt the most comprehensive account of the life and work of Charles de Boos to have been compiled to this point in time.

Peter Crabb,
Canberra,
Autumn, 2022.

Introduction

No person's story can be divorced from the stories of other people, family members, friends, and others, the people they associated with. It cannot be divorced from the places in which the person lived and visited. It cannot be divorced from the times in which they lived, and the times which led up to them and through which their ancestors lived. Every person's story must be set in context, in the geographies and histories that are integral parts of their story.[2]

Writing biography is no easy task. Historians "can never be in that moment they study".[3] Further, biographies are limited by the available sources; to go beyond these, is to engage in speculation and perhaps even to write fiction.[4] The sources, the records of the time in which the subject lived, must be granted primacy. But these can be very limited, and they can be conflicting. At the same time, however, "Biography is an act of re-creation".[5] Griffiths has noted that "writing history is a highly creative act and that its artistic aspirations are perfectly consistent with the quest to represent the past truthfully".[6] We have "to respect the alterity of the past, to be aware that hindsight brings with it distinct dangers, in leading us to fail to understand how the world appeared to people in the past".[7]

A "not-so-ordinary individual"[8]

Charles de Boos was certainly no "ordinary individual". Relatively early in his life, in the middle of an account of some of the people he had mixed with whilst a member of the British Auxiliary Legion fighting in the Carlist wars in Spain, he wrote of having lived "a somewhat motley existence".[9] The phrase could be applied to his whole life, but it would be a gross understatement for what was a remarkable, complex, multi-faceted, and interwoven life. He lived through and participated in important periods in the history of Europe and even more so that of Australia. It was a life lived to the full, in all the locations in which parts of it were spent.

---

2 - Lee 2009, 104; Meister 2018; Renders, de Haan and Harmsma 2017; Allbrook and Nolan 2018.
3 - Brodie 2015, xi.
4 - Curthoys and Docker 2006.
5 - Marr 2016.
6 - Griffiths 2016, 2; Stanley 2014.
7 - Curthoys and Docker, 2006, 140.
8 - Curthoys and McGrath 2009, 187.
9 - His own words, *The Argus*, May 8, 1852, page 4.

Chapter One

Normandy and the early de Boos

We know that the ancestors of Charles de Boos lived in a number of places in Upper Normandy in northern France, but to put even an approximate date on their origins is much more difficult. For one thing, it was not until the mid-16th century that there was any requirement in France for the recording of births, marriages and deaths.[1] Further, most of the records from this time have been lost. So, it is unlikely that it will ever be possible to find 'a first ancestor'. And what of the name? Some family histories speculate that it originated from the town of Boos, south-east of Rouen, in the late 14th century. This would explain the presence of the particle 'de', rather than the suggested association with upper-class nobility.[2] In the 16th and early 17th centuries, there are records that show numerous people named de Boos concentrated in the nearby small settlement of Criquebeuf-sur-Seine, just south of Rouen.[3] This was the birthplace of the earliest de Boos that has been found, namely Guillot, born about 1530; he had a large number of descendants.[4] Other de Boos were present in Boos and nearby settlements.

Boos, Criquebeuf-sur-Seine and these other nearby places are located on the flood plain of the lower Seine. From five to ten kilometres wide and essentially to the south of the river, it is marked by several very large, incised meanders before it reaches its estuary that extends from Tancarville to Le Havre (Figure 1.1).[5] It has long been an area of mixed farming and small villages. Very early on, the production of textiles was part of the peasants' self-sufficiency activities, initially with wool from their own sheep, and from the late-14th century, from hemp.[6] Flax, grown particularly on the

---

1 - In 1539, baptismal registers were required to include birth date; from 1563, godparents' names were to be recorded; and from 1579, marriage and death records were required.

2 - familytreemaker.genealogy.com/users/m/o/o/Robin-Moore/GENE1-0003.html , accessed July 19, 2014; gepatronyme.com/cdip/originenom/particules.htm, accessed July 27, 2014. There is no de Boos in a list of 'The Protestant Nobility in Normandy (XVIIth century)', http://huguenots.free.fr/france/normandie/caux/nobles.htm , accessed July 27, 2013.

3 - http://en.geneanet.org/search/ame=DEBOOS&country , accessed July 20, 2014.

4 - http://gw.geneanet.org/francosmont?lang=en&p=guillot&n=deboos , accessed July 26, 2014.

5 - Frémont 1977, 75-85; Ormsby 1950, 142-149; Vidal de la Blache 1903.

6 - Bois 1984, 196.

flood plain of the Seine due to the need for water for retting, provided the raw material for spinning and weaving linen cloth, as around Boos.[7] In the late 15th century, cloth manufacture developed quickly in the rural areas, especially around Rouen.[8]

The other significant concentration of people named de Boos was in a small part of Le Pays de Caux, north-west of Rouen. Le Pays de Caux is an extensive gently undulating chalk plateau, with an altitude of between 100 to 200 metres.[9] It is drained by numerous north and south-flowing streams, most of them deeply incised into the plateau.[10] To the north and west, the plateau is bounded by the cliffs of the Côte d'Albâtre and La Manche (the English Channel), by the River Béthune and the Pays de Bray to the east, and to the south by the valley of the lower Seine.[11]

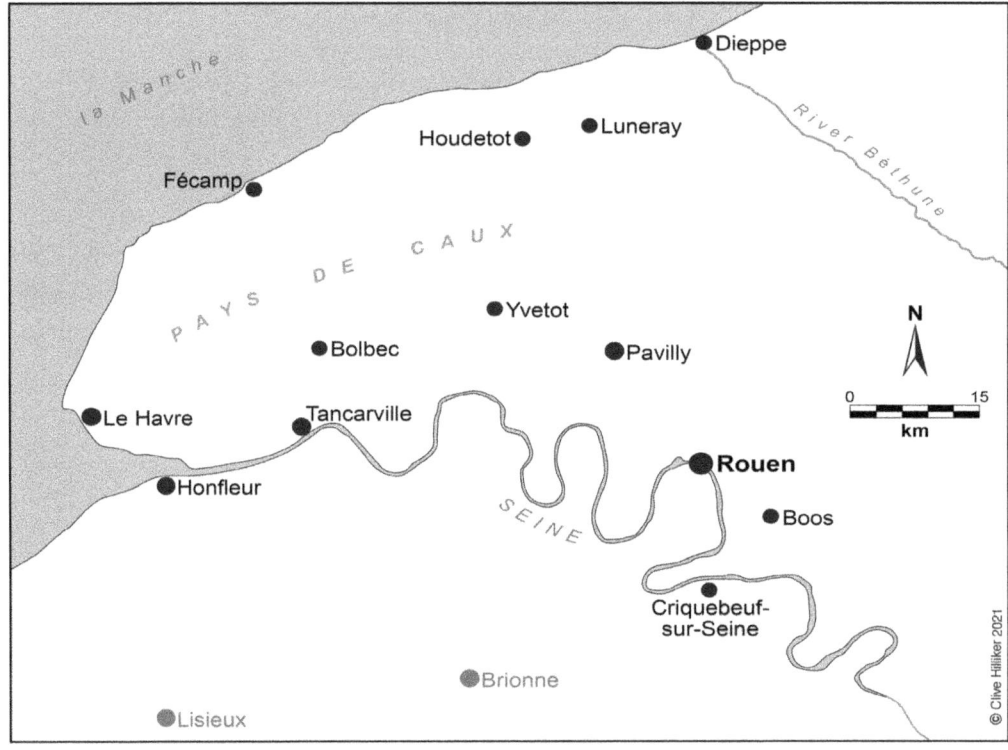

Figure 1.1. *Some of the major and other locations in Upper Normandy and Le Pays de Caux.*

---

7 - Bois 1984, 110. Today, Boos is a farming centre and light industrial town, with about a quarter of the commune occupied by Rouen Airport. https://fr.wikipedia.org/wiki/Boos_(Seine-Maritime).

8 - Bois 1984, 115.

9 - 'Le Pays de Caux', *Atlas des Paysages de Haute-Normandie*. www.atlaspaysages.hautenormandie.fr/ ; Braudel 1988, 49.

10 - 'Les Petites Vallées Affluentes de la Seine', *Atlas des Paysages de Haute-Normandie*. www.atlaspaysages.hautenormandie.fr/ .

11 - Frémont 1977, 118-125; Evans 1959.

The rich soils are the basis of the plateau's arable farming. Dating back to around the 10th century, the land was farmed under a feudal system. The peasants occupied barely self-sufficient small holdings and were subject to unbearable taxation by the lords.[12] As in much of Western Europe, feudalism began to slowly break down in Le Caux from early in the 14th century. By the 17th century, small scale commercial and largely self-sufficient farming had emerged. Interspersed in the arable landscape were small groups of trees, remnants of former forests, and rows of trees and tall hedges.[13] These provided windbreaks that gave protection for the crops and farmsteads from the frequent westerly winds.[14] The farmsteads, with their windbreaks, out-buildings and orchards, known as 'les clos-masures', are still the most characteristic feature of Le Pays de Caux (Figure 1.2). Small villages on the plateau were little more than close groupings of several 'clos-masures'.

Figure 1.2. 'Un clos-masure'. With farming methods constantly changing, farms getting larger, and their numbers declining, the historical significance and unique heritage value of 'les clos-masures' have been recognised with their proposed UNESCO heritage listing. An important step was taken in May 2021 with the completion of a report to government and an inventory of the more than 10,000 properties. Source: Armand 2017; Renout 2018; Normand 2021.

Most of the larger settlements were on the floors of the incised river valleys, where there was sufficient water for domestic use and for early industrial activities. From the late 13th century, numerous grain mills powered by waterwheels were present along the rivers of Le Pays de Caux, associated with small market towns, such as Bolbec and nearby Gruchet-le-Vallasse.[15] On the plateau itself, limited water supplies were an on-going handicap for agriculture and any larger population numbers.

---

12 - Frémont 1981; Frémont 1977, 118-125; Bois 1984, 175.

13 - Bois 1984, 159-164.

14 - Vernon 2014.

15 - Bois 1984, 230-234.

During the 14th and 15th centuries, and again in the 16th, there were some terrible and tragic periods in Le Pays de Caux and nearby areas. Catastrophic crop failures caused soaring grain prices and reduced per capita food supplies resulted in famine and starvation. There were also outbreaks of plague. These and other issues fueled social disorder, further disrupting what economic activity persisted.[16] Such periods of economic and social unrest at times resulted in significant movements of people, as when people from Criquebeuf-sur-Seine, Boos, and nearby places moved to parts of Le Pays de Caux. Taking their skills with them, they contributed to the developing textile industries, especially to the market towns in the valleys as well as to smaller places on the plateau. Initially, they were peasant or 'cottage' industries.[17] As the textile industries grew, the small settlements located in the valleys changed from market towns to industrial ones. The developing industries provided work for the rural poor, and even though wages were low, they were higher than for rural work. At the same time, they were lower than in urban areas, making the locations attractive to the manufacturers. The swift flowing streams coming off the plateau turned countless water wheels that powered the textile and paper mills (some converted grain mills) at such places as Clères, Pavilly, Bolbec (Figure 1.3), Gruchet-le-Vallase, St. Romain, and Montivilliers, and lower down the valleys at Duclair, Caudebec, and Lillebonne, near their confluences with the Seine.[18]

Figure 1.3. *18th century Bolbec, located in the narrow valley of the river of the same name, with the wooded valley sides and the plateau of the Pays de Caux; a clos-masures can be seen in the bottom of the illustration. Source: from L'Atlas de Trudaine, 1745-1780, in 'Les Petites Vallées Affluentes de la Seine', Atlas des Paysages de Haute-Normandie. Agence Folléa-Gautier, Montrouge, 2010. Page 190. www.atlaspaysages.hautenormandie.fr/ .*

---

16 - Bois 1984, vii, 165, 308-309, 338-339; Waddington 1862.

17 - Corvisier 1974.

18 - Ormsby 1950, 145.

Among those who moved were people with the name de Boos, almost certainly including the original ancestors of Charles. They were to be found in places just to the north of Lillebonne, including Saint-Antoine-la-Forêt, Saint-Nicholas-de-la-Taille, Gruchet-le-Vallasse, Bolbec, and Lintot (Figure 1.4).

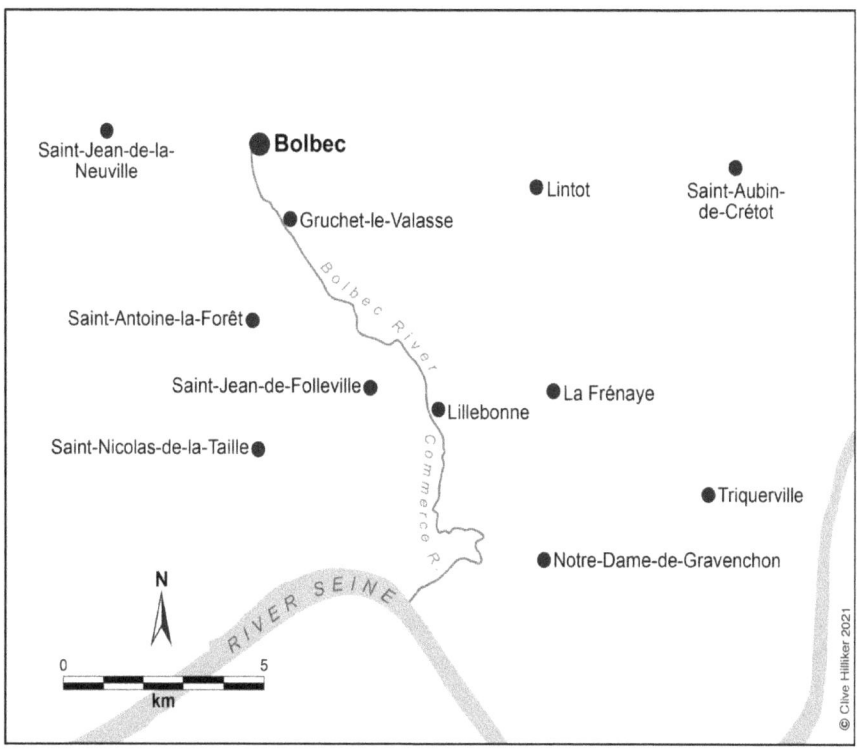

Figure 1.4. *Places in Le Pays de Caux associated with the ancestors of Charles de Boos, along with Boos and Criquebeuf-sur-Seine which are shown in Figure 1.1.*

The Reformation

Without wanting to downplay earlier periods of horrendous disruption, other far more significant changes took place from the early decades of the 16th century, in Normandy, across France, and in neighbouring countries. This was The Reformation.[19] As throughout Europe, the Catholic Church held a dominant position in the government, life and society of France, but this did not prevent the establishment of Protestantism, largely under

---
19 - Mentzer and Van Ruymbeke 2016.

the influence of Martin Luther, Huldrich Zwingli, Jacques le Fevre, and especially John Calvin (1509-1564), a native of Picardy. The first French translation of the Bible was made in 1523. Protestantism (or Calvinism) appealed to people "in crowded cities where employment failed to match the needs of a rising population and the expectations of skilled workers … [in places such as] Senlis, Orléans, Rouen and Tours. 'It was not solely against doctrinal corruptions and against ecclesiastical abuses but also against misery and iniquity that the lower classes rebelled', wrote Hauser. 'They sought in the Bible not only for the doctrine of salvation by grace but for proofs of the primitive equality of all men'".[20] But all classes of people became Protestants, in cities and rural areas. Through the early and mid-16th century, numbers grew and spread throughout France. By around 1570, the number of Huguenots (as the French Protestants had become known[21]) reached a high of some 1.8 million, about 10 percent of the French population, with some 1,200 churches.[22]

Normandy was one of the parts of France where Protestantism was favourably received, in both urban and rural areas. As early as 1536, Geoffrin Decoudray was preaching the 'new ideas' in Luneray and Bacqueville.[23] In 1559, the travelling preacher, Jean Venable, visited Dieppe, Le Havre and Rouen.[24] He distributed French-language versions of the Scriptures and is credited with starting a number of Protestant churches.

> With some 70,000 inhabitants, open to the trafficking of foreign seamen and merchants, Rouen was early exposed to Protestant ideas. It was also an administrative centre, the seat of a parlement [a local or regional parliament] and an archdiocese. From sophisticated parlementaires and experienced merchants at the summit, down through a range of bourgeois and artisans to the cloth workers and the casual labour of the docks, Rouen proved to have zealous converts in all classes. … Moreover, Rouen's influence across the province, along with the free intermingling of traders and seamen in the ports of Le Havre, Dieppe and others, ensured that Protestantism would gain a foothold there.[25]

---

20 - Treasure 2013, 107; Hauser 1899.

21 - Davies and Davies 2000, Chapter 4. The name 'Huguenot' seems to have originated in Geneva about 1532 and first used in France about 1550. Originally, it may have been a derogatory term; subsequently it has been used with pride. For an outline etymology, see https://en.wikipedia.org/wiki/Huguenots , accessed April 12, 2021.

22 - Van Ruymbeke and Sparks 2003; Mentzer and Spicer 2002.

23 - Nash 2007.

24 - Madelaine 1906, pages 29-32.

25 - Treasure 2013, 108.

By 1565, there were some 16,000 Protestants in Rouen, over a fifth of its population,[26] and some 12,000 in Dieppe.[27] The situation was similar in the nearby recently industrialised small towns. The tight-knit craft and artisan groups were other contributory factors. Venable also visited the small towns in Le Pays de Caux, including Luneray, Caudebec, Fécamp, Montivilliers, Lillebonne and Bolbec. By 1660-1670, the Synod of Normandy embraced 43 temples and a Protestant population of 42,200, including 18,800 in the rural areas.[28] The largest congregations were in Rouen, Le Havre and Dieppe.[29] The Temple of Lintot, established in 1578, was probably the largest rural one. It was the religious and spiritual centre for large numbers of people from much of Le Pays de Caux, with over 3,000 communicants; it must have been a substantial structure.[30]

The Wars of Religion

For France, an almost entirely Catholic country, the significance of the Protestant population was much greater than its size would suggest. Though never more than a small minority, the Protestants were not welcome. They were seen as a challenge to the all-powerful Catholic Church and the royal rulers. They were subject to increasing persecution. The writings of Luther and Calvin were banned, as was the French-language version of the Bible. The Massacre at Vassy, in Lower Normandy, in 1562 was the first of the 'Wars of Religion' that bitterly divided the French people for some 200 years.[31] The start of the wars exacerbated the on-going unsettled conditions dating from the late 15th century, causing significant migrations of people within France, especially Protestants, including those who moved from the valley of the Seine to Le Pays de Caux.

The peace agreement of Saint-Germain in 1569 was short-lived, and divisions between the Catholics and Protestants soon escalated. They culminated in the St. Bartholomew Day massacre in Paris on August 24, 1572, when some 3,000 Protestants were killed. As the news spread, an estimated 10,000 Protestants were killed in numerous provincial cities and rural areas.[32] In addition, large numbers were imprisoned, their homes

---

26 - Meuvret 1965; Treasure 2013, 150; Benedict 1975.
27 - Nash 2007.
28 - Benedict 1991; Madelaine 1906.
29 - http://temples.free.fr/ , accessed July 26, 2014; Madelaine 1906, 111, 157-158, 349-356, 359- 379; "Bolbec: les temples", http://temples.free.fr/temples/Bolbec.htm ; Nash 2007.
30 - http://huguenotsinfo.free.fr/temples/XVII/temples_17/Lintot17.htm , accessed July 26, 2014.
31 - Holt 1995.
32 - Benedict 1978, 1985; Gwynn 2011, 17-20.

and businesses destroyed. The Edict of Nantes, promulgated in Nantes in Brittany, on April 13, 1598, was an effort to stem the violence, its religious, civil, judicial, and military clauses giving some protection to the Huguenots.[33] But it was not an easy peace and proved to be only a temporary respite from persecution.

Later, the persecutions resumed, culminating in the Revocation of the Edict of Nantes in 1685 which, along with other actions, totally banned all Protestant worship. At the time, there were an estimated 800,000 to 1,000,000 Protestants in France.[34] People were killed, imprisoned; men put as galley slaves; women had their heads shaved and were imprisoned; churches, businesses, homes and French-language Bibles burned; and emigration made illegal. For close to a century, it was a period of horrors.

Normandy did not escape the persecutions. One of the most murderous of the provincial massacres was in Rouen on September 17-20, 1572.[35] The personal attacks were ferocious; hundreds of people lost their lives. There was much property damage.[36] "Rouen had had the largest reformed community in France: 16,000 before the massacres; barely 3,000 avowed Huguenots after".[37] The city was deprived of an important part of its middle and trading classes, and along with many of the nearby towns, large numbers of artisan dyers and weavers. The violence was not confined to the cities, but also affected such places as Bolbec, Luneray, Caudebec, Fécamp and Montivilliers, where most of the industry and commerce were in the hands of Protestants.[38]

From Normandy and other parts of France, tens of thousands left their homeland. Most, however, remained, "struggling to survive, in their native land, resisters of two kinds: the bold, even desperate, resorting to arms; the passive majority, more cautious, not necessarily less courageous".[39] The people were held together by their religious faith, their extended families, and their work, both farming and textile manufacturing.[40] Many converted to Catholicism, more for survival than anything else. Some moved to other

---

33 - Van Ruymbeke 2003, 3; Coertzen 2013; Sutherland 1987.
34 - Mentzer and Spicer 2002, 224.
35 - Benedict 2004.
36 - Mollat 1979, 184-188.
37 - Treasure 2013, 174; Waddington 1862, 19, 72-75.
38 - Madelaine 1906, 206.
39 - Treasure 2013, 376.
40 - Bost 1984, 2-4, 227-282.

parts of the country. Still others hid their Protestantism and maintained their faith in secret. It was the period of 'The Church of the Desert'.[41]

Protestantism survived

Yet, in spite of everything, Protestantism survived. Bolbec, a long-established market town which, by the 1600s, had become an important textile producing centre, provides an illustration of its survival.

> *It was in the shadow of these woods[42] or at the bottom of some of the quarries that the Huguenots of Le Pays de Caux practiced their religion and retained the constitution of their Church, carefully avoiding compromising with their neighbours and always behaving with the calm strength and cold wisdom which are one of the distinctive features of the Norman temperament. The quarries of the abbey of Valasse, a short distance from Bolbec, often sheltered many groups gathered to hear some preacher from the 'Désert', who came to visit his scattered flock and celebrate holy communion with them.[43]*

In 1852, in *La Normandie illustrée*, Amélie Bosquet described Bolbec as "the masterpiece of Protestantism. This little corner of land, all industry and manufacturing", a revival that was in large measure due to the Protestants.[44]

> *Bolbec was then the main protestant centre of Normandy; its location in a narrow valley with difficult access, its distance from the large towns, the woods which covered the surrounding countryside and which made it easier for religious groups, all of which contributed to the maintenance of a protestant population after the revocation of the Edict of Nantes. The head for business, the interest in industry which seemed almost to have been hereditary in the protestant families of Normandy, were safeguarded in Bolbec and continued to develop there, and so already by their work, their thrift and their integrity, the protestants of the area laid down the foundations of the great industrial fortune which have since made Bolbec one of the richest towns in the Lower Seine department.[45]*

In 1715, Louis XIV announced that he had put an end to the Protestant religion in France. He was wrong, as "The Revocation and events thereafter rekindled Huguenot determination and, in this sense, proved counterproductive".[46] By 1744, there were over 4,400 Protestants in Le

---

41 - https://museeprotestant.org/en/notice/the-church-of-the-desert-in-the-heroic-period-1715-1760/ . They likened themselves to the ancient Israelites living in 'The Desert'.

42 - The names of several places near Bolbec, such as Saint-Antoine-la-Forêt, Saint-Eustache-la-Forêt, Saint-Nicolas de la Taille, etc., certainly suggest that the countryside was once covered in woods. The same can be said for names in the ancient Forest of Lillebonne.

43 - Translated from Waddington 1862, pages 118-119.

44 - Bost 1984, 1; Manneville 1987.

45 - Translated from Waddington 1862, pages 118-119; 115-117; Vatinel 1989; Corvisier 1974.

46 - Mentzer and Spicer 2002, 225.

Pays de Caux, especially in Bolbec, Luneray and Gruchet-le-Vallasse.[47] And by surviving, they made possible the later growth and prosperity of the textile industries.

Figure 1.5. *Bolbec, showing urban development spreading from the Bolbec Valley on to the plateau and the agricultural lands of the plateau beyond, August 2012. Source: L'Europe Vue du Ciel, 54470 Hagéville, France: leuropevueduciel.com*

Today, the valley towns are manufacturing centres and dormitory settlements for Rouen, having grown significantly, spreading on to adjoining parts of the plateau (Figure 1.5). Away from the valleys, however, the hamlets, villages and especially the numbers of farmsteads, les clos-masures, are all in decline. The 'clos-masures' have been modernised. Small-scale agriculture

---

47 - Steele 2009.

has given way to much larger operations. Rural employment has declined.[48] The population is ageing as young people move away. Yet much of the rural character of Le Pays de Caux remains.[49]

Early de Boos

In the 16th and early 17th centuries, there were several discrete de Boos families especially in the Lintot district,[50] though few by the end of the 17th century.[51] The early ancestors of Charles de Boos had maintained their Protestant faith and survived the Wars of Religion. They were residents of two small places near Bolbec: the farming community of Saint-Antoine-la-Forêt, west of the Bolbec River (Figure 1.6), and Gruchet-le-Vallasse, which is now virtually continuous with Bolbec, with its economy based on forestry, farming and light industry.

As far as can be determined, the earliest ancestor of Charles is a **Jean de Boos (1)**[52] (1591-1627), who was married to Marie Dufour (1594-); they were residents of St. Antoine-la-Forêt. **Abraham (2)** (1611-1671) was the third of their four children. In 1627, he married Suzanne Lesage (1614-1672) in 1627; both were very young. They had at least five children, all born in Saint-Antoine-la-Forêt and most likely baptised in the Temple of Lintot.[53] **Abraham (3)** (1638-1678), the second youngest, married Marie Goupil (1641-1689) on April 26, 1654, in the Temple of Lintot.[54] **Abraham (4)** (1660-1746) was born in Gruchet-le-Vallasse, the middle one of their three children.[55]

Abraham (4) was a 'fileur de tisserand' (a spinner / weaver), who seems to have lived much of his life in Gruchet-le-Vallasse. He married Susanne Hatanville (1659-) of Bolbec on January 11, 1681. They had at least four

---

48 - Employment in rural activities in Upper Normandy (agriculture, fishing, forestry) in 1896 totalled 117,000, 31% of the working population; in 1968, the figures were 78,000 and 13% (Frémont 1977, 32).
49 - Frémont 1981.
50 - Bernard 1981, 1987. Faced with fragmented and inconsistent material, most of it compiled by other genealogists (often with limited research skills), the following account is the best that can be achieved with the resources available.
51 - Madelaine 1906. And very few by the 18th century. See Anne Morddel's 'The French Genealogy Blog', https://french-genealogy.typepad.com.
52 - The numbers in brackets are for the direct ancestors of Charles Edward de Boos.
53 - huguenots-france.org/english/normandie/caux/lintot , accessed June 15, 2014. 'Lintot Parish Records', Film 1356282.
54 - 'The Protestants of Bolbec and Surrounding (xvii century): Lintot's Temple'.huguenots-france.org/english/normandie/ , accessed February 25, 2013; http://trees.ancestrylibrary.com/tree/16854242/ , http://huguenots.free.fr/france/normandie/caux/lintot/pag27.htm#37 , accessed July 27, 2013.
55 - An Abraham de Boos was recorded as living in Bolbec, October 9, 1668; St Antione la Forêt, February 12, 1673; St Nicolas de la Taille, October 28, 1674; and St Antione la Forêt, June 29, 1681. huguenots-france.org/english/normandie/caux/lintot , accessed June 15, 2014.

children, all born in Gruchet-le-Vallasse: **Abraham (5)** (1690-1738) was the second. Some records say that Susanne Hatanville died in 1695, but Victor Madelaine indicates she was still alive in 1699.[56] Around 1740, when he was some 80 years old, Abraham (senior) was spoken of as an 'old religeuse'[57] in his petition for payment from the estate of his cousin Jean, 'un apothicaire' (an apothercary). Jean had died, and Abraham must have been his heir, as he was finally paid a considerable sum of money. He used this to pay the debts of his son Pierre, who had died in June 1739, after being married for only nine years, leaving a widow and three children.[58]

Figure 1.6. *Saint-Antoine-la-Forêt, located on the plateau, and, at the top of the photograph, part of the much larger Gruchet-le-Vallasse, in the valley of the Bolbec River, May 2012. A 'clos-masures' can be seen in the upper-left of the photograph.* Source: L'Europe Vue du Ciel, 54470 Hagéville, France: leuropevueduciel.com

---

56 - 'WILDTR-2(10)_2013-11-26', http://trees.ancestrylibrary.com/tree/63798752/ , accessed June 15, 2014. According to Madelaine 1906, 454, in 1698-99, the family was living in Gruchet-le-Vallasse and listed as "Abraham Debos, et Suzanne Hattenville, sa femme; Abraham, son fils; quatre filles: Madeleine, Marie, Suzanne et Anne". Another record suggests she was still alive when her husband died in 1746. They were married for close to 65 years.

57 - This suggests he may have had some position in the church, though 'Un religeuse' means a monk or friar, terms more associated with the Catholic Church.

58 - "Genealogy Report: Descendants of Louis Eudes". https://www.genealogy.com/ftm/m/o/o/Robin-Moore/GENE1-0001.html, accessed July 18, 2019.

These members of the de Boos family were part of the French Reformation. How they in particular maintained their Huguenot faith, where they were married and their children baptised following the closure of the Lintot Temple, and how they survived the persecutions and the devastations of the Wars of Religion and under what conditions, are questions that cannot be answered. They were remarkable people.

Chapter Two

The Huguenot Diaspora and the London Huguenots

Whilst most Huguenots remained in France, for many, the response to the increasing violence was migration to other countries. The 'First Refuge' or exodus occurred from the 1530s to 1590; by the late 1560s, an estimated 20,000 Huguenots had left France.[1] Much larger numbers were to follow. In the short period from about 1680 through to the 1710s, as many as a third of French Huguenots left their homes, around 200,000 people, over 100,000 in the two years 1685 to 1687.[2] Some French cities, like Rouen and Nantes, lost over half their populations; 9,000 of the 12,000 silk workers in Lyon left, and Tours suffered an even greater loss. Over a period of no more than thirty years, this massive Huguenot exodus, the Second Refuge or more often called *le Grand Refuge*, was "the third largest one-shot migration in early modern Europe".[3] It was migration for the maintenance of their religious faith.[4]

Many countries were destinations for the Huguenot Diaspora. Neighbouring ones with significant numbers of Protestants were understandably favoured, including what are now the Netherlands, Germany, Switzerland, England, Ireland, and the Scandinavian countries. Some travelled much further, to North America, the Cape of Good Hope (now South Africa), and other places. Being much more than simply a religious and linguistic minority, the Huguenots took with them their crafts, skills, and many other abilities. They had been France's most industrious commercial class and their migration cost France dearly. For the host countries, there were tremendous benefits.[5] As well as their churches, they set up schools and hospitals. They took silk-weaving, chocolate manufacture, and watch making to Switzerland; sugar

---

[1] - Van Ruymbeke 2003, 6.
[2] - Gwynn 1983; 'The Huguenot Refuge'. www.museeprotestant.org/en .
[3] - Van Ruymbeke 2003, 6.
[4] - Mentzer and Van Ruymbeke 2016, 1-14; McKee and Vigne 2013.
[5] - Davies and Davies 2000, Chapters 5, 6 and 7; Scouloudi 1987.

boiling, linen, and the country's first bank to Ireland. For England, they provided a major economic stimulus, with their skills as financiers, makers of precision instruments (telescopes, watches, clocks, guns), fine jewellery, gold and silversmiths, silk weavers, dyers and clothiers, and cabinet makers.

England was a major destination for the first and second 'Refuges', as well as before and after them. The migrants of earlier periods, both Walloons[6] and Huguenots, laid the foundations in London and some English provincial cities for the much larger numbers that followed. In May 1593, a government census in London recorded a 'stranger' community of 7,000 people. Between 1670 and 1710 alone, over 50,000 people crossed the Channel to England and another 10,000 made it to Ireland; "they reinforced the existing settlements of Canterbury, Southampton, Norwich and, above all, London. New settlements were established in Bristol, Exeter, Plymouth and elsewhere".[7] By the end of the 17th century, some twenty-eight French churches had been established in London, with up to another twenty in other parts of England, along with one in Edinburgh.[8] There were others that had earlier come and gone, as at Sandtoft and Sandwich, as well as what Gwynn describes as "ephemeral congregations" at seven other locations.[9]

Being the focal points of their communities, the French churches were critical to the initial survival of the Huguenot refugees. It has been said that the most important achievement of the initial wave of migrants "was the elaboration of a stable network of institutions [churches] where French-speaking refugees could find appropriate help, shelter, and support".[10] Whilst assimilation into English society was to take a few generations, the migrants were faced with a religious dilemma, whether to maintain non-conformity or to adopt Anglicanism. The majority position was non-conformity, worshipping as they had done in France. At different times, however, there were incentives to change or remain non-conformist. Not every English king was entirely favourably disposed to the newcomers, and numbers crossing the Channel varied accordingly. But in April 1687, James II removed "the barriers to non-conformity", and "As soon as official policy

---

6 - French-speaking people from parts of what is now Belgium that are adjacent to France.
7 - Nash 2009, 21-22; Cottret 1991.
8 - Colchester, Thorpe-le-Soken, Canterbury, Faversham, Dover, Rye, Ipswich, Norwich, Thorney, Southampton, Bristol, Barnstaple, Bideford, Dartmouth, Exeter, Plymouth, and Stonehouse.
9 - Gwynn 2011, 47.
10 - Quoted in Van Ruymbeke 2003, 8.

changed – actually within a matter of days – people started to turn up from the continent".[11] In 1687, 2,497 refugees arrived at the Threadneedle Street Church in London, compared with 607 in the previous year and 283 in 1685.[12]

However, despite the incentives to become part of the Church of England, the majority remained non-conformists, at least initially. And "although second-generation refugees felt increasingly comfortable in English society",[13] second and third generation Huguenots "turned towards religious pluralism, and at best kept an occasional membership in the local French church while being a full-fledged member of another denomination".[14] Next to religion, "the French language was an essential defining element of the Huguenot group identity". But "once the mother tongue of most members was no longer French",[15] the French churches lost their position and numbers declined significantly.

Yet even with the assimilation of second and third generation immigrants, and members attending both the French Church and the Church of England, there was a

> desire to maintain the Reformed core of the church. They may not have been willing to obey the strictures of the discipline when put into practice against them, but in their desire to have their children baptised in the church, their continued participation in the church even while attending their local English services, and their many testamentary donations to the church poor, they still expressed a commitment to the church and the Protestant "Cause" that it symbolised and that had originally brought their parents to England. This was important for the future. When the Huguenot refugees from Louis XIV's France began to flood into London in the 1680s, they were greeted by a functioning and well-administered Reformed church which had not disappeared from sight during the years of sparse immigration in the mid-seventeenth century and which still played an important role for the increasingly anglicised descendants of the original immigrants. … [The Church was] vitally important for the peaceful reception, maintenance, and integration of the thousands of Huguenots who washed up on English shores in the Second Refuge.[16]

---

11 - Gwynn 2006.
12 - Gwynn 2011, 45.
13 - Van Ruymbeke 2003, 8.
14 - Gwynn 1983.
15 - Van Ruymbeke 2003, 9-10.
16 - Littleton 2003, 106-107.

The London Huguenots

At the beginning of the eighteenth century, probably as many as 25,000 Huguenots were living in London, accounting for some five per cent of city's population.[17] Whilst united by their faith and church, in many other ways they were by no means a unified group of people, and the differences that existed in France were carried with them to London. There was significant variation in their wealth, knowledge, and skills, and consequently what they were able to contribute to English society and its economy. Interestingly, these differences found expression in different parts of London.[18] The West End, Westminster and Soho were newly built at the beginning of the eighteenth century; in 1700 there were 14 French churches, seven conformist (Anglican) and seven non-conformist.[19] The area was populated by a very mixed population of Huguenots. Many were craftsmen, producing luxury goods; some were skilled in other areas. It was a vibrant and sophisticated community, with regular interaction with the English. Their assimilation into English society was smooth, aided by being Protestants with "attitudes to such matters as money, work and the family ... very similar to those of the host community".[20]

The East End, and especially Spitalfields, was the location of the other major Huguenot community. With up to half of London's Huguenot population, it was very different from Westminster and Soho. The residents were predominantly poorer, most employed as artisans and labourers. This large community

> *depended almost exclusively on one industry – silk weaving (in its many branches). The effect was to form a more homogenous and conservative community that maintained its Calvinism and its Frenchness somewhat longer. This was assisted by the continuous arrival of new refugees well into the eighteenth century. ... Moreover, many of these refugees came from one province, Normandy, and therefore the tendency to a more tightly-knit community was understandable. As they spread into the neighbouring areas of Bethnal Green, Shoreditch and Mile End, the Huguenots began to intermarry with the English generally after at least two generations. Another factor which kept an awareness of their Huguenot descent alive was the 'French Hospital' or La Providence, an old people's home [established in 1718] which insisted on all applicants giving proof of Huguenot descent.*[21]

---

17 - Gwynn 1983; Gwynn 2011, 43-45; Nash 2009, 21-22.
18 - Gwynn 1998.
19 - Gwynn 2011, 134.
20 - Nash 2009, 22; Nash 2021.
21 - Nash 2009, 22.

In the late seventeenth and early eighteenth centuries, the silk industry boomed, especially in the Spitalfields district, where Huguenot weavers were attracted "by lower rents, weaker guild control, and the presence of sympathetic English non-conformists who practised similar types of Protestant worship".[22] Spitalfields was a ghetto dominated by the silk trade (Figure 2.1). The people were predominantly poor, but the district

> *always included a great contrast of rich and poor. The wealthy master weavers, throwsters and dyers lived in Spital Square (now demolished) and in Church and Princes Streets (now known as Fournier and Princelet Streets). Some of these fine 18th century houses still survive [Figure 2.2]. Poorer weavers lived in courts and alleyways, and in the neighbouring areas of Shoreditch, Mile End and Bethnal Green. The master weavers often owned the houses and sublet them to their workers, which put them in a very dependent position.*[23]

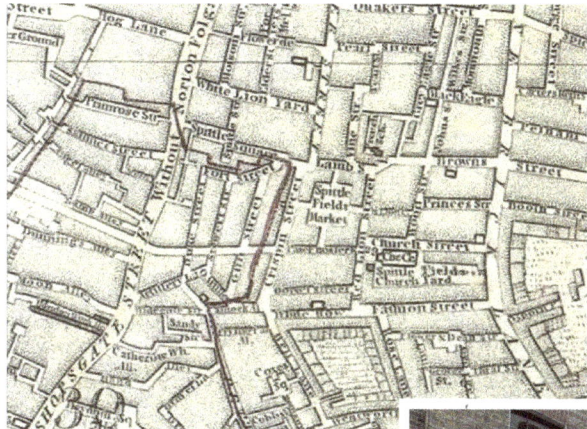

Figure 2.1. Map of the Spitalfields Area, 1787. Source: https://commons/wikimedia.org/wiki/File:Map of Spitalfields Area - 1787.jpg

Figure 2.2. Part of Fournier Street, Spitalfields, one of the best-preserved examples of early Georgian townhouses in Britain. Built in 1725 and formerly known as Church Street, it is named after George Fournier, a man of Huguenot extraction. Photograph c.2015? Source: https://www.the500hiddensecrets.com/united-kingdom/London/discover/historic-streets

Though both groups were Huguenots, the situation was little different to that of many of their French ancestors in Le Pays de Caux. From relatively early in the 18th century, unrest developed in the industry, largely over low

---

22 - Nash 2005; Rothstein 1987; Page 1911.
23 - Nash 2005.

and declining rates of pay. The consequent poverty culminated in riots, and the decline and eventual demise of the silk industry.[24]

The original French Church was located in Threadneedle Street in the City of London. It was founded in 1550, in a building dating back to the thirteenth century. This was destroyed in the Great Fire of London in September 1666, along with all its records, but a new church was completed in August 1669 (Figure 2.3). Through to the late eighteenth century it was the Huguenots' main place of worship and the focal point of their community. This was true for many of the East End Huguenot population, even though it was located some distance west of Spitalfields. Of its membership in the early 18th century, some 82% of those with a named trade were associated with weaving. Threadneedle Street was the mother church for the numerous other French churches established over the following years, including as many as nine in Spitalfields.[25]

Figure 2.3. The French Church of Threadneedle Street in the 1700s.
Source: www.tevelein.net/Pages?FamilyRecThreadaneedle.htm , accessed July 18, 2019.

---

24 - Nash 2005, 4; 'The Worshipful Company of Weavers: History', www.weavers.org.au , accessed November 27, 2016; Page 1911; *London Gazette*, January 26, 1768, number 10802, page 2; Winter 1993, 58, sourced from an anonymous publication by 'A Working Man', *Scenes from my Life*, London, 1858.

25 - Moens 1896; Gwynn 2011, 131; Littleton 2003.

At has been seen, the Huguenots initially retained their identity, and it would be difficult to say how long it was before it was really 'lost'. But with the gradual realisation that there was no going back to France and the appreciation of the benefits of assimilation, in terms of changing religion, changing occupations, and changing residential locations, in probably no more than two to three generations, the Huguenots were gradually absorbed into English society.[26] Even with the continuing changes, the Huguenot identity lasted longer in London's East End, helped by their charities and organisations, and their dominant position in the silk industry and other textile manufacturing.[27]

---

26 - Labrousse 1987, 151.

27 - Nash 2005.

Chapter Three

The London de Boos: a fortunate Family

A Refuge

The large Huguenot community found a refuge in London. Fleeing persecution, they had migrated from all parts of France, but at least half of those living in the East End in the 18th century came from Normandy, with a high proportion of them from Le Pays de Caux.[1] Apart from the churches, other groups were formed to provide "secours mutuels", such as 'la Société Normande', 'la Société de Réfugiés normands', 'le Club Normand', and 'la Société de Lintot'. These groups were limited to descendants of religious refugee families from Normandy. In 1855, the membership list of 'la Société Normande' included the names of Gosselin, Ferry, Levavasseur, Mousset, Le Brument, Frigout, Geaussent, Durand, Levesque, Rondeaux, Hautot, Lesage – and de Boos.[2]

The de Boos were just one of the extended Huguenot families that made their homes and played various roles in the silk-dying and weaving industries in the Spitalfields district.[3] As Gwynn has observed, in eighteenth century London,

> *Spitalfields looked and sounded different from the rest of the city. There were three reasons for its distinctive appearance: its comparative newness, since it was only in the second half of the seventeenth century that open fields had been transformed into housing; its Huguenot settlement, for the weavers kept gardens and were noted for their fondness for flowers; and the weaving craft itself, which meant that many houses came later to have garrets in the roof. The weavers' looms could chatter loudly …*[4]

---

1 - Nash 2007; Cottret 1991, 186.

2 - Waddington 1862, 17-18; Madelaine 1906, 205.

3 - A case in London's Central Criminal Court, the Old Bailey, on October 29, 1806, concerned the theft of silk from the business of James de Boos, a silk dyer; ten years later, on December 3, 1817, another case concerned the theft of goods from the silk-dying business of James, John and George de Boos. The transcript of the latter trial provides a fascinating insight into the operations of the de Boos brothers' business, the many specialist jobs which then existed, and the role of public houses as meeting places for the specialist traders. 'The Proceedings of the Old Bailey, London's Central Criminal Court, 1674 to 1913', www.oldbaileyonline.org/browse.jsp?name=18061029 ; www.oldbaileyonline.org/browse.jsp?name=18171203 , accessed June 6, 2020.

4 - Gwynn 1998, 38.

But change and assimilation in the wider London society were inevitable. Descendants of original settlers moved away from the Spitalfields district to other parts of London, and they moved into other occupations. The use of the French language declined. The Huguenots became part of other Christian denominations, especially the Church of England.[5] Even the Threadneedle Street Church changed, from 1840 moving to various locations, until finally relocating to Soho Square in Westminster in 1893.[6]

The earliest record found of a de Boos in London is Mary de Boos, a widow resident in the Parish of St. Katharine Cree (to the west of Threadneedle Street), who died on April 18, 1603. She would have been part of the 'First Refuge'. More people with the name de Boos migrated as part of the much larger *'Grand Refuge'* in the late 17th century, especially following the Revocation of the Edict of Nantes in 1685. Specifically, they included Jeanne, the younger daughter of Abraham (3) and Marie Goupil. She married Jacques Fossé, a weaver, at the Threadneedle Street Church on December 18, 1689; both came from Saint-Antoine-la-Forêt.[7] At the baptism of their first child, Suzanne, on February 3, 1692, the god parents were given as Jean de Boos and Suzanne de Boos, relatives who had also moved to London.[8] Jeanne was followed to London by her nephew, **Abraham (5)**, the older son of Abraham (4), the 'old religious', though just when is not known.

The London Ancestors

It was probably during the first decade of the 18th century that **Abraham de Boos (5)** (1690-1738) left Gruchet-le-Vallasse and moved to London, where he subsequently owned a textile dying business. On May 21, 1716, he married Magdaleine Eude at the French Church of Threadneedle Street (Figure 3.1).[9] She was born in London on January 27, 1692, baptised at La Patente French Church on February 3, 1692,[10] the daughter of Jacques Eude (of Senully, Basse Normandie) and Madelaine Launé (of Autretot, Haute

---

5 - Gwynn 2006.
6 - It is the only surviving French protestant church in London: Chater 2012, 19-20.
7 - Colyer-Fergusson 1906, 17.
8 - Colyer-Fergusson 1906, 110.
9 - Colyer-Fergusson 1916, 4. In the record of the marriage, Abraham is described as a 'natif de Gruchet'. Non-Conformist and Non-Parochial Registers, 1567-1970.
10 - Minet and Waller 1898, 6.

Normandie) who were married at the La Patente Church, September 14, 1690, and living in Spitalfields.[11] They had five children, **Charles (6)** and his twin brother Jean being the youngest.[12] Magdaleine died in Spitalfields in 1771, aged 79.[13]

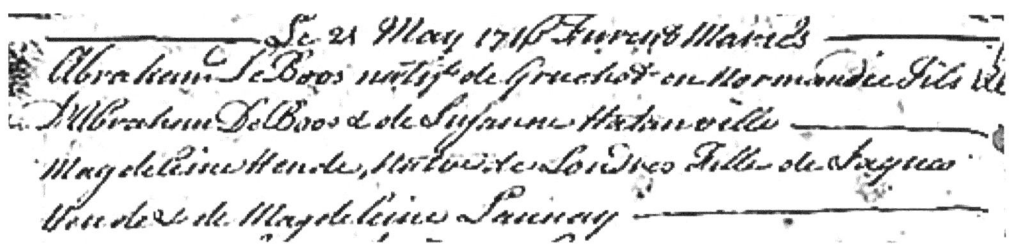

Figure 3.1. Record of the marriage of Abraham de Boos and Magdaleine Heude. Source: England and Wales, Non-Conformist and Non-Parochial Registers, 1567-1970: Piece 4588: Chapel of the Hospital, Spitalfields (Walloon and French Protestant), 1707-1752. http://interactive.ancestrylibrary.com/2972/40612 .

Jean married Catherine Gosselin (1743-1816) on April 8, 1763, at St. Matthew Bethnal Green on September 22, 1743.[14] He continued his father's dye business and probably became quite prosperous; at some stage, he made a visit to France in an unsuccessful attempt to retrieve lost family property.[15] In the 1783 edition of *The New Complete Guide to all Persons who have any Trade or Concern with the City of London and Parts Adjacent*,[16] John (Jean) and his brother Charles are listed as weavers and textiles makers at 24 Wood Street, Spitalfields.[17] Jean was buried on December 27, 1798, at Christ Church, Spitalfields.

Charles de Boos (6) (1738-December 1840) and Marie Gosselin (1745-1816), the sister of Catherine, were married on May 26, 1765, at Christ Church with St. Mary and St. Stephen, Spitalfields.[18] Marie was baptised at the French Church of Threadneedle Street, though by the time of her

---

11 - Minet and Waller 1898, 168.

12 - Colyer-Fergusson 1916, 38, 48, and 61.

13 - http://trees.ancestrylibrary.com/tree/33698979/person/28109423952 .

14 - Jean is the ancestor of John (1819), Charlotte Mary (1815), Matilda (1817), and Henry (1828) de Boos, all siblings, who moved to Euroa, Victoria (see Appendix 3.1). They were children of George and Charlotte Mary (Delaforce): personal communication, "Descendants of Abraham de Boos", compiled by Peter Waite, whose late wife was a descendant of Charles Edward de Boos; https://www.british-history.ac.uk/survey-london/vol27/pp24-38 .

15 - "Genealogy Report: Descendants of Louis Eudes". https://www.genealogy.com/ftm/m/o/o/Robin-Moore/GENE1-0001.html , accessed July 18, 2019.

16 - 16th edition, printed for T. Longman et al., London.

17 - 'U.K. and U.S. Directories, 168—1830': http://search.ancestrylibrary.com/cgi-bin/ , accessed November 19, 2013.

18 - http://trees.ancestrylibrary.com/tree/16854242/ ; see also 31347548.

marriage, she was a member of St Matthews Church, Bethnal Green.[19] Charles and Marie had at least eight children, all of whom are recorded in the baptism registers of the Threadneedle Street Church; a number died when they were very young.[20] **Abraham (7)** was their fifth child.

Abraham de Boos (7) (January 18, 1774-January 13, 1828) and Martha Jane Redman of Bishopsgate (1775-1861) were married on June 12, 1796, at St. Mary's Whitechapel, Middlesex.[21] They had at least four children, all recorded in the baptism registers of the Threadneedle Street Church: **Abraham Charles (8)** was the oldest. When Abraham (7) died, he was living in Pearl Street, Spitalfields. By this time, the family was almost certainly attending a Church of England rather than the French church in Spitalfields. At the 1841 Census, Martha was living at 46 Albermarle Street, Hanover Square, the home of her son Abraham Charles. She died in 1861 and was buried at St. Giles, Camberwell.

A Fortunate Family

Abraham Charles (8) (May 25, 1797-November 2, 1840) married Mary Ann Baker in 1818, when she was 20 years old.[22] They had seven children: **Charles Edward Abraham** (Augustus) (1819-1900); Eliza Susan (1822-1891); Thomas John Redman (1825-1899); Henry Woodstock (1828-1908); Adolphus Burge (1832-?); Emily Montague Buckstone (1833-after 1858); and Augustus Barnet John(s) (1836-1871).

Unlike Abraham Charles and his ancestors, none of his children are recorded in the baptism registers of the Threadneedle Street Church.[23] If they were not already, Abraham Charles and his wife appear to have become members of the Church of England, given where their children were baptised. Charles and Eliza were baptised at St. Mary at Lambeth, Surrey; Thomas at Christ

---

19 - At her marriage, she signed her name as 'Mary'.
20 - Colyer-Fergusson 1916.
21 - 'Binning William Family Tree': http://trees.ancestrylibrary.com/tree/3065747 , accessed November 11, 2013. Also 'Black-Olufson Family Tree', ancestrylibrary.com.au/family-tree/person/tree/23424320/ accessed July 18, 2019; 'Crickshank Family Tree', http://trees.ancestrylibrary.com/tree/18539556 .
22 - 'Black-Olufson Family Tree': http://trees.ancestrylibrary.com/tree/23424320 , accessed November 18, 2013. She was the daughter of Christian Baker (1780-). No clear record of her birth has been found, but her mother may have died at her birth, as a Mary Ann Baker died in January 1799, in Lambeth, and may have been buried at St. Mary's, Lambeth. Her residence was given as "Butts" (Newington Butts, a former village in what was then rural Surrey). 'Find my Past', accessed June 12, 2014.
23 - Information from 'Family Search' and http://trees.ancestrylibrary.com/tree/16854242/ , accessed June 12, 2014.

Church, Southwark; Henry at St. Margaret's Westminster;[24] Adolphus at St Martin-in-the-Fields, Westminster; and Emily and Augustus (on the same occasion) at St. James, Piccadilly, Westminster.[25]

Initially, they lived at various addresses in Lambeth. By 1828, they had moved to Stepney, on the north side of the River Thames, at the time a district that was more rural than urban, "a patchwork of market gardens".[26] This may well have been the location Charles Edward was reminded of when visiting Goulburn, in southern New South Wales, in late 1870 – early 1871. He was stimulated to write about his memories of gardens in London in which he had played as a young boy nearly forty years earlier.

> *From the nature of the climate all kinds of English fruits, shrubs, and flowers can be grown here; and I can scarcely conceive a greater pleasure to the old Englishman, who has been many years confined to the purlieus of Sydney, to come upon a country like this, and see the cherries, currants, and gooseberries of his native land, growing in as great profusion as ever he saw them in the gardens of the old country. In the spring, he will see the lilac in full bloom: and if that don't take his thoughts back home, then he has no heart. I don't know that I ever saw a sight that more impressed me that when, some ten or twelve years ago, after having spent the then half of my life in the colony, I came across the first lilac tree which I had seen in flower since leaving England. The well-remembered flowers and the delicious perfume which they exhaled brought a half-choking lump into my throat, and made the tears well up into my eyes. In an instant the memory of days and weeks and months of happy childhood flashed through my mind, bringing back visions of green and well-kept hedges, of sweet-scented flowers, of the old walnut tree and its autumnal threshings, of the play-ground with its sadly crippled lilac tree in one corner, and its much-punctured cherry tree in the other – the one crippled for its flowers and twigs, the other punctured for that schoolboy delicacy, its gum. It was too late to see lilac in flower in Goulburn, but I saw with equal pleasure many of the old English favourites, somewhat exotic-looking, but still flourishing here when they would have perished in Sydney.*[27]

These brief memories indicate not only a happy childhood, but an almost idyllic location in which to grow up, at least for a young boy. Subsequently, the family moved to addresses in Charing Cross, Hammersmith, and finally the West End of London at 46 Albermarle Street, close to the corner with Piccadilly (Figure 3.2).[28]

---

24 - 'Black-Olufson Family Tree': http://trees.ancestrylibrary.com/tree/23424320 , accessed November 18, 2013. See also http://trees.ancestrylibrary.com/tree/67337802 .
25 - Details of the last three children from 'England, Births and Christenings, 1538-1975', on the 'Family Search' website.
26 - Winter 1993, 5.
27 - *Sydney Morning Herald,* January 28, 1871, page 7.
28 - 'Black-Olufson Family Tree': http://trees.ancestrylibrary.com/tree/23424320 , accessed November 18, 2013. The original building in Albermarle Street was destroyed by bombing on November 15, 1940 (Sangster 2020).

At the time of his marriage, Abraham Charles was a merchant's clerk; by 1825, his occupation was given as accountant. In 1832, on the baptism records of his three youngest children, his occupation was described as 'Gentleman', a term of indeterminant definition.[29] Whatever his actual occupation, he must have prospered, given his residence in London's West End and the money spent on educating his children. Abraham Charles and his family were clearly a fortunate one.

Abraham may have had other sources of income. Between 1836 and 1839, there were reports of him and others being involved in "keeping a common gaming-house, called the Berkeley Club House, in Albermarle-street".[30] They were charged in the Middlesex Sessions with "nuisance and misdemeanour, in keeping common gaming houses for unlawful games of chance and hazard", but there did not seem to have been any convictions.[31]

Figure 3.2. 47 and 46-45, Albermarle Street, London, c. 2020. The original early eighteenth-century terrace houses at numbers 46-45 were destroyed by bombing in 1940; they would have been similar to 47, which is now a Grade II British Listed Building. The new building at 46-45 dates from 1955-57. Source: www.bing.com/images/ ; historicengland.org.uk/

---

29 - Richard John (2011): 'Who were gentlemen in the nineteenth century?' https://richardjohnbr.blogspot.com/2011/08/who-were-gentlemen-in-nineteenth.html , accessed May 12, 2020.

30 - *Sun* (London), September 21, 1837, page 4.

31 - *The Chartist* (London), March 9, 1839, page 4. See also *Morning Advertiser* (London), September 20, 1836, page 3, and *The Globe,* September 28, 1837, page 4.

Abraham Charles died on November 2, 1840, at the relatively young age of 43 years.[32] About a year after his death, Mary Ann married James Hux (1801-1864) at the Church of St. Paul, Hammersmith, on December 1, 1841.[33] He was a chronometer, watch and clock maker.[34] They had a daughter, Helen (1843-1901), who married Louis Williams Cuddeford, a school master, in Uxbridge on December 11, 1869. At the 1851 and 1861 Censuses, James and Mary were living at 20 Down Street, Piccadilly.[35] James died on November 3, 1864, and was buried at All Souls, Kensal Green; his effects were valued at £6,000. Mary Ann died only nine months later, on August 2, 1865, when living at 1 Mall Terrace, Kensington, with her effects valued at £2,000. She was also buried at All Souls, Kensal Green.[36]

The Siblings of Charles Edward de Boos

Not much is known about most of the siblings of Charles Edward de Boos, especially his sisters. **Eliza** de Boos married Augustus Radcliffe of Pentonville on September 14, 1844, at St. Paul's, Hammersmith.[37] They were married for 47 years until her death in 1891. Augustus was a "Patent Glaziers' and artists' diamond manufacturer, wholesale and for exportation".[38]

At the age of fifteen, **Thomas** became a solicitor's clerk. His 'Articles of Clerkship', dated July 3, 1840, cost his father £120 for the five-year period with Charles Boydell, Attorney and High Court Solicitor. A letter written in 1848 stated: "Tom de Boos passed his examination in January and has taken chambers in St. James St. Bedford Row No 16. He has since gathered round him an excellent [word unclear] and could do a vast amount of business if he had the means. As it is, he is cramped awfully".[39] He married

---

32 - *Sun* (London), November 4, 1840, page 4; 'Black-Olufson Family Tree': http://trees.ancestrylibrary.com/tree/23424320 , accessed November 18, 2013.

33 - 'Family Search', accessed June 14, 2014. Black-Olufson Family Tree on Ancestry, accessed June 12, 2014. Also, www.ancestry.com 'London. England, Church of England Marriages and Banns, 1754-1932, St. Paul, Hammersmith', accessed July 24, 2018. At the 1841 Census, James Hux was living at Suffolk Place, Islington.

34 - James was a brother of John Hux, whose second wife was Mary Martha de Boos, the youngest child of Abraham (7); by his first wife, he had a son, John Augustus Hux (Crabb 2020).

35 - *London Post Office Directories*. www.ancestry.com . It is not entirely clear where they were living, Down Street or Hanover Square. Was Down Street the business address?

36 - Sources accessed through Ancestry, June 12, 2014.

37 - *Sun (London)*, September 28, 1844, page 8.

38 - *Post Office Directory, 1843, page 338*. UK, City and County Directories, 1766-1946. www.ancestry.com.au .

39 - Part of a letter from Harry Rogers to George Isaacs (alias A. Pendragon, author of *The Queen of the South*), dated July 25, 1848, in the State Library of South Australia. The three were friends in London. Information provided by Anne Black, University of Adelaide, July 19, 2013; Black 2020, Chapters 1-2. Also, though a resident of South Australia, Isaacs was in Victoria from 1852 to 1855, spending some time on the goldfields. Given his connection with Thomas, did Isaacs have any contact with Charles (Black 2020, 46-47)?

Caroline Radcliffe (a sister of Augustus Radcliffe) on March 19, 1850, in St. Martin-in-the-Fields, Westminster. In 1868, they were living at 23 Hanley Road, Hornsey Road, Middlesex. The 1871 Census stated that he was a Solicitor Manager and living in Camberwell; by the 1881 Census, he was living at Ivy House, Tottenham, Middlesex; and ten years later, he was living in Acton. He died on September 22, 1899, at 'Windermere', St Mary's Grove, Gunnersbury, Middlesex.[40]

Henry followed his older brother to Australia in 1849 (Figure 3.3).[41] He seems to have had various occupations before joining the New South Wales Government public service. After occupying numerous positions, in 1878 he was appointed mining registrar and warden's clerk at Gulgong, in central New South Wales, where he stayed until he retired in 1892 (Appendix 3.1).[42] For part of the time, the Mining Warden there was the Australian author, Thomas Browne (alias Rolf Boldrewood).

Figure 3.3. Henry de Boos. Source: https://www.wikitree/com/wiki/De_Boos-15

---

40 - 'William Kinglake DeBoos Family Tree', 31347548; see also 'Prendergast-Dick Family Tree', 60955323.
41 - Trinder and Fearnley 2005, Reference / Reel 1276.
42 - From *Government Gazette*, March 8, 1878, *Sydney Morning Herald*, March 9, 1878, page 8; *Evening News*, April 30, 1875, page 2.

At the 1841 Census, **Adolphus** was at College House in Fore Street, Edmonton, a live-in school run by Darius White. In 1868, he was reportedly living in Chile. There is a 'Family Search' record of an Adolfo de Boos and his wife Carolina Fernandez living in Valparaiso in 1887.[43]

At the time of the 1851 Census, **Emily** was at a residential school in Great Marlow, Buckinghamshire. In 1856 she went to New York, seemingly on her own, "where she assumed and afterwards sometimes went by the name of Stocker".[44] Letters to her brother Augustus indicated that over the next two years, she lived in Chicago, Buffalo and Montreal, as well as New York.[45] After 1858, nothing further was heard from her.[46] Was she the Emily who was looking for work in New York in May 1858 (Figure 3.4)?

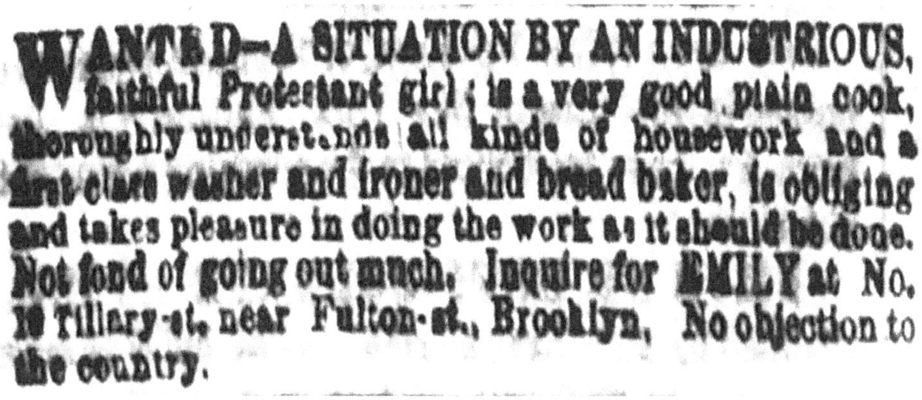

Figure 3.4. Was this Emily de Boos? New York Times, May 29, 1858, page 6.

---

43 - High Court in Chancery, 1868 D114. De Boos v. de Boos and Others, dated October 3, 1868. Ref.: C16/487 C693213. The National Archives, London; see also www.familysearch.org/tree , accessed May 13, 2020.

44 - It would have been very unusual in 1856 for a 23-year-old woman to travel on her own to another country. High Court in Chancery, 1868 D114. De Boos v. de Boos and Others, dated October 3, 1868. Ref.: C16/487 C693213. The National Archives, London.

45 - Searches on www.newspapers.com and numerous genealogy web sites for Emily de Boos and Emily Stocker proved fruitless, except for the one advertisement.

46 - High Court in Chancery, 1868 D114. De Boos v. de Boos and Others, dated October 3, 1868. Ref.: C16/487 D114. The National Archives, London.

In the 1861 Census, **Augustus** was listed as a watch and clock maker, living as a lodger at New Quebec Street, Marylebone. However, at the time of his marriage to Mary Ann Smoker on February 5, 1863, at the Saint Mary Magdalene Parish Church, Woolwich, Augustus was a Bombardier in the Royal Horse Artillery.[47] In 1868-69, advertisements in numerous newspapers, though no London ones, indicated a jewellery and clock business was still operating from 20 Down Street, Piccadilly, by a Mr. de Boos.[48] Was this Augustus? At the 1871 Census, he was a 'watchmaker', but living with his family in Torquay, Devon.[49] Only a few months later, in the October, he died in Wandsworth, aged 35 years.

Some further light is shed on the family by a case in the High Court in Chancery in August 1868, brought by Thomas de Boos against his uncle Edward de Boos and his siblings Eliza (and her husband Augustus Radcliffe) and Augustus, along with Charles, Henry, and Adolphus (the last three "when they shall come within the jurisdiction" of the Court). On May 5, 1846, Thomas had transferred to Edward shares in the London and Westminster Bank in Trust to make provision for his mother, Mary Ann Hux, up to the time of her death. Following her death and the presumed death of Emily, the terms of the Trust were that the funds be divided equally between the siblings, but this had not been done. Edward stated that he could not "safely distribute the said shares and funds except under the direction of this Honourable Court".[50] Unfortunately, the outcome of the case has not been found.

The family life of the de Boos in London was clearly a far cry from that of their Huguenot ancestors, young and old, in London and before that in northern France. It had been a long and arduous journey from Le Pays de Caux to the West End of London. But travel must surely have been in the blood of many of the Huguenots. Most of Abraham Charles' children left London, four to very distant locations. For them, it is unlikely that there would have been any subsequent personal contact, except for Charles and

---

47 - Ancestry.com. London, England, Church of England Marriages and Banns, 1754-1932, Saint Mary Magdalene Parish Church, Woolwich.
48 - Among others, *Bicester Herald*, April 24, 1868, page 3; *Bradford Observer*, January 8, 1869, page 1.
49 - http://trees.ancestrylibrary.com/tree/16854242/ .
50 - High Court in Chancery, 1868 D114. De Boos v. de Boos and Others, dated October 3, 1868. Ref.: C16/487 D114. The National Archives, London. Edward was the sole Executor.

Henry in Australia. Their journeys may not have been so arduous as those of some of their ancestors, but the distances travelled were certainly much greater.

Chapter Four

Leaving Home: School and the Carlist Wars

Addiscombe

According to his obituary and sources published during his lifetime, Charles de Boos was educated in Addiscombe, near Croydon, some distance from the family homes in Stepney and the West End of London.[1] Whilst not the only 'school' that can be located in Addiscombe at the time, he most likely went to the East India Company Military Seminary, which existed from 1809 to 1861 to train officers for the Company's private army and was similar to the then Royal Military Academy at Woolwich (Figure 4.1).[2] (The Company also had a college at Haileybury, Hertfordshire, for training civilian staff.) It was a residential establishment, and when he went there, Charles would have been, at most, fourteen years of age.

The Seminary was much more than a military training establishment. Bourne described it as "not a true military college at all, but a militarized public school".[3] It was by no means a free education (£50 a term by 1835), and a good prior 'classical' education was necessary for entry, an indication that from the start of his schooling, de Boos had received a good education. Also, admission was by patronage on the recommendation of a Director of the Company, something that almost certainly involved a financial inducement.[4] Standards were high: "Entry was by way of public examination with further public examinations at the end of each term. Failure meant immediate expulsion from the college!"[5] Once there, during

---

1 - For example, Heaton 1879, 54; *Windsor and Richmond Gazette* (NSW), July 20, 1889, page 1; December 17, 1892, page 19.

2 - 'Addiscombe Military Academy': http://en.wikipedia.org/wiki/Addiscombe_Military_Seminary , accessed June 30, 2021. There were two other schools in the area, both Church of England institutions, Archbishop Tenison's (1714, Selborne Road) and Whitgift (1596/1600, North End, Croydon), but these were more associated with nearby Croydon than Addiscombe. So, why was it said that he went to school in Addiscombe – a place that was unlikely to have been known to many people in Australia – if it was a school in the no doubt more well-known Croydon? See also Keay 2010.

3 - Bourne 1979.

4 - Information by Tony Fuller, May 2000: http://archiver.rootsweb.ancestry.com.th/read/INDIA/2000-05/0958404186 , accessed May 5, 2012; Fuller 2001.

5 - Canning & Clyde Road Residents Association 2000, 25.

the two years of study, the cadets studied a broadly-based curriculum that included physics, mathematics, chemistry, geology, French, Latin, and Hindustani, as well as military subjects such as musketry and gun drill. It was a curriculum that provided a basis for many of his activities in later life.

It is unlikely that material published during his lifetime would have stated he was educated in Addiscombe if this had not been the case, even though this has not been confirmed from any independent sources. His name is not included in the lists of cadets in contemporary editions of the annual *East-India Register and Directory*[6] or in the lengthy history compiled by Vibart,[7] though it has not been possible to search the records of the East India Company.[8] So, having an education in Addiscombe remains something of a mystery.

Figure 4.1. Addiscombe Place, the main building of the East India Company Military Seminary, with a group of cadets, 1859. Source: Vibart 1894.

---

6 - *The East-India Register and Directory* for the years 1832 through to 1837, compiled by G.H. Brown and/or F. Clark. East India Company, London. The assistance of Dorian Leveque of the APAC Reference Services, The British Library, is gratefully acknowledged for providing this material, February 13, 2016.

7 - Vibart 1894.

8 - These voluminous records are housed in The National Archives, Kew, England: Farrington 1976; Canning & Clyde Road Residents Association 2000.

The Start of his Travels

After Addiscombe, the life of the young Charles took a most unusual turn, namely his participation in the Carlist Wars in Spain. These arose out of a complex mix of factors, both within Spain and beyond.[9] They were part of the transition to a more liberal and secular society in Europe that occurred during the nineteenth century and "the defensive reaction of a traditional society to the threat to its existence posed by liberal political, social, economic, and religious policies".[10] The trigger to the first of the wars was the promulgation of the *Pragmática Sanctión* by King Ferdinand VII that allowed his daughter Isabella to become Queen following his death, thus preventing his brother, Don Carlos, becoming king. On the death of Ferdinand on September 29, 1833, three-year old Isabella became queen, with her mother Maria Cristina, acting as Regent. The response of the traditionalist Carlists was to try to gain power from the liberal Christinos by military means, and so began the first of the Carlist Wars. They had strong support, and with their conquering the Basque country, Maria Christina sought help from London and Paris.[11] The requests for direct help were refused, but permissions were given for the involvement of the French Foreign Legion and the formation of the British Auxiliary Legion in 1835. Paid by the Christinos, the foreign forces were much resented by the Carlists. It was a highly controversial move, but a force of some 9,600 men and 400 officers was assembled in a few weeks under the leadership of George de Lacy Evans, a half-pay lieutenant and radical member of the House of Commons.

Variously known as the 'Auxiliary Legion' or 'British Legion', the British Auxiliary Legion was a largely volunteer force without any previous military experience.[12] Many were urban unemployed, in poor physical condition, and were variously described as "destitute and in rags", "rough citizens", and "the scum of the earth".[13] Further, most of the officers had no previous military service. Among the exceptions were a few on leave from the East India Company. Lasting from 1833 to 1839, it was a brutal war, with

---

9 - 'First Carlist War': http://en.wikipedia.org/wiki/First_Carlist_War , accessed August 6, 2010.
10 - Coverdale 1984, 3.
11 - Coverdale 1984, 173.
12 - 'Auxiliary Legion': http://en.wikipedia.org/wiki/Westminster_Legion , accessed August 6, 2010.
13 - Holt 1967, 85-86.

frequent disregard for any of the conventions of war; an estimated 130,000 were killed and many others injured.[14] Of the British Legion, over 600 died in action, but another 1,850 died of disease.[15] However, the Legion's "service in Spain may be regarded as having made a small but definite contribution to the success of the Queen Regent's armies".[16]

Charles de Boos' participation in the Wars was stated in a number of items published during his lifetime: for example, a report of a visit to an old friend in Richmond, New South Wales, in 1892 stated "He served in the British Legion in the Carlist war during the years 1835-6-7", finishing with the rank of Captain.[17] However, thus far, no mention of his participation has been found in the records of the British Auxiliary Legion.[18] An information sheet issued by The National Archives entitled *The British Auxiliary Legion and the Carlist War 1835-8* stated that "No reference to records relating to individual British soldiers taking part in the Carlist War can be found in records held by The National Archives", no doubt because they were paid by the Queen of Spain.[19] The absence of his name in any records does not exclude his participation. And in a newspaper article published in 1852, writing of a camp-fire meeting with convict stock-keepers most likely in New South Wales, some comments made by de Boos must surely refer to incidents during his time fighting in the Carlist Wars.

> *I by no means pretend to sanctity; I have sat at a camp fire surrounded by convict stockkeepers, and have heard tales and language that thrilled my blood; I have mixed with the military atheists of Napoleon's grande armee, - men whose religion was formed in the no creed days of the first revolution, and have listened, not without horror, to the words of impiety that fell from their lips; I have been at the picquet fire[20] in the midst of low London blackguards dignified with the name of soldiers, and have heard with disgust the bestiality with which their conversation was mingled; but never, in the whole course of a somewhat motley existence, have I heard such brutal, filthy, and profane expressions as are – I will not say used – but, in common use – on the*

---

14 - Coverdale 1984, 3.
15 - Holt 1967, 164; Lardner 1837.
16 - Holt 1967, 167; Brett 2005; Fagette 1975; Henty 1902; Sommerville 1839.
17 - *Windsor and Richmond Gazette*, December 17, 1892, page 19; July 20, 1889, page 1; *Daily Telegraph*, October 31, 1900, page 6.
18 - Research undertaken by Michael Gandy at The National Archives, Kew: personal communication, July 14, 2011. This was a very limited search, as there are many other records in these Archives. See also Anon. 1836; Heaton 1879, page 54, states "1835-36 and 1837".
19 - http://yourarchives.nationalarchives.gv.uk/index.php?title=The_British_Auxiiary_Legion_and_the_Carlist _War_1835-8 , accessed July 14, 2011; Spencer 1997; Gibson and Medlycott 2001.
20 - A military term: an infantry post on the outpost line from which sentries or groups of watchers were sent out, to give warning of an advance by the opponents. www.theodora.com/encyclopedia/p/picquet_picket.html , accessed August 2, 2015.

> *Diggings, introduced of course into the Victorian vocabulary by some of the choicest selections from Van Diemen's Land. To let you judge of the extent to which this is carried, I may tell you that on more than one occasion, I have been compelled to walk away to escape hearing the Port Arthur quotations of these gentry.*[21]

The involvement of de Boos in the Carlist Wars raises many questions. Given that the Seminary in Addiscombe was the training institution for the East India Company's army, why did he go to Spain rather than India? Surely if he had completed his two years' education at the Seminary, he would have been obligated to join the Company's army. And what was he doing being involved in such a war at only some 16 years of age? Had it anything to do with his Huguenot ancestry, a support for liberalism, an opposition to oppression associated with Catholicism? Did he see it as adventure and a way to earn some money? His young age may have helped him to survive the fighting and disease. The military training received at Addiscombe would have provided a basis for his participation, and there may have been a connection with officers from the East India Company. What was the nature of his involvement? Was it with one of the cavalry regiments? This could have provided him with his first contact with horses which were to play such an important part in his later life.

After the Carlist Wars

If de Boos had wanted adventure, he certainly had it during the Carlist Wars. So, what did he do after the end of his involvement, probably in 1837? From his later writings, there are hints that he travelled to other parts of Europe. For example, in 1866, when commenting on the fenced and gated town of Stroud in the Hunter Valley, he observed:

> *I had seen fortified towns in France, and other Continental countries. I had seen the portcullis hung aloft as if threatening every moment to fall and shut out the wicked world beyond; and I had ridden over the bridge with a due respect to the caution "Il est defend de trotter sur le pont", which, backed up by the very presence of a huge six feet gendarme, looming still bigger under the huge cocked hat, it was impossible to ignore; but I never felt such awe and astonishment, even at the vast battlements and the huge ordnance that mounted them, as I did at this remarkable fenced-in town of New South Wales.*[22]

---

21 - *The Argus*, May 8, 1852, page 4.
22 - *Sydney Morning Herald*, August 3, 1866, page 3.

How much of England did he know? Of Hartley, near Bathurst, he wrote that "the turreted belfry of an old-fashioned church, [was] such as you find buried in a mass of elms and chestnuts in some remote Leicestershire village".[23] Such observations raise yet more questions about the two years of his life from 1837. Was this when he undertook further travels in England, France and "other Continental countries"? Nothing else is known about this time. All we have is a comment in his obituary, that he found "little to attract him in the old country".[24]

In 1839, he sailed for Australia. As indicated earlier, he was not the only one of his family to travel overseas. Henry followed him, as did other London relatives. Emily made her home in the United States, while Adolphus found his way to Valparaiso in Chile. The diaspora continued.

---

23 - *Sydney Morning Herald*, October 12, 1865, page 2.
24 - *Sydney Morning Herald*, October 31, 1900, page 7.

Chapter Five

Early Years in Australia, 1839-1850: Sydney, the Hunter Valley, a Family

Just a few weeks after his twentieth birthday, on June 16, 1839, de Boos sailed from London on the 192 tons barque *Australasian Packet*, and after a voyage of just over four months, arrived in Sydney on October 22, 1839. He was one of 16 people who travelled steerage, plus six in cabins, and was one of ten passengers who signed a very effusive letter of appreciation to the vessel's Captain on their arrival in Sydney:

> SIR, - Our pen is but feeble to express the satisfaction we feel, at your kindness, and at your many efforts to render us not only, comfortable, but happy, during the time employed in traversing so vast a portion of the globe. We may say without exaggeration, that few, if any passengers who have sailed from England, have experienced more attention from their commander than we have, both from your self and your officers. Even during the rudest weather our comfort has been looked after with the keenest solicitude. ...[1]

Why Sydney, New South Wales? He could hardly have travelled further from his family in London, no doubt with little prospect of seeing any of them again.

What did he find on his arrival? Though in many ways an 'English' city, Sydney would have been a far cry from London and the other places he had visited in England and on the continent. In 1839, Sydney was well on the way in its change from a penal colony to a settlement for free settlers, change that owed much to Governor Lachlan Macquarie in an earlier decade (1810-1821). The population grew from around 5,000 in 1821, to 16,000 in 1831, and 35,000 in 1843, though the ratio of males to females of five to one was an ongoing concern for the Colony's administrators. The transportation of convicts ended in 1840 and the City of Sydney was formally established in 1842. The city grew (Figure 5.1) and small settlements were established beyond the immediate suburban areas, such as

---

1 - *Sydney Gazette*, October 26, 1839, page 3; *Australian*, October 26, 1839, page 3; *Australasian Chronicle*, October 29, 1839, page 3. For a description of the vessel, see the *Sydney Gazette*, October 29, 1839, page 3.

Parramatta and further out, Richmond and Windsor in the Hawkesbury Valley.

Trade of all kinds formed the basis of the city's economy and developing society. The port was where goods were brought into the colony, where goods were shipped out, wool being the main commodity, and where supplies were taken on, such as by the American and other visiting whalers in Walsh Bay and Chowder Bay. There were numerous Australian whaling stations in Mosman Bay and shipyards on the Balmain peninsula.

Somewhat surprisingly, the later writings of Charles de Boos contain hardly anything about early Sydney. An exception is his observation that when he travelled out of Sydney "at the end of 1839", it was in "one of the old fashioned gigs" and Camperdown was "then considered out of town, and a regular country trip to the Sydney Cockney".[2]

Figure 5.1. 'City of Sydney, N.S.W. from the Government Paddock, Parramatta Street'. John S. Prout, 1844. T. Bluett, Printer, Hobart. Source: NLA PIC Drawer 48# S1616.

What did he do?

Just what de Boos did during his first years in New South Wales remains unclear. In commenting on this time, his obituary stated:

> *In those days the theory was that an energetic Englishman had only to take up pastoral pursuits in order to make a fortune, wherewith he could return in a few years to his ancestral home. Amongst the persons who realised that this theory does not always hold water was young De Boos, who found that the country he had taken up in the Hunter River district brought him no means of livelihood.*[3]

---

2 - *Sydney Morning Herald*, January 20, 1871, page 5. The writer is not named.

3 - *Sydney Morning Herald*, October 31, 1900, page 7.

Apart from this, no other source has been found to support statements about his supposed farming venture in the Hunter River district. Other statements along these lines, often somewhat elaborated, appear to be based solely on this one comment. For example, Crittenden stated that de Boos "tried his hand as a farmer on the rich alluvial soil on the great river flats".[4] Nothing has been found in his writings that suggests he had engaged in "pastoral pursuits" or any other form of farming. In the 1850s and 1860s, he travelled through the district on a number of occasions whilst working for the *Sydney Morning Herald*, but there is no mention of an earlier time in the Hunter River district.[5] In fact, when sailing up the lower Hunter from Newcastle to Morpeth in 1857, he wrote at length about his observations of farming on the river flats, without any indication of having had any involvement with such activities, though he did observe that "Ten years have passed since I last visited Maitland".[6]

The statement that he farmed in the Hunter Valley raises too many questions for it to be credible. When was this time in the Hunter River district? Where was his land? Did he buy or rent the land? What did he try to do with it? Other than the fact that he had no prior knowledge of farming, if he was a farmer for a period, why did the venture fail? And again, if he was in the Hunter Valley during those four years, why was there no mention of him in the local press? In short, apart from his obituary, nothing has been found to suggest that he undertook any form of farming in the Hunter Valley.

His obituary also stated that he became a journalist. He knew shorthand; in fact, he was the first journalist in Australia to have this knowledge.[7] He also had an excellent command of the English language, whilst a reporter's job provided him with the opportunity to travel in his new country. If he worked for the *Sydney Monitor* and the *Sydney Gazette*, as some sources indicate, then this would have been in those first few years, as the *Monitor* ceased publication on December 29, 1841 (it started on May 19, 1826), and the *Gazette* on October 20, 1842 (it started on March 5, 1803). In *The*

---

4 - Crittenden 1996b.

5 - *Sydney Morning Herald*, April 23, 1866, page 3; April 25, 1866, page 2; May 3, 1866, page 2; and May 4, 1866, page 5.

6 - *Sydney Morning Herald*, April 20, 1857, page 2. He also observed with respect to Singleton, that it had "altered but very little during the last nine or ten years".

7 - Shorthand was introduced in 1837 by Sir Isaac Pitman. Did Charles de Boos learn it in England before he left for Australia, or was it something he did on the long voyage to Australia?

Oxford Companion to Australian Literature entry on the *Monitor*, there is no mention of him, but the one for the *Sydney Gazette* names Charles de Boos as one of a number of "significant contributors", along with Henry Halloran, Edward O'Shaughnessy, Michael Massey Robinson, and Charles Tompson.[8] It is not known if he worked for any other contemporary newspapers after the *Monitor* and *Gazette* ceased publication, though Heaton stated that he also worked for the *Sydney Herald*, the predecessor of the *Sydney Morning Herald*.[9]

There is other material that suggests he could not have been in the Hunter River district in those early years. Many years later, he wrote of his first trip to Goulburn:

> The trip to Goulburn is a very different thing now [early 1871] to what it used to be when I first travelled that road, at the end of 1839. It was the first journey I made into the south country, and I remember all the incidents of it as well as if they had only happened yesterday.[10]

Why did he go to Goulburn, and how did he pay for the trip - as a reporter? In an 1865 article in the *Herald*, when writing about the Lake George area, not far from Goulburn (Figure 5.2), he says, "It is more than twenty years ago [pre-1845] since I last visited this spot".[11] Was it on one or both of these trips that he also visited the nearby Bungendore area, which, along with Lake George, provided the location for his first novel, *The Stockman's Daughter* (see Chapter Twelve)? Or were there later occasions? Did the story of the bushranger Jacky Jacky contribute to *The Stockman's Daughter*?[12]

Apart from his work, whatever it was, he had other activities. An item published many years later, referring to the time when George Gipps was Governor of New South Wales (1838-1846), stated that a Mr S. Phillips, the first secretary of the Parramatta District Hospital, "was the first to start an amateur dramatic company in Parramatta, and his little band of performers had the honor of playing before Governor Gipps on more than

---

8 - Wilde, Hooton and Andrews 1994, 734.

9 - Heaton, 1879, 54. Other contemporary newspapers were the *Australasian Chronicle* (April 2, 1839 – October 7, 1843), the *Australian* (October 14, 1824 – September 23, 1848), the *Colonist* (January 1, 1835 – December 31, 1840) (incorporated into the *Sydney Herald* in late 1840): the *Commercial Journal and Advertiser* (August 13, 1835 – November 1, 1845), and the *Sydney Herald* (commenced April 18, 1831); Isaacs and Kirkpatrick 2003; Kirkpatrick 2016.

10 - *Sydney Morning Herald*, January 20, 1871, page 5.

11 - *Sydney Morning Herald*, August 16, 1865, page 5.

12 - *Australian Chronicle*, January 19, 1841, page 3; *Sydney Herald*, January 20, 1841, page 2.

one occasion". One of the company members was "Mr. de Boos ... for many years connected with the 'Sydney Morning Herald'".[13]

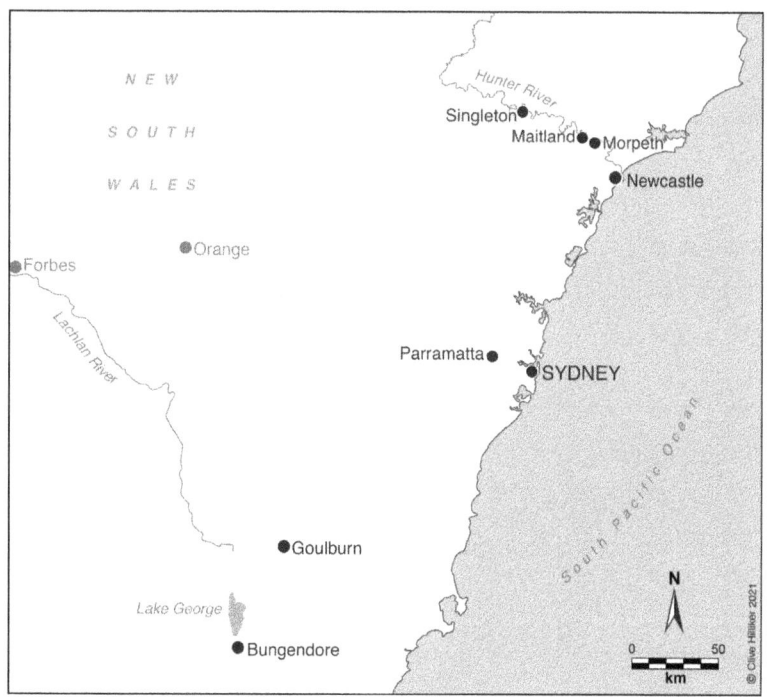

Figure 5.2. Places de Boos is known to have visited during his early years in New South Wales.

During 1841 and 1842, there is only one occasion on which his name has been found in contemporary newspapers and other records.[14] In 1842, an advertisement appeared in the *Sydney Gazette* that included his name:

> FOR SALE, Three allotments of land at Smithfield – For particulars apply to Mr. C. De Boos, Brodie & Craig's Buildings, Bathurst Street, or at the Office of this Paper.[15]

This rather puzzling advertisement raises yet more questions. He was working for the *Sydney Gazette*, but it seems unlikely that he was working for Brodie & Craig, a firm of builders.[16] Did he occupy a room in the building, for work and/or residence?

---

13 - *Cumberland Argus*, June 27, 1896, page 6.

14 - His name is not in the Index of the New South Wales 1841 Census, though only heads of households / premises were recorded by name.

15 - *Sydney Gazette and New South Wales Advertiser*, August 6, 1842, page 3.

16 - By 1844, Hugh Brodie and Archd. Craig were listed as builders at Barker Street (Low 1844, 23 and 33). In 1835, Craig was listed as a carpenter, with an address in Bathurst Street (O'Shaughnessey 1835).

Two months after this advertisement appeared, the *Sydney Gazette* ceased publication. For the next four years, there are very few mentions of de Boos in any contemporary materials. On three occasions, letters addressed to him were detained at the Sydney General Post Office.[17] One was of particular interest as it was a letter for "Mr. C. Deboos, New Zealand", detained "in consequence of the sea postage not having been paid".[18] As mentioned below, there is further evidence that he travelled to New Zealand, but nothing else is known about this.[19] In December 1844, he was elected to a committee to prepare a petition to the Colonial Legislature as the first step in the Incorporation of the town of Parramatta.[20] A week later, an advertisement appeared for the New Year's Day Parramatta Hack Races in which 'Mr. C. DeBoos' was named as 'Secretary'.[21] Was he living in Parramatta for a time?

These 'snippets' leave a lot of time unaccounted for over a period of four years. Apart from New Zealand, did he travel anywhere else? Did he return to England, following the death of his father and his mother remarrying? Especially given the type of person he was, it seems unlikely that his name would not have appeared somewhere and at some time in at least one of the newspapers of the day, regardless of what kind of activity he may have been engaged in. This largely 'absent' period continues to be a mystery.

The Hunter Valley

Then, 'out of the blue', in August 1846, de Boos' name appeared in advertisements in the *Maitland Mercury* as 'Secretary pro tem' of the Acting Committee of the Maitland Jockey Club and, later in the month, as 'Secretary' of the Club.[22] Surely, he would have had to have been in Maitland for some time before taking on this job. But why go to Maitland in the first place?

---

17 - *Sydney Morning Herald*, February 10, 1843, page 4; *NSW Government Gazette*, February 7, 1845, page 145.
18 - *Australasian Chronicle*, April 11, 1843, page 4.
19 - A "Mr. De Bois" sailed for the Bay of Islands on the barque *Magnet*: he was the only passenger listed *(Sydney Morning Herald*, October 28, 1842, page 2). Was this him? A search for 'de boos' and 'de bois' on the National Library of New Zealand Papers Past website produced no results.
20 - *Parramatta Chronicle*, December 14, 1844, page 1.
21 - *Parramatta Chronicle*, December 21, 1844, page 3.
22 - *Maitland Mercury*, August 8, 1846, page 3; August 12, 1846, page 3; and August 29, 1846, page 3.

Numerous advertisements in the local newspaper and in *Bell's Life of Sydney and Sporting Reviewer* for the Maitland Jockey Club indicate that he undertook this task for about a year.[23] During this time, he was clearly active in the local community. In August 1846, he attended a lecture on New Zealand in Maitland; in seconding the vote of thanks, de Boos stated that he had visited New Zealand.[24] At a later date, he attended a dinner in Singleton given for the visit of the Governor to the Hunter Valley. He returned thanks to a toast for "The *Maitland Mercury*, and the liberty of the press" and proposed a toast for those who had prepared "a dinner so extensive".[25] It seems unlikely that he would have done this without some prior connection with "the press". Or, and this is pure speculation, was he then working for the *Maitland Mercury* (first published on January 7, 1843)

The last advertisements to include his name as Secretary of the Maitland Jockey Club were for the Maitland Annual Races on August 24-26, 1847.[26] Efforts to find other references to Charles de Boos in numerous records in the Hunter Valley proved unsuccessful.[27]

Is it this period and his involvement with horses and the Maitland Jockey Club that gave rise to the statement in his obituary that he took up farming in the Hunter Valley? This may have provided him with a link to 'the land', but hardly in the capacity of a farmer. It could also have been the period when he became familiar with "the topography and culture" of the Hunter River district,[28] which some years later provided the setting for his major novel, *Fifty Years Ago* (see Chapter Thirteen).[29] Further, there is no evidence to support statements that, in the Hunter Valley, "he had lively experiences with bushrangers", or that "On one occasion he was shot by them but not seriously hurt; ... [and] afterwards ran them down and captured them".[30]

---

23 - It was reported that the Maitland Jockey Club was newly formed on June 3, 1846 (*Maitland Mercury*, June 6, 1846, page 4), even though other reports indicate it was in existence as early as 1843. In its first two months, there were two other Secretaries before Charles de Boos had the job.

24 - *Maitland Mercury*, August 29, 1846, page 4.

25 - *Maitland Mercury*, February 10, 1847, page 2; *Sydney Morning Herald*, February 12, 1847, page 3.

26 - *Maitland Mercury*, August 14, 1847, page 1, and August 21, 1847, page 1; *Bell's Life in Sydney and Sporting Reviewer*, June 26, 1847, page 4; *Maitland Mercury*, September 22, 1847, page 4.

27 - Research undertaken through the Maitland & District Historical Society (visited on August 15, 2012) and the Maitland & District Genealogical Society, personal communication, Maree Solomon, October 10, 2012.

28 - Clancy 1999a.

29 - *Fifty Years Ago: an Australian tale* was first published in 1866-67. See Chapter Thirteen.

30 - Clancy 1999a.

Later, in the 1850s and 1860s, he travelled through the area on a number of occasions whilst working for the *Sydney Morning Herald*, but as mentioned above, there are no references to earlier visits except those to Maitland and Singleton.

After a year or so working and obviously being active in the local community, de Boos left Maitland. Why or where he went immediately are not known, as again there is another gap in the information about him, this time of about seven to eight months.

Regarding these 'missing' months, was it the period when his travels included the Lake George – Bungendore area? There is evidence that his travels also included the Lachlan district. In the 'Author's Preface' to the first chapter of "The Yo-Yo. A Legend of the Lachlan District", serialised in the *Sydney Morning Herald* and *The Sydney Mail* in 1861-62 (see Chapter Twelve), de Boos wrote that "The first four chapters of this sketch, … were written some fifteen years ago", which was 1847.[31] He stated that the story had been told to him by "Mr. Bumblebunkumeree the eminent Aboriginal naturalist", "many years ago, by a camp fire in the wild bush of the district".[32] But what was he doing in the Lachlan district?

Back to Sydney

Sydney continued to change, becoming more deserving of its city status (Figures 5.3 and 5.4). What work de Boos did on his return is, once again, not known. However, he was soon active in community affairs. In March 1848, he was one of a group of people involved in looking into setting up a building society, being named a member of the provisional committee.[33]

On May 17, 1848, de Boos married Sarah Stone at St James Church of England, King Street, Sydney, by Special Licence, the service being conducted by the Rev. Charles Priddle (Figures 5.5 and 5.6). She was twelve years younger than Charles. He almost certainly met her at the King's Arms

---

31 - *Sydney Morning Herald*, November 29, 1861, page 8.
32 - *Bell's Life in Sydney*, November 30, 1861, page 2.
33 - *The Sydney Chronicle*, March 2, 1848, page 3.

Figure 5.3. George Street, Sydney, looking North. J. Tingle, c. 1850. Sands & Kenny, Sydney. NLA PIC Drawer 2637# S2101.

Figure 5.4. The part of Sydney with which Charles de Boos was particularly associated in the late 1840s. Extract from 'Map of the City of Sydney' by W.H. Wells. W. Baker, Sydney, 1843. State Library of New South Wales, Sydney, MZ/M2 811.17/1843/1.

1. *King's Arms Inn, 278-280 Pitt Street.*
2. *St James's Church, King Street.*
3. *The Metropolitan Offices, 337 George Street (opposite the Cathedral).*
4. *Brodie & Craig's Building, Barker and Bathurst Streets.*
5. *Sydney Gazette Offices, Lower George Street.*

Inn on Pitt Street, where her father, William Stone, was the landlord from 1840 to 1846.[34] After William died, his wife Mary was the landlord from 1847 to 1858. Sarah and Charles' first child, Mary Ann Agnes, was born on March 19, 1849, and baptised at St James Church on April 8, 1849. In the Baptism Register, their address was given as 280 Pitt Street (the King's Arms Inn) and her father's occupation as 'Newspaper Reporter'. But for which paper?[35]

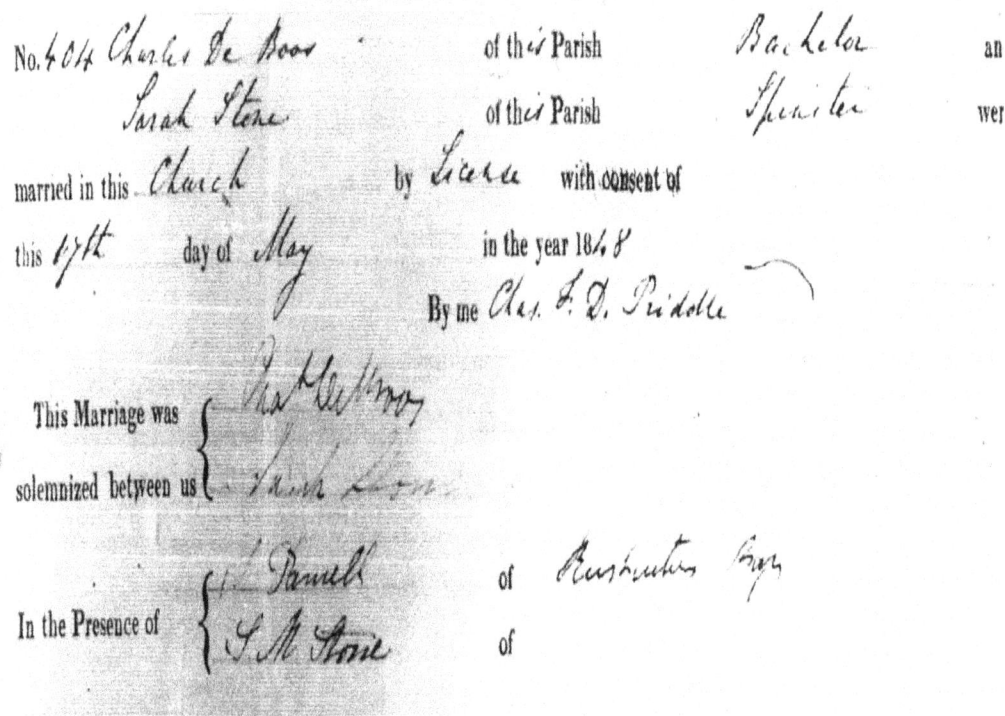

Figure 5.5. St James Church of England Register record of the marriage of Charles de Boos and Sarah Stone. Source: Microfilmed Records of Marriages in the Parish of St. James, Society of Australian Genealogists, SAG Reel 61 Marriages 1839-1853.

---

34 - Low 1844, 104.

35 - Contemporary newspapers, 1849: *Bell's Life in Sydney* (1845-70); *People's Advocate* (1848-1856), *Sydney Morning Herald* (1831-).

Figure 5.6. St. James Church, King Street, Sydney, 1856, by S.T. Gill. Allan & Wigley, Sydney, 1856. Source: NLA PIC Volume 196# S4021.

His own newspaper: *The Metropolitan*

His involvement with newspapers took a further step later in 1849 with the appearance of a *Prospectus of a new weekly journal of politics, literature, science and the arts to be entitled The Metropolitan* (Figure 5.7).

The first issue appeared on Saturday afternoon, August 18, 1849. It gained widespread publicity, with advertisements in the *Sydney Morning Herald*,[36] where it was announced as "a new weekly journal of politics, literature, science, and art", and in news items in other papers. One item stated that "The new Sydney paper, The Metropolitan, is said to be the organ of the Sydney Reporters, who have formed themselves into a 'Professional Library Society'".[37] An item on the paper in the *Goulburn Herald* noted that "Mr. de Boos is well-known as a reporter to the Press".[38] He was clearly experienced, well known, and well regarded. A brief description of the first issue noted:

> *It is printed on a double Crown sheet, and folded into sixteen pages. The leading matter consists of four articles – on the Police establishment of Sydney; the new Postage Bill; the City Council; and Mr. Lowe's resolutions on the Constitution. We must not omit to notice some very pretty stanzas on a love affair, and subscribed by the well known initials "E.K.S.".*[39]

---

36 - August 15, 1849, page 1; September 6, 1849, page 3.

37 - *The Argus*, August 11, 1849, page 2; August 25, 1849, page 2; *Maitland Mercury*, August 22, 1849, page 2; *Moreton Bay Courier*, September 8, 1849, page 3; September 15, 1849, page 3; *Goulburn Herald*, August 25, 1849, page 5.

38 - *Goulburn Herald*, August 25, 1849, page 5.

39 - *Moreton Bay Courier*, September 8, 1849, page 3.

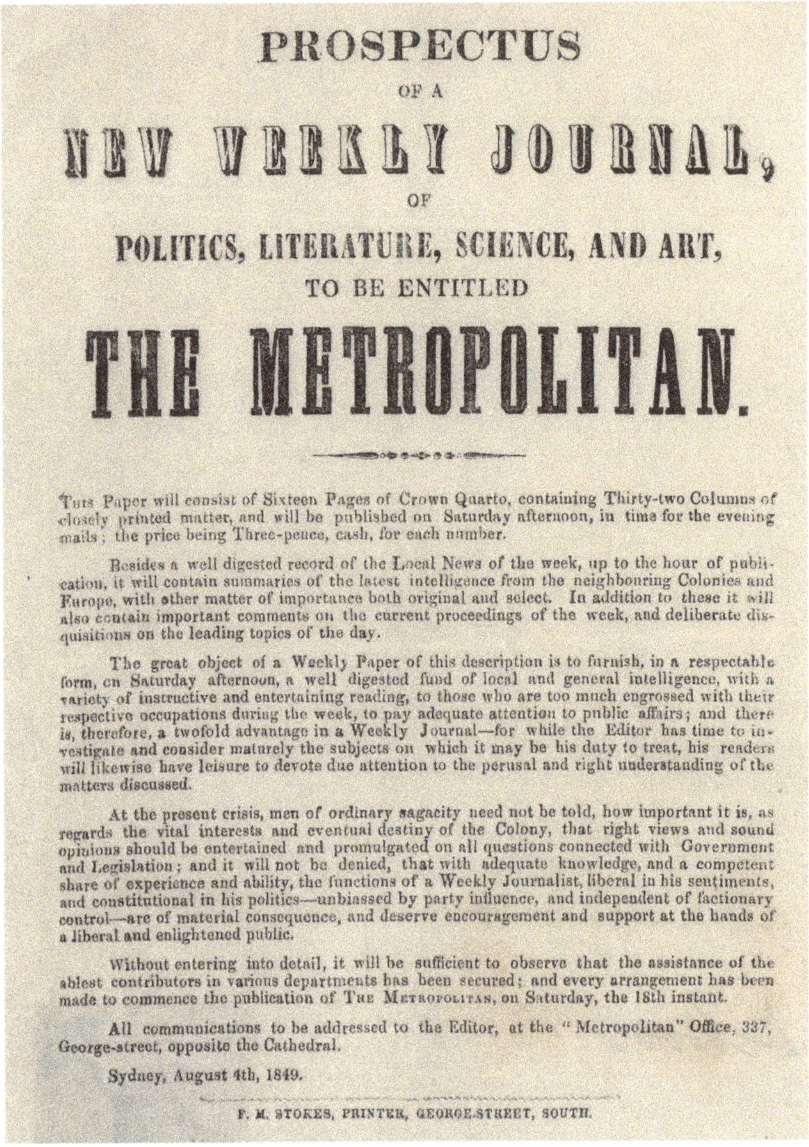

> **PROSPECTUS**
> OF A
> **NEW WEEKLY JOURNAL,**
> OF
> POLITICS, LITERATURE, SCIENCE, AND ART,
> TO BE ENTITLED
> **THE METROPOLITAN.**
>
> This Paper will consist of Sixteen Pages of Crown Quarto, containing Thirty-two Columns of closely printed matter, and will be published on Saturday afternoon, in time for the evening mails; the price being Three-pence, cash, for each number.
>
> Besides a well digested record of the Local News of the week, up to the hour of publication, it will contain summaries of the latest intelligence from the neighbouring Colonies and Europe, with other matter of importance both original and select. In addition to these it will also contain important comments on the current proceedings of the week, and deliberate disquisitions on the leading topics of the day.
>
> The great object of a Weekly Paper of this description is to furnish, in a respectable form, on Saturday afternoon, a well digested fund of local and general intelligence, with a variety of instructive and entertaining reading, to those who are too much engrossed with their respective occupations during the week, to pay adequate attention to public affairs; and there is, therefore, a twofold advantage in a Weekly Journal—for while the Editor has time to investigate and consider maturely the subjects on which it may be his duty to treat, his readers will likewise have leisure to devote due attention to the perusal and right understanding of the matters discussed.
>
> At the present crisis, men of ordinary sagacity need not be told, how important it is, as regards the vital interests and eventual destiny of the Colony, that right views and sound opinions should be entertained and promulgated on all questions connected with Government and Legislation; and it will not be denied, that with adequate knowledge, and a competent share of experience and ability, the functions of a Weekly Journalist, liberal in his sentiments, and constitutional in his politics—unbiassed by party influence, and independent of factionary control—are of material consequence, and deserve encouragement and support at the hands of a liberal and enlightened public.
>
> Without entering into detail, it will be sufficient to observe that the assistance of the ablest contributors in various departments has been secured; and every arrangement has been made to commence the publication of The Metropolitan, on Saturday, the 18th instant.
>
> All communications to be addressed to the Editor, at the "Metropolitan" Office, 337, George-street, opposite the Cathedral.
>
> Sydney, August 4th, 1849.
>
> F. M. STOKES, PRINTER, GEORGE-STREET, SOUTH.

Figure 5.7. Prospectus of The Metropolitan, 1849. Source: State Library of New South Wales, Sydney, PAM 84/790.

The "pretty stanzas" resulted in an unusual response to the paper in the *Bell's Life in Sydney and Sporting Reviewer*, in the form of a poem entitled 'The Forsaken One', "suggested on reading some delicious stanzas in no. 1 of the 'Metropolitan'".[40] No copies of *The Metropolitan* have survived, and it is unlikely that more than four editions were published, on August 18, August 25, September 1, and September 8, 1849 (Figure 5.8).

---

40 - *Bell's Life in Sydney and Sporting Reviewer*, August 25, 1849, page 3.

After this unsuccessful venture, did he return to work again for one of the contemporary newspapers, or did he work in The King's Arms Inn? These are more unanswered questions. So, too, is the reason for another departure from Sydney in April 1850.[41]

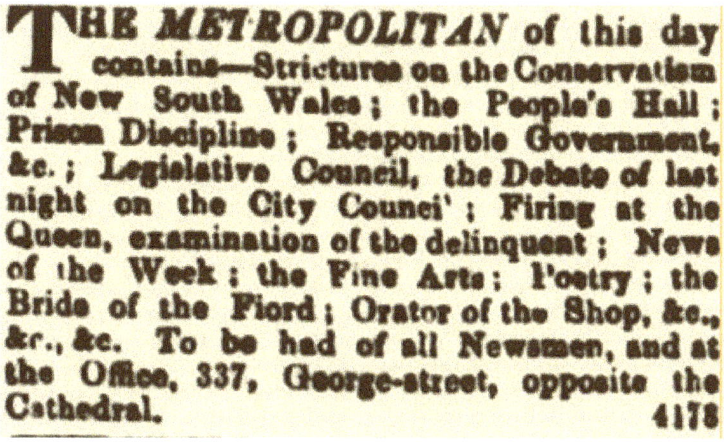

> THE *METROPOLITAN* of this day contains—Strictures on the Conservatism of New South Wales; the People's Hall; Prison Discipline; Responsible Government, &c.; Legislative Council, the Debate of last night on the City Council; Firing at the Queen, examination of the delinquent; News of the Week; the Fine Arts; Poetry; the Bride of the Fiord; Orator of the Shop, &c., &c., &c. To be had of all Newsmen, and at the Office, 337, George-street, opposite the Cathedral.   4178

Figure 5.8. An advertisement for The Metropolitan, outlining the contents of the fourth, and almost certainly the last issue. Sydney Morning Herald, September 8, 1849, page 1.

---

41 - *Sydney Morning Herald*, April 22, 1850, page 2.

Chapter Six

Melbourne, 1850-1856: Newspaper Reporter and Colonial Government Official

Leaving Sydney on April 21, 1850, Charles de Boos, his wife and daughter, finally arrived in Melbourne on May 10, 1850.[1] Bad weather caused a normal voyage of just over a week to last nineteen days. Three days after leaving Sydney, the 154 tons brig *Dart* "put into Twofold Bay, on the far south coast of New South Wales, on the 25th, and sailed on the 27th ultimo for Melbourne"; on May 4th, it was off Babel Island;[2] on the afternoon of the 7th, the vessel was "inside the Heads"; on the 10th, it finally docked in Melbourne.

Melbourne in 1850 had a population of about 23,000 people, just over half that of Sydney. "Fitzroy, Richmond and Collingwood were thriving suburbs and nearby Brighton, 'the third town of Port Phillip', had some two thousand people. Most of the central square mile was now built up with an incongruous mixture of architectural styles; in the whole town there were three times as many stone and brick houses as weatherboard, but only one roof in forty was slated and not shingled. … Most of the main streets were metalled and well kept by the Town Council".[3] Essentially, it was a trading port and business centre for the pastoral industry.

No more than a year after the de Boos family arrived in Melbourne, every facet of life in Victoria changed dramatically. First, the massive and devastating fires that culminated in 'Black Thursday', February 6, 1851, gave the early settlers a new appreciation of the dangers of their new home.[4] Much more significant, however, were the discoveries of gold from early 1851. Victoria soon accounted for a third of the world's gold production. Melbourne grew

---

1 - *The Argus*, May 8, 1850, page 2; May 11, 1850, page 2.

2 - *Sydney Morning Herald*, May 6, 1850, page 2; May 13, 1850, page 2. Babel Island is a small island of some 440 ha off the east coast of Flinders Island, clearly well off the route to Melbourne.

3 - Serle 1963, 1-8, 66-72; Broome et al. 2016; Davison 2016; Grant and Serle 1957.

4 - Approximately a quarter of Victoria was burned over some weeks, culminating in 'Black Thursday, when the shade temperature in Melbourne reached 47°C. 'Black Thursday bushfires', https://en.wikipedia.org/wiki/Black_Thursday_bushfires .

at an almost unbelievable pace. Huge numbers of people arrived from all over the world; between 1851 and 1861, Victoria's population increased from around 85,000 to over 540,000. The rushes were on.

> *The discovery of the Victorian Gold Fields has converted a remote dependency into a country of world-wide fame; it has attracted a population, extraordinary in number, with unprecedented rapidity; it has enhanced the value of property to an enormous extent; it has made this the richest country in the world; and, in less than three years, it has done for this colony the work of an age, and made its impulses felt in the most distant regions of the world.*[5]

For the fortunate ones, there was the accrual of significant wealth.[6]

Figure 6.1. Collins Street from Russell Street, looking west, Melbourne. S.T. Gill (1853). Source: NLA PIC PIC Solander Box C19# S701.

Melbourne became an 'instant city' (Figure 6.1), but it was far from a welcoming place for the vast majority of the new arrivals, as the location simply could not cope with such large numbers of people. It "experienced all the usual problems of urban development – providing food and water, housing, sanitation, social security and public order – all at once".[7] One response to the accommodation problem was the creation of 'Canvas Town' on the St Kilda Road, which by 1853 housed more than 7,000 people (Figure 6.2). Many years later, de Boos described the temporary settlement in his novel *Mark Brown's Wife* (see Chapter Twelve).

---

5 - Committee on the Claims to Original Discovery of the Gold Fields of Victoria. *Sydney Morning Herald*, March 28, 1854, page 2. The Report was first published in *The Argus*, March 24, 1854, page 5.

6 - McCalman, Cook and Reeves 2001; Bate 1988; 2001; Blainey 2006; en.wikipedia.org/wiki/History_of_Melbourne.

7 - Davison 2016.

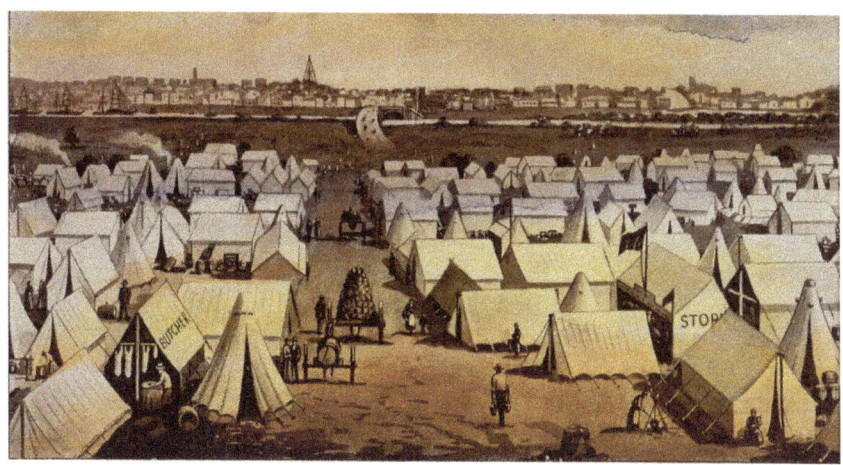

Figure 6.2. 'Canvas Town, between Princes Bridge and South Melbourne', c.1855, by De Gruchy & Leigh, lithographers, Melbourne. Source: H25127 Pictures Collection, State Library of Victoria, Melbourne.

The early 1850s was a critical time in Victoria's history in other respects, with its separation from New South Wales in 1851 and the establishment of the Legislative Council. "The first parliament was made up almost entirely of lawyers, successful businessmen, affluent squatters and merchants. They may have represented the 80,000 people who lived in the colony in 1851, but they hardly represented the 300,000 in 1855".[8] The new constitution of 1855 added the Legislative Assembly to the colony's administration.

The Victorian Gold Rushes

From 1849 to 1851, Melbourne newspapers published various reports, comments and editorials on gold and its discovery. Gold was allegedly discovered in the Pyrenees, near Avoca, in the late 1840s, but there was little or no substantiation of the finds.[9] The first of a number of Government-established 'Gold Committees' was not satisfied by the Pyrenees claims either.[10] *The Argus* seemed somewhat pleased that, by late July 1851, it could say, "The Gold fever has now considerably abated. … Hopes are less bright – fears are less gloomy – the mind's eye of the public less dazzled by the golden glare – and the subject can now be discussed somewhat rationally and calmly".[11]

---

8 - '*History of Melbourne*', www.onlymelbourne.com.au/history-of-melbourne-581 .

9 - The Argus, February 2, 1849, page 2; February 16, 1849, page 2; February 23, 1849, page 2; March 23, 1849, page 2.

10 - *The Argus*, February 20, 1849, page 2; June 8, 1849, page 2; December 11, 1849, page 2; May 23, 1851, page 2 July 8, 1851, page 2; July 11, 1851, page 2; July 18, 1851, page 4; July 29, 1851, page 4; *Geelong Advertiser*, July 7, 1851, page 2.

11 - *The Argus*, July 25, 1851, page 2.

How wrong was Edward Wilson, the Editor![12] Within a matter of days, gold finds were made and confirmed at Clunes (early on, sometimes referred to as the Pyrenees) and Anderson's Creek (sixteen miles north of Melbourne, and later named Warrandyte).[13] These finds really marked the beginning of gold mining in Victoria. Though both were only briefly successful, they vie with each other as to which was the first find. A few years later, the *Committee on the Claims to Original Discovery of the Gold Fields of Victoria* was unable to decide on one particular find as being the first in Victoria.[14]

Figure 6.3. Places on the Victorian gold fields visited by de Boos, as well as other places with which he was associated during his time in Melbourne.

Following the initial finds, the next ones were in the Ballarat area, starting near Buninyong in August 1851 (Figure 6.3).[15] The consequent movement

---

12 - Bate 1988, 2001.

13 - *The Argus*, July 17, 1851, page 2; July 26, 1851, page 2. See the comparative comments regarding Clunes and the Victoria Diggings by 'Our Special Correspondent' (*The Argus*, August 22, 1851, page 2); extract from a letter regarding the Victoria Diggings (*The Argus*, August 29, 1851, page 2); Serle 1963, Chapter 3.

14 - *The Argus*, March 24, 1854, page 5; *Sydney Morning Herald*, March 28, 1854, page 2.

15 - *The Argus*, September 8, 1851, page 2: report by 'A.C.' written on September 4 and reprinted from the *Geelong Advertiser*. *Geelong Advertiser*, September 9, 1851, page 2; October 7, 1851, page 2; both articles by 'A.C.' (Alfred Clarke),

of people was considerable; for example, "About two hundred persons left Melbourne yesterday, to follow in the wake of those whom the prospect of immediate and boundless wealth has attracted to the shrine of the golden Juggernaut at Ballarat".[16] In October 1851, alluvial gold was discovered along Forest Creek, and large numbers of people made their way to what became known as Mount Alexander, stretching from what are now Chewton to Castlemaine.[17] At the time, it was the world's richest shallow alluvial goldfield. A tranquil wooded valley was rapidly transformed, with the search for alluvial gold along the waterways and the near total destruction of the forests to provide timber to construct the mines and fuel for the steam-driven machinery.[18] The discovery resulted in perhaps the largest peacetime migration of the 19th century. By the end of November, the population was some 15,000; mid-December, approaching 25,000; and by 1852, the population of the area was put at 40-60,000 people.

The first gold finds in the Bendigo area were announced in December 1851,[19] but it was five months later when the first big find was made at Eaglehawk Gully. By the following month, up to 5,000 diggers a week were arriving in the area. Some of the initial alluvial finds were short-lived, but within two to three years, the focus shifted to underground working of the rich quartz reefs. The Ovens Valley gold rush followed the discoveries on Reid's Creek and then Spring Creek in February 1852, what is now Beechworth. These were quickly followed by finds at nearby Yackandandah, Nine Mile Creek, Snake Valley, Woolshed Valley (El Dorado), and Three Mile Creek. By January 1853, an estimated 8,000 miners were camped on the Beechworth goldfields. New finds and re-workings of previous ones continued in the Ovens Valley and the Buckland Valley (a tributary of the Ovens) through the 1850s.[20] There were large numbers of German, American and Chinese miners; in 1857, the Chinese were subjected to brutal attacks in an attempt to drive them out of the Buckland Valley.

The gold rushes had significant impacts on all other sectors of the Victorian economy as people left their jobs for the diggings.

---

16 - *The Argus*, October 8, 1851, page 2; December 4, 1851, page 2; December 8, 1851, page 2; December 11, 1851, page 2; December 18, 1851, page 2; December 24, 1851, page 3; December 29, 1851, page 3.

17 - *The Argus*, from late 1851 through to the end of 1852; Hocking 1994; Annear 1999; Goodman 1994; Stone 2011.

18 - Serle 1963, 71-72.

19 - *The Argus*, December 13, 1851, page 2.

20 - http://www.beechworth.com.au/Beechworth-History/ ; Woods 1985; Griffiths 1987.

The market economy ceased to function for those with money and no interest in gold. Servants could not be hired at any wage. Boats lay idle in the harbour, their masters unable to keep their crew for the next leg of their journey. Even the pastoralists who ruled the global wool trade were left without men.

> To keep his administration running La Trobe [the Governor] pulled the only lever available to him in a high-wage society without workers – he doubled the salary of public servants.[21]

Life on the Goldfields

Conditions on the goldfields were hard: crime, sly grog, bad roads, poor mail services, poor health, and even starvation.[22] The supply of water for mining and for domestic purposes was a major concern, though by no means the only one.[23] But the biggest issue was the licence, which cost £1.10.0 per month, and had to be paid by every adult on the goldfields, unsuccessful as well as successful miners and even those not involved in mining. It had to be carried at all times; if it could not be produced on demand from the police or inspectors, the person was arrested and fined. The increase in the licence fee to £3 galvanised the miners into significant protest action. After a number of local gatherings, what became known as the 'Monster Meeting' was held at Golden Point, Mount Alexander (what is now Chewton), on December 15, 1851, when up to 14,000 people gathered in opposition to the increase in licence fees (Figure 6.4).[24] A number of resolutions were carried unanimously, the most important being: "That this meeting deprecates as unjust, illegal, and impolitic, the attempt to increase the licence fee from 30s. to £3".[25] The location is now part of the Castlemaine Diggings National Heritage Park; apart from the regrowth of vegetation, there has been little alteration to the immediate landscape (Figure 6.5). A large commemorative stone with two plaques marks the spot (Figure 6.6), with a quote from the address given by Mr Booley, one of the speakers: "There are few people who understand what a

---

21 - Goodman 2018.
22 - *The Argus*, March 13, 1852, page 4; Serle 1963, 72-85.
23 - *The Argus*, October 25, 1851, page 2.
24 - www.egold.net.au/biogs/EG00230b.htm , accessed May 27, 2015.
25 - *The Argus*, December 18, 1851, page 2.

Government is, or what it ought to be. It should be the chosen servants of a free people". The gathering's resolutions fell on deaf ears.

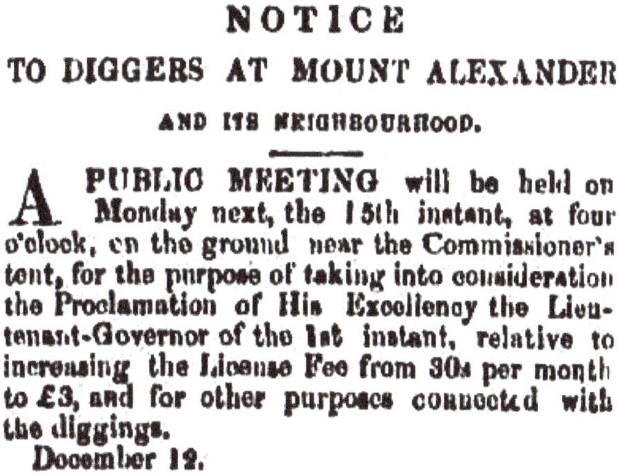

NOTICE
TO DIGGERS AT MOUNT ALEXANDER
AND ITS NEIGHBOURHOOD.

A PUBLIC MEETING will be held on Monday next, the 15th instant, at four o'clock, on the ground near the Commissioner's tent, for the purpose of taking into consideration the Proclamation of His Excellency the Lieutenant-Governor of the 1st instant, relative to increasing the License Fee from 30s per month to £3, and for other purposes connected with the diggings.

December 12.

Figure 6.4. The Argus, December 12, 1851, page 3.

Figure 6.5. The site of the 'Great Meeting of Gold Diggers' at Mount Alexander, December 15, 1851, at the junction of the Forest and Wattle Creeks, in what is now Chewton. Photograph: Peter Crabb, May 10, 2011.

The initial response of the Government was far from favourable (such as "calling on the Legislature to authorise the Governor to expect from you whatever license he may think proper to levy"[26]), as evident when Dr Webb

---
26 - *The Argus*, December 30, 1851, page 2.

Figure 6.6. Memorial Stone at the site of the 'Great Meeting of Gold Diggers' at Mount Alexander, December 15, 1851. Photograph: Peter Crabb, May 10, 2011.

Richmond reported back to a meeting organised by the United Miners' Association at Flagstaff Hill, Ballarat, on December 29, 1851. In response, several resolutions were carried unanimously, including:

> *That this meeting resolves to pay no license, or other impost on the gold, until a final adjustment of the license question takes place.*
>
> *That this meeting views with disgust the arbitrary and illegal seizure of gold by Commissioner Fletcher, from Lambrick, Lang, and Wilson, three members of this Association, and that the President and Council be entrusted to take such steps, on the part of the Association, for its restoration to the injured parties as they may consider necessary.*[27]

The activities of the Gold Commissioners who administered the goldfields also came in for much criticism, as indicated in a 'Scraps from the Ovens' column.

> GOLD COMMISSION.
>
> *It is reported that the Resident Commissioner, Mr. Turner, is about to be removed from the Ovens gold-field, and that his successor is to be Mr. Clow, who has, it is said, managed to involve himself in a serious row with certain other officials at Balaarat [sic]. Mr. Turner has done very little here to raise the utility of the Gold Commissioner in public estimation. Though he probably considers himself a useful public servant, and has no doubt every desire to support the dignity of the Commission, his pompous*

---

27 - *The Argus*, December 30, 1851, page 2.

> *manner and mode of addressing those whom he considers his inferiors, have by no means been appreciated at the Ovens. Mr. Clow's performances here last year during the memorable visit of Mr. Wright to the Ovens, are still fresh in the memory of many here; and should his reported appointment turn out to be correct, the Ovens miners will be no gainers by the change. A resident commissioner should be a man of great judgement and some little talent, always accessible to the humblest applicant, and still not prone to scheming and chicanery. The necessity for the Goldfields will, no doubt, become quickly apparent to a new Governor of Victoria. Then, and not till then, we may expect a better state of things throughout the gold department.[28]*

The situation continued until the positions were abolished in 1855.[29]

A Reporter for *The Argus*

On May 15, 1850, just five days after his arrival in Melbourne, it was announced that Charles de Boos "has been appointed Reporter to the *Argus*", along with Graham Finlayson and George Ashton, and the re-appointment of Henry Edminston.[30] Whether or not de Boos had arranged the job with *The Argus* before he left Sydney is not known. His cousin, John de Boos, may have played a role, as he and his family were already in Melbourne, and he was working for *The Argus* (Appendix 3.1).[31]

The Argus was first published on June 2, 1846, and soon replaced the *Melbourne Morning Herald* as the city's main newspaper (Figure 6.7).[32] The editor, Edward Wilson, was later described as "certainly dogmatic and intolerant, and cruel and unforgiving to his enemies. [But] His journalism was brilliant".[33] Over the five years to 1855, Wilson and *The Argus* led the opposition to the government and Governor Charles La Trobe.[34] It was "radical and partisan, opposing the powerful squatting interest and all attempts to introduce convict labour".[35] Serle described *The Argus* as "the bane of the government",[36] but acknowledged that the newspaper also "helped create a robust and effective political discourse at a time

---

28 - *The Argus*, January 25, 1854, page 5.
29 - Hamilton 2015, 24-26, 56.
30 - *The Argus*, May 15, 1850, page 3.
31 - John and Mary (nee Lane) de Boos and their three children arrived in Melbourne on January 4, 1850. *Sydney Morning Herald*, January 19, 1850, page 4.
32 - Porter 2003; Dunstan 2003; Kirkpatrick 2016, 33-37; Gardiner 1967.
33 - Serle 1963, 18-19; Serle 1976.
34 - The first Lt-Governor of Victoria, La Trobe, like de Boos, was also of Huguenot descent (Cameron 2019).
35 - Dunstan 2003; *The Argus*, March 6, 1854, page 4.
36 - Serle 1963, 18.

Figure 6.7. The offices of The Argus, 74-76 Collins Street, Melbourne, c.1858. Source: Image b20011, State Library of Victoria, Melbourne.

when there were few political forums and colonial authority was relinquishing power, though initially only to certain favoured interest groups".[37]

Initially, de Boos was engaged in general reporting. From the beginning, he was more than prepared to defend his position and integrity. In early 1851, there was a dispute between *The Argus* and the *Port Phillip Gazette* and its editor, William Kerr, over the publication of material from the 'Conference of Delegates from the Australasian Colonies on the Transportation Question', held in Melbourne on February 1, 1851, with criticism of *The Argus* and its reporters.[38] However, as "One of the reporters to the *Argus*", de Boos stood by his story, as documented in a Letter to the Editor, headed 'The Rebuke'. He concluded, "I should not have troubled you with these facts, were it not that it is hardly the correct thing for Mr. Kerr to shelter himself by bringing a poor devil of a reporter into a scrape".[39]

The Argus and the Diggers

The Argus was highly critical of the government's attitude to the gold miners, as indicated in more than one editorial. For example, "Thanks to the mismanagement, the vacillation, the niggardliness, the down-right

---

37 - Dunstan 2003. As far as is known, no archival records of the company that published *The Argus* exist, in relation to the company itself or its employees. Personal communication, Katie Flack, Australian History & Literature Team, State Library of Victoria, email November 26, 2012.

38 - *Port Phillip Gazette*, February 6, 1851, page 2; February 7, page 2; and a *Supplement* to the paper, February 1, 1851.

39 - *The Argus*, February 7, 1851, page 2; February 8, 1851, page 2.

imbecility of the Executive, the diggings have long been, and now are, in a very critical state".[40] For Serle, the paper was more than simply supportive of the diggers, claiming "that the contribution made by *The Argus* to growing discontent on the goldfields was considerable, with the diggers 'inflamed by exaggerated reports of the venality and inefficiency of the gold field administration'".[41] He noted that "All the correspondents to some extent pleaded the digger cause and, with an eye to sales, slanted their reports. Some *Argus* reports must be read with special caution, but in this period the *Herald* and *Geelong Advertiser* reports generally have the ring of veracity".[42] William Kelly had put forward similar views of *The Argus* in 1859, more than a century earlier.

> *There was such a relentless persistence in its tone, the diggers were cajoled into the belief that it was genuine earnestness. All legitimate authority was abused with such a seeming heartiness that imperial connexion came to be a question of debate on the gold-fields. And the license tax (a most odious imposition in the eyes of the diggers) was so held up to public execration as an infamous and illegal exaction, that the vast community of diggers, gradually and adroitly warmed up from a gentle simmer to a full boil, rushed madly, with arms in their hands, in open rebellion to procure its abolition.*[43]

The Argus supported the diggers and the large meetings held to press their claims, particularly for a reduction in the licence fees.[44] These gatherings, along with many others, such as on the Ovens,[45] were peaceful events. There were also public meetings in Melbourne in support of the diggers and seeking justice for them.[46] There was the formation of the Anti-Gold-License Committee.[47] These numerous public meetings highlighted the opposition to the Colonial Government, and the *Report of the Select Committee of the Legislative Council for the Better Management of the Gold-Fields* was savaged by *The Argus*.[48] In its words, the Committee traced "the recent disorders at the gold-fields to the proceedings of the sister legislature of New South Wales; to the ill luck of the diggers; to the misrepresentations of the Press;

---

40 - *The Argus*, March 16, 1852, page 2.
41 - Dunstan 2003, quoting Serle 1963; Serle 1976.
42 - Serle 1963, 26.
43 - Kelly 1859, 104. There was also strong criticism of *The Argus* from the Editor of *The Courier* in Hobart (May 4, 1855, page 2).
44 - *The Argus*, July 21, 1853, page 5.
45 - *The Argus*, April 8, 1853, page 9; August 26, 1853, pages 4-5.
46 - *The Argus*, August 5, 1853, page 4; September 6, 1853, page 5.
47 - *The Argus*, September 12, 1853, page 5; October 21, 1854, page 6.
48 - "The Management of the Gold-Fields" (Editorial on *Report of the Select Committee of the Legislative Council for the Better Management of the Gold-Fields*), *The Argus*, November 2, 1853, page 4.

but *attributing no portion of the blame to their own immaculate body*".[49] The Press was then charged with inventing the grievances of the diggers. *The Argus* did "not believe that a more thoroughly disgraceful document [had] ever before issued from a Legislative Council".[50]

Most of the public meetings mentioned thus far predated the very different Red Ribbon Rebellion at Bendigo in August 1853 and the rebellion of gold miners at Eureka Lead, which culminated in the Battle of the 'Eureka Stockade' on December 3, 1854, with the deaths of twenty two miners.[51] The reasons for the civil unrest were the familiar ones: the cost of the miner's licence (30 shillings a month); the lack of any representation for the miners; and the actions of the government and its agents. The *Report of the Commission Appointed to Enquire into the Condition of the Gold Fields of Victoria* was presented to the Government just over three months later.[52] It was very critical of the situation and of the colonial government.[53] Clearly, successive Victorian governments had not learned from the many problems associated with the goldfields. There was much validity in the many criticisms published in *The Argus*. Then and since, however, other views of the diggers and their actions were expressed.

> *Remarkably, the individual miner had now become a symbol of freedom and resistance to oppression, rather than of private wealth seeking at the expense of public resources. The common sense of colonists, and most historians since, became that individual gold seeking was the most natural response to gold, and that proposals to tax or limit individual gold seeking in the name of the greater public good were simple masks for imperial and class oppression. The license was replaced in Victoria in 1855 with a Miner's Right, sold for one pound and valid for one year, conferring also the right to vote. The 1857 amendments to the 1855 Gold Fields Act further specified that the Miner's Right gave the right to put up a building, cut down trees for personal use, and 'divert and use' water for mining purposes on Crown Land.[54]*

For de Boos, his support for the diggers came from his concerns for the under-privileged and issues of inequality.

---

49 - *The Argus*, November 2, 1853, page 4.

50 - *The Argus*, November 5, 1853, page 4.

51 - *The Argus*, October 21, 1854, page 4; November 22, 1854, page 4; December 2, 1854, page 5; "Fatal Collision at Ballaarat", *The Argus*, December 4, 1854, page 5; December 5, 1854, pages 4; December 6, 1854, pages 4-5; Hamilton 2015, 24-26. There is no evidence that de Boos was at the Eureka demonstrations.

52 - *Report of the Commission Appointed to Enquire into the Condition of the Gold Fields of Victoria*. Ordered to be printed, March 29, 1855. Government Printer, Melbourne, 1855.

53 - *The Argus*, April 10, 1855, page 5.

54 - Goodman 2018.

The Newspapers and their Reporters

Gold was 'gold' for the contemporary newspapers. It took up a large proportion of the printed pages and just about everything imaginable associated with the precious metal was covered: editorials,[55] specific reports; short reports in the 'Domestic Intelligence' columns; the 'Gold Circulars'; reports from the other colonies and overseas (New South Wales, California, New Zealand); 'Original Correspondence' (letters to the Editor); and countless advertisements for everything connected with gold and its mining, such as the needed clothing and equipment and even 'how-to' books (Figure 6.8a-d). In fact, advertisements of all kinds filled up most of the papers. 'News' rarely occupied more than two pages in *The Argus*; and some issues were nothing but advertisements.

Gold kept the many *Argus* reporters very busy from mid-1851 through to 1853, but why so many were required to write about the same events in the same places is somewhat difficult to understand; on occasions, reports on the same matter from two or three reporters followed each other on the same page. Few were known by name, and more than one person was given the title of 'A Correspondent', 'Another Correspondent', 'Our Own

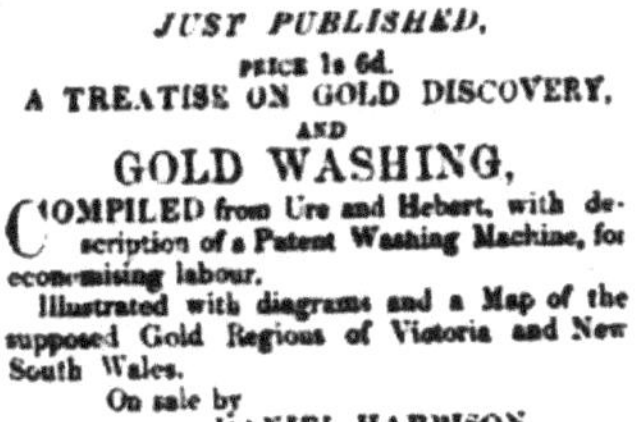
JUST PUBLISHED,
PRICE 1s 6d.
A TREATISE ON GOLD DISCOVERY,
AND
GOLD WASHING,
COMPILED from Ure and Hebert, with description of a Patent Washing Machine, for economising labour.
Illustrated with diagrams and a Map of the supposed Gold Regions of Victoria and New South Wales.
On sale by
DANIEL HARRISON,
34 Collins-street, West,
and by all Booksellers.
Sent free by post, on receipt of 1s. 8d. in stamps.

Figure 6.8a. The Argus, July 25, 1851, page 4.

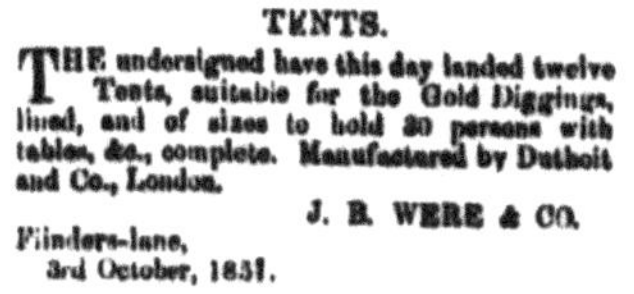
TENTS.
THE undersigned have this day landed twelve Tents, suitable for the Gold Diggings, lined, and of sizes to hold 20 persons with tables, &c., complete. Manufactured by Duthoit and Co., London.
J. B. WERE & CO.
Flinders-lane,
3rd October, 1851.

Figure 6.8b. The Argus, October 6, 1851, page 3.

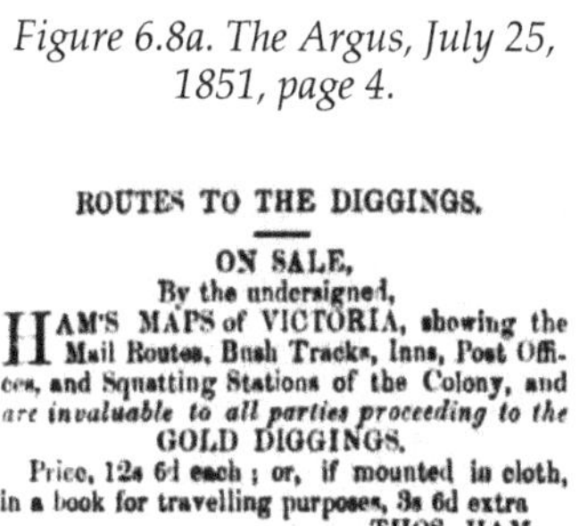
ROUTES TO THE DIGGINGS.
ON SALE,
By the undersigned,
HAM'S MAPS of VICTORIA, showing the Mail Routes, Bush Tracks, Inns, Post Offices, and Squatting Stations of the Colony, and *are invaluable to all parties proceeding to the* GOLD DIGGINGS.
Price, 12s 6d each; or, if mounted in cloth, in a book for travelling purposes, 3s 6d extra
THOS. HAM.

Figure 6.8c. The Argus, February 10, 1852, page S1.

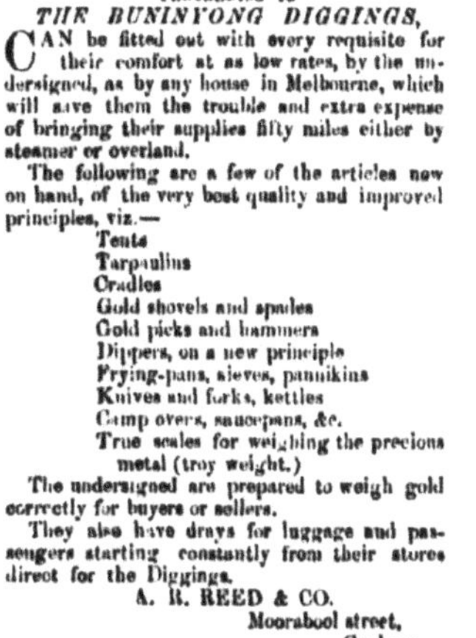
GOLD SEEKERS
PROCEEDING TO
THE BUNINYONG DIGGINGS,
CAN be fitted out with every requisite for their comfort at as low rates, by the undersigned, as by any house in Melbourne, which will save them the trouble and extra expense of bringing their supplies fifty miles either by steamer or overland.
The following are a few of the articles now on hand, of the very best quality and improved principles, viz.—
Tents
Tarpaulins
Cradles
Gold shovels and spades
Gold picks and hammers
Dippers, on a new principle
Frying-pans, sieves, pannikins
Knives and forks, kettles
Camp ovens, saucepans, &c.
True scales for weighing the precious metal (troy weight.)
The undersigned are prepared to weigh gold correctly for buyers or sellers.
They also have drays for luggage and passengers starting constantly from their stores direct for the Diggings.
A. R. REED & CO.
Moorabool street,
Geelong.

Figure 6.8d. The Argus, October 6, 1851, page 3.

55 - For example: *The Argus*, October 8, 1851, page 2; January 2, 1852, page 2; February 13, 1852, page 2; February 16, 1852, page 2; March 4, 1852, page 2); en.wikipedia.org/wiki/Australian_gold_rushes.

Correspondent', or some other similar term, making their identification and that of their particular work even more difficult. Despite the number already reporting on the goldfields, in March 1852, the Editor of *The Argus* announced yet another person would be reporting on the Mount Alexander goldfields:

> *To do something to clear up the doubts that exist upon the subject ... of the richest gold mine in the world, we have dispatched a gentleman to Mount Alexander as a special commissioner for this journal, with instructions to make a complete tour of the various places where the search for gold is carried on; to inform himself accurately of everything of interest at each; and to furnish full and authentic reports of what he sees and hears. Our emissary is a gentleman long known to us, and as a man of intelligence and integrity, we can pledge ourselves to the truthfulness of his statements.*[56]

'Our emisary', or 'Our Special Commissioner', wrote thirteen reports that appeared in *The Argus* from March 16 to May 19, 1852 (Appendix 6.1), and though mainly about Mount Alexander – Forest Creek, the later ones also covered the Bendigo area. The 'Special Commissioner' was not named, but it was Charles de Boos (who along with his cousin John are two of the few reporters known by name[57]), as he indicated many years later:

> *At the latter end of 1851 I was commissioned specially by the Argus paper in Victoria to make a tour through the Gold Fields of that Colony, and to make a report thereupon. In pursuance of that commission, I visited Ballarat, Forest Creek, and Bendigo, the only Gold Fields then opened, and spent between four or five months upon that business. Again, two years later [i.e., 1853-54], I visited the Gold Fields on a similar mission for the Argus, this second time going more particularly through the Ovens Gold Field. My personal acquaintance with the Victorian Gold Fields ceased about 1854.*[58]

Textual analysis and at least some of the content confirm that these articles are the work of de Boos, as are those by 'Argus SC' (Figure 6.9). Already the established reporter, the gold rushes added significantly to his workload, as well as starting a life-long association with gold mining and gold miners. From August 5 to August 16, 1851, a series of four articles on 'The Clunes Diggings' appeared in *The Argus* followed by one on Anderson's Creek, written by 'Our Special Correspondent' (Appendix 6.2). Analysis indicates that these articles and some of the subsequent ones about Ballarat (Appendix 6.3) are the work of de Boos (Figure 6.10). This clearly suggests that Charles and John were the first reporters at the first two important gold finds in Victoria, an interesting coincidence.

---

56 - *The Argus*, March 16, 1852, page 2.
57 - Regarding John de Boos, see Appendix 3.1; *The Argus*, August 16, page 2; August 18, page 2; August 22, 1851, page 2.
58 - Gold Fields Royal Commission 1871, 151.

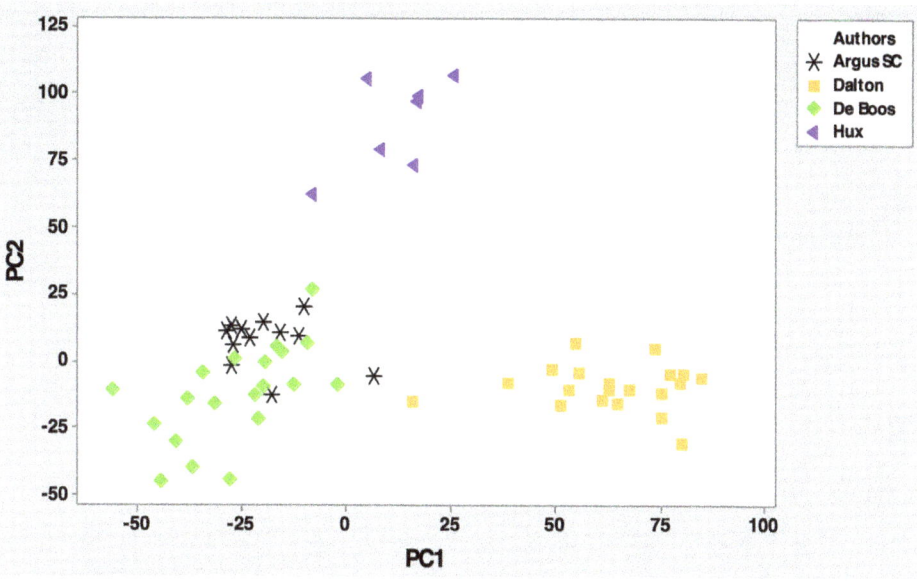

Figure 6.9. Differentiating the writings of de Boos from some other known reporters (the Hux and Dalton articles were about the NSW goldfields). 'Argus SC' was a 'Special Correspondent' for The Argus, in this case another title given to de Boos. Source: Dr Alexis Antonia, Centre for Literary and Linguistic Computing, University of Newcastle.[59]

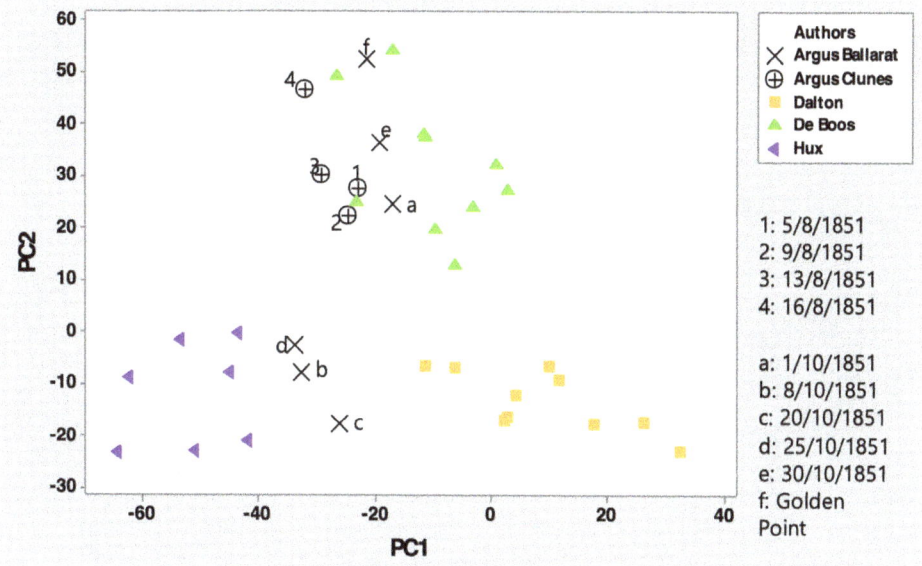

Figure 6.10. de Boos on Clunes and Ballarat; analysis based on 100 function words. Source: Dr Alexis Antonia, Centre for Literary and Linguistic Computing, University of Newcastle.

---

59 - For information on the analytical methods, see Crabb, Antonia and Craig 2014. For information on Hux, see Crabb 2020; on Dalton, see Dalton et al. 2016; Crabb et al. 2019.

From early 1852, there were increasing numbers of reports on the Ovens diggings. For some two years from late 1852, over 100 columns headed 'Scraps from the Ovens' appeared in *The Argus*, almost all of them written from Spring Creek by 'Our Own Correspondent'.[60] Many other reports were written by various correspondents, who were given a variety of titles. They also covered other nearby goldfields, such as McIvor, Mitta Mitta, Wangaratta, and Omeo. However, in spite of de Boos' own words, nothing relating to the Ovens Gold Field has yet been found that can be clearly attributed to him.

What did de Boos write about?

The bad roads were a constant cause for comment, and not just by de Boos; thick dust when it was dry, mud up to the axles of drays when it was wet. So, when he found some road work that had actually been planned and then undertaken, he could hardly contain his surprise![61] Mail services were poor, especially at Bendigo, where people also had to contend with the high cost of food and other supplies. He provided graphic descriptions of the environmental consequences of gold mining along Forest Creek.

> *The road, which winds along the Creek through the Diggings, is, from the constant traffic, ten times more dusty than even dusty Melbourne and the heavy gusts of wind which pour through the gulleys with great violence, whirl it up in clouds and scatter it far and near upon everything around. The newly erected tent does not therefore long retain its brilliant whiteness, a few blasts powder it effectually, and give it the same sombre indescribable dusty hue that distinguishes its neighbours, and soon take off every appearance of freshness. In the same way such trees as have escaped the axe are dusted to an unnatural brownness, and look more like the desperate attempts at vegetation made by the stunted shrubs of a Hackney roadside villa, than the giant growth of an Australian forest. Even off the road, the earth is so trodden and worn by the thousands of feet that are constantly passing and repassing, that not the faintest sign of verdure remains upon the ground, all being bare and dusty; while on the southern side of the Creek, the hills are so pierced, and the subsoil so tossed and tumbled about upon their face, that they look like nothing but gravel or chalk pits and stone quarries. When to this is also added the constant feeding of the innumerable horses which throng the Diggings, eating off the grass on the few hills that have not been ransacked, and even cropping the shoots of the few shrubs that grow amongst the rocks, baring them of every particle of verdure, and the rude rough look of the jagged rocks which protrude from the bare surface, anything but a refreshing picture meets the eye.[62]*

---

60 - From December 10, 1852, through to December 27, 1854.
61 - *The Argus*, April 21, 1852, page 4.
62 - *The Argus*, March 22, 1852, page 2; Lawrence and Davies 2019; Lawrence, Davies and Turnbull 2016a; 2016b.

He commented at some length on the problems caused by very dry conditions and the lack of water, for mining and for people, resulting in dysentery and other health issues. de Boos was particularly concerned with the social conditions, especially for women and children. "In no part of the Victoria Diggings is there more crime, violence, and lawlessness, than at Bendigo";[63] things were somewhat better at Mount Alexander. He laid the blame on excessive alcohol consumption and especially the illegal 'sly grog shops', many of which operated with impunity; a lack of police and law enforcement officials; and the numbers of ex-criminals from New South Wales and especially Van Diemen's Land.[64] The effects of the latter's foul language and behaviour on other people was of great concern to de Boos.

The licencing system, which applied to everyone on the goldfields, came in for particular criticism, for its cost, application, and its inconsistent enforcement. The behaviour of the Commissioners and the Licencing Officers left much to be desired.

> *What will be said to a case which I myself witnessed! Three men, whom I saw enter upon the Diggings, with their bundles on their backs, having just arrived from Melbourne, were met by a constable only a few minutes after they had passed me, and were apprehended for not having a licence. And yet these men had not actually had time to take out a licence, and were in fact arrested on the road to the Commissioners. Again, a dray was stopped coming on to, and before it had reached the Diggings, and the owner was seized, and I believe fined for being without the potent sign manual of the Commissioner. Nor will it suffice to have paid the fee, as diggers have, in more than one instance, been fined for being without a licence, not because they had not one, but because they had it not about them, and the constables were too eager for their half penalty either to accompany the man to his tent or allow him to send a friend to procure the protecting document. Such scenes as these are being daily, nay hourly, enacted, and what impression think you they can have on the minds of men who are compelled to witness their performance. Nor can the victims raise their eyes in hopeful appeal to the tribunal before which they are judged, since 'Commissioner's Law' has become on the Diggings a bye word for absurdity or oppression owing to the gross cases of illegality and arbitrary abuse of power that the canvas walls of the Commissioner's Court have seen perpetrated.*[65]

And if such cases were not bad enough, in early 1852, Governor Sir George Gipps decided to strictly enforce the rules and the collection all the relevant fees.

---

63 - *The Argus*, May 6, 1852, page 4.
64 - McCalman 2021.
65 - *The Argus*, May 5, 1852, page 2.

Of special interest is the fact that the writings of de Boos on the early Victorian goldfields are complemented by the sketches of S.T. (Samuel Thomas) Gill. Both were in the Forest Creek and nearby areas at the same time (August to October 1852) (Figure 6.11). Gill's *The Diggers and Diggings as they were in 1852* suggests he had very similar views to de Boos on many issues (Figures 6.12 and 6.13).[66] He "recorded the unfolding environmental

Figure 6.11. Forest Creek, Mount Alexander Diggings from base of Red Hill near the Argus Office looking towards Castlemaine, July 1852, by S.T. Gill. The red sign on the building on the left reads "To Argus Office". Macartney & Galbraith, Melbourne, 1852. Source: National Library of Australia, PIC Solander Box C19# S84.

Figure 6.12. Diggings at Little Bendigo, Forest Creek, 1852, by S.T. Gill. Source: Gill 1855; National Library of Australia, nla.gov.au/nla.obj-135654217/view

Figure 6.13. Fryers Creek, Mount Alexander Diggings, by S.T. Gill. Macartney & Galbraith, Melbourne, 1852. Source: National Library of Australia, nla.gov.au/nla.obj-135678637/view

---

66 - Gill 1855; Grishin 2015.

catastrophe on the goldfields, where the trees had largely been felled, streams clogged, and the human anthill had eroded the surface. … It was in the 1860s that Gill's style and ideology became firmly cemented as he adopted the stance of a democratic socialist, one who was critical of racism [especially against the Chinese], who defended the rights of Australia's Indigenous peoples, protested at social inequality, and was critical of the land use and environmental destruction caused by the European settlers".[67] He portrayed life as it was on the goldfields, and he included more women in his work than any other colonial artist.

Just when de Boos stopped working for *The Argus* is not known. Did his statement that his "personal acquaintance with the Victorian Gold Fields ceased about 1854" also mark the end of his work for the paper? As early as 1853, the position of *The Argus* on various issues began to change. Wilson "was appalled by the armed resistance at the Eureka Stockade in October 1854, when several hundred men proclaimed their intention to establish the Republic of Victoria. From that time on *The Argus* was firm in support of La Trobe's successor, Governor Hotham, and the forces of law and order".[68] In a major change of policy, *The Argus* adopted a highly critical stance towards the diggers and transferred its support to the Colony's mercantile interests. This resulted in a number of key staff leaving *The Argus* and joining a new paper, *The Age*. Given his support for the diggers, de Boos was likely one of those who left, though there is no evidence that he joined *The Age*.[69]

Working for the Victorian Legislative Council

Some three months after de Boos moved to Melbourne, Victoria ceased to be part of New South Wales and became a separate colony by an Act of the British Parliament, signed by Queen Victoria on August 5, 1850. It was some time before this news reached Melbourne, and not until July 1, 1851, that the enabling legislation was passed by the NSW Legislative Council. Initially, self-government was limited to the Lieutenant-Governor and a Legislative Council. de Boos was appointed "Government Reporter to the

---

67 - Grishin 2016.
68 - Hirst 2003; 2002.
69 - Dunstan 2003.

Council" in November 1851.[70] What was the nature of this work? Was it solely for the Legislative Council, or was it to provide reports of debates which were published in *The Argus*, at a time before there was an official Hansard? In the Government's estimates of expenditure, his salary appears to have gone from an initial £200 per year to £700 in 1855, an indication of the high salaries and other inducements that had to be provided to keep essential jobs in Melbourne filled in the face of the attractions of the gold rushes.[71]

The coincidental employment of de Boos by *The Argus* and the Victorian Legislative Council raises some interesting issues. How was he able to do both jobs? How could he have had the time to be involved in the work with the Legislative Council and, at the same time, be an active reporter, especially reporting that required travelling well beyond Melbourne? Were they both part-time positions or were they in some way complementary? In addition to this, there was the clearly antagonistic relationship between *The Argus* and the Government, or rather the kind of people and their characters who made up the Legislative Council, a conservative squattocracy and lawyers.[72] In commenting on a statement from the paper's Geelong correspondent, the Editor of *The Argus* stated:

> We never differed from our correspondent as to the 'duplicity and faithlessness' of our Executive Council. On the contrary, we believe both by its constitution and its actions, that the La Trobe element is there in a majority; and that while such a predominance continues, duplicity and faithlessness will be the prevailing characteristics of that body; still doubtless, slightly relieved occasionally by the direst imbecility.[73]

The Victorian Legislative Council met for the first time on November 11, 1851. There were certainly long periods when the Council did not sit (up to eight months at a stretch), but it was in those periods that the

---

70 - *Melbourne Morning Herald*, November 5, 1851, page 2. The item also reported that Captain [Lewis] Conran had been appointed "Sarjaent-at-Arms in the Legislative Council". The item was repeated in other papers, including the *Sydney Morning Herald*, November 17, 1851, page 3; the *Maitland Mercury*, November 19, 1851, page 3; *Geelong Advertiser*, November 6, 1851, page 2; and the *Colonial Times* (Hobart), November 15, 1851, page 3. However, only Conran's appointment was reported in the *Victoria Government Gazette* (No. 18, November 11, 1851, page 718) and *The Argus*, November 6, 1851, page 2.

71 - From *Parliament of Victoria: About Hansard:* www.parliament.vic.gov.au/hansard/about-hansard, accessed February 5, 2011; "A brief history of The Argus', *The Argus*, June 3, 1946, page 11; *Victoria: Votes and Proceedings of the Legislative Council, 1851-52*, Government Printing Office, Melbourne, 1852; 'Estimates of the Ways and Means and of the Probable Expenditures of the Colonial Government of Victoria, for the year 1853'. *Victoria: Votes and Proceedings of the Legislative Council, Session 1852-53*, Volume 1. Government Printing Office, Melbourne, 1853. Only two people had a higher salary, another had the same (Butterfield 1854, 163).

72 - For example: "We trust that the Council may be able to survive its decided over-dose of lawyers" (*The Argus*, November 8, 1851, page 2).

73 - *The Argus*, January 21, 1852, page 2.

meetings of numerous Select Committees were held.[74] These would surely have required de Boos to be in Melbourne, leaving little time for him to be a reporter. There were probably very few periods when neither the Council nor one or more committees were not sitting.[75] So what were his employment conditions that enabled him to have two apparently full-time jobs at the same time?

At the end of 1854 and into January 1855, there were large cuts to the numbers employed in the Public Service, with others having salary cuts of up to fifty per cent, measures that came in for much criticism.

> GOVERNMENT DISMISSALS, COLONIAL ENTERPRISE, AND THE LAND.
>
> *That the dismissed Government employés have just ground for complaint in the treatment they have received at the hands of the Executive Government, we fancy no one impartially viewing the circumstances of the case can deny. They have been appointed to a service which had come to be generally recognised as permanent one. They had afforded no pretext for dissatisfaction; and they have had dismissal administered to them, on the principle of that singular impartiality which treats all claims alike, making no difference between the novice and the experienced between those who could plead length of servitude as a reasonable ground of protection from arbitrary caprice, and those who could boast but the appointment of yesterday.*[76]

Did de Boos remain in his job? Heaton stated that he held his government job until 1856, but early 1855 seems much more likely.[77]

There is at least one piece of evidence that he also undertook other casual work. The 1852-53 report of the 'Melbourne, Mount Alexander and Murray River Railway Company' included a cost item of £14.18.0 for "Mr DeBoos' short-hand writer's account for reports".[78]

For the second time, his own newspaper

In May 1855, the first of a number of reports appeared in Melbourne of a new weekly newspaper, *The Telegraph and Sporting Times*. In advance of the first issue, it was widely publicised:

---

74 - Ray Wright 2001, 144-152.
75 - Enquiries to the Legislative Council of Victoria yielded no other information relating to the time de Boos spent working for the Council. Emails from Andrew Young, Acting Clerk, May 21, 2015, and Jon Breukel, Acting Manager, Parliamentary Library and Information Services, May 25, 2015.
76 - *The Argus*, January 4, 1855, page 4.
77 - Heaton 1879, page 54.
78 - *The Argus*, March 24, 1853, page 9.

> *The prospectus of a new weekly journal, The Telegraph, has been issued. The first number will make its appearance on the first Saturday in July, and the journal will be conducted by Mr. de Boos, formerly shorthand writer in the Legislative Council, and for many years connected with the colonial press.*[79]

> NEW WEEKLY NEWSPAPERS. *Two new hebdomadals are to make their appearance on Saturday next, the Telegraph and the Pictorial Times. The former, a sporting paper, is under the editorship of Mr. C. de Boos; the latter, as the name purports, is to be an illustrated publication. 'There's room enough for all'.*[80]

The paper was a joint venture of de Boos and Thomas Henry Jones.[81] *The Argus* of July 5, 1855, contained three separate advertisements for the paper.[82]

The first issue appeared on July 7, 1855, and was well received, with summaries and complimentary reviews in a number of newspapers (Figure 6.14).[83] de Boos was described as "a skilful veteran of the press in Victoria, and perhaps the most clever reporter in the colony", and "well known to fame in Sydney".[84] The review in *The Argus* was particularly favourable, suggesting that de Boos continued to be on good terms with his former employers:

> *THE TELEGRAPH. – Mr. De Boos has started a weekly newspaper, entitled The Telegraph and Sporting Times, of which the first number was published on Saturday. The Telegraph, though of small size, contains a great deal of pleasant matter. The history of the week, under the different heads of "Home", "Mining", and "Colonial", contains a lively and comprehensive review of the principal events of the preceding seven days. The first three chapters of "The Stockman's Daughter: a Tale of the New Country", are full of promise. No. 1 of "Chapters from Life, by an Old Reporter", has all the verisimilitude of personal reminiscence. "Our First Leader" has the merit of modesty; and a few pithy remarks are made in reference to the Finance Commission. The sporting intelligence is rather scant, no fault, however of the Telegraph; but a review of "our public amusements" furnishes more abundant subject of remark. Amid the local intelligence one or two venerable "Joes" have found their way into the company of new and effective allusions to passing events and prominent personages.*

---

79 - The Cornwall Chronicle [Launceston], May 26, 1885, page 3.

80 - *The Argus*, Tuesday, June 26, 1855, page 5.

81 - *Telegraph and Sporting Times*. *Print:* Jones, Thomas Henry of 89 Stephen Street, Melbourne, and De Boos, Charles Edward of Fitzroy Street, Collingwood. *Publ:* Jones, Thomas Henry and De Boos, Charles Edward of 2½ Bourke Street, Melbourne. At Little Bourke Street, in premises occupied by Messrs Abbot and Co. at the back of the General Post Office, Melbourne. *Remarks:* Jones and De Boos are also the Editors" (Darragh 1997, 95).

82 - *The Argus*, July 5, 1855, page 8. The advertisements also listed some of the content: "The 'Stockman's Daughter" a colonial tale, in the *Sporting Times*, Saturday next"; "Punch in Victoria. – See the *Telegraph and Sporting Times* of Saturday next"; "The *Telegraph and Sporting Times* will appear on Saturday next, July 7".

83 - *Geelong Advertiser*, July 11, 1855, page 2.

84 - *Colonial Times* (Hobart), July 16, 1855, page 4; *People's Advocate*, July 21, 1855, page 14.

There is a somewhat too exclusively sporting letter from "Our Sydney Correspondent", and "Bridle-rein" contributes a graphic sketch of a popular character. We anticipate for our new contemporary a highly successful career.[85]

> THE TELEGRAPH AND SPORTING TIMES.—The first number of this Weekly Journal is before us,—as indicated by its title, a very happy one, by the bye, it is devoted to all subjects comprised in the term "Sporting." The appearance of the journal is business-like, and the first issue is replete with much original matter, containing the first chapter of a tale, entitled "the Stockman's Daughter," and first paper of a series under the heading of "Chapters from Life," exceedingly well written. The editorial matter is sensible, without pretensions, and the sporting intelligence ample. General information of local matters is well digested, and a precis of English Sporting Intelligence, will be found grateful to the admirers of manly sports. Quips, cranks, puns, and satires, "shooting folly as it flies," peep out from innumerable paragraphs, and excite risibility, despite the depression prevalent. Under the management of Mr. Charles Edward de Boos, a skilful veteran of the press in Victoria, and perhaps the most clever reporter in the colony, there is guarantee "that if he cannot command success, he will deserve it," and we heartily commend the product of his labors, to the patronage of our sporting friends.

Figure 6.14. Geelong Advertiser, July 11, 1855, page 2.

The first issue must have sold well, as a few days after its publication, more workers were required by the paper's printers: "Compositors Wanted on the *Telegraph and Sporting Times*. M.M. Abbott and Co., Printers, Melbourne".[86] This advertisement would suggest that there was at least one more issue, but the paper did not have the "highly successful career" anticipated by *The Argus*. It soon became one more of the many short-lived newspapers during this period in Victoria. No copies of the paper are known to exist.[87]

On August 1, 1855, the dissolution by mutual consent of the partnership between Jones and Charles de Boos relating to the *Telegraph and Sporting Times* was announced.[88] Two subsequent public notices suggest a somewhat contradictory story of what happened following the dissolution. Given the somewhat strong statement by de Boos, all was not well between him and Jones (Figures 6.15 and 6.16).[89] This is yet another incident in the life of de Boos about which the full story is unknown.

---

85 - *The Argus*, July 9, 1855, page 5; *People's Advocate*, July 21, 1855, page 14.

86 - *The Argus*, July 10, 1855, page 1.

87 - For guidance on information relating to early Victorian newspapers and *The Telegraph and Sporting Times* in particular, thanks are due to Zoe Velonis, State Library of Victoria, Melbourne, emails, February 2, 2010, and June 14, 2011.

88 - *The Age*, August 9, 1855, page 1; *Victoria Government Gazette*, August 10, 1855, page 2033.

89 - *The Argus*, August 10, 1855, page 8. 'Defalcation' is defined as 'misappropriation of money, etc., held by a trustee or other fiduciary'.

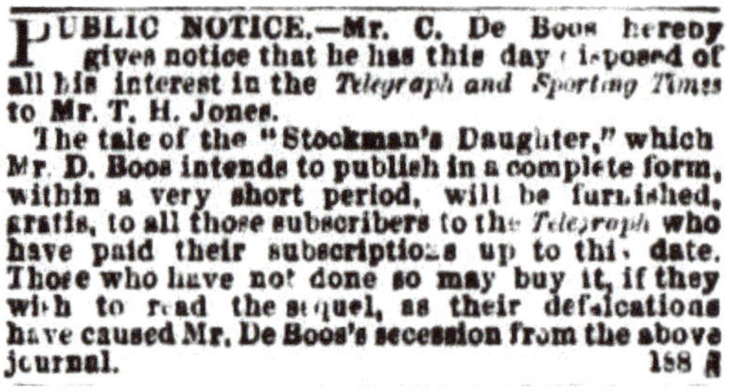

> PUBLIC NOTICE.—Mr. C. De Boos hereby gives notice that he has this day disposed of all his interest in the *Telegraph and Sporting Times* to Mr. T. H. Jones.
>
> The tale of the "Stockman's Daughter," which Mr. D. Boos intends to publish in a complete form, within a very short period, will be furnished, gratis, to all those subscribers to the *Telegraph* who have paid their subscriptions up to this date. Those who have not done so may buy it, if they wish to read the sequel, as their defalcations have caused Mr. De Boos's secession from the above journal.

Figure 6.15. The Argus, August 10, 1855, page 8.

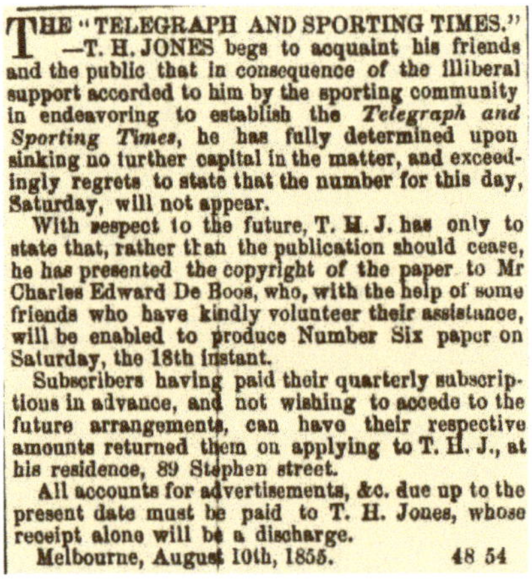

> THE "TELEGRAPH AND SPORTING TIMES."—T. H. JONES begs to acquaint his friends and the public that in consequence of the illiberal support accorded to him by the sporting community in endeavoring to establish the *Telegraph and Sporting Times*, he has fully determined upon sinking no further capital in the matter, and exceedingly regrets to state that the number for this day, Saturday, will not appear.
>
> With respect to the future, T. H. J. has only to state that, rather than the publication should cease, he has presented the copyright of the paper to Mr Charles Edward De Boos, who, with the help of some friends who have kindly volunteer their assistance, will be enabled to produce Number Six paper on Saturday, the 18th instant.
>
> Subscribers having paid their quarterly subscriptions in advance, and not wishing to accede to the future arrangements, can have their respective amounts returned them on applying to T. H. J., at his residence, 89 Stephen street.
>
> All accounts for advertisements, &c. due up to the present date must be paid to T. H. Jones, whose receipt alone will be a discharge.
>
> Melbourne, August 10th, 1855.

Figure 6.16. The Age, August 11, 1855, page 8.

Family life

Initially, Charles and his family lived at 110 La Trobe Street, East.[90] His income was clearly sufficient for his wife to employ one or more servants to help with looking after their child and undertake "all work".[91] Their second daughter, Sarah Susannah, was born at the family residence on August 24, 1851.[92] Mrs de Boos was in need of more help.[93] In 1852, they were living in Collingwood, where they had a horse or rather "A flee-bitten grey mare" (Figure 6.17). On June 19, 1853, Charles Edward, jun., their third child, was born at the family residence in Little Brighton, Melbourne.[94] Indicating again his community involvement, de Boos donated to the Wesleyan Chapel Building Fund in Brighton.[95]

---

90 - July 1851: Victorian Electoral Roll 1851; Gipps Ward; La Trobe Street; "dwelling house".

91 - "WANTED: A female servant, principally to look after a young child. Apply to Mrs. C. De Boos, 110 La Trobe Street, East" (*The Argus*, April 28, 1851, page 3). "WANTED: A general house servant. Apply to Mrs. C. De Boos, 110 La Trobe Street, East" (*The Argus*, July 14, 1851, page 3).

92 - *The Argus*, August 26, 1851, page 2.

93 - "WANTED: A servant of all work. Apply to Mrs. C. De Boos, 110 La Trobe Street, East. None need apply but those who can give satisfactory references" (*The Argus*, October 18, 1851, page 3).

94 - *The Argus*, June 21, 1853, page 2.

95 - *The Age*, December 30, 1854, page 5.

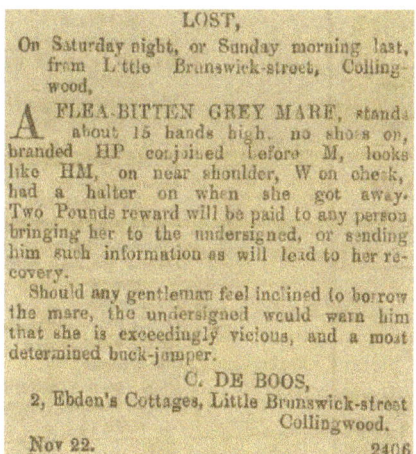

Figure 6.17. The Argus, November 26, 1852, page 8.

After the failure of his newspaper venture, the rest of his time in Melbourne during 1855-1856 is something of a mystery. Once again, how was he able to support himself and his family? The question is made even more puzzling by an insolvency case. Raised initially in the Supreme Court in July 1855, de Boos was subsequently in the Insolvent Court, seeking payment of a debt of £318 from a Jacob Beer.[96]

> *The insolvent has been a farmer at Little Brighton. Mr. Frame, solicitor, now supported insolvent, who was present in person. Mr. De Boos proved a debt of £318, for costs of an Equity suit and money lent. No other debts were proved. The insolvent attributed his ruin to the above equity suit. He had cultivated the land for about four years, when a flaw was discovered in the lease, and he was ejected from the land.*[97]

This report raises many questions. The de Boos family had lived in Little Brighton for a time in 1853-1854. But who was Jacob Beer and what was his relationship with de Boos? de Boos had been well paid by the Colonial Government, but how did he have over £300 to lend? The failure of his newspaper may well have driven de Boos to seek payment of the money owed to him.

On October 23, 1855, their fourth child and second son, Francis George, was born at their Collingwood home.[98] By the following year, they had moved again (11 Argyle Street, Melbourne).[99] He was described in the

---

96 - *The Argus*, July 28, 1855, page 6.
97 - *The Argus*, September 12, 1855, page 5; *The Age*, September 12, 1855, page 5.
98 - *The Argus*, October 24, 1855, page 4.
99 - Victorian Electoral Roll, 1856-57: St. Mark's Division, includes Charles Edward de Boos (Reporter); Household; 11 Argyle Street. Source: NLA mcN.477. Publication of the roll seems to date from mid to late 1856.

Electoral Role as a 'Reporter', but was he an employed or unemployed one? If the former, which paper was he working for? In early April, at a complimentary dinner given by residents of the Fitzroy Ward in recognition of the service of their representative on the Melbourne City Council, Mr Groom, "Mr. De Boos" was a vocal soloist, singing 'Rule Britannia', 'The Marseillaise', and 'The British Grenadiers'.[100]

Not long after this, Charles and family returned to Sydney. No record of their voyage has been found.

Conclusion

During his six years in Melbourne, de Boos was intimately involved in a period of remarkable change in Victoria. It became a separate Colony, and he was one of the first employees of the initial institutions of self-government. He worked for one of the Colony's major newspapers, at a time when these were the only means of providing information to the general population. Further, given the inadequacies of the government institutions, newspapers, and *The Argus* in particular, were the major avenues of criticism of and opposition to the government. Most significantly, this was the period of the initial gold rushes in Victoria, which had major secondary effects. The attraction of gold meant that many people left their employment in established activities and essential services, with consequent labour shortages in rural areas and in Melbourne. In an endeavour to overcome these, wages rose rapidly and significantly, doubling within two to three years. It is hardly surprising that initially there was much criticism of the 'gold fever' and what it would do to individuals and society as a whole.

> *Newspaper and parliamentary debates of the period feature anxious monologues on the imminent threats to law and order created by 'the rush to be rich'. The clergymen, the social engineer and the moralist lamented the unholy obsession with the 'lottery of gold digging' and warned of the consequences, both in this life and the next, of succumbing to gross materialism. Champions of the gold culture claimed that it fostered independence, ingenuity and 'manliness' and praised an environment in which the advantages of inherited privilege meant nothing to an individual's chances of success. For supporters and opponents of gold culture alike, the perceived 'democracy' of the goldfields was an inexhaustible topic for discussion.*[101]

---

100 - *The Argus*, April 5, 1856, page 4.
101 - McCalman, Cook and Reeves 2001, 2.

As a reporter and also later as a novelist, especially in *Mark Brown's Wife*, de Boos was an active participant in and observer of this tumultuous and chequered period in Victoria's early history.[102] Yet why he and his family left Melbourne at such a time to return to Sydney is just one more of the many unknowns in the life of Charles de Boos.

---

102 - McCalman, Cook and Reeves 2001.

Chapter Seven

A Reporter for *The Sydney Morning Herald*, 1856-1872

> *In 1856, ... I returned to Sydney, and during the first recess of Parliament I visited for the Herald the whole of the Gold Fields of the Colony, except those in the Braidwood District, which were then flooded. And since then I have visited as Special Reporter for the Herald all the newly-discovered Fields. I went also to Caloola [sic, should be Canoona], near Rockhampton. ... My last visit to the Gold Fields was to Tambaroora, Gulgong, Trunkey, and indeed nearly the whole of the Western District.[1]*

Charles de Boos and family returned to Sydney after April 1856. Initially, he may have worked for *The People's Advocate*,[2] given its serialised publication of his first novel, *The Stockman's Daughter*.[3] However, this cannot be substantiated, whilst suggestions that he worked for *The Empire* are not correct.[4] Just when he joined John Fairfax & Sons and the *Sydney Morning Herald* is not known (Figure 7.1).[5] In an article dated May 16, 1857, he commented on having done "nine months reporting in the Legislative Council", which gives a starting date of September-October 1856, more or less ruling out any, or very little, work for other publications.[6]

This chapter considers one of the major parts of his life, the sixteen years from 1856. It begins with a brief look at the early Colonial Parliament of New South Wales, the setting for his work as a parliamentary reporter. This work extended over all of his time with the *Herald* and is outlined in the second part of the chapter. Thirdly, the chapter examines 'Free Selection',

---

1 - Gold Fields Royal Commission 1871. Evidence by de Boos, pages 151-154.

2 - Prior to early January 1856, it was named *The People's Advocate and New South Wales Vindicator* (Walker 1976, 62-68). It was published weekly by Edward Hawkesley (editor) and Francis Cunninghame (printer) from December 2, 1848, until its final edition on December 27, 1856. Like de Boos, Hawksley fought with the British Auxiliary Legion in the Carlist Wars: did they meet in Spain? en.wikipedia.org/wiki/The_People's_Advocate_and_New_South_Wales_Vindicator , accessed May 31, 2013.

3 - 'The Stockman's Daughter', Appendix 12.13. *The Stockman's Daughter: a tale of the new country* was republished by the Mulini Press, Canberra (de Boos 2009).

4 - *Evening News*, October 31, 1900, page 4. *The Empire* was published December 28, 1850, to February 14, 1875, except for the period August 28, 1858, to May 23, 1859.

5 - An enquiry to Fairfax Media provided no information: "Fairfax Archives and personnel records are reasonably good for the 1900s but there is almost nothing prior to this", as was confirmed by a search for relevant material (Chris Berry, Director, Information Services, Fairfax Media, personal communications, August 19 and 23, 2013).

6 - *Sydney Morning Herald*, May 16, 1857, page 7. This would have meant that he had writings published at the same time in the *Advocate* and the *Herald*; Kirkpatrick 2016, 49-55.

a topic that, in one way or another, engaged much of his reporting and other writing. The fourth and largest part is devoted to his work beyond Sydney, which involved considerable travelling to report particularly on the goldfields as well as many other issues in the Colony. Largely in the context of gold mining, he gave much attention to the natural environments and the impacts of mining and to the social conditions on the diggings, especially for women and children. Beyond the Colonial Parliament, he was a 'country' reporter, his travels taking him to most of the eastern half of New South Wales. In the final sections, some of his other work is outlined and his retirement that was not a retirement is discussed.

Figure 7.1. Pitt Street from Hunter Street, looking north, with the new offices of the Sydney Morning Herald, on the corner with O'Connell Street. S.T. Gill (1856), Allan & Wigley, Sydney. Source: National Library of Australia, PIC Volume 1# U126 NK9593/21.

The Early Colonial Parliament

New South Wales attained responsible government in 1856. Before then, the colonial legislature consisted of the partly elected Legislative Council. With the new constitution, this became the Upper House, with the new Legislative Assembly the Lower House. "Generally speaking, members were drawn from three broad groups in society: the pastoral and landholding section, the professions and trade and commerce", though in the Upper House, those representing "the interests of property" were in the majority.[7]

---
7 - Loveday and Martin 1977.

There were no political parties as such, though a division of sorts emerged in the mid to late 1850s.

> The 'liberalism' and 'conservatism' of the mid-fifties are best described as two broad movements of thought which were an essential part of the atmosphere in which the new parliament began its deliberations. Though real enough as general touchstones for classifying candidates in the election of 1856, they were too ill-defined to offer a basis for party action in the campaign. No organization existed to claim either of them as its own. ... The election of 1856 thus did not decide who was to form the first ministry under responsible government. ... [F]actions, not parties, ... developed to give order and meaning to the wrangle for political power.[8]

These factions and their leaders, both liberal and conservative, were constantly changing. The most long-lived, dating from the 1856 election, was that of Charles Cowper, the moderate liberal, and John Robertson, who was described as "decidedly liberal".[9] The 'liberals' supported reform of the Upper House, the opening up of land to settlement by farmers, and measures that would benefit working men and the poorer sections of the community. The liberals' opponents were called 'constitutionalists' or, more pejoratively 'conservatives'. They opposed democracy and universal suffrage, they had close links with the large land holders (for example, Wentworth, Macarthur, Oxley, Campbell, and Berry), and wanted a colonial aristocracy, believing that "a society could only be ordered and stable if its social classes were clearly defined and hierarchically ranked".[10] In 1851, "sheep graziers, and particularly squatters, were the holders of the vast bulk of settled land in New South Wales. ... [U]nder leases, 180 million acres were held by 1,800 people out of a population of 200,000"; W.C. Wentworth held some 500,000 acres as a squatter.[11] But the conservatives became powerless, as they "had increasingly lost touch with reality".[12]

A Parliamentary Reporter

Reporting on the debates of the New South Wales Legislative Assembly was de Boos' main task, for which his knowledge of shorthand - the first reporter employed by the *Herald* with such knowledge - would have been

---

8 - Loveday and Martin 1966, 23 and 26.
9 - Loveday and Martin 1966, 28, quoting Robertson from *Maitland Mercury*, April 30, 1857, page 4.
10 - Paraphrased from Loveday and Martin 1966, 10-16; Dyster 1988.
11 - Hamilton 2015, 11-12.
12 - Loveday and Martin 1966, 17.

a great benefit, as these reports were the 'Hansard' of the day.[13] However, there were those who questioned the accuracy of some of his reporting. For example, John Robertson, the Minister of Land and Works, denied the accuracy of de Boos' reporting of a speech he had made, but de Boos was able to refute the allegations.[14] *Bells Life in Sydney* had its own take on the dispute:

> ROBERTSON VERSUS DE BOOS.
>
> *The complainant is the celebrated Minister of Lands and Works. The defendant is a publican who reports for the S.M. Herald. The complainant attended the meeting of the great unwashed at the Lyceum on Monday evening, for the purpose of spouting. The defendant also attended the meeting for the purpose of reporting. The complainant put on a more than usually tristful countenance next morning over his roll and coffee at reading his speech in the Herald. Having munched his breakfast he wrote a note complaining to the proprietor of our Pitt street contemporary that the reporter had 'cut him short', and misrepresented him. The public(an) reporter sent a missive to the press denying the Minister's impeachment. Thus the public are gratified with reading this intensely interesting original correspondence, and the typos of our grand-maternal contemporary are not kept waiting for copy.[15]*

Later in the year, it happened again. A 'Letter to the Editor' from 'The Parliamentary Reporters of the *Herald*', strongly attacked a statement by Premier Charles Cowper in "the House", and vigorously maintained their independence, individually and collectively:

> *There has never been a whisper to us that a political bias should guide the important duty we have to perform, and not one of us would hold our situation for a single hour, if we could feel amenable to the ungenerous, the humiliating insult with which the Premier of the colony has vainly endeavoured to brand us.*

They were Ed. K. Silvester, A.D. Murphy, Samuel Cook, Daniel Melhado, Stephen Hayes, Chas. De Boos, George Eld, and Edward Reeve.[16] Six years later, a libel case was brought against John Fairfax and some of the *Herald*'s reporters, Samuel Cook, Charles de Boos, James Haddon, and Edward Reeve, over their supposed inaccurate reporting, this time by Daniel Dalgleish.[17] In a letter to the Editor, the four reporters again maintained

---

13 - *Sydney Morning Herald*, July 4, 1910, page 9; Souter 1981, 70. In New South Wales, 'Hansard' did not start until 1879.
14 - *Sydney Morning Herald*, June 9, 1858, pages 5 and 4.
15 - *Bells Life in Sydney*, June 12, 1858, page 3.
16 - *Sydney Morning Herald*, December 23, 1858, page 5.
17 - Ferguson 1972.

the accuracy of their reporting.[18] Work in the Legislative Assembly was not without other costs, as de Boos observed in one report from his first extended travels:

> I picked up about a pennyweight of gold in an old cart-track, after a shower of rain, in the short space of five minutes. This, for one whose eyesight has not been most materially improved by a nine months' reporting in the Legislative Council, was not so very bad; and I have no doubt that persons with sharper powers of vision than I possess might have gathered more.[19]

'Free Selection'

From 1861, two related topics occupied much of de Boos' recording of parliamentary debates, his other reporting, and his other writing (see Chapter Twelve). These were 'Free Selection' and its key proponent, John Robertson. Given their widespread relevance to the work of de Boos and to contemporary politics and governance in New South Wales, they merit consideration.[20]

From the 1820s, the pastoral industry played a major part in the early settlement of New South Wales. Vast tracts of land were pre-emptively taken up by 'squatters' as sheep runs, before there had been any surveys and without the occupiers having any form of title to use the land. They became wealthy pastoralists, effectively 'locking up' large areas and keeping other settlers out. The response to this was the *Waste Lands Occupation Act 1846*, which, among other things, enabled pastoralists to obtain leases for up to fourteen years. This gave them security of title, though limited, but with the government maintaining ownership of the land. In political terms, the squatters formed a major part of the conservative side of colonial politics.[21]

The New South Wales election of 1860 saw the clear defeat of the conservative and pastoral interests and the overwhelming re-election of the Cowper-Robertson liberal ministry. The following year, the Cowper government pushed two acts through the Colonial Parliament: the *Crown Lands Alienation Act 1861*, which dealt with the sale of land, and the *Crown*

---

18 - *Sydney Morning Herald*, October 22, 1864, page 1; November 28, 1864, pages 2-3; *Sydney Mail*, November 26, 1864, page 11; and subsequent articles.
19 - *Sydney Morning Herald*, May 16, 1857, page 7.
20 - Holmes 2000; Robinson 1974.
21 - Loveday and Martin 1966, especially 31-33; Hamilton 2015, 67-68; Hardy 1855.

Lands Occupation Act 1861, which dealt with the leasing of Crown Land.[22] The minister responsible was John Robertson, who, in 1858, had been part of an earlier Cowper ministry as Secretary for Lands and Public Works. Robertson was determined to break the squatter-pastoralists' monopoly on land holding, and to see a more egalitarian distribution of land and land ownership.[23] He wanted to give people with limited capital a fair chance to possess and cultivate land.[24] Also, "owing to the decline in the amount of alluvial gold discovered in the latter part of the fifties, there was a large number of unemployed or semi-unemployed gold diggers in the colonies, and the Selection Acts were designed to settle these people on the land as small farmers".[25] Above all, Robertson wanted to see an increase in closer settlement, in arable farming and in agricultural development, which the *Waste Lands Occupation Act* had failed to achieve.[26]

The new legislation allowed any person to enter the Crown land squatting runs of a pastoralist and 'select' an area, priory to survey, in order to establish a farm and buy land in freehold from the Crown.[27] This was the principle of 'free selection before survey' or 'Free Selection'.[28] The *Occupation Act* permitted anyone to select between 40 and 320 acres of land (except urban land), on condition of paying one-quarter of the purchase price after survey, undertaking improvements to the value of £1 per acre, and living on the land for three years, thus obtaining freehold. "The conditions were designed to ensure that only *bona fide* farmers took up selections – that squatters, and those who would blackmail the squatters, were excluded".[29] However, the view of the squatters was "that free selection before survey will be injurious to them – that it will colonise their districts with cattle stealers – and the litigation about boundaries will be interminable".[30]

The Acts were bitterly opposed by the pastoral interests, and they highlighted the strong divisions between 'liberals' and 'conservatives'.[31] For the liberals,

---

22 - At different times, Robertson and Cowper both held the position of Premier.

23 - Baker 1958; Nairn 1976.

24 - "Free Selection Before Survey, as Explained by Mr. Robertson at Muswellbrook". *Freeman's Journal*, December 8, 1860, page 34.

25 - Baker 1958.

26 - Baker 1958.

27 - Wright 2005a.

28 - *Crown Land*. NSW Land Registry Services, Sydney, 2017; *Conditional Purchase of Crown Land Guide*. NSW State Archives and Records, Sydney.

29 - Baker 1958.

30 - *Freeman's Journal*, December 8, 1860, page 34.

31 - Wright 2005a.

the Robertson Land Acts promoted land reform, enabling poorer people to own and cultivate land, though if they failed to cultivate it, the land was forfeited. The Acts were "a powerful symbol of democracy", designed to attack the privileges of the squatters.[32] Not so for the conservatives. For them, "It was an initiative that promised to dictate the future terms of the political agenda by shifting the primary end of legislation to the conditions of the poor and working classes".[33] For Robertson, everything was positive:

> ... if a man is willing to develop the resources of the country, we ought to let him select the land wherever he likes and on the easiest terms. They who undertake to clear, cultivate and convert the useless bush into a farm, surely deserve more encouragement by the Government than the mere land speculator.[34]

The controversies gave rise to much comment in the newspapers of the day, not least the *Sydney Morning Herald*. In a number of editorials,[35] it argued strongly that the conditions were impracticable, and that the measures would not achieve the reformers' intentions of attacking "unequal conditions".[36] In the view of the *Herald* and de Boos, "the Anglo-Celtic working class had been harmed by the Robertson Land Acts".[37] de Boos was particularly concerned for "the *bona fide* selectors, who have honestly gone upon the land and as honestly endeavoured by hard work and perseverance to get a living from it".[38] For example, at the Wingecarribee Swamp (near Bowral), "what on earth could ever have induced the free-selectors to come here ... the poor man would starve before he had an acre cleared, or so much as a cabbage grown".[39] The position taken by de Boos was not so much backing a conservative cause, as an indication of his concerns over what happened to the selectors. Particular issues were their lack of knowledge and capital; the small size of their selections, which he termed 'cabbage patches'; the impossibility of their tasks; and the corruption in the administration of the land laws.[40] He very quickly saw the consequences of the legislation and

---

32 - Wright 2005a; Buck and Wright 2005, 5.

33 - Buck and Wright 2005, 2.

34 - Extract from a speech, "Free Selection before Survey as explained by Mr. Robertson at Muswellbrook". *Freeman's Journal*, December 8, 1860, page 34.

35 - *Sydney Morning Herald*, February 14, 1861, page 5; February 16, 1861, page 4; November 8, 1861, page 5.

36 - Baker 1958.

37 - Wright and Buck 2001.

38 - *Sydney Morning Herald*, August 18, 1865, page 2. In addition to the *bona fide* ones, he identified three other groups of 'free selectors': "those who already have land and have selected additions to their present property [and] second, the schemers, and – to use an expressive word in use amongst the settlers – the duffers".

39 - *Sydney Morning Herald*, July 5, 1865, page 5.

40 - He was not alone in his criticism. *Sydney Morning Herald*, June 21, 1866, page 5; June 27, 1866, page 2.

the strong advocacy of Robertson for the 'Free Selectors', views vindicated some years later. In 1883, an inquiry into the state of public lands and the administration of the land laws, undertaken by Augustus Morris and George Rankin, found that only a small percentage of 'Free Selection' applicants had actually established a homestead and more than fifty per cent of them lacked the necessary capital. The scheme was plagued by corruption and maladministration. It had far from assisted the settlement of land in New South Wales.[41] In fact, by 1883, "Large-scale pastoral occupation accounted for a greater proportion of the land than in 1861".[42] Over twenty-five years later, de Boos wrote that since the *Land Acts* had been passed, "the colony has been nothing but a source of heart-burning and strife. Amendment after amendment has been made, only driving matters from bad to worse, until now both selectors and squatters are discontented and almost defiant".[43]

One other matter became almost central to the political antagonism between the liberals and conservatives over the *Lands Acts*.[44] It was 'the poor man'. The term had originated in England but gained particular currency in New South Wales in the mid-nineteenth century, being "a rhetorical figure for the unemployed and propertiless".[45] The free selector was 'the poor man'.[46] Not only was 'the poor man' the subject of comment in de Boos' 'Random Notes', he also appeared in de Boos' satirical writings and social commentary (see Chapter Twelve). Much of the political satire "purported to prove that the poor man had not benefited from his life on the land as a small-scale agriculturalist", that he, "the working class", had failed to improve his standard of living, and more importantly, had failed to improve the land.[47] de Boos also applied the term to the individual gold miner, whose days, he said "were over". Not everyone agreed with de Boos, but increasing numbers of people were accepting the fact that mining required capital and that meant large companies or at least multiple men working together.[48]

Then there was John Robertson, the proponent of the Acts. Robertson has been described as "the great apostle of social equilibrium through land justice ... [who became] one of the great land reformers of the nineteenth

---

41 - Morris and Rankin 1883.
42 - Buck and Wright 2005, 22.
43 - de Boos 1889.
44 - Buck 1996.
45 - Wright and Buck 1998.
46 - Buck and Wright 2005, 1-29.
47 - Wright and Buck 2001.
48 - *Sydney Morning Herald*, May 30, 1866, page 5.

century".⁴⁹ But he was far from free of criticism, and as much as de Boos was critical of the *Land Acts* themselves, he was more than critical of Robertson. He sarcastically described him as a "Heaven-born genius".⁵⁰ A visit to Scone, Robertson's home town, was an opportunity not to be missed by de Boos, as, "alas, a prophet has no honour in his own country; and the great prophet of the land law is actually pooh-poohed in Scone".⁵¹

The strong criticisms of the *Land Acts* are one thing, but were they that closely associated with Robertson to account for the antagonism towards him found in the *Herald* and other contemporary newspapers? It would not seem so, as the antagonism started well before 1861. For example, in 1858, the *Herald*'s Editor wrote of "The boisterous, puerile impudence of this precious specimen of the Cabinet [Robertson]".⁵² Equally scathing and more sarcastic was the radical Daniel Deniehy writing in *The Southern Cross* in 1860.⁵³ Other views of Robertson have been presented.⁵⁴ Why Robertson was subjected to such personal antagonism is not a matter for here, but the 1883 inquiry by Morris and Rankin ended his parliamentary career.

'Our Special Commissioner' and 'A Wandering Reporter'

By the time de Boos returned to Sydney, there had been numerous discoveries of gold in New South Wales, later documented by the Rev. W.B. Clarke.⁵⁵ In July 1857, an editorial in the *Herald* included a response to the increasing amount and inconsistency of information about the New South Wales goldfields.

> It has been our constant effort to furnish our readers with information respecting our Gold-fields; to create no unnatural stimulus to mining pursuits, and yet to give fair pay to our mineral resources. It was in keeping with this policy that we despatched a special commissioner to collect, at the different gold-fields, the more important facts, to ascertain the feelings and wishes of the miners, and thus to assist the merchant and the legislator, as well as the labourer. A Commissioner – such was the distinction first claimed by the Times for its agents – has functions different from that of ordinary reporting. His duties are more remote, less liable to oversight, and therefore peculiarly

---

49 - Nairn 1976.
50 - *Sydney Morning Herald*, July 19, 1865, page 5.
51 - *Sydney Morning Herald*, May 4, 1866, page 5; July 25, 1865, page 2.
52 - *Sydney Morning Herald*, June 9, 1858, page 4.
53 - *The Southern Cross* newspaper was published in Sydney from 1859 to 1861. The article by Deniehy "Mr. Robertson in His Glory" was reprinted in Martin 1884, 140-142.
54 - For example, Nairn 1976.
55 - The Appendix to Clarke (1871) lists the locations of all the gold findings in New South Wales up to that time and the dates when the discoveries were made.

confidential. He is bound to see with his own eyes, to collate and estimate the facts he may gather, and penetrate through the illusions of selfishness, slander, and timidity, in search of the substantial and permanent.[56]

The task and title of 'Our Special Commissioner' were given to de Boos, very similar to that given him earlier by the Editor of *The Argus*. His abilities as a reporter and the knowledge gained from the Victorian goldfields, made him well qualified for this new undertaking. Under the heading 'The Gold-Fields of New South Wales', his 24 articles were published in the *Sydney Morning Herald* from April to August 1857 (Appendix 7.1). They constitute the most comprehensive documentation of the Colony's goldfields that, up to the time, had been written.[57] For the time, and the means of travel available, the journey was a remarkable one (Figure 7.2).

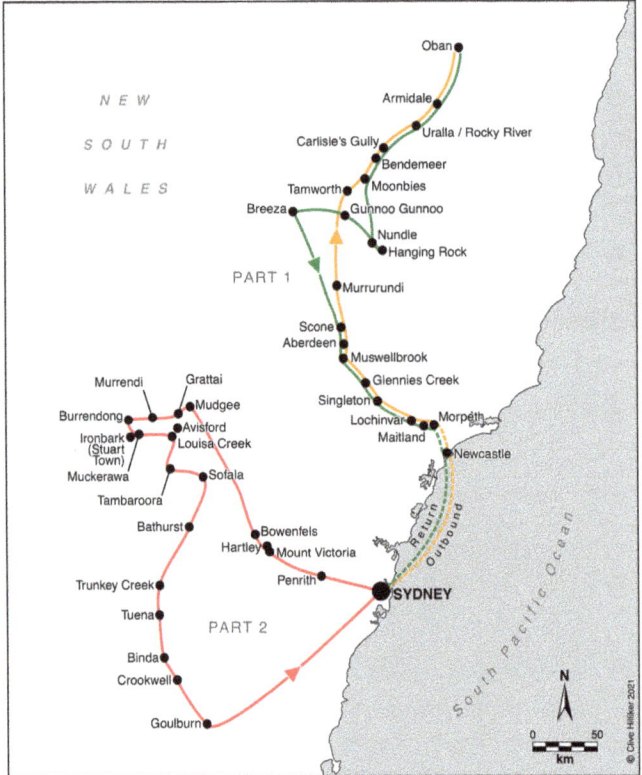

Figure 7.2. Some of the places visited by de Boos for his reports on 'The Gold-Fields of New South Wales', 1857. Note that it was a two-part trip. The condition of the roads resulting from extremely wet weather made it impossible for him to go directly from Breeza to Mudgee, as planned; it was easier to return to Sydney and resume his journey from there.

---

56 - *Sydney Morning Herald*, July 23, 1857, page 4.

57 - For a commentary on the series, see: www.goldtrails.com.au/gold-heritage/heritage-chronology/ , accessed January 22, 2017. There were two earlier series, but they were both limited to the Western Gold Fields. A short series by a "commissioned" but unknown reporter appeared in the *Sydney Morning Herald* from November 12, to December 1, 1852. The longer series appeared in *The Empire*, October 21, to November 30, 1852, and was written by Angus Mackay. It was reprinted as a 68-page pamphlet the following year (Mackay 1853).

The following year, he undertook the longest trips he ever made in Australia, to report on the Canoona gold rush on the Fitzroy River in Queensland (then still part of New South Wales). For some months prior to his visit, various reports and letters appeared in the *Sydney Morning Herald* relating to the 'Fitzroy Diggings'. They were not without concern, particularly because of the very mixed views being presented.[58] As a consequence, de Boos, once again as the *Herald*'s 'Special Commissioner', was sent north to investigate and provide "the earliest and the fullest intelligence" on the Fitzroy goldfields.[59] In the space of just over two months, he actually made two trips to the Fitzroy (Appendix 7.2). He recounted his experiences in a series of ten articles entitled the 'Fitzroy Diggings', published in the *Herald* between early October and early December 1858 (Appendix 7.3).[60] Some 15,000 people went through Rockhampton to Canoona, but there was very little gold and most of the men were left destitute. It was 'boom to bust' within a few weeks, for the miners and for Rockhampton.

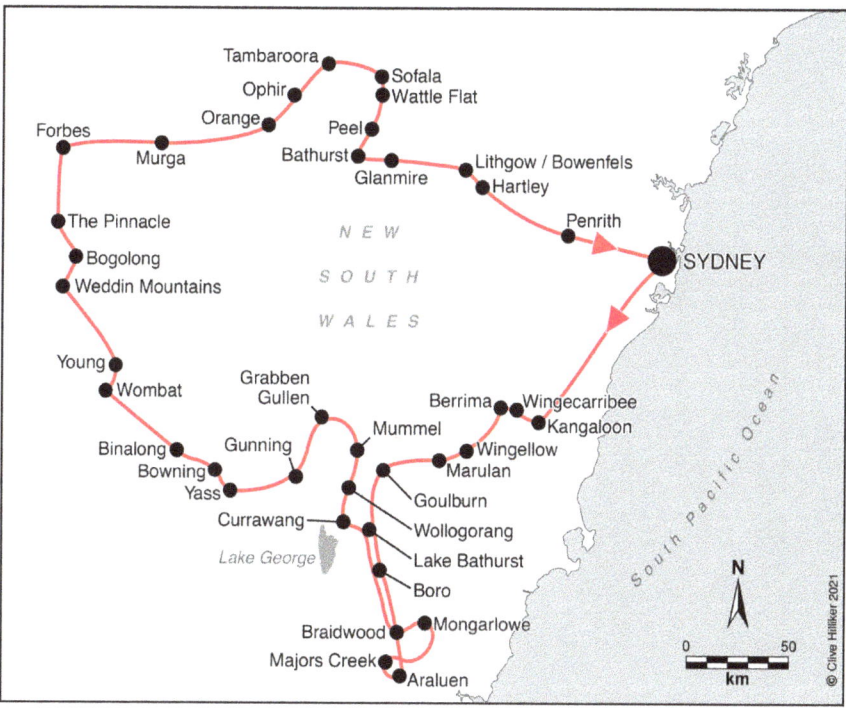

Figure 7.3. *The First Journey of the Herald's 'Wandering Reporter', 1865.*

---

58 - For example: *Sydney Morning Herald*, September 29, 1858, page 4; October 4, 1858, page 4; October 6, 1858, page 5; Pearson 1858; Stone 2014.

59 - *Sydney Morning Herald*, September 25, 1858, page 4. A lengthy article headed "The Fitzroy Gold-Fields" appeared in the *Herald* on October 9, 1858, pages 6-7. Setting out the many statements made on the Fitzroy, including material from de Boos' initial article, and containing a number of warnings to those contemplating visiting the Fitzroy, it took up over one and a quarter pages. There was more material on pages 3 and 4.

60 - Crabb 2010; Rockhampton & District Historical Society 1961; Mr John Fletcher, President, RDHS Inc., personal communication, March 9, 2010.

In early July 1865, it was reported that "The *Herald* [had] dispatched a special reporter for a cruise in the country districts during the Parliamentary recess".[61] The "special reporter" was de Boos, and his "cruise" took some three months through much of central and southern New South Wales (Figure 7.3). The outcome was the first of six series called 'Random Notes from a Wandering Reporter', published in the *Sydney Morning Herald* and *The Sydney Mail* from 1865 to 1874 (Appendix 7.4).

The following year, 1866, he was sent on another 'cruise', and whatever concerns he may have had about being away from home yet again, he was "glad … to see the end of the [Parliamentary] session … [and experience the relief] on being delivered from the ceaseless flow of words that in these degenerate days is dignified by the name of debate".[62] So began his 'Second Series' of 'Random Notes from a Wandering Reporter' (Figure 7.4; Appendix 7.5).

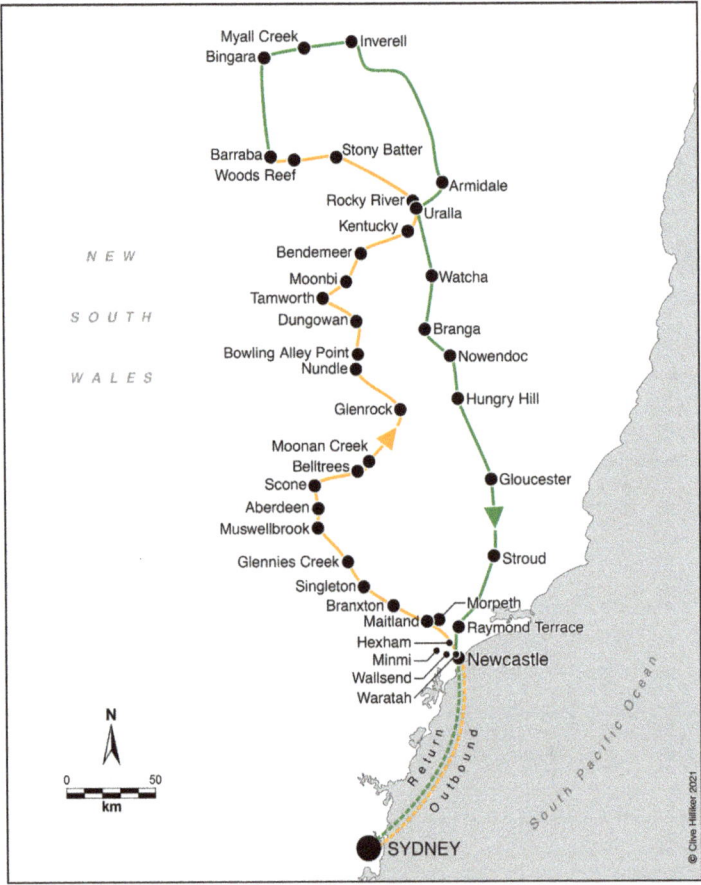

Figure 7.4. *The Second Journey of the Herald's 'Wandering Reporter', 1866.*

---

61 - *The Sydney Mail*, July 8, 1865, page 4.
62 - *Sydney Morning Herald*, April 23, 1866, page 3.

Three more series of 'Random Notes' were published between 1870 and 1872. They were shorter, covering much shorter journeys. In 1870-1871, number three took him to Cudgegong, Gulgong, Tambaroora, Dirt Holes, Hawkins Hill, and Hill End, and there were other articles about the Bowenfels Coal Field in the Lithgow Valley, the Turon Valley, and Goulburn (Appendix 7.6). A shorter trip in late 1871 took him again to Gulgong, Mudgee, Tambaroora, Hill End, and Hawkins Hill (Appendix 7.7). In 1872, he reported on his last journey, which was to Hill End and nearby places, the Wattle Flat goldfield, and the Shale Oil Company at Mt. Victoria (Appendix 7.8).[63]

Between 1859 and 1865, he undertook several other journeys (Figure 7.5). In a series entitled 'Pen and Ink Sketches' (by 'Our Special Reporter', Appendix 7.9),[64] he wrote of Forbes, Orange, the Lachlan Valley, and Tambaroora. He had visited Orange and Forbes before, in 1848.[65] Forbes was "nothing more than the spectre of what it once was. ... Most melancholy, most woe-begone, most dilapidated. Most ragged is its appearance now. ... meeting with the one sole occupant of the town, whose voice was heard in a room of the palace, reciting the verses of the Koran".[66] He was pleased to see the pine forests of the Lachlan Valley, which provided "an agreeable change from the never varying gums" and an important source of timber for the goldfields, as well as cover for such bushrangers as Gardiner, Gilbert and O'Mealley.[67] In the fourth article, he mentioned "Your recent gold-fields reporter, Mr. Hux, who was with me at the time".[68] He also reported on coal mining in the Hunter Valley,[69] the Fitzroy Iron Mines, near Berrima,[70] and a short series of "Stray Notes on a Week's Ramble on the Western Line".[71]

---

63 - *Sydney Morning Herald*, January 17, 1872, page 5; *Sydney Morning Herald*, March 8, 1872, page 5. Note his comment to the Gold Fields Royal Commission 1871: "My last visit to the Gold Fields was to Tambaroora, Gulgong, Trunkey, and indeed nearly the whole of the Western District", pages 151-152.

64 - de Boos had indicated to the Royal Commission that this term was used to identify him.

65 - *Sydney Morning Herald*, November 26, 1863, page 5.

66 - *Sydney Morning Herald*, December 14, 1863, page 8.

67 - *Sydney Morning Herald*, December 29, 1863, page 2.

68 - *Sydney Morning Herald*, December 29, 1863, page 2. Hux had reported on the Kiandra, Lambing Flat (Young), and Lachlan gold rushes for the *Herald*. He was related to de Boos through marriages of their parents (Crabb 2020).

69 - *Sydney Morning Herald*, May 12, 1860, page 8. The same 'Special Reporter' had earlier been sent to the lower Hunter valley and Newcastle area to report on "the ministerial deliverances at the recent re-elections:" *Sydney Morning Herald*, March 17, 1860, page 4; March 21, 1860, page 4; March 22, 1860, page 5.

70 - *Sydney Morning Herald*, June 2, 1865, page 5; June 6, 1865, page 5; June 7, 1865, page 2. Also published as two articles in *The Sydney Mail*, June 3, 1865, page 9: June 10, 1865, page 3. Though the writer described himself as a "business man", comments in a much later article by de Boos suggest he was the writer of the articles. *Sydney Morning Herald*, December 5, 1874, page 6.

71 - *The Sydney Mail*, November 28, 1868, page 12; December 12, 1868, page 6; January 2, 1869, page 11.

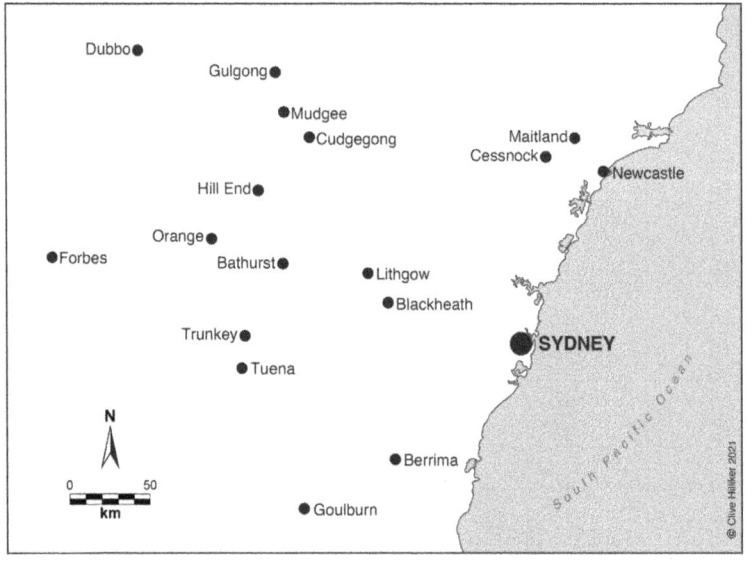

Figure 7.5. Some of the places in New South Wales visited by de Boos on his other travels.

The distances de Boos travelled were remarkable. For example, his reports on 'The Gold Fields of New South Wales' involved traveling over 2,100 km., using every form of available transport: coastal steamer, rail, coach, horseback, and on foot. He did not like sea travel, as there were almost always "disagreeable consequences". On one of his worst trips, "six months' agony [was] intensified into that short passage from Sydney Heads to Newcastle".[72]

With most of his travelling on horseback and on foot, the 'roads' figure frequently in his writings. 'Roads' was a euphemistic term: there were the "main" roads, "the minor roads, the disused roads, and the no roads of the colony".[73] Barely visible tracks were made even more difficult by wombat holes. 'Roads' took him across rivers, creeks and swamps. The state of the 'roads' was largely determined by the weather. When it was dry, there was dust and flies: "you are attacked by fly after fly until you are driven to the utmost limit of ill-temper, and drive your spurs into your horse's sides with a kind of forlorn hope that rapidity of motion will free you of your tormentors".[74] And there was drought, which destroyed crops.[75] Near

---

72 - *Sydney Morning Herald*, April 20, 1857, page 2; October 5, 1858, page 4; December 7, 1858, page 4.
73 - *Sydney Morning Herald*, July 25, 1865, page 2.
74 - *Sydney Morning Herald*, May 4, 1866, page 5.
75 - *Sydney Morning Herald*, May 11, 1866, page 5.

Barraba, there was "not a bite of grass within five or six miles", and his horse went without food for more than two days.[76]

In wet weather, the roads were treacherous; one 'road' he described as "a most extraordinary compound state of water and mud".[77] His mare could be "slopping and puddling" and almost knee-deep in the mud; at the end of a day in such conditions, she could be "a perfect picture of misery".[78] At times, de Boos was no better off himself. Travelling across the Branga Plains with the 'scab inspector',[79] "I was a miserable man ... with chattering teeth, for wet as we were every breath of the cold westerly wind went through us as though it were piercing us with icicles".[80] Crossing rivers when they were in flood was particularly dangerous, as when he came off his horse in the flooding, silt-laden Tilbuster Creek, near Armidale, an experience he described in graphic detail.

> *The creek was much swollen by the rains, and had been still more so, as it appeared from the vast gaps in the banks washed down by the current. I kept rather too low down the stream, and did not fancy the crossing-place that offered itself at the spot where I reached it. Going still further down, for nearly a mile, I could see no place that offered a reasonable chance of crossing, the banks being steep, or where they shelved, showing only long deltas of mud. At last I reached a spot that I thought would exactly suit. Two long points, of what apparently were fine firm shingle or pebbles, almost reached each other, leaving not more than three feet of water to pass over. I spurred my mare down the bank, very much against her inclination, and the first step on what I thought shingle sank the poor animal up to her knees in mud. However, it was getting late, and on I spurred. We crossed the water, and reached the opposite point of deceptive beach. With a heavy plunge she tried to mount it, but sank up to her haunches behind, and nearly to the point of the shoulder in front, and there stuck fast. I knew my weight must settle her down all the deeper, and preclude every chance of extrication, so without a moment's hesitation I mounted on top of the saddle, à la Ducrow, and took a jump as far towards the bank as I could. My leap so far favoured me as to bring me nearer to the bank, but the additional impetus given to my weight in the descent, sent me over the knees into the mud. I tried to scramble out. It was no go. I was held fast by the legs, and bade fair to become a martyr in the public service. I still held the bridle of the mare, and looking round on her to see how she got on, the thought suddenly flashed across me that I was directly in the line between her and the bank, and that if she, in her struggles to get out, should reach me, she might possibly knock me over in the slough and provide me with anything but an eligible grave at the same time as she settled me. This thought had no sooner entered my mind than, by a kind of galvanic action of*

---

76 - *Sydney Morning Herald*, June 2, 1866, page 8.
77 - *Sydney Morning Herald*, June 26, 1857, page 4.
78 - *Sydney Morning Herald*, May 4, 1857, page 2.
79 - 'Scab', a minor form of 'mange', is an infectious disease of sheep. Infected sheep were not allowed to move along public roads.
80 - *Sydney Morning Herald*, July 10, 1866, page 2.

the muscular power, I found myself on the river bank clear of the difficulty; showing thereby the wonderful effect that a little wholesome looking things fairly in the face will have upon nervous gentlemen. When safely landed, I gave a few encouraging chirrups to the mare, who again took heart of grace, and as I could now help her with the bridle, a few stout struggles landed her also safely on the bank, though so weak as scarcely to be able to stand. I myself was in a pretty plight. Smothered in mud from nearly the waist downwards, whilst large gouts of the same odoriferous deposits spotted the rest of my person, being the more remarkable about my face, I presented anything but the imposing appearance of a Special Commissioner.[81]

If the roads were bad for a horse, they could be even worse for a 'coach', another somewhat euphemistic term.[82] On his trip from Morpeth to Maitland in 1857, de Boos travelled in "a narrow vehicle, called, by courtesy only, an omnibus".[83] On a journey to Cudgegong, it took twelve hours to cover fifty miles, the road being "in a worse state than any other road in the Colony".[84] Further, journeys were often at night, and in winter could be extremely cold. After reaching Goulburn on a trip from Berrima, he wrote "that I got off the coach, that I got upon my feet with a kind of misty impression that I was standing on the stumps of my knees, and that all below these was only 'of the stuff that dreams are made of'". Only after breakfast and becoming "thoroughly warm … did I get into that equable, calm, and amiable frame of mind that is my usual characteristic".[85]

de Boos' travels covered the period of the introduction and slow expansion of railways in New South Wales. There were many similarities between rail and coach travel. Journeys were often at night. On a trip from Sydney, "I was unable in spite of all my anxiety to see anything, and in a most intense state of disgust and disappointment I reached Goulburn".[86] He had an almost equal dislike of early starts. The ride through the Blue Mountains was a rough one, through cuttings, on embankments, and around many curves, resulting in a "succession of sharp jerks, now to one side, now to the other, as the curve is to the right or left". Safety was a real concern.[87]

---

81 - *Sydney Morning Herald*, May 11, 1857, pages 2 and 3.

82 - Travelling by coach / omnibus: "Braidwood to Sydney" by Henry Thomas Fox, pages 76-79; "The Barbarous mail-coach" by John Robert Gidley, pages 72-75 in Keesing 1967. "I may say I have seen the public carriages of a good many countries, some of them not very advanced in civilization; but in discomfort, insecurity, unpunctuality, and general barbarism, the mail between Bathurst and Sydney far surpasses them all" (1853). *Extracts from a Journal of a Visit to New South Wales in 1853. Fraser's Magazine*, November-December 1853; *Sydney Morning Herald*, April 20, 1857, page 2.

83 - *Sydney Morning Herald*, April 20, 1857, page 2.

84 - *Sydney Morning Herald*, July 5, 1870, page 5.

85 - *Sydney Morning Herald*, July 13, 1865, page 2; June 27, 1857, page 6.

86 - *Sydney Morning Herald*, January 20, 1871, page 5.

87 - *Sydney Morning Herald*, December 12, 1868, page 6.

What did de Boos write about?

Just about everything! In addition to the roads, there were few topics that de Boos did not write about from his journeys as a 'Special Commissioner', a 'Wandering Reporter', and other names he was given. Just a few illustrations must suffice.

Places he visited

Herald readers must have had mixed reactions to his descriptions of the towns he visited. Some were complimentary: the agricultural community of Murrurundi was "as romantic a looking village as can be found in the whole interior".[88] Armidale was an "exceedingly pretty looking town", its prosperity supported by the surrounding districts' farming activities and, more recently, the nearby Rocky River goldfield.[89] In 1857, Bathurst was "the finest of our inland towns" and an important business centre for the Western Districts.[90] Some eight years later, the residents were waiting for the railway, but when it would arrive was "as hopelessly unknown as the sign 'X' in an algebraical surd".[91] By 1874, however, "Bathurst [was] not a lively city", for though there were good commercial facilities, there was little available in the way of amusement and entertainment. The Cobb & Co. coach building factory and Mr. Denny's foundry and engineering works were important industries and employers.[92]

de Boos was not so kind to other places. "Berrima is dead, dull, and miserable as ever";[93] Aberdeen has "a very high-sounding name, but it is a diminutive place of no importance";[94] Scone was another "long straggling village – and has nothing particular about it to render it remarkable", while Lochinvar was "a miserable little village".[95] He wrote a complimentary account of Yass, but Gunning was "another of those little pottering towns that do more harm than good".[96] As for Barraba, he wondered "Why it

---

88 - *Sydney Morning Herald*, April 23, 1857, page 5.
89 - *Sydney Morning Herald*, May 1, 1857, page 2.
90 - *Sydney Morning Herald*, July 29, 1857, page 2; July 23, 1857, page 4; and August 3, 1857, page 2.
91 - *Sydney Morning Herald*, October 12, 1865, page 2.
92 - *Sydney Morning Herald*, November 2, 1874, page 2.
93 - *Sydney Morning Herald*, July 6, 1865, page 8.
94 - *Sydney Morning Herald*, May 4, 1866, page 5.
95 - *Sydney Morning Herald*, April 23, 1857, page 5.
96 - *Sydney Morning Herald*, August 16, 1865, page 5.

was ever established".[97] He was "astonished" to find that Inverell had been established on a floodplain (and even more so that the site was selected by the district's Commissioner for Crown Lands). It was therefore "exceedingly liable to be inundated whenever that treacherous river, the Macintyre, may be forced by rains over its ordinary banks" (Figure 7.6).[98] Major's Creek had "a most melancholy and deserted appearance", while the township of Mongarlowe was "only a very miserable affair".[99]

Gloucester did not impress. It was largely owned by the Australian Agricultural Company (A.A.C.), whose land totally surrounded it and extended south beyond Stroud (Figure 7.7).[100] In spite of the opportunities provided by the location, there is "scarcely a sign of vitality. … Nothing could more clearly show the suicidal policy of shutting up the lands of the colony than the present condition of this township. It has been established over twenty years, and yet remains in about the same state as when the first rush of inhabitants, in all the exuberance of hope, settled upon it".[101] Stroud was another A.A.C. town, but one he found particularly interesting, as it was a 'fenced town', with gates on the access roads which were locked at night. It reminded him of the fortified towns he had seen many years earlier in France and other European countries. However, the fence and gates at Stroud clearly caused him some unease:

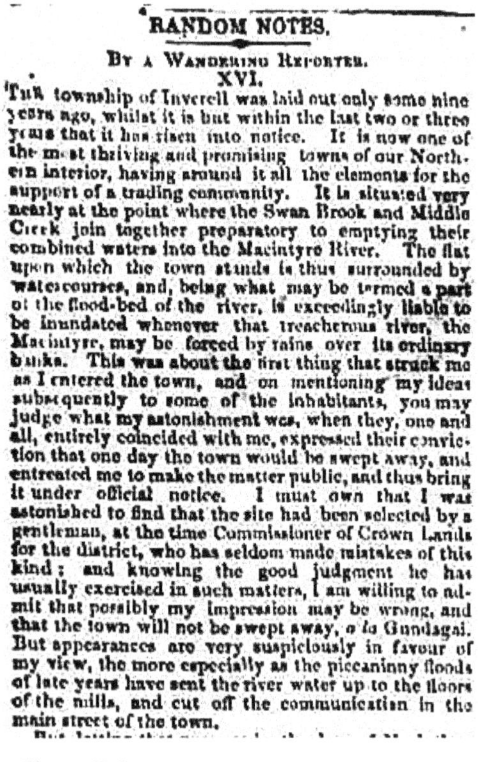

RANDOM NOTES.

BY A WANDERING REPORTER.

XVI.

THE township of Inverell was laid out only some nine years ago, whilst it is but within the last two or three years that it has risen into notice. It is now one of the most thriving and promising towns of our Northern interior, having around it all the elements for the support of a trading community. It is situated very nearly at the point where the Swan Brook and Middle Creek join together preparatory to emptying their combined waters into the Macintyre River. The flat upon which the town stands is thus surrounded by watercourses, and, being what may be termed a part of the flood-bed of the river, is exceedingly liable to be inundated whenever that treacherous river, the Macintyre, may be forced by rains over its ordinary banks. This was about the first thing that struck me as I entered the town, and on mentioning my ideas subsequently to some of the inhabitants, you may judge what my astonishment was, when they, one and all, entirely coincided with me, expressed their conviction that one day the town would be swept away, and entreated me to make the matter public, and thus bring it under official notice. I must own that I was astonished to find that the site had been selected by a gentleman, at the time Commissioner of Crown Lands for the district, who has seldom made mistakes of this kind; and knowing the good judgment he has usually exercised in such matters, I am willing to admit that possibly my impression may be wrong, and that the town will not be swept away, *a la* Gundagai. But appearances are very suspiciously in favour of my view, the more especially as the piccaninny floods of late years have sent the river water up to the floors of the mills, and cut off the communication in the main street of the town.

Figure 7.6. Sydney Morning Herald, June 18, 1866, page 8.

97 - *Sydney Morning Herald*, June 13, 1866, page 2.

98 - *Sydney Morning Herald*, June 18, 1866, page 8.

99 - *Sydney Morning Herald*, July 19, 1865, page 5.

100 - The Australian Agricultural Company was established in 1824 as a land development company through an act of the British Parliament and with the assistance of a Crown Grant of one million acres in the Port Stephens area of New South Wales. www.aaco.com.au .

101 - *Sydney Morning Herald*, August 3, 1866, page 3.

The fencing in had a most depressing effect upon me, and disturbed my nightly slumbers by dreams of lockings up, and cageings, and fastenings, in all of which I was an imprisoned victim. I was not sorry, therefore, to quit this ominous spot, though I assure you I had some misgivings as I approached the gate, lest the gentleman in authority here, might have taken it in his head to fasten me in. I was intensely relieved when at last I got through the barricade, and heard the gate bang behind me; I pursued my way with a sense of freedom and liberty that I had not before experienced throughout all my wanderings.[102]

He wrote about Goulburn on a number of occasions and was not always complimentary: it was "not a lively town – I beg its pardon – city, I should have said". It does not "offer very much in the way of amusement to the visitor. … it has been built upon the old primeval Botany Bay principle, and has its

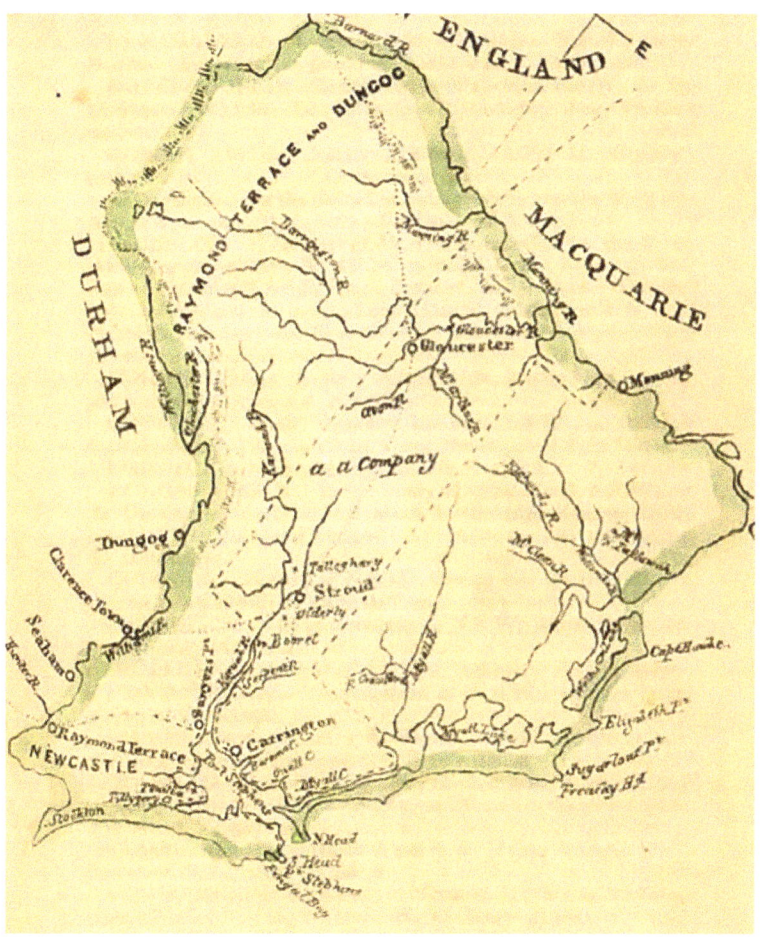

Figure 7.7. Contemporary map of the County of Gloucester, with an indication of the area of land owned by the Australian Agricultural Company in the County. Source: Wells 1848, between pages 184 and 185. Original maps by J. Allan, Lithographer, Hunter Street, Sydney.

---

102 - *Sydney Morning Herald*, August 3, 1866, page 3.

gaol and Court-house directly in the centre of the city",[103] as in Bathurst, "as though their presence were necessary to keep us in restraint".[104] de Boos liked his pipe, but "The great occupation of the people of Goulburn seems to be smoking. Were pipes and tobacco abolished, the men of the Queen of the South would perish from nicotinian inanition".[105]

In 1871, he found the town of Blackheath in a very sad state, with its facilities no longer needed as a consequence of the railway, a topic he had commented on in an earlier report.

> *The old inn looks like some spot upon which the curse of an evil deed has fallen. With cessation of the traffic over the mountains by way of the road ended also the day of public-houses, and this, amongst others on the line was done up. It has been long tenantless, and is fast going to ruin.*[106]

For de Boos, travelling was not always pleasurable. Leaving Barraba, he was not in a good state of mind: "I had been so long absent from anything approaching to civilised society that what with my own mishaps, the starvation of my horse, and my consequent mental uneasiness, my record of days became exceedingly complicated and confused".[107]

Overnight accommodation for himself and his horse was frequently worthy of comment. Between Sofala and Bathurst, he spent a night at James Short's Inn, because his horse was "dead beat", and it was dark when he arrived. He had a miserable night, due to noise, drunkenness and "orgies", and he made serious complaints about the landlord's behaviour.[108] The inn at Breeza was "a miserable sample of country hostelry". By contrast, at Tuena, "I reached 'mine inn', in which I took 'mine ease', with a feeling of luxury and comfort from the privations of two days that any one, looking at the miserable style of diggings' public-houses, would have thought it impossible to experience".[109] Non-commercial accommodation was frequently much better, whether it was a shepherd's hut or a wealthy squatter's home (Figure 7.8).

---

103 - *Sydney Morning Herald*, January 28, 1871, page 7.
104 - *Sydney Morning Herald*, August 18, 1857, page 4.
105 - *Sydney Morning Herald*, January 28, 1871, page 7.
106 - *Sydney Morning Herald*, February 25, 1871, page 6.
107 - *Sydney Morning Herald*, June 13, 1866, page 2.
108 - *Sydney Morning Herald*, July 29, 1857, page 2; July 23, 1857, page 4; August 3, 1857, page 2.
109 - *Sydney Morning Herald*, August 5, 1857, page 5.

Landscapes observed

He traversed and wrote about many different types of landscapes: the Hunter River flats between Newcastle and Morpeth; numerous other river valleys and, in some, their farming activities; the many ranges he had to climb and descend to cross from Sydney and the Hunter Valley to the inland plains, with their pastoral activities (in one day he passed over 11,000 sheep that were on the move).[110]

From Moonbie to Nundle, he rode through over 35 miles of "rough rocky mountain country".[111] From Govett's Leap, near Blackheath, he described some of the scenery and its luxuriant vegetation.

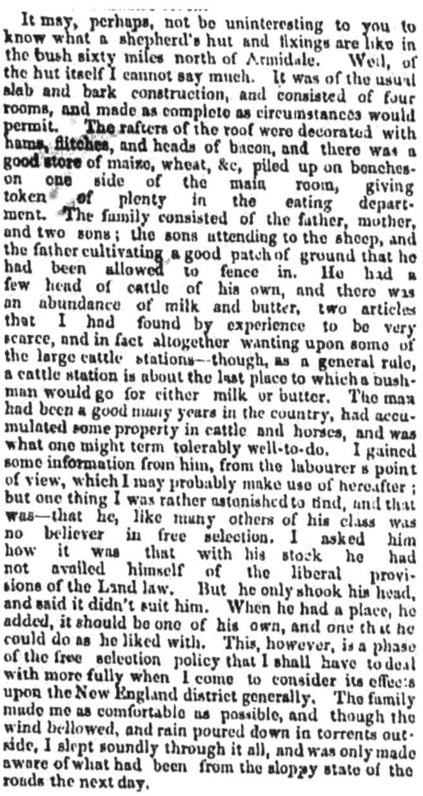

> It may, perhaps, not be uninteresting to you to know what a shepherd's hut and fixings are like in the bush sixty miles north of Armidale. Well, of the hut itself I cannot say much. It was of the usual slab and bark construction, and consisted of four rooms, and made as complete as circumstances would permit. The rafters of the roof were decorated with hams, flitches, and heads of bacon, and there was a good store of maize, wheat, &c, piled up on benches on one side of the main room, giving token of plenty in the eating department. The family consisted of the father, mother, and two sons; the sons attending to the sheep, and the father cultivating a good patch of ground that he had been allowed to fence in. He had a few head of cattle of his own, and there was an abundance of milk and butter, two articles that I had found by experience to be very scarce, and in fact altogether wanting upon some of the large cattle stations—though, as a general rule, a cattle station is about the last place to which a bushman would go for either milk or butter. The man had been a good many years in the country, had accumulated some property in cattle and horses, and was what one might term tolerably well-to-do. I gained some information from him, from the labourer's point of view, which I may probably make use of hereafter; but one thing I was rather astonished to find, and that was—that he, like many others of his class was no believer in free selection. I asked him how it was that with his stock he had not availed himself of the liberal provisions of the Land law. But he only shook his head, and said it didn't suit him. When he had a place, he added, it should be one of his own, and one that he could do as he liked with. This, however, is a phase of the free selection policy that I shall have to deal with more fully when I come to consider its effects upon the New England district generally. The family made me as comfortable as possible, and though the wind bellowed, and rain poured down in torrents outside, I slept soundly through it all, and was only made aware of what had been from the sloppy state of the roads the next day.

Figure 7.8. Sydney Morning Herald, June 18, 1866, page 8.

Casting my eye below, I look into an abyss twelve hundred feet deep. The giant trees which are there growing thickly in all the luxuriance of a sheltered position and a well-watered soil, and which must form a dense forest of most magnificent timber, appear to be nothing more than diminutive saplings. So close are the trees that nothing but a mass of verdure is seen below, and it is only by the difference of shade that I can note the varying and ridgy nature of the glen. But from below comes the hoarse murmur of a stream as it rattles its way through rocks and other obstacles; and there is the sound of a sharp dash of water brought to the ear, and drawing attention to the direction whence it proceeds. It is one of the several falls – the largest of them – and I am in a splendid position to see it. The stream is swollen by the late rains, and grumbles loudly through its rocky bed as though complaining of the leap it is compelled to take, then swirls over the rock with a swift and almost silent murmur springs out into the void, as though desirous of showing no hesitation, over that which is inevitable. For a brief space it flashes and sparkles through the air, then comes with a sullen dash upon the debris below, shines for a moment over the broken rocks, and disappears amongst the timber. Its murmurings, however, mingle with the solemn and continuous splash of the descending waters, and come mellowed by distance into music, and form a not inappropriate accompaniment to the scene around.[112]

---

110 - *Sydney Morning Herald*, May 1, 1857, page 2.
111 - *Sydney Morning Herald*, May 16, 1857, page 4.
112 - *Sydney Morning Herald*, February 25, 1871, page 6.

In his account of the ride from Tuena to Goulburn, he stressed the detail of the landscapes that were so often unseen by most observers, and for which written descriptions could be so inadequate: "To the unpractised bushman, one gully may seem exactly the same as another, the difference being imperceptible to him, whilst to the old denizen of the forest every minute detail speaks aloud. ... Nor, do I think the pen could adequately convey all that which only the eye of the experienced traveller can mark".[113] But there are times when his pen does achieve that. His travelling was slow: he had time to stop, to view, to observe, to take in, and he had "a thorough knowledge of the Australian bush".[114] Of his ride from Tambaroora adjacent to the valley of the Turon River, he wrote extremely eloquently of the location's scenery, as well as the old Ophir Diggings, which he believed had "not yet been half worked".[115]

> To the right, or N.W., a deep valley may be traced for many miles, the huge mountains towering up on either side to an enormous height, whilst here and there one more vast than its fellows juts prominently forward, and throws out long branches or spurs, which, falling by degrees, gradually sink into the valley. A couple of hundred yards further on, and I came upon the edge of the real descent, which falls to the south-east, and then a view of unparalleled beauty and grandeur met my sight. The course of the Turon could be traced upwards for many miles, which in the back-ground, the heavy ranges of the Crown Ridge, from whence it takes its source, were marked out strongly upon the horizon, though blue with the distance. In every direction the winds and turns of the numerous ridges could be followed with ease, the great height at which I stood above causing them to be displayed before me as though upon a map, from their first starting from the river bed until, rising gradually, they joined themselves with the towering mountains of the main range. This, again, could be followed into the far distance, until the eye, wearied with the extended view, lost it in the confused mass of mountains that blackened the horizon. In the foreground, appearing almost at my feet, the waters of the Turon flowed swiftly by, glistening in the sunlight, showing out brighter from the darkness that, from where I stood, appeared to hang over the deep valley through which it coursed. To the right, the valley of the Lower Turon, was discernible for some distance down, an occasional ray of light, flashing up from the depths, marking the presence of the stream, until the view was broken by an abrupt turn of the river.[116]

Near Inverell, he was surprised to see thousands of sheep on the move, and, in the absence of any fencing, eating - stealing - the grass of landholders along their way.

---

113 - *Sydney Morning Herald*, August 18, 1857, page 4.
114 - Hamer 1957a.
115 - *Sydney Morning Herald*, September 26, 1865, page 2; Higgins 1990.
116 - *Sydney Morning Herald*, July 20, 1857, page 2; October 28, 1870, page 5.

Whilst I was riding along and complacently regarding the feed on either side of the road, and fancying in my innocence the splendid stand-by of feed that the occupier of the run would have for the winter, I raised my eyes and saw the advance guard of a flock of sheep. On it came and passed me, and was followed by another and another, till five flocks, numbering I suppose eight or nine thousand sheep had gone by. To see how the feed, the luxuriance of which I had previously admired disappeared before the advance of this army of locusts had overspread the line of road was something very nearly approaching to a caution. I don't know what the feelings of a run owner – especially if he has to pay anything like a largely increased rental under the valuation – would likely to be; but I do know this that I felt that there must be something radically wrong in a system that allowed of such a wholesale confiscation of grass as I here witnessed.

But these eight or ten thousand sheep are a mere nothing, for on subsequent enquiry, I learnt that there were no less than a hundred and forty to a hundred and fifty thousand sheep on their travels from the far Western districts round the edges of New England, Clarence and Macleay districts – sheep that had been taken on the road to procure the feed and water that had altogether failed on their own runs.[117]

Gold and the goldfields

Everything concerned with the goldfields and gold mining was subject matter for de Boos. There were the different methods of mining, all undertaken by human labour, with axes, picks and shovels. Alluvial mining involved washing and sifting materials from the beds and banks of creeks; the different methods he observed on the Oban Diggings in 1857 are described in great detail.[118] 'Surfacing' was working material close to the surface of the ground with a spade. 'Stripping' consisted of removing the alluvial soil lying on the drift or 'washdirt' in which the gold was found, often to a depth of 25 feet to 35 feet. These were also termed deep leads or buried rivers. The material removed was carried away to form immense mounds, or 'tips', often up to 20 feet high.[119] In some locations like Majors Creek, the evidence of such mining can still be seen (Figure 7.9). Underground or reef mining, digging shafts and tunnels, was frequently very difficult, and often without success.

Water was an essential pre-requisite for all forms of mining. It was essential for washing the gold from the ore. It was needed for crushing the host rocks before the washing could take place. In brief, without water, there was no mining and no gold production. On numerous occasions, de Boos

---

117 - *Sydney Morning Herald*, June 14, 1866, page 2.
118 - *Sydney Morning Herald*, May 4, 1857, page 2; May 11, 1857, page 2.
119 - *Sydney Morning Herald*, July 17, 1865, page 5.

commented on the importance of water and the problems when there was none.[120] For example, at Nundle in 1866,

Figure 7.9. Part of the Majors Creek valley. In the centre and background are some of the large mounds or tips produced from 'stripping'. Source: Peter Crabb, July 1, 2018.

> *The whole appearance of the place – no business doing either in public-house or store, no work going on, heaps of quartz lying uncrushed, whilst the water-wheels stand motionless, cracking beneath the fierce rays of the sun – is wretched and miserable in the extreme. Talk of a deserted village, why all Goldsmith's poetry could never give such an absolute picture of desolation as would one glance at a diggings standing still for want of water.*[121]

---

120 - *Sydney Morning Herald*, May 21, 1866, page 2.
121 - *Sydney Morning Herald*, May 21, 1866, page 2.

At the Hanging Rock diggings on the Peel River, he was very complimentary of the role of the American Water Company in ensuring "a steady and continuous supply of water" by means of numerous reservoirs and some 42 miles of "ditches" (just one of the complex works constructed to provide miners with water at a number of locations).[122] At more than one location, he had similar concerns regarding the availability and quality of water for domestic purposes.

Araluen extended over six kilometres along the Araluen River. It was one of many places that suffered from the vagaries of water availability, from far too little to far too much, the narrow nature of the valley resulting in often extreme floods (Figure 7.10). The vast majority of the 3,500 to 4,000 people (catered for by 28 public houses) were engaged in gold mining, but some were occupied with agriculture, including a number of Italians who had been very successfully producing grapes for three years, with more vines being planted, in spite of "all the obstacles that red tape and circumlocution of that very circumlocutory branch of the public service, the Lands Office, could find … who in their humble way had done far more substantial good to the colony … than had the whole body of miners who, during the past three years, had been engaged upon upturning the valley".[123]

Figure 7.10. Flooding in the Araluen Valley, August 2020. It has been much worse than this. Source: https://aboutregional.com.au/

---

122 - *Sydney Morning Herald*, May 16, 1857, pages 4 and 7.

123 - *Sydney Morning Herald*, July 17, 1865, page 5; July 19, 1865, page 5. See comments on 'The Midge Correspondence' in Chapter Twelve.

de Boos was well aware of the dilemmas that gold mining created, as he had observed earlier in Victoria. On the one hand, there were the economic benefits for the Colony and, to varying degrees, for its residents. On the other, there was the damage to the natural environment resulting from all forms of gold mining. In almost every instance, a gold find was followed by the wholesale clearance of vegetation, not only to get at the gold, but also to provide timber for constructing buildings, for fuel, for shoring-up holes and mines, and for building water diversion works. As much of the mining was for alluvial gold, the natural states of the waterways were destroyed; for some distance below Muckerawa, the Macquarie River had "its bed unmade for it".[124] At the Hanging Rock diggings, "Holes sunk in every direction, hillsides cut down, gullies completely washed away to a depth of twenty feet down to bare rock, and the whole appearance of the country changed from the beautiful green of the native bush, to the red hue of the gold mine".[125] On the Rocky River Diggings, close to Uralla, it was "only with much difficulty that a person on horseback can make his way across amongst the numerous holes and heaps of refuse or washing dirt."[126] Muckerawa "must have been a picturesque spot when first opened as diggings, but now every charm has been destroyed by the ruthless hand of the miner ... I think that of all the diggings I have visited in New South Wales, that of Muckerawa has been the most completely ransacked".[127] At Louisa Creek, "Every sign of verdure has also been buried under the red gravelly earth thrown out from the holes, which are so thickly sunk that in many places barely a sufficient dray road is left".[128] The gold licence contained no environmental obligations.

By 1870, the Turon Valley was no longer the beautiful area he had described just a few years earlier. "Much of the wild beauty of the scene has departed. Every accessible slope has been denuded of its timber; its face [marks] the action of the gold fever, even as the scarred face of the sufferer from small-pox shows the ravages of that fell disease".[129] Yet again, here was the dilemma with which de Boos was frequently confronted, namely the consequences of

---

124 - *Sydney Morning Herald*, September 28, 1865, page 2.
125 - *Sydney Morning Herald*, May 16, 1857, page 7.
126 - *Sydney Morning Herald*, May 12, 1857, page 3.
127 - *Sydney Morning Herald*, July 2, 1857, page 2.
128 - *Sydney Morning Herald*, July 7, 1857, page 3.
129 - *Sydney Morning Herald*, October 28, 1870, page 5; September 30, 1865, page 4; Higgins 1990.

gold mining: "much of its [the Turon's] wild and savage grandeur has gone from it, but the evidences of civilization more than compensate for the loss. ... some pretty white-washed cottage, with its garden fence running down to the very water's edge ... [and, across the river] the very antipodes of the Anglo-Saxon neatness ... a Chinese encampment ... one large hut, which accommodates any number of Celestials".[130]

However, de Boos was not a lone voice when it came to issues of the impact of mining on the natural environment, as a comment found by David Goodman indicates.

> Today even the most elementary environmental sense should lead us to re-evaluate with a little more sympathy the losing side of these nineteenth-century arguments about gold and democracy. We remember the Eureka rebellion very well in Australia as a key moment in the history of Australian democracy. Arguments like this from the Hobart Courier [May 4, 1855] are nowhere in the national memory of Australia: 'The gold diggers cannot be permitted to use the public lands for private advantage without contributing rent in some shape or other to the public purse'. Why on earth – in this more environmentally conscious age – do we not remember, and even cautiously honour, that side of the argument?[131]

Mining other minerals

de Boos' writing on mining was not limited to gold, with articles on the coal industry in the Hunter Valley;[132] Newcastle, "the coal seaport ... grimy with coal dust, of which its people carry about samples on various parts of their dress";[133] the Bowenfels Coal Field in the Lithgow Valley;[134] shale oil production near Mt Victoria;[135] and cinnabar, the principal ore of mercury, at Cudgegong.[136] From the Orange district, he wrote about the copper mining at Cadia and other nearby locations.

---

130 - *Sydney Morning Herald*, October 28, 1870, page 5.
131 - Goodman 2018; 'Melbourne Gold Export Duty', *The Courier* (Hobart), May 4, 1855, page 2.
132 - He had "no intention of treating the matter in a scientific point of view. That I must leave to more learned pens than mine. I never had any aptitude for learning hard names, and from my boyhood up have had a very wholesome horror, begotten no doubt in the ancient days of King Birch, of those terrible jaw breakers upon which it seems necessary that science should be founded" *(Sydney Morning Herald*, August 6, 1866, page 2); *Sydney Morning Herald*, August 10, 1866, page 5; August 13, 1866, page 2.
133 - *Sydney Morning Herald*, August 20, 1866, page 6.
134 - *Sydney Morning Herald*, August 11, 1870, page 5; August 15, 1870, page 5.
135 - *Sydney Morning Herald*, March 8, 1872, page 5.
136 - *Sydney Morning Herald*, July 9, 1870, page 6.

Administration of the goldfields

As he was later to put to the 1871 Royal Commission, there were significant problems with the administration and regulations of the goldfields, so much so that they worked to the disadvantage of the individual miner.[137] They were based on the *Gold Fields Management Act, 1852*, and its regulations, and their frequent changes and amendments.[138] There was turmoil over licence fees for miners and everyone else who earned a living on the goldfields, including ministers of religion. The system was dependent on Gold Commissioners, who had to cover large areas, and unpaid magistrates, who were unqualified to deal with mining issues. The importance of the Gold Commissioners was illustrated by the "great ferment" that arose on the Peel River diggings in 1866 at the removal of Gold Commissioner Frederick Dalton from his position based in Nundle.[139] de Boos believed there should be distinct courts specifically to deal with mining issues.

> ... *mining disputes are for the most part of so complicated a character, and the regulations are so incomprehensible to those who have not studied them, and so utterly contradictory to those who have done so, that the unpaid magistracy will be sure to shun mining cases, as they would shun the Father of Evil. In fact, any magistrate who is not fully up in all mining matters will find the whole thing a chaos of confusion; and unless he has the Regulations by heart and at his finger's end, he might as well look into the Koran as into them to guide him in his dilemma.*[140]

A particular problem was the frontage system of mining claims.[141] It originated in Ballarat to solve local difficulties, but soon resulted in even greater problems, with overlapping claims and interminable litigation (Appendix 7.10). It was almost certainly to the detriment of gold mining there. It was abandoned in Victoria in 1866. It was adopted in New South Wales in 1862, but, as in Victoria, it resulted in problems and much litigation. Yet it was some years before it was abandoned. As early as 1863, de Boos attributed the decline of Forbes entirely to the 'frontage system' of mining claims.[142] At a later date, he had some very caustic comments about the system:

---

137 - Gold Fields Royal Commission 1871, 151-154.
138 - *Sydney Morning Herald*, December 25, 1852, page 4; August 1, 1866, page 6.
139 - *Sydney Morning Herald*, May 24, 1866, page 3.
140 - *Sydney Morning Herald*, May 30, 1866, page 5.
141 - Veitch 1911, 111-112, 136; Armstrong 1901, 32-35; Hamilton 2015, 84.
142 - *Sydney Morning Herald*, December 25, 1863, page 2.

The real truth is – and the regulations are so mystified and mystifiable that this truth has only just dawned upon me – that all the mischief that has followed upon them has been owing to an attempt made through them to establish in New South Wales that ruin of all gold-fields, the frontage system. After it had been extensively applied in Victoria, had been found to work ruinously there, and had been utterly and completely given up, its superior excellence seems suddenly to have struck the head of the Lands Department, and being a new thing, that might possibly pass for an original idea, was forthwith seized upon with avidity. How it has worked we see in the vast wastes of turned up land now lying unworked and unworkable upon what were once our gold-fields.[143]

Given the significance of gold mining to the Colony, de Boos was also highly critical of the lack of government geologists in New South Wales, certainly when compared with Victoria and Queensland. In one of his columns, he noted that "were it not for the Rev. W.B. Clarke and other scientific gentlemen who, without remuneration, for the pure love of science, and with a desire to benefit the country, occasionally publish their opinions to the world, we should be altogether in the dark with regard to many matters, the knowledge of which is of the utmost consequence to the miner".[144]

Aboriginal people

Whilst frequently using the colloquial language of the times, de Boos often commented favourably on the Aborigines and those who treated them with some dignity. At Glenrock Station, south-east of Nundle, he was highly complimentary of the owner, his family and staff, including an Aboriginal family, not least the complete absence of social distinctions between any of them.[145] At the Oban Diggings, he described factually "a large tribe of blacks", 70 to 80 people, which had stopped nearby, noting the work done for some of the diggers and station owners, the men cutting trees and the women doing washing and cooking.[146] He had also seen Aboriginals as bullock drivers.

He visited the then peaceful location of Myall Creek, site of "one of the few prolonged hand to hand struggles between the aboriginal savage of Australia and the white usurper of his domain".[147] His response to the

---

143 - *Sydney Morning Herald*, May 30, 1866, page 5.
144 - *Sydney Morning Herald*, August 11, 1870, page 5.
145 - *Sydney Morning Herald*, May 11, 1866, page 5.
146 - *Sydney Morning Herald*, May 11, 1857, page 2.
147 - *Sydney Morning Herald*, June 14, 1866, page 2; Tedeschi 2016; www.myallcreekmassacre.com ; https://en.wikipedia.org/wiki/Myall_Creek_massacre .

infamous massacre of numerous blacks, including women and children, by a group of local white men, was somewhat different to that of many of his contemporaries:

> ... horrible as it must have been to contemplate such a massacre of strong men who might, and who did resist, what pen can ever describe the frightful inhuman slaughter that followed, when the men of the tribe being laid low, the women and children were deliberately shot down one by one, unresisting and pleading for mercy.[148]

On his trip to the Fitzroy, de Boos acknowledged that the local Aborigines were "fierce and implacably hostile" towards the Europeans who had taken over their land. The killing of a number of whites raised real issues of security for life and property, but the material evidence of the death of at least one Aborigine caused de Boos to observe that "there is something exceedingly shocking to the feelings of civilised man in such a destruction of human life".[149]

The Chinese Miners

During the time de Boos was employed by the *Herald*, the Editor was the Rev. John West,[150] a Congregational minister, a "man of high principle and humane feeling".[151] Prior to the conclusion of the reports on 'The Goldfields of New South Wales', West wrote a long editorial based largely on de Boos' writings. It included an extended and essentially supportive discussion of the Chinese gold miners and their relationships with the Europeans. West stated that there was ample room on the goldfields for all of them, Europeans and Chinese, "if they can only be kept apart". West pondered restricting more Chinese immigration for a somewhat unusual reason, namely that "it is quite clear that the principles of Christianity and of civilization are far too little developed to enable us to ensure the race against oppression while they pursue a wandering life".[152] The Europeans still had much to learn. Relationships between Europeans and Chinese varied significantly from place to place. Nowhere were they worse than at Lambing Flat (Young), where the persecution of the Chinese in 1861

---

148 - *Sydney Morning Herald*, June 14, 1866, page 2.
149 - *Sydney Morning Herald*, October 16, page 5.
150 - John West was editor of the *Sydney Morning Herald*, 1855-1873 (Reynolds 1967). West was followed as Editor by Andrew Garran and William Curnow, both non-conformist ministers (Souter 1981, 591-594; Reynolds 1967).
151 - Walker 1976, page 60.
152 - *Sydney Morning Herald*, July 23, 1857, page 4; July 18, 1857, page 4.

was unreservedly condemned, as was the inaction of the Government.[153] de Boos strongly criticised the hatred of the Chinese, the wrecking of their market gardens, and the fact that they had "been driven out to the farther end of Wombat, a ploughed line marking the demarcation between them and the Europeans".[154]

Over time, the Chinese miners gradually figured more prominently in the writings of de Boos. He indicated their numbers on the various goldfields: for example, of the 1,700 miners in the Bathurst district, two-thirds were Chinese; in the Araluen district, there were some 1,000 European miners and 600 Chinese.[155] He wrote of the quantity and value of the gold they produced (which they did not disclose), and the rules by which they undertook their communal operations. Writing of Raggety Point in 1857, he was very complimentary of "these indomitable diggers … [who] … work most assiduously in the face of all difficulties".[156] From Bowling Alley Point to the Monroe's Creek area, the Chinese and Europeans work "on an equal footing and in the most amicable manner",[157] and "They proceed very systematically, and work out their claims most completely".[158] Further, regardless of location, it was "altogether a mistake to say that the Chinese will work for less than a European".[159] In the Forbes district, the Chinese miners and market gardeners operated without any trouble.[160] At Dirt Hole, near Tambaroora, where a large proportion of the miners were Chinese, they were well regarded for their "order, sobriety, steadiness, and perseverance". The main complaint there came from the publicans, because they had to pay a license fee whilst those operating some twenty Chinese opium-smoking tents did not.[161]

---

153 - Souter 1981, pages 54-62; *Sydney Morning Herald*, February 11, 1861, page 4; July 5, 1861, page 5; Crabb 2020; Schamberger 2015.

154 - *Sydney Morning Herald*, August 16, 1865, page 2; August 14, 1865, page 2; January 14, 1864, page 2. The local newspaper, *The Miner and General Advertiser*, took a very different view, being very much against the Chinese miners. Editorials were highly racist: for example, "it remained for our latter-day rulers [the Colonial government], to let loose on the gold-digging community – men and women – a filthy, heathen, obnoxious, and alien race, and to maintain them by force of law in the midst of a Christian people" (September 18, 1861, page 2; February 20, 1861, page 3; July 6, 1861, page 2; July 27, page 2); Kirkpatrick 2000.

155 - *Sydney Morning Herald*, July 19, 1865, page 5.

156 - *Sydney Morning Herald*, July 9, 1857, page 8.

157 - *Sydney Morning Herald*, May 21, 1866, page 2; May 23, 1866, page 3.

158 - *Sydney Morning Herald,* May 21, 1866, page 2; May 23, 1866, page 3.

159 - *Sydney Morning Herald*, May 28, 1866, page 2.

160 - *Sydney Morning Herald*, August 16, 1865, page 2.

161 - *Sydney Morning Herald*, July 15, 1857, page 2.

At Tambaroora, relations could not have been better and were an example to those in other locations. The kindness of the Europeans towards the Chinese, especially with respect to issues of their health and suicides, are warmly reported.

> *One case of leprosy occurred here some three years back, and caused a great deal of excitement. The Chinese themselves were the first to acknowledge it, and, of course, the first to shun the unhappy victim of disease; and the medical practitioner recognised it, though he was only called in after the death of the man to make the matter sure. With the egotism that marks those who know the full effects of this dread disorder, the Chinamen left their countryman alone, and untended, and he would have died of starvation instead of disease had it not been for some good Samaritans of Europeans, who took him some food and gave him attendance; and that charity which, by a high authority, is said to cover a multitude of sins, in their case covered them with a protecting armour, and shielded them from the effects of this fell and foul disease. This is the way that the men of Tambaroora act towards a man like themselves, though he chances to be born in China.*[162]

Whilst gold mining may have been their main activity, the Chinese contributed significantly to other parts of the local economies.[163] As Don Watson observed many years later, for most of the goldfields,

> *the Chinese were essential to local economies, and, as providers of fresh food, probably to public health. As the goldrushes faded, the great majority of them returned to China. The few thousand who remained either moved to city Chinatowns or found niches in the rural economy. Hardworking and resilient, experts in irrigation, terracing and horticulture, long after the goldrushes were over, Chinese gardeners grew the bulk of the vegetables and fruit for many country towns.*[164]

Social Concerns

The involvement of de Boos in the Fitzroy gold rush made a significant impression on him, and his reports demonstrate his concerns for all of those involved.[165] He was greatly concerned over the destitute state of most of the miners because of its essential failure. Nowhere was his concern for the less fortunate more evident than in his account of an incident on his trip 'Up the Fitzroy'. A dead body, unrecognisable due to its decomposition, was seen floating "amongst the reeds and lilies that border the river". The detailed description leaves little to the imagination, but it is the reaction of de Boos to the body that merits repeating:

---

162 - *Sydney Morning Herald*, September 30, 1865, page 4.
163 - Wilton 2004.
164 - Watson 2014, 135; Gittins 1981.
165 - For a much more detailed account of the Canoona trip, see Crabb 2010.

> *The thought that this poor fellow, who had thus perished alone in the wild bush, with no eye to witness his agonised struggles for life, with no friend or mate to search for his remains, and found at last by strangers in such a state as to prevent the possibility of recognition – that he had, perhaps, left behind him in his search for gold a mother – brothers, sisters – and perhaps a wife and children – whom in his sanguine dreams he had hoped to place beyond the chance of future want, and who perhaps are even now waiting in anxious expectation of his return – to think all this, and to know that neither friends nor relatives would ever hear the certainty of his fate, saddened both my companion and myself, and for a considerable time afterwards ducks and teal were allowed to rise from the water without our paying them the slightest attention.*[166]

Difficult though the Fitzroy trips were for de Boos, he fared better than most of the miners, and his continuing concern for the destitute ones was evident in a letter he wrote to the *Herald*'s Editor, appealing for funds to assist them.[167]

In 1860, he was most likely the person sent "to furnish particulars of a rather more tangible and substantial character relating to the coaling industry of the Hunter Valley". The outcome was a very detailed report, along with accounts of the principal collieries, entitled "A Visit to the Newcastle Collieries".[168] But as well as the mining, the accounts tell of the miners and other matters. He was far from impressed with the miners' living conditions at some of the collieries. At none of the mines did "the provisions for the comfort of those employed bear the slightest comparison with the complete and admirable provisions for procuring and shipping the coal expeditiously and cheaply".[169] There was also the issue of coal dust: "Everywhere there is the black griminess of coal, and you will hardly meet a buxom matron or a blooming maiden who does not bear a smudge mark of black somewhere upon her visage".[170] In marked contrast was the care given to its workers by The Shale Oil Company, near Mt. Victoria. They had comfortable residences; there was a small store, but no public-house; a Public School; a doctor was available; and there were occasional visits from clergymen. In an effort to have a steady fixed population of workers, men

---

166 - *Sydney Morning Herald*, November 27, 1858, page 5; Anon. 1859. Frederick Sinnett, writing for *The Argus* and later published privately (Sinnett 1859), covers similar ground in his much shorter accounts of "the insane rush to the place". However, they do not compare with the vivid and comprehensive accounts of de Boos.

167 - *Sydney Morning Herald*, December 30, 1858, page 5. A Diggers Employment Committee was subsequently established to assist destitute miners (*Sydney Morning Herald*, February 28, 1859, page 4). Was de Boos involved?

168 - *Sydney Morning Herald*, May 12, 1860, page 8. The same 'Special Reporter' had earlier been sent to the lower Hunter valley and Newcastle area to report on "the ministerial deliverances at the recent re-elections," *Sydney Morning Herald*, March 17, 1860, page 4; March 21, 1860, page 4, and March 22, 1860, page 5.

169 - *Sydney Morning Herald*, May 12, 1860, page 8.

170 - *Sydney Morning Herald*, August 13, 1866, page 2.

employed by the Company were being offered freehold plots of land, at a nominal price, sufficient for a house and garden.[171]

On the diggings, he commented frequently on living conditions, especially when people were living in 'tents'. The situations of women and children were of particular concern to him. Even though de Boos had held a publican's licence, he more than once wrote of the large numbers of inns: for example, on the Rocky River Diggings, which extended "for a distance of fully seven miles" along the river, there were licences for 18 inns for a population of about 1,600 people.[172] In Gulgong, he was not impressed by men "walking about with their hands in their pockets" when there was prospecting that could be done.[173] Yet many places were peaceful communities, such as the Oban diggings, despite having "neither commissioner nor constable, clergyman or schoolteacher".[174] On rare occasions, he had a pleasant surprise, such as at Rocky River.

> I heard the notes of a fine-toned piano-forte rattling out a lively polka as I passed. This caused me almost involuntarily to look around upon the wild hills and the primeval forest that on all sides hemmed in this little oasis of civilization; and I thought of the wonderful effects of gold in so soon making such a change, and I pictured to myself the astonishment with which some patriarchal opossum must have listened from the branches of his favourite gum-tree to the unwonted sound of ball-room music.[175]

Bushrangers

Bushrangers were frequently noted. Travelling north-east from Scone, 'Captain Thunderbolt' (the alias of Frederick Ward) became a topic of discussion, de Boos observing, "I longed for nothing better than half-an-hour's conversation with Mr. Ward".[176] There were rumours that he did have some contact with him, but this is unlikely, in spite of one unsubstantiated report.

> Mr. de Boos could claim to have received the queerest commission from a newspaper on record. In the early bushranging days he was instructed by the 'Sydney Morning Herald' to allow himself to be captured by the bushrangers in order to make copy out

---

171 - *Sydney Morning Herald*, March 8, 1872, page 5.
172 - *Sydney Morning Herald*, May 12, 1857, page 3.
173 - *Sydney Morning Herald*, July 13, 1871, page 5.
174 - *Sydney Morning Herald*, May 11, 1857, page 2.
175 - *Sydney Morning Herald*, May 12, 1857, page 3.
176 - *Sydney Morning Herald*, May 9, 1866, page 2.

of his experiences. Somehow or other however the adventure did not come off. Perhaps bushrangers were wise as well as daring and knew better than to tackle a newspaper man for plunder. [177]

Even if he had met him and lived to tell the tale, would he have told it?[178] Quite apart from any unlikely meeting, de Boos had sufficient to write about regarding the impact of 'Thunderbolt' on travellers and local residents, especially those in isolated places, and how they coped with him. He also wrote of Mary Ann Bugg, "Ward's mistress … The poor, ignorant aboriginal woman turn[ed] out to be a well educated half-caste … she was Thunderbolt's chief lieutenant and right hand man".[179] He also wrote of bushrangers Gardiner, Gilbert, and O'Mealley in the Lachlan Valley,[180] Ben Hall in the Braidwood area,[181] and others in the Nundle district,[182] though he does not appear to have written of the exploits in the Braidwood area of the Clarke Gang, "arguably the worst and most troublesome bushrangers of all time".[183]

Tambaroora, Hill End, and Hawkins Hill: a case study

Between 1857 and 1872, de Boos visited the Dirt Hole, Tambaroora, Bald Hills and Hill End district more than any other locations (Figure 7.11). His reports provide an account of the many changes on the goldfields over that period.[184]

In 1857, de Boos wrote a detailed account of "The Dirt Hole, Tambaroora, and the Bald Hills [gold fields which] form one continuous line of diggings for a distance of about seven miles".[185] A large percentage of the miners were Chinese, and as noted above, relations between them and the Europeans were very good. It was a highly productive field, with a population of about

---

177 - "Notes and Notions" by Quilp. *National Advocate* (Bathurst), November 1, 1900, page 2. This was written at the time of the death of de Boos.

178 - On 'Captain Thunderbolt', see Hamilton and Sinclair 2009; Baxter 2011; McHugh 2011; *Canberra Times*, June 28, 2010. Was he killed, or did he escape to North America? Efforts by Hamilton and Sinclair to see all of the relevant archival papers were refused by the NSW Government, in spite of a Legislative Council order for them to be made available. As far as is known, this continues to be the case; no reasons have been given.

179 - *Sydney Morning Herald*, May 11, 1866, page 5.

180 - *Sydney Morning Herald*, December 29, 1863, page 2.

181 - *Sydney Morning Herald*, July 19, 1865, page 5.

182 - *Sydney Morning Herald*, May 21, 1866, page 2.

183 - Smith 2015; *Sydney Morning Herald*, January 15, 1867, page 5.

184 - Crabb 2014 and 2015a; *Hill End Historic Site*. NSW National Parks and Wildlife Service, Hurstville, 2006.

185 - *Sydney Morning Herald*, July 15, 1857, page 2.

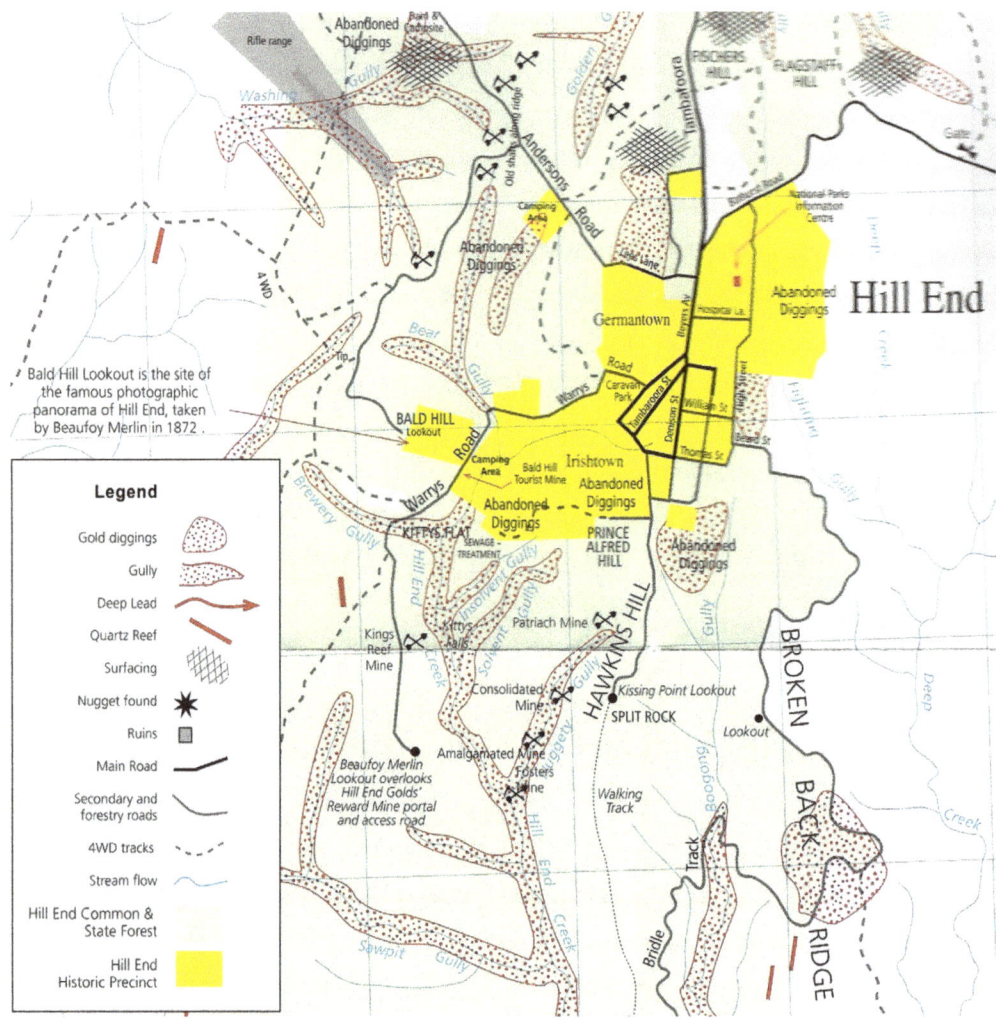

Figure 7.11. The Hill End Goldfield. Source: Stone (2014): Gold Atlas of New South Wales. Outdoor Press, Euroa. Section 2.

2,000 people, of which two-thirds were diggers.[186] de Boos visited the area again in September 1865[187] and in July-August 1870.[188] By 1870, much of the district had "a most unpromising look of decadence. From end to end of the valley, … nothing is to be seen but one uninterrupted line of worked-out ground. … Saplings have grown up amongst the deserted holes which line the course of the stream, and serve, to some extent, to veil the nakedness of the land; but still the inexorable barrenness of a broad belt of the centre of the valley is not concealed, and gives birth to that peculiarly depressing feeling which the sight of a worn-out gold-field is so calculated

---

186 - *Sydney Morning Herald*, July 15, 1857, page 2; September 30, 1865, page 4.
187 - *Sydney Morning Herald*, September 26, 1865, page 2; September 28, 1865, page 2; September 30, 1865, page 4.
188 - *Sydney Morning Herald*, August 8, 1870, page 5; August 11, 1870, page 5; August 15, 1870, page 5.

to inspire".[189] However, the mining had moved down-stream to Hill End and Hawkins Hill, and de Boos was pleased to see his earlier assessments, that this was "one of the finest and richest reefing districts, not only in New South Wales, but in the whole continent of Australia", were being realised.[190] Down-stream to Hawkins Hill was "one continuous line of workings".[191]

By 1871, he regarded the Hill End goldfield as "the most important at the present time … the sights I have seen here down some of the rich shafts were quite sufficient to turn the brain of any person given to speculation".[192] In five reports, de Boos provides a remarkably detailed account of the reef mining area of Hawkins Hill, with notes on all of the underground mines (Figure 7.12; Appendix 7.7).

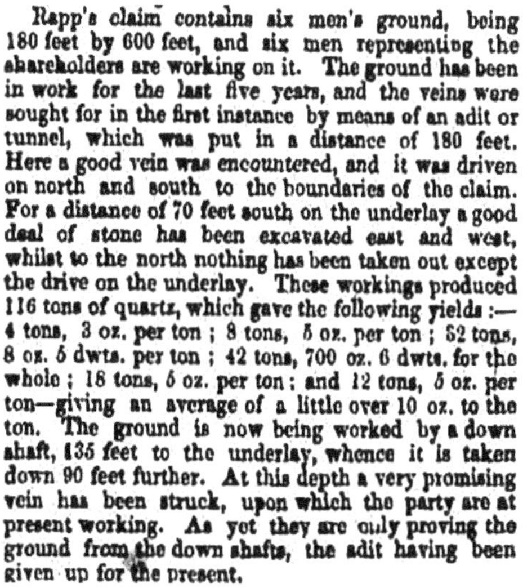

> Rapp's claim contains six men's ground, being 180 feet by 600 feet, and six men representing the shareholders are working on it. The ground has been in work for the last five years, and the veins were sought for in the first instance by means of an adit or tunnel, which was put in a distance of 180 feet. Here a good vein was encountered, and it was driven on north and south to the boundaries of the claim. For a distance of 70 feet south on the underlay a good deal of stone has been excavated east and west, whilst to the north nothing has been taken out except the drive on the underlay. These workings produced 116 tons of quartz, which gave the following yields :— 4 tons, 3 oz. per ton ; 8 tons, 5 oz. per ton ; 52 tons, 8 oz. 5 dwts. per ton ; 42 tons, 700 oz. 6 dwts. for the whole ; 18 tons, 5 oz. per ton ; and 12 tons, 5 oz. per ton—giving an average of a little over 10 oz. to the ton. The ground is now being worked by a down shaft, 135 feet to the underlay, whence it is taken down 90 feet further. At this depth a very promising vein has been struck, upon which the party are at present working. As yet they are only proving the ground from the down shafts, the adit having been given up for the present.

Figure 7.12. A description of one of the underground mines on Hawkins Hill: Rapp's Claim. Sydney Morning Herald, August 7, 1871, page 2.

He went underground at "about a dozen" of them, despite the personal discomforts, both going down and coming up.

> *It may seem an easy enough thing to descend so trifling a distance as 200 feet by an ordinary ladder, but when that ladder is placed perpendicularly, being secured to the timbers of the shaft, and not placed at an angle of easy gradient, as our superterrestrial ladders are planted, the matter becomes much more serious than people generally are inclined to consider it. It is trying to the muscles of one unaccustomed to the peculiar kind of exercise, and especially trying to the wind, if the individual attempting the feat is out of training. The ladders, as I have said, are placed perpendicularly against the*

---

189 - *Sydney Morning Herald*, August 8, 1870, page 5.
190 - *Sydney Morning Herald*, August 8, 1870, page 5.
191 - *Sydney Morning Herald*, August 11, 1870, page 5; August 15, 1870, page 5.
192 - *Sydney Morning Herald*, July 26, 1871, page 5.

side of the shaft, and consist each of fourteen rounds or steps. Then occurs a platform where a rest can be obtained if necessary, with an oval opening in it just large enough to admit the passage of an ordinary sized man, but utterly prohibiting the passage of any individual at all inclined to obesity. From the platform, the ladder descends on the other side of the shaft for fourteen rounds when, another platform occurs, and the ladder descends on the opposite, thus alternating from side to side from every platform. For the last thirty feet or so, the ladders are laid on the side of the underlying rock for about twenty feet, and the remaining distance has to be descended by the means of the acrobatic performance I have previously described, that is, a lowering oneself by the rope, with the body thrown out at an angle, the feet keeping time in the descent with the hands. ...

If the descent by the ladder way was difficult, the ascent was, I assure you, very much more trying. Whether I had got stouter whilst down below, or whether the peculiar position in ascending makes any difference, I am not prepared to say. Your reader may take either alternative as suits him; but this I can say that the orifice on the landings seemed to be much too small for me to pass through – nay, they seemed to get smaller and smaller as I ascended, and to jam my knees as I bent them in mounting the last few rounds. When I got to the surface I felt, as a man usually does feel when he has completed a tough job, that if there had been only two more ladders to mount I must have caved in. I have had the same feeling on reaching the top of a hill – not one of your toy hills about Sydney, but a good old man hill, such as Monkey Hill on the Turon, or Hawkins' Hill, or those pretty hills between Hargraves and Tambaroora – I have felt as if another hundred yards of ascent would have done me up, though probably that distance would have made no particular difference except to render me more tired.[193]

Alluvial gold was found in the Hill End district in 1851, but through the 1850s-1860s gradually gave way to near surface and then deeper reef mining, it being the first reef mining area in Australia. 1871-1874 were the boom years at Hill End.[194] The district's population reached some 8,000 people, making it

Figure 7.13. Central Hawkins' Hill by Beaufoy Merlin. Source: Holtermann Collection, State Library of New South Wales, Sydney, ON 4 Box 71 No G, collection.sl.nsw.gov.au/

at the time one of the largest inland towns in New South Wales. Over 50 tonnes of gold were produced, 12.4 tonnes coming from Hawkins Hill (Figures 7.13 and 7.14). This included the largest piece of reef gold ever

---

193 - *Sydney Morning Herald*, August 4, 1871, page 5; July 26, 1871, page 5; Hamilton 2015, 121, 124-130.

194 - Jinks 2005a; *Hill End Gold Deposits*. Primefact 569. Department of Primary Industries, Sydney, 2007; Mayne 2003.

discovered in the world: the 286 kg 'Holtermann Nugget' or 'Beyers and Holtermann nugget', as it became known, was found at the 'Star of Hope' Mine on October 19, 1872 (Figure 7.15).[195]

Figure 7.14. Gold mines on Hawkin's Hill, Turon Valley in the background, 1872, by Beaufoy Merlin. Source: Holtermann Collection, State Library of New South Wales, Sydney, ON 4 Box 49 No 45, collection.sl.nsw.gov.au/

Figure 7.15. Bernhardt Holtermann with 'The Holtermann Nugget', Hill End, c. 1872. Source: State Library of New South Wales, Sydney. PIC/12254/264 LOC Album 1136.

de Boos paid a further visit to Hill End at the beginning of 1872, his report being the first of a number grouped together as Series Five of 'Random Notes by a Wandering Reporter' (Appendix 7.10). It was his last visit to Hill End and his report was a very upbeat and complimentary one.

> Seen from the top of the Bald Hill, south-west of the town, and the highest point of the range, the picture is a most pleasing one, as almost every store, house, or hut is brought into view; whilst the sun, shining upon the galvanized iron so plentifully used in roofing, remind one of some of those fabled cities of the East, where the houses were of silver and the streets paved with gold.[196]

---

195 - Davies 2013; *Hill End Gold Deposits*. Primefact 569. Department of Primary Industries, Sydney, 2007; *Australian Town and Country Journal*, November 2, 1872, page 559.

196 - *Sydney Morning Herald*, January 17, 1872, page 5.

But from 1874, Hill End's heyday was over.[197]

This last visit to Hill End was just three months before the photographer Beaufoy Merlin visited the area taking some of his famous photographs, now perhaps better known as part of the Holtermann collection.[198] A number of lithographs were copied from Merlin's photographs and published in *The Australian Town and Country Journal* and other newspapers.[199] Evidence of mining from this period can still be seen, along with that of current exploratory work.

In 1872, a series of articles by another reporter, entitled "A Trip to Hill End", appeared in the *Sydney Morning Herald* and *The Sydney Mail*.[200] In the *Mail*, the first of the articles was accompanied by a 'Supplement', a lithograph of Hawkins Hill, with all the gold mines identified.[201]

Recognition of the special nature of Hill End came on April 2, 1999, when the Hill End Historic Site was listed on the New South Wales State Heritage Register (Figures 7.16, 7.17, 7.18).[202]

Figure 7.16. Clark Street, Hill End, 1872. Source: Hill End & Tambaroora Gathering Group, Sydney. https://www.heatgg.org.au

---

197 - Hodge 2009; Stone 2014.
198 - Davies 2013. It is not known if de Boos met Merlin or Holtermann.
199 - *Australian Town and Country Journal*, March 30, 1872, page 40; May 29, 1872, page 816.
200 - *Sydney Morning Herald:* I, May 21, 1872, page 5; II, May 23, 1872, page 3; III, May 25, 1872, page 7; IV, May 27, 1872, page 2; V, May 28, 1872, page 2; VI, June 3, 1872, page 9; VII, June 4, 1872, page 2; VIII, June 6, 1872, page 5; IX, June 10, 1872, page 6; X, June 11, 1872, page 6; XI, June 13, 187, page 3; XII, June 18, 1872, page 3. *The Sydney* Mail: May 25, 1872, page 660; June 1, 1872, pages 692-693; June 8, 1872, pages 724-725; June 15, 1872, pages 756-758.
201 - Supplement in *The Sydney Mail*, May 25, 1872.
202 - https://www.weekendnotes.com/hill-end-historic-site

Figure 7.17. Mining Registrar's Office, Hill End, 1872. Source: Hill End & Tambaroora Gathering Group, Sydney. https://www.heatgg.org.au

Figure 7.18. An old miner's cottage, little changed from when it was built in the late 1860s. Source: Hill End & Tambaroora Gathering Group, Sydney. https://www.heatgg.org.au

Some other work

In between his reporting of parliamentary debates and his travels to different parts of the Colony, de Boos found time to do other things related to his employment with John Fairfax & Sons.

In September 1870, an 'Intercolonial Industrial Exhibition' was held in Sydney, under the auspices of the Agricultural Society of New South Wales. It received extensive coverage in the *Sydney Morning Herald*, with one issue having eight pages of articles about New South Wales, written by staff of the *Herald*.[203] If he wrote nothing else, Charles de Boos was most likely the author of the section on 'Gold'. The following year, the articles were re-published as part of an 821-page volume titled *The Industrial Progress of*

---
203 - *Sydney Morning Herald*, September 6, 1970, pages 2-3; September 7, 1870, pages 4, 5, 7-14; September 27, 1870, page 4.

New South Wales: being a Report of the Intercolonial Exhibition of 1870, at Sydney; together with a variety of papers illustrative of the Industrial Resources of the Colony.[204] With the authors identified, this is one of the few occasions on which the names of so many *Herald* reporters were set out. Described as "members of the literary staff of the *Herald*", they were Howard Reed, Samuel Cook, Charles St. Julian, Charles de Boos, George Eld, Edward Reeve, W.E. Langley, Charles Robinson, and Edward Burton.[205] The volume also contained a report of the Intercolonial Exhibition, a collection of 'Special Papers', and a large coloured map of the Colony; the editors were 'Professor Smith and Mr. Howard Reed'.[206]

Retirement from the *Herald* and the Fairfax company

On May 27, 1872, a 'Note' appeared in the *Herald* stating that de Boos had retired.[207] A few days earlier, on May 16, 1872, "a testimonial was presented to Mr. Charles De Boos, on his retirement from the reporting staff of the *Herald*" (Figure 7.19).

> *Address from the Literary Staff and Heads of Departments connected with The Sydney Morning Herald to Charles de Boos, Esquire, of Stanmore.*
>
> *Dear Sir,*
>
> *Understanding that you have just relinquished the position occupied by you on the Sydney Morning Herald - with which you have been so long and so honorably identified - we beg to avail ourselves of this opportunity to give a united and cordial expression to our personal consideration and sincere respect, desiring to place on record, not only our high opinion of your professional ability, but also our regard for your many other estimable qualities.*
>
> *Associated, as many of us have been with you, for many years past, in connection with the Herald, it is a gratification to us to think that we still occasionally have the pleasure of seeing you, as we understand that you propose to remain in this Colony. Trusting that every prosperity may reward your energy, and attend upon your talents in the new sphere of life you have chosen.*
>
> *We remain, Dear Sir, yours very sincerely,*
>
> *Signature.*
>
> *On behalf of the Literary Staff and Heads of Departments connected with the Sydney Morning Herald.*

---

204 - Government Printer, Sydney, 1871. *Sydney Morning Herald*, April 18, 1871, page 2. The article on Gold is at pages 436-443. There is also a longer article by Clarke (1871) which includes an Appendix listing the locations of all the gold findings in New South Wales and the dates when the discoveries were made.

205 - *Sydney Morning Herald*, April 18, 1871, page 2; April 19, 1871, page 9; *The Sydney Mail*, April 27, 1871, page 231.

206 - Professor John Smith was the first Professor of Chemistry at the University of Sydney (Hoare and Radford 1976).

207 - In 'Notes of the Week'. *Sydney Morning Herald*, May 27, 1872, page 2.

It is surprising that there was not a more extended notice of his retirement, though it was included in the 'Chronicle of Occurrences' for 1872.[208]

The sixteen or so years spent working for John Fairfax & Sons, from 1856-1872, was a remarkable period in the life of de Boos. It can also surely be described as a frenetic one. He reported the debates of the New South Wales Parliament; no other reporter was more widely travelled, covering much of the eastern half of the Colony; and he reported on the goldfields and many other aspects of life in the Colony. Few reporters would have written more. In terms of gold, de Boos was probably the most prolific and knowledgeable reporter in the twenty years or so from the early 1850s. As to why he left the *Herald*, this is yet another unanswered question in the life of de Boos, but it may well have had much to do with the declining health of his wife (see Chapter Eight).

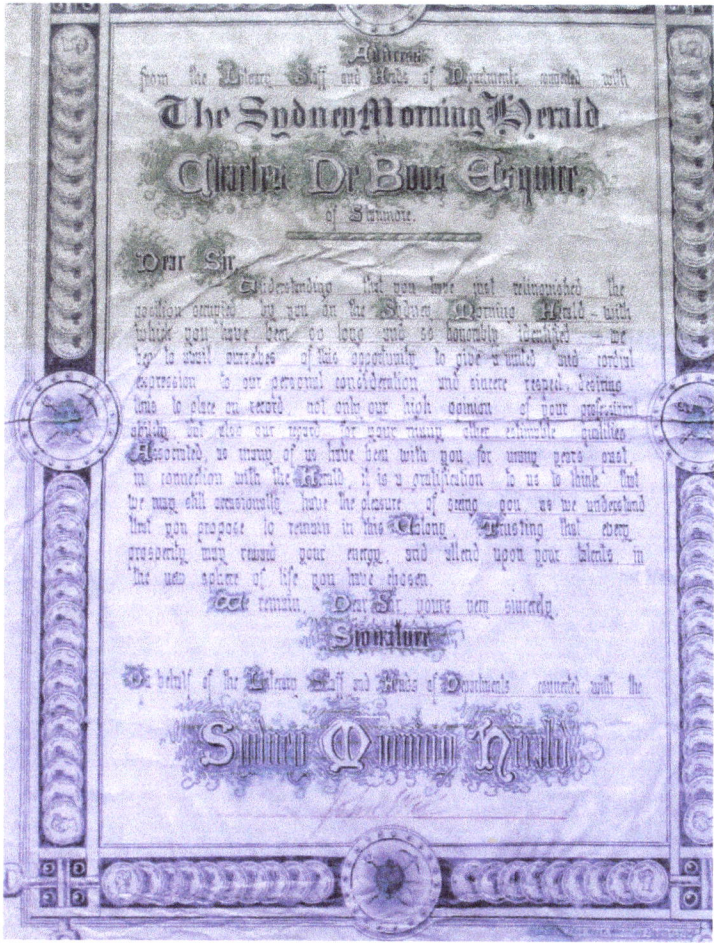

Figure 7.19. Testimonial presented to Charles de Boos, May 16, 1872. Copy courtesy Mr Geoff Murray, personal communication, March 11, 2010.

However, as discussed in the next chapter, the problem with the 'official' retirement of de Boos is that it is far from clear that he did actually retire.[209]

---

208 - *Sydney Morning Herald*, December 31, 1872, page 3.
209 - *Sydney Morning Herald*, May 27, 1872, page 2.

Chapter Eight

Life and Family in Sydney, 1856-1875

In 1856, Sydney was a much-changed city to the one de Boos had left five years earlier. Coincidentally, as in Mt Alexander in 1852, Samuel Gill was also 'in town' to record many of the new buildings and landscapes (Figures 8.1 and 8.2). Over the near-twenty years de Boos lived in Sydney, the city and surroundings continued their rapid changes.

Figure 8.1. George Street from King Street, looking south, Sydney. Allan & Wigley, Lithographers, Sydney, Sydney, 1856. Source: National Library of Australia, PIC Volume 1 #123 NK9593/18

Figure 8.2. Circular Quay, Sydney, by S.T. Gill (1856), Allan & Wigley, Sydney. Source: National Library of Australia, PIC Volume 196# S4031.

"The new sphere of life": involvement in gold mining

In the Address presented to de Boos on his departure from the *Sydney Morning Herald*, his colleagues wished him "every prosperity in the new sphere of life you have chosen" (see Chapter Seven). But what was this?

In the early part of 1872, a company of 'Mining Brokers and Agents' was established named 'De Boos and Gritton', with offices in Greville's Chambers, Sydney.[1] As well as being involved in share dealings and company transactions, the business was a publicist for the gold mining industry. For example, "Rich stone is reported to have been struck in Campbell's lease, Big Oakey Creek, between Sofala and Wattle Flat. Specimens have been received, and may be seen at Messrs. De Boos and Gritton's office".[2] Along with E. Greville and E.N. Emmett, de Boos wrote to the Agricultural Society of New South Wales suggesting "the society should offer medals for the best specimen of gold in quartz, for the best series of strata passed through in sinking upon alluvial deposits, and for the best general collection of mineral specimens. After some discussion, it was decided that medals for such exhibits should be offered".[3]

In the months before and after he left the *Herald*, de Boos became personally involved in the gold mining industry and several companies in particular. The full extent of his involvement is difficult to determine, in part because his oldest son was also named Charles Edward. Whilst Charles Edward Junior was only 19 years old in 1872, he was certainly involved in mining not long after this. (How de Boos and/or his son were able to finance their involvement is another unknown.) Along with others, he jointly held a number of mining leases, particularly in the Tambaroora – Hill End area, all of which seem to have been subsequently cancelled or forfeited due to non-compliance with the lease conditions.[4] He wrote a letter in support of the share sale for a company mining Creighton and Beard's gold claim

---

1 - *Sydney Morning Herald*, March 2, 1872, page 3; March 22, 1872, page 1; April 10, 1872, page 4; April 11, 1872, page 1.
2 - *Sydney Morning Herald*, April 23, 1872, page 5; *Sydney Mail*, April 27, 1872, page 532.
3 - *Sydney Morning Herald*, April 13, 1872, page 6.
4 - *NSW Government Gazette*, 186, July 29, 1873, page 2089; 300, August 25, 1876, page 3387; April 21, 1874, page 1172; July 29, 1873, page 2089; February 10, 1874, page 416; *Sydney Morning Herald*, November 11, 1876, page 9; *NSW Government Gazette*, 324, September 15, 1876, page 3678; *Sydney Morning Herald*, September 20, 1876, page 2. An exception may have been Lease 2037, covering 10 acres, quartz, by Price, de Boos & Co., at Bogie Mountain. No record of its cancellation has been found. *NSW Government Gazette*, 159, June 20, 1873, page 1744. There may well have been a conflict of interest for de Boos to hold these mining leases when he became a Mining Warden in 1875 (see Chapter Nine).

on Hawkins' Hill, Hill End;[5] he had significant share-holdings in the Clan Campbell Gold Mining Company in Hill End, the Mulloon Copper Mining Co., and the "Molong Consols" Copper Mining Co. Ltd;[6] and he was a director of a number of other companies.[7]

On August 6, 1872, a debate was initiated in the New South Wales Legislative Assembly by William Forster regarding a mining dispute and various claims involving de Boos and others over a quartz claim at Wythe's Hill, Tambaroora (lease number 1076).[8] The mining lease application made by de Boos and party was disputed by a Charles Williamson and party. During a short debate, Farnell, the Minister for Mines, told Forster that he "had been misinformed on many points". The dispute was won by de Boos. The materials relating to the dispute were requested by Forster and they were compiled in a Legislative Council paper.[9]

Back to reporting?

It seems that "the new sphere of life" did not last very long, with no advertisements for 'De Boos and Gritton' being found after April 27, 1872 (a month before the 'Address' was presented to de Boos).

It is quite likely that, after a break of unknown length, he returned to work for Fairfax & Company, no doubt on a casual basis. This would have been much more convenient for him, especially given that his wife was very ill (see below). The *Sands' Sydney Directories* for 1873 and 1875 stated that his occupation was a 'Reporter' with the *Sydney Morning Herald*.[10] A further series of 'Random Notes' published at the end of 1874 (with the last on January 2, 1875) (Appendix 8.1) contain many indications that they are the work of de Boos.[11] Further, based on construction dates for the

---

5 - For example, *Sydney Morning Herald*, February 16, 1872, page 6; February 21, 1872, page 2.
6 - *NSW Government Gazette*, 291, November 8, 1872, page 2922; 86, April 8, 1873, page 1054.
7 - *NSW Government Gazette*, 140, May 17, 1872, page 1296; *Sydney Morning Herald*, March 1, 1872, page 5; *Evening News*, April 17, 1872, page 2; *Sydney Morning Herald*, December 12, 1873, page 1; April 20, 1872, page 3; *Evening News*, April 30, 1872, page 3; *Sydney Morning Herald*, July 27, 1872, page 8; *Sydney Mail*, May 11, 1872, page 591; *Maitland Mercury*, December 24, 1872, page 2; *The Empire*, April 25, 1872, page 1; *Sydney Morning Herald*, April 20, 1872, page 3.
8 - *Sydney Morning Herald*, August 7, 1872, page 2; *Evening News*, August 7, 1872, page 4; *Votes and Proceedings of the Legislative Assembly*, August 6, 1872, page 356. There is no indication as to why Forster raised this issue.
9 - *Quartz Claim on Turon River. (Correspondence in Reference to Dispute for Possession of.) Votes and Proceedings of the Legislative Assembly, 1872-1873*, Volume 2, pages 861-869. Government Printer, Sydney.
10 - The Directory was not published in 1874.
11 - *Sydney Morning Herald*, November 2, 1874, page 2; December 5, 1874, page 6.

Western Railway, the trip was a contemporary one.[12] However, as to any other writings for the *Herald* and *Mail* between 1872 and 1874, nothing definitive can be said.

A lone report in the *Armidale Express* in September 1873, suggested the involvement of de Boos in yet another publication, a proposed weekly literary review; a prospectus had been issued and the first issue was expected in the same month.[13] However, as nothing further has been found about the proposed journal, it would appear that it failed before it even began.

Beyond employment

Given his work for John Fairfax and Company, his reports on parliamentary debates and the travelling his other reporting involved, it is hard to believe de Boos had time for anything else! But this was far from the case. As outlined below, he accomplished much more over these years. There was his local government service, his community work, running a public house for some of the time, and finding what must have been very limited time for his wife and growing family. And on top of all this, these sixteen years were by far the most productive in terms of his other writing; satire, social commentary, and fiction, a very large corpus of work that is discussed in Chapters Twelve and Thirteen.

Contributing to the community

As his writings for the *Herald* indicate, de Boos was a community minded person, concerned for peoples' lives, especially women and children, and the physical and social environments in which they lived. At the time, such concerns were far from the norm.

The Municipality of Newtown was incorporated on December 12, 1862. In March 1863, de Boos became involved with the first Council in a rather strange way. He and a W. Rowland Hill provided £75 each as surety for the newly appointed Council Clerk, W.H. Mackay.[14] This was a very large

---

12 - The line reached Mount Victoria in 1868, Wallerawang 1870, Tarana 1872, Bathurst 1876, and Orange 1877. https://en.wikipedia.org/wiki/Main_Western_railway_line,_new_south_wales .

13 - *Armidale Express*, September 20, 1873, page 6.

14 - See Newtown Municipal Council meetings minutes for March 5, March 9, and March 16, 1863. www.newtownproject.com.au/2009/05/1863/3/

sum of money, especially as de Boos had been insolvent only a few years previously. Why he did this is not known. The following year, Hill was elected to the Council. In 1866, charges of embezzlement against Mackay resulted in considerable dispute, including the implication of Hill. There were calls for the recovery of sureties from de Boos and Hill, but legal action against them was stayed after payments by them of £2.10.0 and £25.0.0, respectively, to cover the Council's costs.[15] Yet another strange and unexplained incident in the life of Charles de Boos.

In 1870, he was one of 117 signatories to a 'Petition for the Separation from the Borough of Marrickville' of the 'Stanmore Ward' and that it be made a separate municipality.

> *The petitioners state that they are ratepayers within the Stanmore portion of the Borough of Marrickville, and are desirous of the same being separated from that borough and erected into a municipality under the name 'Stanmore'.*
>
> *That their interests are seriously affected by being joined to the said borough.*
>
> *That they have ample grounds of dissatisfaction, as the amount given in the ratebook for Stanmore, together with the Government endowment, shows that only about one-half of said rates collected therein, together with the apportioned endowment, is expended in Stanmore.*[16]

The issue was certainly not resolved to the satisfaction of de Boos and other Stanmore ratepayers, as was clear from the report of a meeting in September the following year.[17] The ratepayers' requests were not successful.[18]

In 1871, de Boos was nominated for the Marrickville Council, but was not elected due to "an informality in Mr. De Boos' nomination paper".[19] The following year, he was successful, being elected with a substantial majority as an Alderman for the Stanmore Ward.[20] He was also Chairman of the Finance Committee.[21] He ended his time as a member of the Council in

---

15 - www.newtownproject.com.au/local-council-info/biographies/18/ ; *Empire*, August 22, 1866, page 5.

16 - *Sydney Morning Herald*, December 2, 1870, page 12; *NSW Government Gazette*, 290, December 1, 1870, pages 2675-2676; September 16, 1871, page 5.

17 - *Sydney Mail,* September 16, 1871, page 912.

18 - *Sydney Morning Herald*, June 6, 1879, page 6.

19 - *Sydney Morning Herald*, February 13, 1871, page 5.

20 - *NSW Government Gazette*, 47, February 16, 1872, page 436; *Sydney Morning Herald*, February 14, 1872, page 5; *The Sydney Mail*, February 17, 1872, page 215.

21 - For example, *Sydney Morning Herald*, February 7, 1872, page 3; February 27, 1872, page 3; May 25, 1872, page 9; September 23, 1872, page 3; October 11, 1872, page 3; November 23, 1872, page 5; January 28, 1873, page 7; February 27, 1873, 7. He didn't attend all meetings: on one occasion, "Mr. de Boos was away in the country", *Sydney Morning Herald*, March 29, 1872, page 2.

June, 1873.²² He must have maintained his local government connections, however, as some years later, he was at a banquet for the Mayor of Randwick,²³ and later still, his abilities were mentioned in a complimentary manner at a special meeting of the Marrickville Municipal Council.²⁴

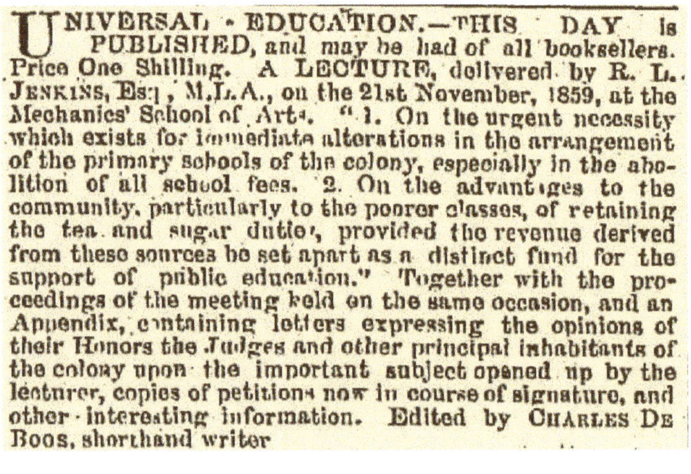

> UNIVERSAL EDUCATION.—THIS DAY is PUBLISHED, and may be had of all booksellers. Price One Shilling. A LECTURE, delivered by R. L. JENKINS, Esq., M.L.A., on the 21st November, 1859, at the Mechanics' School of Arts. "1. On the urgent necessity which exists for immediate alterations in the arrangement of the primary schools of the colony, especially in the abolition of all school fees. 2. On the advantages to the community, particularly to the poorer classes, of retaining the tea and sugar duties, provided the revenue derived from these sources be set apart as a distinct fund for the support of public education." Together with the proceedings of the meeting held on the same occasion, and an Appendix, containing letters expressing the opinions of their Honors the Judges and other principal inhabitants of the colony upon the important subject opened up by the lecturer, copies of petitions now in course of signature, and other interesting information. Edited by CHARLES DE BOOS, shorthand writer

Figure 8.3. Sydney Morning Herald, December 14, 1859, page 8.

He was a supporter of various community projects. In late 1859, he put his shorthand skills to use by taking down the full details of a public lecture on the subject of 'Universal Education'. It was published in the hope of leading "the public mind more pointedly towards the subject of Education" (Figure 8.3).²⁵ He was one of the speakers at the laying of the Foundation Stone of the Marrickville National School, responding to a vote of thanks to 'The Australian Press'.²⁶ He was a generous doner to many appeals, including the Homebush Races;²⁷ the Wivenhoe Estate Fund, set up to prevent the sale of the property of Charles Cowper;²⁸ the Prince Alfred Hospital Fund;²⁹ the fund for building the National School in Marrickville;³⁰ and Mrs de

---

22 - *NSW Government Gazette*, 169, July 8, 1873, page 1887; *Sydney Morning Herald*, May 30, 1873, page 1.

23 - *Australian Town & Country Journal*, February 1, 1879, page 209.

24 - *Sydney Morning Herald*, June 6, 1879, page 6.

25 - *Universal Education: a lecture delivered by R.L. Jenkins on 21st November, 1859 in the lecture hall of the Mechanics' School of Arts, Sydney*, edited by Chas. De Boos. Published by H. Bancroft, Sydney. *Sydney Morning Herald*, December 14, 1859, page 8; *Northern Times* (Newcastle), December 21, 1859, page 2.

26 - *The Empire*, April 10, 1865, page 5.

27 - *Sydney Morning Herald*, April 30, 1859, page 2.

28 - *Sydney Morning Herald*, June 19, 1866, page 1 and page 8; July 7, 1866, page 4. Sir Charles Cowper was a New South Wales politician and was Premier on several occasions; Ward 1969.

29 - *The Empire*, July 15, 1868, page 8.

30 - *The Empire*, February 22, 1865, page 7; *The Empire*, July 20, 1864, page 4.

Boos donated 5/- to the Floods Relief Fund.[31] He strongly supported the construction of a permanent Church of England in Petersham.[32]

He was a very active Freemason and during his years in Sydney, he was a member of the Cambrian Lodge of Australia, No. 656.

Charles de Boos the publican

In late 1857, de Boos took over the licence of 'The Old Bay Horse Inn' on Parramatta Road at the foot of Petersham Hill. It was no small establishment (Figure 8.4).[33] The licence was transferred to de Boos from William Pullen, even though Pullen had only held it for some three months.[34] Given the travelling de Boos did for his work with the *Herald*, he could not have run the inn without a major contribution from his wife Sarah. On May 4, 1858, the licence was renewed for the year through to July 1, 1859.[35] For some unknown reason, on February 1, 1859, it was transferred to an inn in Newtown, which was also called 'The Old Bay Horse Inn', de Boos still holding the licence that was valid through to July 1, 1859.[36] However, in March 1859, the licence was transferred from de Boos to Mary A. Brennan; once again, the reason is unknown.[37]

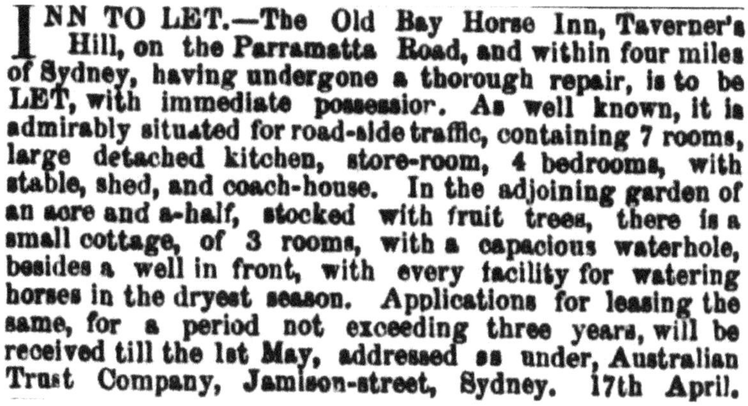

> INN TO LET.—The Old Bay Horse Inn, Taverner's Hill, on the Parramatta Road, and within four miles of Sydney, having undergone a thorough repair, is to be LET, with immediate possession. As well known, it is admirably situated for road-side traffic, containing 7 rooms, large detached kitchen, store-room, 4 bedrooms, with stable, shed, and coach-house. In the adjoining garden of an acre and a-half, stocked with fruit trees, there is a small cottage, of 3 rooms, with a capacious waterhole, besides a well in front, with every facility for watering horses in the dryest season. Applications for leasing the same, for a period not exceeding three years, will be received till the 1st May, addressed as under, Australian Trust Company, Jamison-street, Sydney. 17th April.

Figure 8.4. Sydney Morning Herald, April 18, 1857, page 10.

---

31 - *Sydney Morning Herald*, July 19, 1867, page 8.
32 - *Sydney Morning Herald*, August 12, 1870, page 5.
33 - *Sydney Morning Herald*, April 18, 1857, page 10; *Sydney Morning Herald*, November 9, 1857, page 8.
34 - *Sydney Morning Herald*, December 17, 1857, page 4; September 24, 1857, page 5.
35 - *Sydney Morning Herald*, April 21, 1858, page 8; May 19, 1858, page 6.
36 - 'Certificate to Authorise the Removal of a License'. License No. 1022. Public Licenses Index, State Archives and Records Authority of New South Wales, Sydney.
37 - *Sydney Morning Herald*, March 9, 1859, page 3.

On May 12, 1874, the licence of The Town Hall Hotel, 536 George Street (on the corner with Park Street, "The best position in the city"[38]), was transferred from John Tighe, a brother of Charles's wife Sarah, to de Boos.[39] John had lost the licence just four days after he was found guilty of assaulting Francis Smith, the licensee of the Burrangong Hotel, also on George Street.[40] Less than a year later, the licence was transferred from de Boos to Susan M. Tighe.[41]

Charles de Boos and his family

Over their years in Sydney, entries in the *Sand's Sydney Directories* and the locations of the births of their children, indicate that the de Boos family moved frequently, living at several places (Figure 8.5). William Peter was born at the Old Bay Horse Inn on May 18, 1858.[42] Where they lived immediately after leaving the Old Bay Horse in Newtown in 1859 is not known. Their next known address was 105 Harrington Street, Church Hill (The Rocks), where Emily Eliza was born on May 15, 1861; she died just ten weeks later, on July 30, 1861.[43] From 1863 to 1865, the family home was in Addison Road, Stanmore,[44] where Henry Augustus was born on November 12, 1862, only to die there three months later, on February 13, 1863.[45] The following year Lucille Grace was born on March 17, 1864.[46] Charles was back in Sydney from one of his journeys just in time for the birth of his daughter, Estelle Evangeline, on August 23, 1866.[47] With so many children, it was perhaps not surprising that Sarah advertised for "A General Servant".[48] In 1866, *Sand's Sydney Directories* reported them living in Ross Street, Kingston (Newtown), and the following year in Regent Street, Kingston; from 1868 to 1874, they lived in Middle Street, parallel to Addison Road, Marrickville.[49] Henrietta was born and died within

---

38 - *Sydney Morning Herald*, August 13, 1875, page 7.
39 - *Sydney Morning Herald*, May 13, 1874, page 7; *Sydney Morning Herald*, July 3, 1874, page 1. *NSW Government Gazette*, 209, September 2, 1874, page 2647.
40 - *Sydney Morning Herald*, May 8, 1874, page 2.
41 - *Sydney Morning Herald*, February 24, 1875, page 5.
42 - *Sydney Morning Herald*, May 22, 1858, page 1.
43 - *Sydney Morning Herald*, May 17, 1861, page 1; July 31, 1861, page 1.
44 - Addison Road is variously recorded as being in Stanmore and in Marrickville.
45 - *Sydney Morning Herald*, November 13, 1862, page 1; February 16, 1863, page 1.
46 - *Sydney Morning Herald*, March 19, 1864, page 9.
47 - *Sydney Morning Herald*, August 24, 1866, page 1.
48 - *Sydney Morning Herald*, October 30, 1867, page 8.
49 - *Sand's Sydney Directories*, John Sands, Sydney. But see another address for Charles de Boos in 1873 at Victoria Street, Paddington (*New South Wales Government Gazette,* 86, April 8, 1873, page 1054).

Figure 8.5. Places where Charles de Boos and family lived during their time in Sydney, 1856-1875. Source: from Map of Port Jackson and City of Sydney by James A. Willis (1867). Engraved by G.W. Sharp and printed from stone by J. Sharkey. Published by James A. Willis, Darlinghurst. NLA MAP F 109.

1. 1856-1857 and 1874-1875 The Town Hall Hotel, 536 George Street (on the corner of Park Street), Sydney
2. 1857-1859 'The Old Bay Horse Inn', Taverner's Hill, on Parramatta Road, Petersham
3. 1859 'The Old Bay Horse Inn', Newtown
4. 1859-1863 105 Harrington Street, Church Hill
5. 1863 to 1865 Addison Road, Stanmore
6. 1866 Ross Street, Kingston, Newtown
7. 1867 Regent Street, Kingston, Newtown
8. 1868-1874 Middle Street, Marrickville

an hour on November 22, 1867. On November 8, 1869, an un-named daughter was still-born at the Middle Street residence.[50] Another daughter, Aimee Theodora, was born at the family's Marrickville home on June 25, 1871, only to die after four weeks on July 23.[51] Later in the year, there was another advertisement for "a Female Servant".[52]

---

50 - *Sydney Morning Herald*, November 9, 1869, page 1.

51 - *Sydney Morning Herald, June 27, 1871,* page 1; *Sydney Morning Herald,* July 24, 1871, page 1.

52 - *Sydney Morning Herald*, September 13, 1871, page 8.

In June 1860, "Charles de Boos, of Sydney, shorthand writer" was called before the Insolvency Court, with liabilities of £108.5.7 and estimated assets (the "value of personal property") of only £15.0.0.[53] The matter was mentioned a number of times in the *Herald*'s records of court proceedings between June 20 and July 5, 1860.[54] At the final Court hearing, "Three debts were proved, and [the] insolvent was allowed his household furniture and wearing apparel".[55] The cause of the financial problems is unknown, and there is nothing to suggest they were long-lasting.

As if Charles and his family had not experienced enough personal tragedy, on December 10, 1872, Sarah died at "her temporary residence", 587 Bourke Street (on the corner with Arthur Street), Surry Hills, aged 41 years (Figure 8.6). Whose home this was, is not known.[56] The family home was still in Marrickville.[57] She had been ill with "hydatid disease of the liver [for] several years", which may have contributed to three of her last five children living for such short periods. Nonetheless, in earlier years, there must have been happier times, judging by "the wild Indian yell with which I was greeted by my youngsters on entering my own door", as de Boos returned from one of his many trips.[58]

In August 1874, an unusual advertisement appeared: "Cash purchaser for small COTTAGE with good yard; Piper or Moncur streets, Woollahra. Particulars to Mr. De Boos, Post-office".[59] Was he acting for a third party; was it for Charles, junior, or another member of the family; or was he considering a place of his own, even though at the time he was the licensee of The Town Hall Hotel?

Occasionally, there were reports of his older children's activities. A 'de Boos' played for Marrickville Cricket Club.[60] Francis was successful in the Public

---

53 - Insolvency Index, File No. 04964, Sequestration, but nothing found in Insolvency Index, 1842-1887: www.records.nsw.gov.au/state-archives . Accessed August 1, 2013. Reported in *New South Wales Government Gazette*, 1860, page 1219.

54 - *Sydney Morning Herald*, June 20, 1860, page 3; June 25, 1860, page 4; July 2, 1860, page 5; *New South Wales Government Gazette*, 118, June 26, 1860, page 1203.

55 - *Sydney Morning Herald*, July 5, 1860, page 2.

56 - Unfortunately, the *Sand's Sydney Directory* was not published in 1860, 1862, 1872 and 1874, in one way or another, all significant years in the life of Charles de Boos. It also means that there is no record of who lived at 587 Bourke Street. The 1871 *Directory* indicated that at this address, on the corner with Arthur Street, there was only vacant land, though by 1875, two dwellings had been built.

57 - *Sydney Morning Herald*, December 11, 1872, page 10; December 30, 1872, page 10.

58 - *Sydney Mail*, September 14, 1861, page 2.

59 - *Sydney Morning Herald*, August 4, 1874, page 1.

60 - *Sydney Morning Herald*, February 16, 1871, page 5.

Examinations at Sydney University, and he was also a member of the Sydney Grammar School Cadet Corps shooting team.[61] Later, William was among the names in the list of Public Examinations for Latin and History of England.[62] There was much less mention of de Boos in the newspapers through 1873 and 1874. One reason at least would have been that he had a family to care for: Mary 23, Sarah 21, Charles 19, Francis 17, William 14, Lucille 8, and Estelle 6. But what work did he do to enable him to care for them?

A reporter finally retired

At the beginning of 1875, Charles de Boos finally retired from life as a reporter, a personal involvement in gold mining, and from running The Town Hall Hotel, the licence having been transferred to Susan M. Tighe, his sister-in-law and wife of John Tighe.[63] At the age of 55, he made a major career change, becoming an employee of the New South Wales Colonial Government, a change that also meant a move from Sydney.

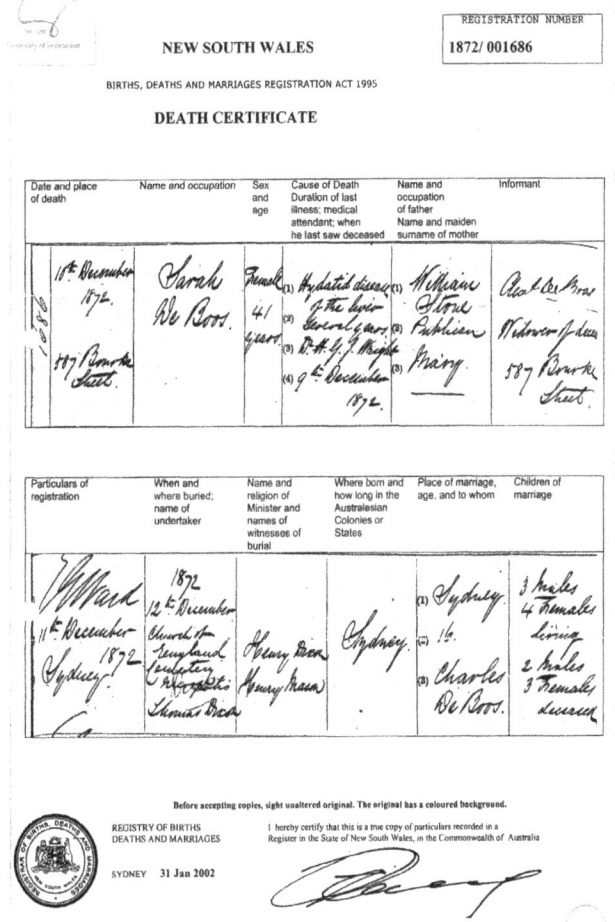

Figure 8.6. Death Certificate of Sarah de Boos. Source: New South Wales Registry of Births, Deaths and Marriages, Sydney.

61- *Sydney Morning Herald*, December 1, 1871, page 3; September 15, 1871, page 4.

62- *Sydney Morning Herald*, November 26, 1873, page 5.

63- *Sydney Morning Herald*, February 24, 1875, page 5; July 24, 1875, page 10. Five months later it was transferred to Eliza O'Loughlin.

Chapter Nine

An Official of the New South Wales Colonial Government, 1875-1889

As noted in previous chapters, de Boos was the last person to give evidence to the New South Wales Royal Commission "appointed to inquire into the working of the present Gold Fields Act and Regulations of New South Wales, and into the best means of securing a permanent water supply for the gold fields of the Colony".[1] The Commission had been established because of numerous problems associated with the management of the goldfields by the Department of Lands and the system of local Gold Commissioners. de Boos' evidence, given over a period of five hours, was clear and forthright, the result of some twenty years of reporting on the goldfields in New South Wales, Queensland, and Victoria. Few others who gave evidence to the Commission would have had such broad and detailed knowledge, or as much personal experience. Among other things, de Boos spoke of the many problems for the diggers with the regulations; unpaid and unknowledgeable Magistrates having to settle disputes; a lack of uniformity over questions of law; and the need for a system of mining districts, each with a Mining Warden and other officers.[2]

The prime conclusion of the Royal Commission was that "the 1866 system had been a complete failure":[3] "the unanimous testimony of all the witnesses whom we have examined … [was] that the present plan of Judicature, established by and existing under the Act of 1866, is worse than useless".[4] That was sufficient reason for a complete overhaul of the existing system. The main recommendations were for the creation of Mining Districts, each under the charge of a Mining Warden who would also be the Police Magistrate for the District. The Wardens would be required to hold periodical Wardens' Courts. At the discretion of the Warden, investigations

---
1 - Gold Fields Royal Commission 1871.
2 - Gold Fields Royal Commission 1871, 369-372.
3 - Hamilton 2015, 117.
4 - Gold Fields Royal Commission 1871, para 33, 135.

could be held in court or on the ground.⁵ Many of the Commission's recommendations were in line with de Boos' evidence.

The major outcome of the Commission was *An Act to make better provision for the regulation of mining, 1874* (37 Vic No. 13), which came into force on May 1, 1874.⁶ Among other things, it created a new Department of Mines and a new management system of eight mining districts: Mudgee, Tambaroora and Turon, Bathurst, Lachlan, Southern, Tumut and Adelong, Peel and Uralla, and New England and Clarence.⁷ Each District was divided into a number of Divisions. Each District had a Mining Warden, together with Registrars, Surveyors, Engineers, and others. On May 12, 1874, provision was made for Wardens' Courts to be held in some 46 locations within the colony.⁸

From items in numerous *NSW Government Gazettes*, the District and Division boundaries were subject to frequent changes, and the Districts of Cobar and Albert were added in 1878 and 1881, respectively.⁹ Over time, there were also numerous changes to the locations of the Wardens' Courts. By late 1879, Wardens were located at Hill End, Braidwood, Trunkey, Young, Armidale, Gulgong, Forbes, Tenterfield, Lismore, Albury, Scone, Tumut, Orange, Carcoar, Bingera, Bullah Delah, Glen Innes, Inverell, and Bourke.¹⁰

A Colonial Government Official

At the beginning of 1875, Charles de Boos started a new career with the New South Wales Colonial Government, being one of the early appointments as a Mining Warden. This clearly owed much to his knowledge of gold mining and the evidence he gave to the Royal Commission. He would have had fewer qualifications for the associated appointment of Police Magistrate, though he was not alone in this. Often such positions were ones of political patronage, though not in the case of de Boos. In many respects,

---

5 - Gold Fields Royal Commission 1871, paras 37-42, 157-159.
6 - *New South Wales Government Gazette*, 90, April 23, 1874, pages 1193-1239. Hamilton 2015, 51-52, 160-161.
7 - The district boundaries were set out in words in 'The Second Schedule' to the Act (*NSW Government Gazette*, 90, April 23, 1874, pages 1232-1234).
8 - *NSW Government Gazette*, 112, May 12, 1874, page 1461.
9 - *NSW Government Gazette*, 91, March 29, 1878, pages 1273-74; 72, February 25, 1881, page 1089.
10 - *The Sydney Mail*, December 27, 1879, page 1161.

the police magistrates seem to have been "able to set [their] own rules … the police magistrate [was] an irregular and unusually autonomous public servant".[11] Over the period of nearly fifteen years that he worked for the government, he held numerous positions under the Colony's Department of Mines and Department of Justice. At different times and in addition to his appointments as Mining Warden and Police Magistrate, he held concurrent appointments as one or more of Coroner, Justice of the Peace, Clerk of Petty Sessions, Assistant Registrar of Births, Deaths and Marriages, Agent for the 'Curator of Intestate Estates', and Marriage Celebrant.

His first appointment took him to Braidwood in 1875, where he stayed until 1880. Appointments followed at Copeland (1880-1881), Forbes (1880, a short temporary appointment), Temora (1881-1882), Copeland (1883-1887), Milparinka (1887-1889), and Cobar (1889). His workload was frequently massive. At each appointment, with the exception of Copeland, his responsibilities extended over large areas of country.

Braidwood

In January 1875, de Boos was appointed "a Warden of the Southern and Tumut and Adelong Mining Districts", that is, to work in two Districts.[12] Soon after, on May 27, 1875, he was appointed "a Magistrate of the Colony".[13] He was based in Braidwood,[14] from where he covered a large part of south-east New South Wales, taking in Nowra, Moruya, Mount Dromedary and Nerrigundah (Gulph Creek) on the South Coast, Tumut, Adelong and Kiandra, Queanbeyan and the Upper Murrumbidgee Valley, as well as numerous places much closer to Braidwood: Araluen, Majors Creek, Reidsdale, Bells Creek, Jembaicumbene, Nerriga, the upper Shoalhaven River, the Clyde River, and Mongarlowe (Figure 9.1). One trip took him to Bega for a meeting of the Prospecting Board with the Bega

---

11 - Golder 1991.
12 - *NSW Government Gazette*, 20, January 29, 1875, page 267.
13 - *NSW Government Gazette*, 122, June 1, 1875, page 1591.
14 - The *Braidwood Dispatch and Mining Journal* was published between 1859 and 1958, and as the *Braidwood Dispatch* from 1958-1969. There were two issues a week. Unfortunately, few copies of the paper before August 1888 have survived, largely due to a fire that destroyed the company's Braidwood premises, printing works and records on August 1, 1888 (*Goulburn Herald*, August 4, 1888, page 3). The *Dispatch* resumed publication on August 15, 1888. Consequently, research is dependent on material published in the *Sydney Morning Herald* and the *Queanbeyan Age*, some of it copied from contemporary issues of the *Dispatch*. Reports in the generally weekly 'Braidwood' column in the *Herald* give indications of the varied kinds of activities in which de Boos was involved (for example, see *Sydney Morning Herald*, June 13, 1876, page 3; July 18, 1876, page 3; July 26, 1876, page 3).

Prospecting Association,[15] and another to Albury, in the company of the Under-Secretary for Mines and a geological surveyor.[16] He did not have a lot to do with the Tumut and Adelong Mining District. He had visited a number of these places on his travels as a reporter for the *Sydney Morning Herald* (see Chapter Seven). On his first visit to Braidwood in 1865, he had not been at all complimentary: it "is small, unmistakably so. It is not imposing looking; on the contrary, I might also say that it is dingy and forlorn, with an air like that of a faded beauty, just *un petit peu passe*".[17] A decade later, it had significantly improved.

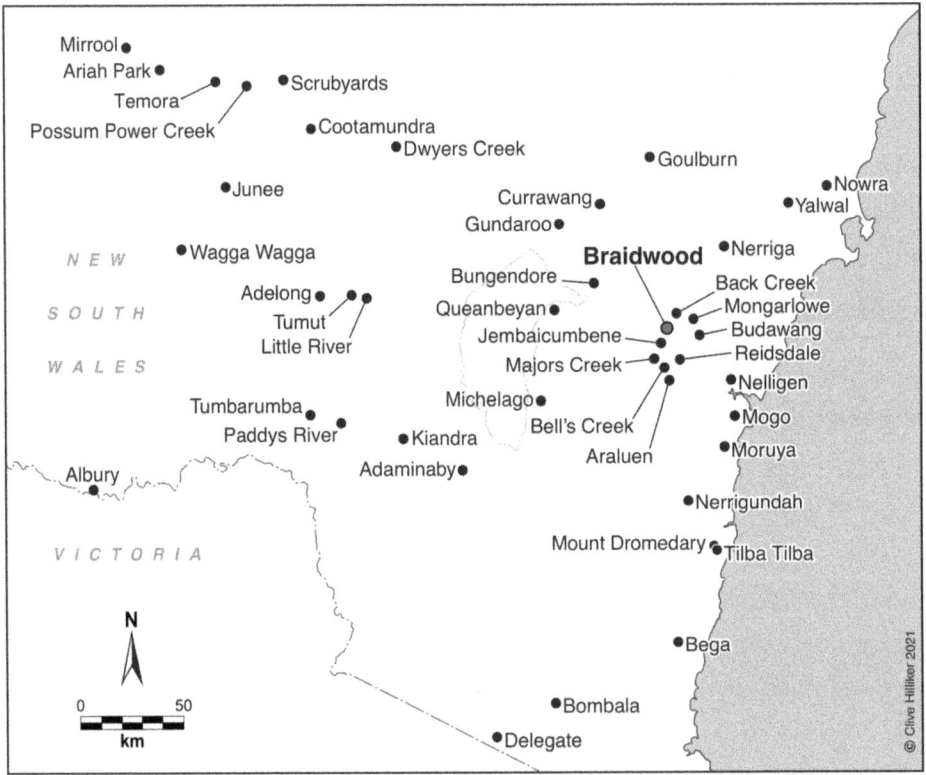

Figure 9.1. Places visited by de Boos during his appointment at Braidwood. Source: based on the Annual Reports of the Department of Mines, 1875-1879, and various newspaper articles.

Not only was his territory large, it was also extremely varied: the coast and near coastal areas of southern New South Wales; the southern coastal ranges and their western approaches; the High Country; and the south-

---

15 - *Sydney Mail*, November 9, 1878, page 750; *Australian Town & Country Journal*, November 16, 1878, page 934.
16 - *Queanbeyan Age*, October 12, 1878, page 1.
17 - *Sydney Morning Herald*, July 24, 1865, page 2.

west slopes. In the upland areas and along the coast there were numerous rivers, their valleys being the locations of much of the gold mining. They often created hazards for the traveler.

> NARROW ESCAPE. Mr. Warden De Boos and a friend in coming from Bungendore to Braidwood on Sunday, the 19th instant, had a very narrow escape from a serious accident. The Braidwood Dispatch says that, in crossing the Mulloon Creek at the Long Swamp by the usual crossing-place, the heavy boulders in the creek checked the way of the buggy; and the horse, in endeavouring to pull out, succeeded in pulling himself out of the harness, some of the gear giving way. The result was that Mr. De Boos and his friend were left in the middle of the creek, whilst the horse, freed of his harness, safely reached the other side, leaving the two disconsolate passengers in the middle of the stream to make the best of their position. No persons were about except two young boys and a woman, who were only too anxious to render assistance that it was not in their power to give, and as the stream came down so strongly that the buggy several times shifted, Mr. De Boos and his friend thought it time to shift also. A lurch more strong than usual induced them to take to the cool element, and they arrived safely ashore. The buggy remained in the creek some four hours, during which time it shifted considerably, and everything in it was ultimately swept clean out by the force of the stream.[18]

The loss of official papers relating to a mining lease at Michelago caused some people a lot of problems.[19] A few months earlier, he had come off even worse, when he was thrown from his horse at Majors Creek. Landing on his face resulted in "a slight concussion of the brain, ... his nose broken, and his two eyes were bruised and discoloured".[20]

By the time he was appointed to Braidwood, the major period of mining was over,[21] certainly on the main fields of Araluen Creek, Major's Creek, Bell's Creek, and along the Deua River. The same was true for Kiandra.[22] The various rushes from 1851 to 1874 were followed by years of slow decline. At its peak, there were over 3,000 people in the Araluen Valley, spread through several small settlements. People from numerous countries lived together with few tensions. Some 30 per cent of the miners were Chinese.

---

18 - *Sydney Morning Herald*, November 24, 1876, page 3.

19 - *Australian Town & Country Journal*, August 25, 1877, page 299.

20 - *Sydney Morning Herald*, June 13, 1876, page 3; *Sydney Mail*, June 24, 1876, page 811.

21 - For a comprehensive history of the goldfields of the Braidwood district and others in south-east New South Wales, see McGowan 2010; 1996b; 2000. Ellis 1989. *Nerriga Gold Deposits*. Primefact 571, NSW Department of Primary Industries, Sydney, 2007. *Annual Report of the Department of Mines, New South Wales, for the year 1875*. Government Printer, Sydney, pages 43-49; *Annual Report of the Department of Mines, New South Wales, for the year 1876*. Government Printer, Sydney, pages 63-65; *Annual Report of the Department of Mines, New South Wales, for the year 1877*. Government Printer, Sydney, pages 89-97; *Annual Report of the Department of Mines, New South Wales, for the year 1878*. Government Printer, Sydney, pages 79-83; *Annual Report of the Department of Mines, New South Wales, for the year 1879*. Government Printer, Sydney, pages 107-115.

22 - Moye 1959/2005; Crabb 2020.

They made a major contribution to the Braidwood area over many years, not just as miners but also as businessmen and market gardeners; a key role in the Chinese community was played by Quong Tart.[23] For some years, the gold fields of the Braidwood area, and especially the Araluen Valley, were the largest in New South Wales: "Escort returns from the banks in Braidwood to the Royal Mint, Sydney between 1858-1874 amounted to 19,596 kilograms (630,088 oz)".[24] Nearly all of the gold was obtained by alluvial mining.

The availability of water for alluvial mining and washing ore was a major issue in south-eastern New South Wales and at every other location where de Boos worked.[25] As he commented in one of his reports from Braidwood, "With no water to enable them to work, miners and their families were moving elsewhere, to other mining areas and other occupations, such as railway construction".

> The small and precarious rainfall, the long continuance of heat and drought, and the prevalence of strong parching winds have been all but fatal to mining industry, in so far as the alluvial workings are concerned. Streams of water that should have continued running until after Christmas were almost dried up in the early spring by the hurricane of westerly wind that came down upon us and continued its devastation for nearly a week, uprooting and tearing limbs off trees, unroofing houses, and worse than all for the miner, parching the earth and licking up even the small amount of water that the few preceding days of rain had given us.[26]

Then the rain would come, and work would be stopped by floods and too much water, as occurred at Araluen in February 1860 and September 1879, causing considerable damage. At a public meeting following the flood, de Boos made it very clear that the "washed-out miners … only wanted relief in the form of work". With "Some one hundred and sixty men out of work, the Government may fairly be called upon to expend money on the roads of the district, and so give employment to the miners, who will otherwise be destitute".[27] But with the floods gone, "the season has been the finest the miners have had for their occupation for many years past".[28] Access

---

23 - Travers 1981; McGowan 2007; McGowan 2008; McGowan 2010.

24 - *Braidwood Gold*. Primefact 559, NSW Department of Primary Industries, Sydney, 2007.

25 - Lawrence, Davies, and Turnbull 2016; 2017.

26 - *Annual Report of the Department of Mines, New South Wales, for the year 1877*. Government Printer, Sydney, pages 89-90.

27 - *Sydney Morning Herald*, September 20, 1879, page 5; September 24, 1879, page 6.

28 - *Annual Report of the Department of Mines, New South Wales, for the year 1879*. Government Printer, Sydney, page 107. *Sydney Morning Herald*, September 24, 1879, page 6.

to whatever water was available often created disputes between miners, which the Warden had to endeavour to solve. For example, commenting on Kiandra in his 1879 report, de Boos wrote:

> *Everything here depends upon the supply of water, so that those who have the first water-rights out of creeks or springs virtually hold the gold-field in their hands. All the disputes that I have heard here are about or in connection with water, and some of the parties have shown themselves to be exceedingly pertinacious in wrong-doing. This is shown from the circumstance that my last four visits to this locality have been necessitated by the disputes of the self-same individuals.*[29]

There were a number of new finds in the area whilst de Boos was Warden, including Warri (between Bungendore and Braidwood); Jerrawa, near Gunning; the lower Clyde River; near Wallaga Lake on the coast; Michelago; Paddys River, near Tumberumba; the Nelson Ranges, near Bega; Nerrigundah; and in "black gold-bearing sand on the beach" at Tilba, near Wallaga Lake.[30] All but one proved to be of little significance. If there was an exception, it was at Dromedary Mountain, near Central Tilba, but even here, in a report to the Under-Secretary for Mines, de Boos expressed his view that it would not "prove a discovery of any excessive value".[31]

In 1878, he held the first Mining Warden's court in Nowra, dealing with issues on the nearby Yalwal goldfield.[32]

His Mining Warden's work was not limited to gold. For example, there was silver in the Dwyer's Creek area near Moruya. For the period 1866-72, the Phoenix Mine at Currawang, near Goulburn, was the largest copper producer in New South Wales. The mine and associated smelting operations had a marked social and environmental impact on the surrounding district. The town's population was well over 400, with two public houses, four

---

29 - *Annual Report of the Department of Mines, New South Wales, for the year 1879*. Government Printer, Sydney, page 113; *Manaro Mercury*, November 26, 1879, page 3.

30 - *Freeman's Journal*, August 28, 1875, page 12; *Albury Banner*, November 20, 1875, page 19; *Goulburn Herald*, November 20, 1875, page 5; *Sydney Morning Herald*, May 30, 1877, page 6; May 29, 1877, page 2; October 23, 1877, page 5; October 23, 1877, page 5; *Australian Town and Country Journal*, June 23, 1877, page 979; August 25, 1877, page 299; *Evening News*, September 6, 1878, page 2; *Sydney Mail*, March 15, 1879, page 432; *Sydney Mail*, November 9, 1878, page 750; *Sydney Morning Herald*, August 28, 1878, page 5; *Sydney Mail*, March 15, 1880, page 930; *Sydney Morning Herald*, June 4, 1880, page 5; *Sydney Daily Telegraph*, July 17, 1880, page 7; Stone 2014.

31 - *Sydney Morning Herald*, May 30, 1877, page 6; *Australian Town and Country Journal*, June 2, 1877, pages 858-859; *Annual Report of the Department of Mines, New South Wales, for the year 1877*. Government Printer, Sydney, pages 92. *Sydney Morning Herald*, May 29, 1877, page 2; May 30, 1877, page 6; August 28, 1878, page 5.

32 - *Telegraph and Shoalhaven Advertiser*, September 11, 1878, page 2.

stores, and a school.³³ de Boos had to deal with a pollution problem at the mine, with leakage from an old shaft getting into Lake George.³⁴

In early 1875, under instructions from the Minister for Mines, de Boos visited the Tarrabandra Marble Company's works at Tumut, where he arranged "for the dispatch of a few slabs of marble to Sydney, for the [Sydney Intercolonial] Exhibition".³⁵ In connection with the Exhibition, the New South Wales Department of Mines published a blue book entitled *Mines and Mineral Statistics of New South Wales*. de Boos was one of the contributors.³⁶

Even after the Royal Commission and the new Mining Act of 1874, de Boos and other wardens still had to deal with almost unending complaints and disputes. There were problems related to the leasing system, to which he was strongly opposed.³⁷ Lease conditions were not adhered to, as occurred in the Braidwood district, creating numerous problems. Disputes over land long used by miners being taken over by 'selectors' in such places as Major's Creek, Long Flat, and Jembaiecumbene were settled largely due to the intervention of de Boos (Figure 9.2).³⁸

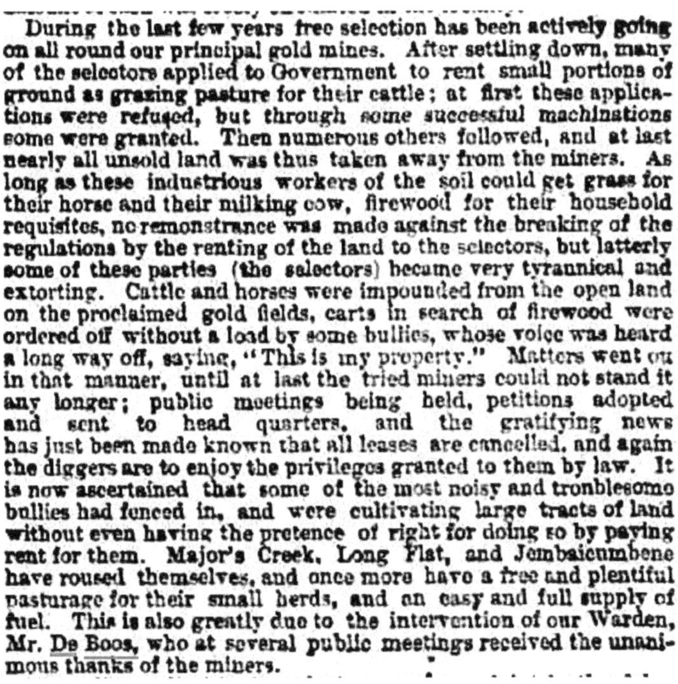

Figure 9.2. Issues over the illegal occupation and use of land. Source: Sydney Morning Herald, October 8, 1878, page 6.

During the last few years free selection has been actively going on all round our principal gold mines. After settling down, many of the selectors applied to Government to rent small portions of ground as grazing pasture for their cattle; at first these applications were refused, but through some successful machinations some were granted. Then numerous others followed, and at last nearly all unsold land was thus taken away from the miners. As long as these industrious workers of the soil could get grass for their horse and their milking cow, firewood for their household requisites, no remonstrance was made against the breaking of the regulations by the renting of the land to the selectors, but latterly some of these parties (the selectors) became very tyrannical and extorting. Cattle and horses were impounded from the open land on the proclaimed gold fields, carts in search of firewood were ordered off without a load by some bullies, whose voice was heard a long way off, saying, "This is my property." Matters went on in that manner, until at last the tried miners could not stand it any longer; public meetings being held, petitions adopted and sent to head quarters, and the gratifying news has just been made known that all leases are cancelled, and again the diggers are to enjoy the privileges granted to them by law. It is now ascertained that some of the most noisy and troublesome bullies had fenced in, and were cultivating large tracts of land without even having the pretence of right for doing so by paying rent for them. Major's Creek, Long Flat, and Jembaicumbene have roused themselves, and once more have a free and plentiful pasturage for their small herds, and an easy and full supply of fuel. This is also greatly due to the intervention of our Warden, Mr. De Boos, who at several public meetings received the unanimous thanks of the miners.

---

33 - McGowan 1996a, 75-92, "Currawang"; this is a very detailed account of the operations. The mines were briefly reopened in 1897 and 1907. *Mulwaree Shire Community Heritage Study*, 2002-2004. Heritage Archaeology, 2004, page 156.

34 - *Sydney Morning Herald*, July 10, 1880, page 3.

35 - 'The Sydney Intercolonial Exhibition'. *Sydney Morning Herald*, March 16, 1875, page 5; April 6, 1875, page 5.

36 - *Albury Banner*, November 13, 1875, page 20.

37 - *Cootamundra Herald*, July 2, 1881, page 9.

38 - *Sydney Morning Herald*, October 8, 1878, page 6; Stone 2014

As a Police Magistrate and Justice of the Peace, he dealt with numerous cases in the local courts, such as whether it was legal to move cattle along a particular stretch of road; people occupying more Government land than they had the right to do; various livestock issues; the improper behaviour of a government official; and a person "suffering from religious mania".[39] There were often inadequate numbers of judicial officers and facilities, not least in the Araluen Valley, in spite of it being such a productive goldfield; de Boos had to work at least one day a week there because of the absence of court officers.[40] There were occasionally 'ceremonial duties' to perform, such as his presence at the opening of the Moruya Bridge, where "he brought the day's festivities to a close".[41]

de Boos was an active member of the communities in which he lived and worked. In Braidwood, he was a senior member of the Masonic Lodge and, along with at least one of his sons, Frank, was involved with cricket.[42]

There is no doubt that there were times when his work was affected by his personal life. With the death of his wife Sarah in December 1872, de Boos was left with a large family to care for, and that would have become no easy task when he had to leave Sydney and move to Braidwood. Whilst it is likely that his two eldest daughters and perhaps William (in view of his legal studies) remained in Sydney, some or all of his other children lived with him at some appointments; at others, they were visitors.

With Mary Ann in Sydney, he was thus left with three sons, Charles, Francis, and William (all under 30 years), and two young daughters (in 1880, Lucille was 16 and Estelle 14). Charles and Francis were with him in Braidwood, as no doubt were his two youngest girls.[43]

The Temora District

As if his area of work was not large enough, in late 1879 de Boos was appointed "a Warden of the Lachlan Mining District", in addition to his

---

39 - For example, *Sydney Morning Herald*, June 13, 1876, page 3; September 25, 1877, page 5; *Maitland Mercury*, June 12, 1886, page 12S; *Evening News*, August 5, 1879, page 4; *Manaro Mercury*, January 1, 1876, page 4.
40 - *Sydney Mail*, July 22, 1876, page 110; July 29, 1876, page 142; *Sydney Morning Herald*, July 18, 1876, page 3.
41 - *Australian Town & Country Journal*, February 5, 1876, page 220.
42 - *Sydney Mail*, December 25, 1875, page 822; March 18, 1876, page 374.
43 - From the *Braidwood Dispatch*, *Sydney Morning Herald*, November 16, 1876, page 2; *Queanbeyan Age*, October 19, 1878, page 2; *Sydney Morning Herald*, March 14, 1876, page 5.

existing appointments.[44] It's unlikely that any other person had appointments to three mining districts at the same time. This coincided with his being ordered to Merool Creek, west of Ariah Park and Temora, on news of a discovery of alluvial gold.[45] He reported that the rush was a dead failure, though from the appearance of the country, he thought that deep leads might be found in the lowlands.[46] For the *Wagga Wagga Express*, "the rush [was] emphatically a 'duffer'".[47]

But things soon changed, with de Boos very much involved in the initial gold rushes in the Temora district.[48] This required a number of long journeys from Braidwood in 1879-80, as on the opening up of the Temora Gold Field he was the first mining warden and police magistrate sent to the area.[49] Various place names were associated with the gold rushes, for example, Temora (early on known as Watsonford) and Scrubyards[50] (proclaimed as the Gundibindyal Goldfield, but also known as the Baker Diggings, Woodstown, and then Woodville),[51] where a town was "laid out by Mr. Margules, the mining registrar".[52] A Warden's Court was established at Woodstown, and Henry Margules was given the temporary appointment as Warden's clerk.[53] A large part of de Boos' 1879 report was devoted to these areas which were well beyond Braidwood.[54] As a magistrate and Justice of the Peace, his work also took him to the Cootamundra Police and Small Debts Courts.[55]

In February 1880, there was a major gold find at Temora. In a telegram sent from Braidwood to the Under-Secretary for Mines, de Boos wrote: "A new

---

44 - *NSW Government Gazette*, 459, December 24, 1879, page 5724; *Sydney Morning Herald*, December 25, 1879, page 3.

45 - *Sydney Morning Herald*, October 30, 1879, page 5.

46 - *Sydney Morning Herald*, October 30, 1879, page 5; November 12, 1879, page 6; November 1, 1879, page 3; *Grenfell Record*, November 1, 1879, page 2; *Australian Town & Country Journal*, November 15, 1879, page 925; *Annual Report of the Department of Mines, New South Wales, for the year 1879*. Government Printer, Sydney, pages 108-110. Merool was 100 miles northwest of Wagga Wagga.

47 - *Wagga Wagga Express*, November 8, 1879, page 4.

48 - Fritsch et al. 1992; Webster 1950; *Sydney Morning Herald*, July 26, 1880, page 3; Swan 1971.

49 - *Australian Town & Country Journal*, December 6, 1879, page 1094; *Sydney Mail*, January 10, 1880, page 84; *Sydney Morning Herald*, August 9, 1880, page 5; *Maitland Mercury*, August 12, 1880, page 7.

50 - 'The Scrub Yards Rush', a long report by 'Our Special Correspondent'. *Sydney Morning Herald*, November 17, 1879, page 7; *Sydney Mail*, November 22, 1879, pages 900-901.

51 - *Australian Town & Country Journal*, November 29, 1879, page 1046; December 6, 1879, page 1094; February 21, 1880, page 359; *Cootamundra Herald*, December 27, 1879, page 4; *Evening News*, January 3, 1880, page 3.

52 - *Sydney Morning Herald*, November 17, 1879, page 7; November 18, 1879, page 5.

53 - *Sydney Mail*, January 3, 1880, page 11; *Evening News*, January 3, 1880, page 3.

54 - *Annual Report of the Department of Mines, New South Wales, for the year 1879*. Government Printer, Sydney, pages 107-115.

55 - *Cootamundra Herald*, February 14, 1880, page 3; April 17, 1880, page 3.

field is reported to me as discovered at Temora, 12 miles from Woodstown. The sinking is 60 feet, through good ground. The prospects are 4 oz. to the dish. I leave for there on Monday".[56] Following this and other finds, the gold field and town developed rapidly, with large numbers of miners arriving from other locations. However, the absence of water meant that, initially, most of the would-be miners had to rely on what resources they had brought with them.[57]

Though divided into three parts, Temora was essentially one long town, with a wide main street (Figures 9.3 and 9.4). The initial conditions in Temora were rudimentary to say the least. The buildings, both public and private, were typical of early gold rush towns, as some early sketches published in *The Sydney Mail* clearly show (Figures 9.5 and 9.6). Much the same could be said of the actual mining operations (Figure 9.7).

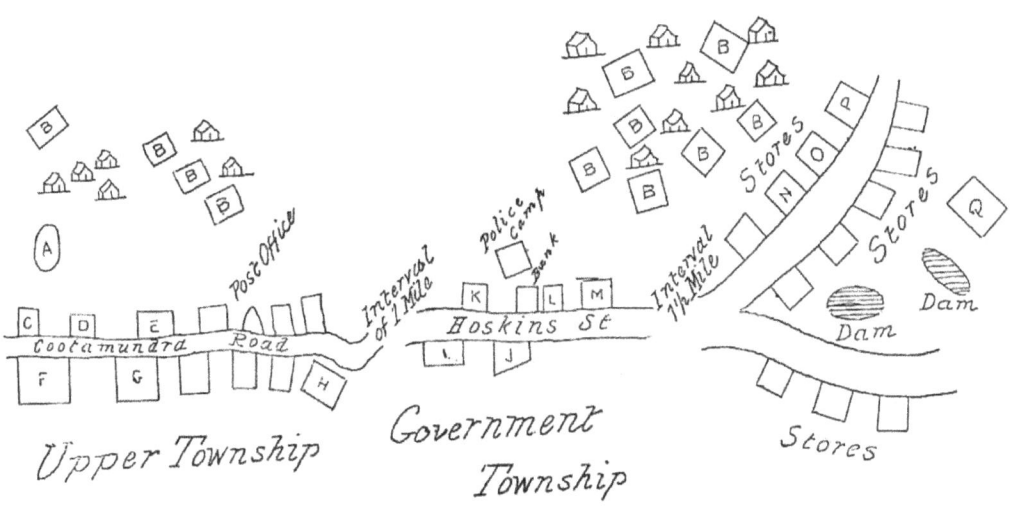

Figure 9.3. Sketch map of Temora township, 1880. Source: The Sydney Mail, July 31, 1880, page 216. See also Christie's Map of Temora Gold Field, County of Bland, Land District of Cootamundry. Compiled and drawn by Wm. Bede Christie, August 10, 1880. Lithographers, Turner and Henderson, Sydney.

A Water dam, B Claims, C Temora Hotel, D Quail's, E Stewart's Hotel, F Hancox's Store, G Butcher's shop, H Billiard Room, I Mr. Purchase chemist, J Gardiner's Store, K Dacey's Store, L Coffee Shop, M Angor's Hotel, N Forrest's Stores ,O Billiard Room, P Butcher's Shop, Q Frenchman's Claim.

---

56 - *Sydney Daily Telegraph*, February 9, 1880, page 3; *Australian Town & Country Journal*, February 14, 1880, page 310; *Cootamundra Herald*, February 14, 1880, page 3.

57 - 'The Temora Rush', *Sydney Mail*, July 24, 1880, page 184; *Sydney Morning Herald*, July 26, 1880, page 3; *Australian Town and Country Journal*, July 3, 1880, page 22.

Figure 9.4. 'Temora in 1880, after the Gold Rush. The main street'. Source: The Sydney Mail, September 16, 1893, page 595.

During the first few months of the Temora goldfield, the location of the nearest Warden's Court was at Woodville ("a place which now seemed to be deserted"[58]), which caused increasing inconvenience to both government officials and miners. After some considerable pressure, including from de Boos, the move to Temora took place at the end of July 1880.[59] By then, Temora's population was approaching 8,000, with increasing numbers of gold finds.[60]

Figure 9.5. The Court House. 'Our special artist in Temora', The Sydney Mail, July 31, 1880, page 201.

Figure 9.6. A miner's family residence. 'Our special artist in Temora', The Sydney Mail, July 31, 1880, page 201.

---

58 - *Cootamundra Herald*, July 31, 1880, page 3.

59 - *Burrangong Argus*, July 24, 1880, page 2; *Cootamundra Herald*, July 31, 1880, page 3.

60 - *Sydney Daily Telegraph*, August 9, 1880, page 3.

Figure 9.7. The 'Golden Gate Claim, 125 feet deep. 'Our special artist in Temora', The Sydney Mail, July 31, 1880, page 201.

A New Appointment

de Boos did not benefit from the move of the Warden's Court, as at the end of July 1880, he was appointed to Copeland in the Upper Hunter Valley. He was held in high regard, and the move was met with "great regret" by the Temora miners.[61] His departure was met with even greater regret from the Braidwood community: "Several public meetings are advertised to petition for his retention here. His decisions have never been appealed against".[62] "The removal of Mr. De Boos from this district (says the *Dispatch*) is looked upon by the diggers as nothing short of a calamity, for one and all had the most implicit confidence in the righteous nature of his decisions".[63]

Back in Braidwood, de Boos was "too ill to proceed to his new appointment".[64] The rigours of his work and travelling since the addition of the Temora district to his responsibilities had taken their toll. On one occasion, after going from Temora to Tumut, he "accomplished the journey from Tumut to Braidwood (250 miles) in twenty-four hours".[65] His health would not have been helped by the nature of his final Warden's Court in Temora, in which his successor participated. As the *Sydney Mail* reported, the new Warden, Mr Warden Sharpe, was a very different kind of government official (Figure 9.8).[66]

---

61 - *Sydney Morning Herald*, July 31, 1880, page 6; 'A Trip to Temora'. *Freeman's Journal*, August 14, 1880, page 17; *Sydney Morning Herald*, July 31, 1880, page 6; *Sydney Morning Herald*, August 9, 1880, page 5; *Sydney Daily Telegraph*, August 28, 1880, page 5.
62 - *Sydney Morning Herald*, August 30, 1880, page 6; *Sydney Daily Telegraph*, August 28, 1880, page 5.
63 - *Wagga Wagga Advertiser*, September 2, 1880, page 2.
64 - *Sydney Morning Herald*, August 23, 1880, page 5.
65 - *Sydney Mail*, May 29, 1880, page 1009.
66 - *Sydney Mail*, August 21, 1880, page 351.

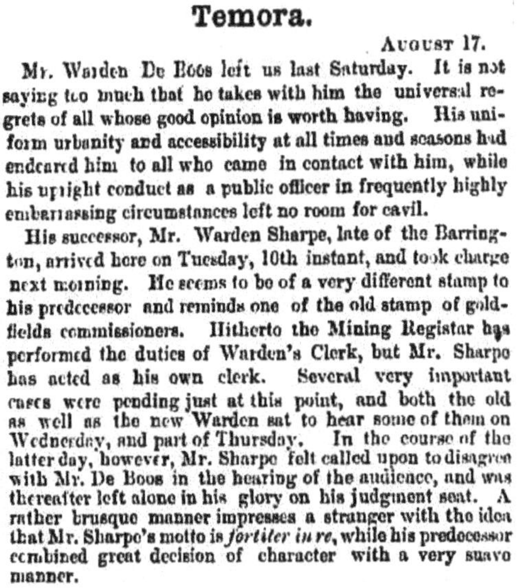

> **Temora.**
>
> AUGUST 17.
>
> Mr. Warden De Boos left us last Saturday. It is not saying too much that he takes with him the universal regrets of all whose good opinion is worth having. His uniform urbanity and accessibility at all times and seasons had endeared him to all who came in contact with him, while his upright conduct as a public officer in frequently highly embarrassing circumstances left no room for cavil.
>
> His successor, Mr. Warden Sharpe, late of the Barrington, arrived here on Tuesday, 10th instant, and took charge next morning. He seems to be of a very different stamp to his predecessor and reminds one of the old stamp of goldfields commissioners. Hitherto the Mining Registrar has performed the duties of Warden's Clerk, but Mr. Sharpe has acted as his own clerk. Several very important cases were pending just at this point, and both the old as well as the new Warden sat to hear some of them on Wednesday, and part of Thursday. In the course of the latter day, however, Mr. Sharpe felt called upon to disagree with Mr. De Boos in the hearing of the audience, and was thereafter left alone in his glory on his judgment seat. A rather brusque manner impresses a stranger with the idea that Mr. Sharpe's motto is *fortiter in re*, while his predecessor combined great decision of character with a very suave manner.

Figure 9.8. Sydney Mail, August 21, 1880, page 351.

Copeland

Located near Gloucester in the Upper Hunter Valley, Copeland was originally known as Back Creek or the Barrington Diggings. The narrow timbered valley had a population of up to 1,100. A brief period of alluvial operations was followed by quartz reef mining.[67] It was a busy time in Copeland following the first discovery of gold in 1876,[68] but mining had just about peaked by 1879.[69] Nonetheless, in 1880, the Centennial claim yielded 155 ounces of gold from 51 tons of stone and the Mountain Maid Company made a profit of £8,887.[70]

Moving to Copeland in August 1880, de Boos held several other positions: Justice of the Peace, Police Magistrate, "Warden of the Hunter and Macleay Mining District", and Coroner "at Copeland, Barrington River, and for the Colony generally".[71] Certainly when compared with his previous appointments, Copeland was a much smaller community, and his work covered a much smaller area. He was actively involved in the community.[72]

---

67 - *Copeland gold deposits.* Primefact 566, NSW Department of Primary Industries, Sydney, 2007.

68 - *Annual Report of the Department of Mines, New South Wales, for the year 1880.* Government Printer, Sydney, pages 171-174.

69 - A series of articles on the history of Copeland by Robin Budge. *Gloucester Advocate*, July 25, 2001, pages 2-3; August 15, 2001, page 4; September 12, 2001, page 10; September 26, 2001, page 5. See also Mitchell 1989; Stone 2014.

70 - *Newcastle Morning Herald*, February 18, 1881, page 2.

71 - *NSW Government Gazette*, 328, August 13, 1880, page 4152; *NSW Government Gazette*, 336, August 20, 1880, page 4259; *NSW Government Gazette*, 361, September 10, 1880, page 4668.

72 - *Maitland Mercury*, December 9, 1880, page 7; *Sydney Mail*, December 25, 1880, page 1217;

Close to the end of the year, his second daughter died on December 27, 1880, at her sister's residence in Woollahra. Sarah Susannah was 29.[73] There is little doubt that she would have played a key role in caring for younger siblings, especially after the death of her mother.

Forbes

On November 28, 1880, Frederick Dalton, the Warden and Police Magistrate at Forbes, in the Lachlan Valley, disappeared without trace.[74] Already a Warden of the Lachlan District, de Boos was sent to Forbes and spent some weeks "speedily and satisfactorily" completing Dalton's unfinished work, prior to the appointment of a new Warden.[75]

Copeland

No sooner had de Boos returned to Copeland, than he was on the move again, back to Temora. It was another move that was regretted by the locals. On his departure, a complimentary banquet was given for him, with "all classes of the community joining in expressing their appreciation of Mr. De Boos' many sterling qualities".[76]

Temora

de Boos arrived in Temora on February 22, 1881, to take up his appointment as Warden, Police Magistrate, and Clark of Petty Sessions.[77] By the time of his return, his predecessor, "Mr. Warden Sharpe [had] contrived to make himself unpopular".[78] In contrast, de Boos "was warmly received with cheers by a large number of miners and residents".[79] "Mr. De Boos was held in high esteem by the miners when previously acting as warden. Mild in manner and courteous to everyone, there was utter absence of anything

---

73 - *Sydney Morning Herald*, December 28, 1880, page 1
74 - Dalton, Antonia, Crabb and Craig 2016; Crabb, Dalton, Craig and Antonia 2019.
75 - *Australian Town & Country Journal*, February 12, 1881, page 326; *Evening News*, February 12, 1881, page 3.
76 - *Newcastle Morning Herald*, February 18, 1881, page 2; *Evening News*, February 16, 1881, page 12.
77 - *NSW Government Gazette*, 57, February 11, 1881, page 869; 159, April 14, 1881, page 2193; *Evening News*, January 20, 1881, page 2.
78 - *Burrangong Argus*, February 26, 1881, page 2.
79 - *Goulburn Evening Post*, February 24, 1881, page 4; *Australian Town and Country Journal*, March 5, 1881, page 454.

harsh in his decisions, and a patience in the investigation of cases which could not fail to be appreciated".[80] At his first Warden's Court, he "was congratulated by the lawyers present".[81]

Not long after his return to Temora, there were suggestions that he might be moved again, causing the *Maitland Mercury* to make some caustic comments about the Department of Mines:

> *EFFICIENCY NOT ADVANTAGEOUS. It would seem that Mr. de Boos, the newly appointed P.M. of Temora, is not likely to get mouldy by being kept in one place. He has been three times removed within a few months, and we learn from the Temora Herald that it is in contemplation by the Mines Department to send him to Mount Browne [near Milparinka]; and on this the Herald remarks:-'It is with much regret we learn that we are likely to lose our newly appointed warden, Mr. de Boos, who it is stated in official circles, will, if the Mount Poole diggings prove a payable gold-field, be appointed to that recently discovered Golconda. It is no doubt a crime to be an able officer – at all events we should judge so by the eccentric manoeuvres of the Mines Department who look upon Mr. de Boos as their best man, for they are continually punishing his ability by shifting him to all the cardinal points of the compass, keeping him as a pioneer for the kidgloved wardens and police magistrates who follow in his wake'.*[82]

Temora was a rather different town to the one he had left some six months earlier, as a comparison of Figures 9.4 and 9.9 indicates (see also Figure 9.10).[83] At the height of the rush, there were some 20,000 people in the district, with finds at a number of places being widely reported.[84] It may have been a return to familiar territory for de Boos, but the newly-developing goldfields placed heavy demands on him, his responsibilities extending to Sebastopol, Barmedman and Morangarell (Figure 9.11).[85] There was particular dissatisfaction in Barmedman over the fact that business had to be done in Temora before its own Warden's Court was

---

80 - *Cootamundra Herald*, February 26, 1881, page 6; January 29, 1881, page 3; *Sydney Morning Herald*, January 22, 1881, page 5; *Goulburn Penny Post*, January 27, 1881, page 2; *Goulburn Evening Penny Post*, February 24, 1881, page 4.

81 - *Sydney Morning Herald*, February 25, 1881, page 6

82 - *Maitland Mercury*, March 5, 1881, page 7; *Sydney Morning Herald*, March 1, 1881, page 5; *Goulburn Herald*, March 9, 1881, page 2.

83 - Swan 1971.

84 - *Annual Report of the Department of Mines, New South Wales, for the year 1881*. Government Printer, Sydney, pages 52-54; *Annual Report of the Department of Mines, New South Wales, for the year 1882*. Government Printer, Sydney, pages 55-57; *Sydney Mail*, October 29, 1881, page 748: 'Geological Report of the Temora Goldfield' by C.S. Wilkinson, Geological Surveyor in charge of the Mining Department; *Sydney Morning Herald*, July 26, 1880, page 3; August 9, 1880, page 5; *Australian Town & Country Journal*, July 3, 1880; *Cootamundra Herald*, July 10, 1880, page 6; *Sydney Mail*, August 7, 1880, page 262.

85 - *Temora Star*, October 26, 1881, page 2; June 7, 1882, page 2; June 17, 1882, page 2; *Sydney Morning Herald*, September 24, 1881, page 10; *Evening News*, November 16, 1881, page 7; McLaren 1974.

Figure 9.9. Main street in Temora, 1881. Source: Fritsch et al. 1992, page 35. Note 'De Boos Bros Auctioneers' store next to McCarthy's Commercial Hotel (see Chapter 11).

Figure 9.10. De Boos Street, looking north, the Roman Catholic Church on the right, c. 1880. Sydney Mail, September 16, 1893, page 599.

Figure 9.11. Places visited by de Boos during his appointment at Temora, based on the Annual Reports of the Department of Mines and various newspaper articles.

established.⁸⁶ Also, the absence of a Commissioner of Affidavits created difficulties, until William de Boos (a solicitor and son of Charles) was given the task by the Chief Justice.⁸⁷ Charles de Boos was the only judicial officer in Temora, resulting in comments that "The Government ought at once to appoint a coroner resident here, and some more Js.P., as there is no magistrate nearer than 15 miles away, except Mr. de Boos".⁸⁸ There were additional problems due to the nearest District Court and Court of Appeal being in Cootamundra. It took eight hours on a Cobb & Co. coach to travel between the two towns, yet another indication of the amount of time de Boos spent travelling.⁸⁹ William de Boos was admitted as an attorney by the Supreme Court in Sydney in late 1881.⁹⁰ He then joined his father in Temora, where he became one of very few solicitors who were resident in the town.⁹¹

An on-going concern and the topic of many discussions in the Temora area, official and unofficial, were the limited water supplies, for mining, livestock and domestic use. Further, its quality often left much to be desired. A report from Barmedman noted "The drinking water has a muddy, white appearance by no means inviting, but it is nevertheless, very precious just now".⁹² In the previous year, a report by de Boos and a Works Department engineer recommended the purchase and enlargement of several dams and reservoirs in the district to improve water availability along with further investigation of underground water sources.⁹³

By the time de Boos wrote his 1882 report, Temora was in decline; "the period of decadence has set in sooner than usual, owing, first to the arid nature of the country, and next to the limited area within which work has been prescribed".⁹⁴ Compounding the situation, the main quartz lead had suddenly come to an end. And "With regard to the reefs at Temora proper,

---

86 - *Temora Herald*, June 6, 1882, page 2; *Temora Star*, June 21, 1882, page 2. *Temora Star*, October 14, 1882, page 2.
87 - *Temora Star*, April 26, 1882, page 2; *Temora Herald*, May 12, 1882, page 2.
88 - *Sydney Morning Herald*, April 1, 1882, page 6
89 - *Temora Star*, June 24, 1882, page 3; Webster 1960, 58-59. At least some of Cobb's coaches carried 65 passengers and were drawn by seven horses. *Cootamundra Herald*, May 21, 1881, page 4.
90 - *Sydney Morning Herald*, September 29, 1881, page 4.
91 - The first report of William de Boos appearing in the Warden's Court was in the *Temora Star*, October 15, 1881. page 2.
92 - *Sydney Mail*, April 1, 1882, page 496.
93 - *Sydney Mail*, August 20, 1881, page 338.
94 - *Annual Report of the Department of Mines, New South Wales, for the year 1882*. Government Printer, Sydney, pages 55-57.

I have no great expectation of their turning out anything wonderful".[95] At nearby Barmedman, however, where de Boos had been involved in the establishment of the town and selecting sites for "the Court House, Police barracks and Lock-up",[96] the reefs proved much more rewarding.

There were times when de Boos had to contend with very litigious miners.[97] He complained about the numerous disputes over claims, noting in his 1881 report that "the Warden's Court was for a time inundated with business".[98] Barmedman was no better with its "incessant applications".[99] As the *Cootamundra Herald* reported, he was not helped by the nature of the Mining Act, which "resembled a maze to bewilder far more than a finger-post to guide. Its pages not only puzzle the miners, but wardens and crafty lawyers have often hazy notions of the meaning conveyed".[100] There were 'pegging disputes' relating to the validity or otherwise of original surveys and pegging. 'Jumping disputes' concerned situations "where it was not disputed that the title had been validly pegged and applied for in the first place, but it was contended that the holding had subsequently lost validity", due to abandonment or failure to comply with lease conditions. The competitor would then "overpeg the existing title and allege that, although originally valid, it had ceased to be valid at the time of overpegging".[101] The *Temora Star* observed that "Jumping as a fine art has on no previous period in the history of gold-mining been brought to such a perfection as on Temora".[102] There was also 'dummying', "the practice of acquiring land while concealing the purchase by acting through a 'dummy' ['one put forward to act for others while ostensibly acting for himself'], in order to evade laws limiting the amount of property which could be held by an individual".[103] Dummying, "This evil, which has been the curse of Temora ever since the goldfield was opened", was an on-going problem.[104] The efforts by de Boos to stamp it out were fully supported by

---

95 - Ibid.
96 - *Temora Herald*, October 17, 1882, page 2; McLaren 1974.
97 - Armstrong 1901.
98 - *Annual Report of the Department of Mines, New South Wales, for the year 1881*. Government Printer, Sydney, page 54.
99 - *Sydney Mail*, January 5, 1884, page 21.
100 - *Cootamundra Herald*, June 11, 1881, page 3.
101 - Hamilton 2015, 125. See also *Temora Star*, July 29, 1882, page 2.
102 - *Temora Star*, July 29, 1882, page 2.
103 - Delbridge et al. 1991, 543.
104 - *Temora Herald*, August 8, 1882, page 2; *Cootamundra Herald*, August 5, 1882, page 4.

the *Cootamundra Herald* in 1881,[105] and the following year, the *Temora Herald* described it as a "rampant evil".[106] In the view of one miner, put in a letter to the *Herald*, Temora had "the worst species of land dummies who ever pestered legitimate and bona fide enterprise and labour". Within their leases, "work is only carried on in a most perfunctory manner, just sufficient to enable the hungry land-mongers to lock up their respective areas from men who would work the ground and develop the resources of the district, but who, owing to the avaricious greed, the inertia, and the fervent prayer of these dummy miners (whose sole aim and hope is that speculators may be induced to buy them out), are compelled either to quit the field or to stroll about in reluctant idleness".[107] de Boos was strongly opposed to the leasing system:

> *With reference to his dealing with men by virtue of their miners' rights, he wished to remark that ever since he had gone to Temora he had persistently set his face against leases. The consequence was there had not been a single lease issued upon the goldfield, and there should not be, if he could help it, while he continued to be warden there. All the claims were being worked under miners' rights, and this, he contended was the only way in which a gold-field should be worked. If men took up a claim and failed to set to work upon it at the end of three days they rendered themselves liable to be dispossessed of it, and others could jump it. This system put a stop to that monopoly of which there were such loud complaints, and which so retarded the opening up of new gold-fields; and so far as he was concerned, as long as the mining department continued to stick to him, he should ever set his face against leases.*[108]

Some of his rulings were unusual, especially for the times in which they were made. For example, at the end of February 1882, a case came before the Temora Warden's Court involving shares in a mining claim held by a Robert Harris and by his wife, Elizabeth, and the purchase of the claim by W. Rue. It was a complex case, and initially, de Boos gave no decision.[109] At a subsequent hearing, however, he stated that a married woman could hold a miner's right apart from her husband's right. With agreement of both parties, he put three questions to the Supreme Court, which upheld his decision (Figure 9.12). However, it was later overturned in the Mining Appeal Court by Judge David Forbes, on the grounds that the woman was

---

105 - *Cootamundra Herald*, June 11, 1881, page 3; September 17, 1881, page 6.
106 - *Temora Herald*, November 14, 1882, page 2.
107 - *Temora Herald*, September 19, 1882, page 2.
108 - *Cootamundra Herald*, July 2, 1881, page 9; *Burrangong Argus*, August 27, 1881, page 2.
109 - *Temora Star*, March 1, 1882, page 2.

attempting to defraud her husband's creditors.¹¹⁰ This was a technicality, specific to the particular case. Nonetheless, the general issue of a married woman being able to hold a miner's right and claim was upheld. It was a ruling that generated considerable interest.¹¹¹

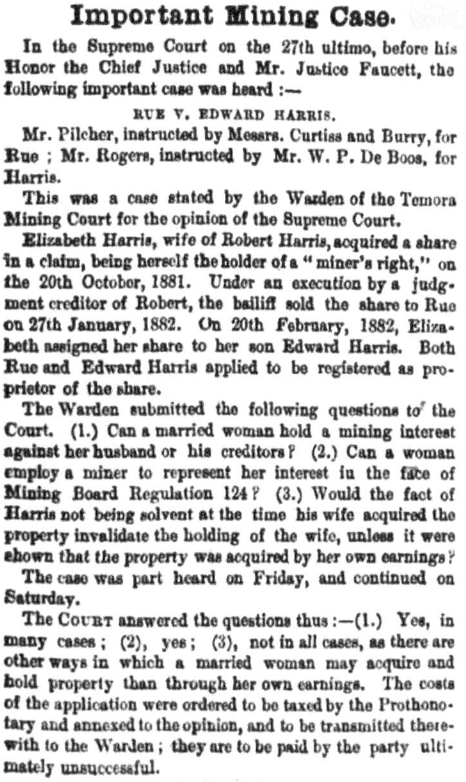

Figure 9.12. Sydney Mail, June 3, 1882, page 897; Sydney Morning Herald, May 29, 1882, page 7. See also Evening News, May 29, 1882, 2; Temora Star, May 31, 1882, page 2; June 3, 1882, page 3; Temora Herald, August 11, 1882, page 2.

Important Mining Case.

In the Supreme Court on the 27th ultimo, before his Honor the Chief Justice and Mr. Justice Faucett, the following important case was heard :—

RUE V. EDWARD HARRIS.

Mr. Pilcher, instructed by Messrs. Curtiss and Burry, for Rue ; Mr. Rogers, instructed by Mr. W. P. De Boos, for Harris.

This was a case stated by the Warden of the Temora Mining Court for the opinion of the Supreme Court.

Elizabeth Harris, wife of Robert Harris, acquired a share in a claim, being herself the holder of a "miner's right," on the 20th October, 1881. Under an execution by a judgment creditor of Robert, the bailiff sold the share to Rue on 27th January, 1882. On 20th February, 1882, Elizabeth assigned her share to her son Edward Harris. Both Rue and Edward Harris applied to be registered as proprietor of the share.

The Warden submitted the following questions to the Court. (1.) Can a married woman hold a mining interest against her husband or his creditors? (2.) Can a woman employ a miner to represent her interest in the face of Mining Board Regulation 124? (3.) Would the fact of Harris not being solvent at the time his wife acquired the property invalidate the holding of the wife, unless it were shown that the property was acquired by her own earnings?

The case was part heard on Friday, and continued on Saturday.

The COURT answered the questions thus :—(1.) Yes, in many cases ; (2), yes ; (3), not in all cases, as there are other ways in which a married woman may acquire and hold property than through her own earnings. The costs of the application were ordered to be taxed by the Prothonotary and annexed to the opinion, and to be transmitted therewith to the Warden ; they are to be paid by the party ultimately unsuccessful.

It wasn't just unusual cases and the failings of the Mining Act that de Boos had to deal with. In September 1881, Margules, the Mining Registrar at Temora, was dismissed because of his illegal transfer of a mining claim that was in the name of Patrick Hannan. In the dismissal letter sent to him, the reasons given were:

1. Making changes in excess of those authorized by the Mining Regulations.

2. Transferring a share without authority from the owner for doing so, as provided by the Regulations.

3. Altering statements relating to holdings under the Mining Act, which at least show great carelessness in their preparation, if such alterations were necessary.

4. The careless and unsatisfactory manner in which you have conducted the duties of your office.¹¹²

---

110 - *Gundagai Times*, October 31, 1882, page 2; *Australian Town and Country Journal*, November 4, 1882, page 876. On Forbes, see *Sydney Morning Herald*, March 8, 1901, page 5.

111 - *Sydney Morning Herald*, May 29, 1882, page 7; *Temora Herald*, June 2, 1882, page 2; *South Australian Register*, May 29, 1982, page 6.

112 - "Mr. H. Margules, late Mining Registrar at Temora (Papers, Minutes, & c.)", *New South Wales Votes and Proceedings of the Legislative Assembly and Papers laid upon the Table during the Session 1881*, Vol. 3. Government Printer, Sydney, page 721.

Opinions of Margules varied considerably. There was certainly support for him: a 'Petition from Citizens and Miners of Temora to The Honorable the Executive Council', signed by 218 people, asked that Margules "be returned as Mining Registrar. … His removal would be regarded by the majority of this field as a great calamity". However, a 'Petition from Residents of Temora to The Honorable the Secretary of Mines', signed by 329 people, stated that Margules was "utterly unfit for the position he holds as an officer of the Government". Over 400 miners signed another petition to the Minister of Mines asking that Margules be dismissed.[113] The matter was raised in the Legislative Assembly.[114]

Yet it was de Boos that Margules was particularly displeased with, as indicated by his letters in the *Temora Star*, disputing some of the Warden's statements.[115] Among other things, the findings of an investigation by de Boos were clearly a major factor in his dismissal. The letters continued after Margules had set himself up as a 'Land and Mining Agent' with an office in Sydney.[116] Some years later, however, the report of a Select Committee of the Legislative Assembly inquiry into the loss by Patrick Hannan of his mining claim due to the illegal action of Margules, upheld Hannan's position and recommended he receive compensation. The Report noted that "Patrick Hannan was deprived of his mining share in the said lease by the illegal action of the Mining Registrar", and the Committee recommended "the case of the said Patrick Hannan to the favourable consideration of the Government".[117]

In Temora, de Boos' community activities were numerous. He was the first President of the committee inaugurated in 1880 to establish a new

---

113 - *New South Wales Votes and Proceedings of the Legislative Assembly*, No. 28, August 19, 1881, page 114. Complaints about Margules and his actions and behaviour were reported earlier in the year: *Cootamundra Herald*, May 7, 1881, page 6; June 4, 1881, page 2.

114 - "Mr. H. Margules, late Mining Registrar at Temora (Papers, Minutes, & c.)", *New South Wales Votes and Proceedings of the Legislative Assembly and Papers laid upon the Table during the Session 1881*, Vol. 3. Government Printer, Sydney, 1881, pages 667-721. The document contained 103 items. "Mr. H. Margules, late Mining Registrar at Temora (Additional papers, & c.)", *New South Wales Votes and Proceedings of the Legislative Assembly and Papers laid upon the Table during the Session 1883-84*, Vol. 4. Government Printer, Sydney, 1884, pages 443-472. The document contained 76 items.

115 - See, for example, *Temora Star*, October 5, 1881, page 3; August 26, 1882, page 2; January 14, 1882, page 2.

116 - *Temora Star*, November 5, 1881, page 1; November 23, 1881, page 2.

117 - "Report from the Select Committee on Patrick Hannan's Mining Claim at Temora, together with the Proceedings of the Committee, Minutes of Evidence, and Appendix". *New South Wales Votes and Proceedings of the Legislative Assembly and Papers laid upon the Table during the Session 1883-84*, Vol. 4. Government Printer, Sydney, 1884, pages 473-491; *Sydney Morning Herald*, July 19, 1884, page 11.

Hospital.[118] He was President of the Temora Jockey Club in 1881 and 1882;[119] President of the Hospital Committee and of the Cricket Club.[120] He was involved in the establishment of the Church of England, and he and his son William were vocalists in concerts for the building fund.[121] Also, he was involved in dramatic presentations by 'The Owl Club', of which he was President.[122] Meanwhile, one of his daughters, most likely Lucille, participated as a vocalist in concerts in aid of the Church of England in Temora and in Cootamundra.[123]

Quite apart from the Margules issue, much of the latter part of his time in Temora was a tumultuous one for de Boos. It merits special attention and is discussed in more detail in Chapter Ten.

Copeland

Given the events of the preceding few months, it was no doubt with feelings of great relief that de Boos returned to Copeland at the beginning of 1883 as Police Magistrate and Clerk of Petty Sessions[124] and "a Warden of the Hunter and Macleay Mining District".[125] He was given other duties: Warden's Clerk and Mining Registrar;[126] Assistant Registrar of Births, Deaths, and Marriages;[127] Licensing Magistrate and Official Member of the Licensing Court (being responsible for the Quarterly Licensing Courts that considered "applications for Publicans, Colonial Wine, Brewers and Spirit Merchants, Booth, Stand, or Packet Licenses, renewals, removals, and transactions of other business");[128] Coroner "at Copeland, and for the Colony generally";[129] and Agent for the Curator of Intestate Estates.[130] He

---

118 - *Temora Star*, October 19, 1881, page 2; January 28, 1882, page 2; February 15, 1882, page 3; February 25, 1882, page 2; *Temora Herald*, April 21, 1882, page 3; *Australian Town and Country Journal*, August 9, 1905, page 29.

119 - *Australian Town & Country Journal*, December 17, 1881, page 1186; *Temora Star*, December 10, 1881, page 2; August 30, 1882, page 2; *Temora Herald*, September 1, 1882, page 2.

120 - *Temora Star*, October 19, 1881, pages 2 and 3.

121 - *Temora Star*, August 2, 1882, page 2; January 20, 1883, page 3.

122 - *Temora Star*, September 7, 1881, page 2; *Cootamundra Herald*, September 14, 1881, page 1; *Temora Star*, August 30, 1882, page 2; *Temora Herald*, September 22, 1882, page 2.

123 - *Temora Star*, December 31, 1881, page 3; April 5, 1882, page 2; *Cootamundra Herald*, March 25, 1882, page 6.

124 - *NSW Government Gazette*, 533, December 29, 1882, page 6859.

125 - *NSW Government Gazette*, 46, February 6, 1883, page 666; *Sydney Daily Telegraph*, February 3, 1883, page 6, from *NSW Government Gazette*, February 2, 1883.

126 - *Goulburn Herald*, March 13, 1883, page 2.

127 - *NSW Government Gazette*, 46, February 6, 1883, page 689.

128 - *NSW Government Gazette*, 369, August 31, 1883, page 4764; 486, August 30, 1886, page 5853.

129 - *NSW Government Gazette*, 198, May 15, 1885, page 3168; *Maitland Mercury*, June 23, 1885, page 3.

130 - *Sydney Morning Herald*, September 25, 1886, page 5.

was sworn in as Police Magistrate for Copeland at the Singleton Quarter Sessions court.[131]

It was not a large area to deal with (Figure 9.13), but that didn't mean it was free of problems, especially from the miners at the Wangat reefs north of Dungog:

> *The miners here seem to be most litigiously disposed, and have been engaged as much in quarrelling and Court work as in reefing. So much has this been the case that I have been called upon to settle more disputes in this locality than in all the rest of the Copeland division put together.*[132]

By 1882, the mainly reef/quartz mining in the Copeland area was past its peak, and though his Warden's reports on new ventures were very detailed, he was not often optimistic.[133] There was gradual decline, with drought and

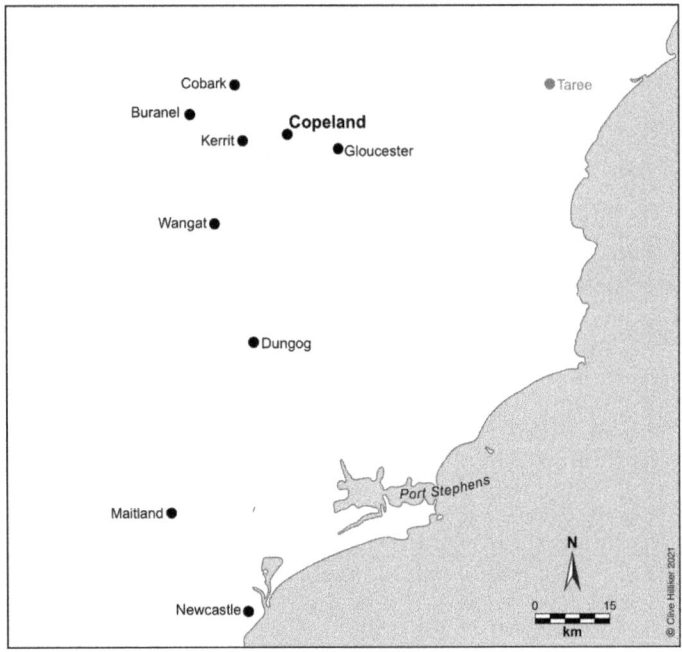

Figure 9.13. Places visited by de Boos during his two appointments at Copeland, based on the Annual Reports of the Department of Mines and various newspaper articles.

---

131 - *Maitland Mercury*, June 23, 1885, page 3.

132 - *Annual Report of the Department of Mines, New South Wales, for the year 1880*. Government Printer, Sydney, page 174.

133 - *Annual Report of the Department of Mines, New South Wales, for the year 1883*. Government Printer, Sydney, pages 97-99; *Annual Report of the Department of Mines, New South Wales, for the year 1884*. Government Printer, Sydney, pages 93-95; *Annual Report of the Department of Mines, New South Wales, for the year 1885*. Government Printer, Sydney, pages 87-89; *Annual Report of the Department of Mines, New South Wales, for the year 1886*. Government Printer, Sydney, page 87; *Sydney Morning Herald*, September 20, 1884, page 15; *Daily Telegraph*, September 20, 1884, page 6.

a lack of capital, the high cost of mining the gold veins, and the collapse of companies; more money could be made in coal mining lower down the Hunter Valley.[134] What remains of the gold mining period has been almost entirely overgrown, though the Mountain Maid Mine, now in the Copeland Tops State Conservation Area, has been partially restored and is open to visitors.

de Boos clearly had time for other activities, as reported in a 'travelogue' article on "Stroud, Gloucester, Copeland".

> *Copeland … seems wedged in at the base of the hills that tower around it on every side. One of the first buildings passed is the Court House, perched on the side of a considerable rise. The appearance of the building is greatly enhanced by the gay appearance of the flowers, which are attended by the police magistrate (Mr. de Boos), who takes considerable pride in his garden. Farther on are several stores and the hotels, the road, as it seems is usually the case in most mining townships, being very narrow and extremely tortuous. Signs of past prosperity exist in the deserted and dilapidated billiard and oyster saloons …*[135]

Only a few weeks later, however, the situation of the Court House changed dramatically.

> *At about 3 o'clock this morning [April 14] a disastrous fire completely demolished the courthouse. A gale was blowing from the N.E. It is believed that a spark from a brick fireplace in a detached kitchen [only recently built by de Boos] was the cause, as the fire started there. Although great efforts were made, nothing could be saved, not even the books and documents, Warden de Boos and his daughters having barely time to escape. Great regret is expressed here, as the courthouse was the principal ornament at Copeland. By the exertions of many willing hands the police barracks were saved. An inquiry is to be held to-day. The fire is believed to have been purely accidental.*[136]

> *An alarming fire took place here about 4 o'clock on Wednesday morning, burning the court house, one of our best buildings, to the ground. The warden, Mr. Charles de Boos, managed with great difficulty to save the cash box, which contained a large sum of money, and was badly burnt. … Mr. de Boos lost a great deal of his own property by the unfortunate occurrence. … An inquiry was held on Friday, but no decided information could be given as to how the fire occurred, and a verdict was given in accordance.*[137]

---

134 - *Annual Report of the Department of Mines, New South Wales, for the year 1886.* Government Printer, Sydney, page 87.
135 - *Australian Town and Country Journal*, March 20, 1886, page 600.
136 - *Sydney Morning Herald*, April 15, 1886, page 12.
137 - *Australian Town & Country Journal*, April 24, 1886, page 847. The event was widely reported, for example, *Bathurst Free Press and Mining Journal*, April 15, 1886, page 2; *Launceston Examiner*, April 15, 1886, page 2; and *Clarence and Richmond Examiner*, April 17, 1886, page 5.

Nothing is known of the personal impact of the fire on de Boos and his two daughters, but it must have been traumatic. And among the property lost, were there any manuscripts that Charles just might have been working on?

As at previous appointments, de Boos was actively involved in the local community. At the first in a series of concerts in aid of a new hospital, "our worthy magistrate, Mr. de Boos" was thanked for his interest.[138] He was listed as a 'Judge' for the Copeland Jockey Club Races in May 1883,[139] and at the Williams River Agricultural and Horticultural Association exhibition held in Dungog, de Boos was awarded second prize for "Buggy stallion gelding in harness".[140] By the time of his second term in Copeland, his two youngest daughters were almost certainly living in Sydney, but they were frequent visitors to Copeland. At a local concert, 'Miss de Boos' was highly complimented as the organist.[141]

In April 1887, significant cuts to government services and the number of public servants were announced, and among those the Minister of Justice "proposed to dispense with on 30th June" were "C. De Boos, P.M. and C.P.S., Copeland" (as well as "H. De Boos, C.P.S., Gulgong").[142] Coupled with the decline of mining, the cuts were felt significantly in Copeland, and they were compounded by the departure of de Boos. But he was not dispensed with.

Milparinka and Cobar

After the small mining district of Copeland, from July 1, 1887, de Boos was appointed Mining Warden for the Albert Mining District and Police Magistrate and Clark of Petty Sessions in Milparinka, a large district located in the outback of far north-west New South Wales.[143] Later, he was appointed an Agent for The Curator of Intestate Estates,[144] Licensing

---

138 - *Maitland Mercury*, December 9, 1880, page 7.
139 - *Maitland Mercury*, April 10, 1883, page 5.
140 - *Maitland Mercury*, April 16, 1887, page 7.
141 - *Maitland Mercury*, November 16, 1886, page 6.
142 - *Burrowa News*, April 15, 1887, page 2; *Sydney Mail*, April 9, 1887, page 770.
143 - The Albert Mining District was proclaimed in February 1881. *NSW Government Gazette*, 72, February 25, 1881, page 1089. *NSW Government Gazette*, 290, May 17, 1887, page 3367; 363, June 28, 1887, page 4208. *NSW Government Gazette*, 267, May 6, 1887, page 3030. *Daily Telegraph*, May 7, 1887, page 3. *Sydney Morning Herald*, April 24, 1887, page 9.
144 - *NSW Government Gazette*, 549, October 5, 1887, page 6611.

Magistrate for Milparinka and Tibooburra,[145] and assistant registrar of births, deaths, and marriages for the district of Wentworth.[146] He was also appointed Police Magistrate at Tibooburra.[147] Much of his work was relatively close to Milparinka, taking in the Tibooburra area, Warratta, Mount Poole, and Mount Browne, but there were also some very long journeys (Figure 9.14).[148]

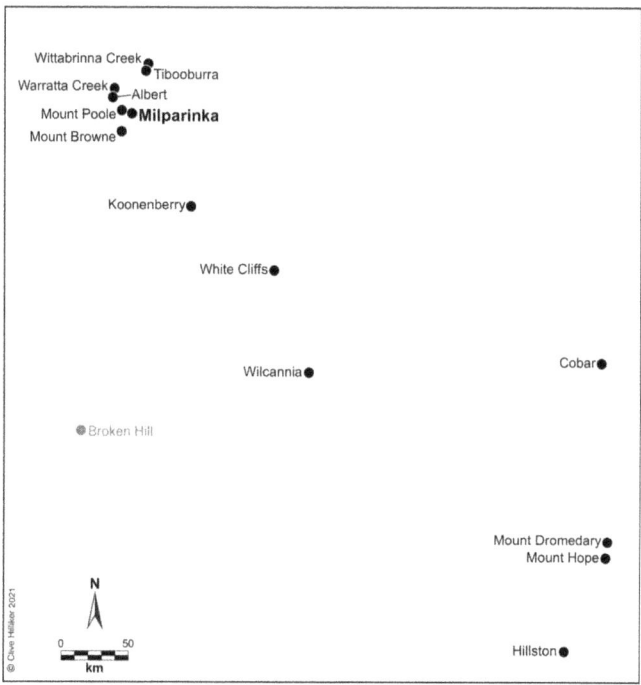

Figure 9.14. Places visited by de Boos during his appointment at Milparinka, based on the Annual Reports of the Department of Mines and various newspaper articles.

The first payable goldfield was found in February 1881 at Mt Browne. Along with others in the area, they were amongst the last alluvial diggings found in New South Wales. The Milparinka area was a very different place to any of de Boos' previous appointments. Sturt had described it as a "stoney, waterless waste", yet the miners came. The conditions must have been abysmal. Shortages of food and water worsened as the population grew. "Prices for basic commodities such as flour, were exorbitant. Diseases,

---

145 - *NSW Government Gazette*, 719, December 13, 1887, page 8292.
146 - *Sydney Morning Herald*, July 9, 1887, page 9.
147 - *Daily Telegraph*, September 10, 1887, page 3.
148 - *Annual Report of the Department of Mines, New South Wales, for the year 1887*. Government Printer, Sydney, pages 105-107; *Annual Report of the Department of Mines, New South Wales, for the year 1888*. Government Printer, Sydney, pages 120-121.

such as cholera and typhoid, were rife on the fields".[149] In the 1882 Annual Report for the New South Wales Department of Mines, the Under-Secretary of Mines stated: "Probably no gold-field has been discovered in the Colony which is calculated to tax the perseverance and ingenuity of the miner to a greater extent than the Albert Gold-field".[150]

The two annual reports written by de Boos from Milparinka provide a picture of a dry isolated location, with the mining being virtually all surface operations and constantly frustrated by a lack of water.[151] In 1888, it rained in January, but there was virtually no more for the rest of the year. For both life and work in this place, nothing was more important than water.

> *And here arises a very serious question. The residents at Mount Browne have been during the whole of the year entirely dependent upon the underground water for their supply for domestic use, as well as for the watering of their cattle and horses. Now, if one, or possibly two, Companies have at work pumps so powerful as to keep down the water so as to allow their claims to be workable, there will be no water for the public. The water being their own private property, the Companies will as much as possible conserve it for their own use when it comes to the surface – for their engine and for puddling. If they have no more than sufficient for these purposes, it is hardly likely that they will let the public have what they want for themselves to make their venture remunerative. The shallower shafts now used will be drained dry, and then comes the question, how is household water to be obtained? It may be said probably that a well could be sunk in some other locality beyond the reach of the draining action of the Company's pumps. But who is to do it? There is nothing in the Mining Board Regulations to provide for the taking up of a well or water-shaft. Such an idea was never mooted before the Mining Board.*
>
> *… Such a field as Mount Browne, so different from any other in the Colony, was certainly never dreamt of in the Mining Board philosophy. If a water reserve be proclaimed it would be open to all, and no person would have a right to sink a well and claim the monopoly of the water. And even if permits were given by the Government endless disputes would arise; and, with the well-known wrong-headedness of miners, the moment the reserve was made there would be a general concurrence of opinion that there on that spot and below that reserve was to be found the best run of gold in the district. The question is one that will arise, though perhaps not immediately; but it is one that ought to be met in some shape, if the Mount Browne Company, being successful, should get into a heavy swing of work.[152]*

---

149 - www.outbacknsw.com.au/mining-heritage.html , accessed March 1, 2016; McQueen 2007; Johnson 1881; *Town and Country Journal*, August 6, 1881, page 262; October 29, 1881, page 838.

150 - *Annual Report of the Department of Mines, New South Wales, for the year 1882*. Government Printer, Sydney, 1883. Page 11.

151 - *Annual Report of the Department of Mines, New South Wales, for the year 1887*. Government Printer, Sydney, 1888. pp. 105-107. *Annual Report of the Department of Mines, New South Wales, for the year 1888*. Government Printer, Sydney, 1889. Pages 120-121.

152 - *Annual Report of the Department of Mines, New South Wales, for the year 1888*. Government Printer, Sydney, 1889. Page 121.

Established in the early 1880s, Milparinka was the first town on the Albert Goldfield, along with Albert, Mount Browne, and Tibooburra (Figure 9.15). All grew and declined in tune with the state of gold mining.[153] No local newspaper was available in Milparinka until just before de Boos left.[154] Mining was initially by surfacing and there were largely unsuccessful attempts at reef mining (there was some underground mining at Mt. Browne).[155] But by 1893, mining was largely abandoned.[156]

Figure 9.15. Milparinka from the air: the Albert Hotel and Milparinka Museum in the centre; old Court House, Police Barracks and Cells, and ruins of Post Office to the left, 2020. Source: https://topwiretraveller.com/milparinka/

Interestingly, de Boos was the Mines Department representative on the board of the then new Mount Browne Prospecting Company, which was "subsidised by the Government".[157] This was surely a very unusual move by the Colonial Government.

> A large public meeting has been held at Milparinka with reference to testing the deep ground at Mount Browne Goldfields. Mr. Chambers was in the chair. It was agreed to form a Company, to be called the Mount Browne Gold-mining Company, with a nominal capital of £3,000, to work in conjunction with the Mines Department. Mr. de Boos, the Mining Warden on the Albert Goldfields, is to have a seat on the Board as a representative of the Minister of Mines. The Government Prospecting Board, comprising the Under-Secretary of Mines, the Chief Geologist, and the Inspector of Mines, is expected to visit the goldfields, which have been much kept back by dry seasons and want of capital.[158]

---

153 - "Albert Gold-Field, N.S.W." *South Australian Register*, April 9, 1883, page 6; Stone 2014.

154 - *The Milparinka Advertiser and Tibooburra Recorder*. Copies are rare, with an incomplete collection for the period, May 20, 1889 – April 14, 1890, available in the State Library of Victoria.

155 - McQueen 2008.

156 - MacTaggart 2014.

157 - *South Australian Register*, November 21, 1887, page 6; *Annual Report of the Department of Mines, New South Wales, for the year 1887*. Government Printer, Sydney, page 106; McQueen 2007.

158 - *South Australian Register* (Adelaide), August 25, 1887, page 5.

In May 1889, de Boos made one of his longest overland journeys, a round trip of over 1,600 km. Travelling south-east through White Cliffs and Wilcannia, he visited Mount Hope, Mount Dromedary, and Hillston. His report to the Mines Department covered the geology and topography of the County of Blaxland, copper mining at Mount Hope, gold mining at Mount Dromedary, and enquiries he had made about gold finds at Nabba.[159] "There are two townships in the vicinity; one containing 100 and another 150 inhabitants. Since the fall in the price of copper both townships have been in a languishing condition", though two copper mines were still operating in Mount Hope.[160] At Mount Hope, de Boos also "held an inquiry into the objections preferred against Jasper J. Tullia, mining registrar", noting also that the absence of a local mining registrar was causing "considerable trouble and expense".[161]

At Milparinka, as Police Magistrate, de Boos had some difficult cases to deal with, including "A sensational case of suicide" by a seventeen year old woman,[162] and the theft of a gold nugget weighing 12 ounces that gained Australia-wide publicity. The latter had an unusual outcome: "After the case had been disposed of, the purloined nugget was sold for £47, and the proceeds were divided between Murray [the plaintiff] and the prisoner".[163] A more pleasant task was his role as a marriage celebrant: "The Warden has had a busy time during the past month in the way of marriages, having celebrated four, which is something unusual for Milparinka".[164]

On June 4, 1889, de Boos was appointed warden of the Cobar Mining District, seemingly in addition to his Milparinka appointment.[165] His area of responsibility was expanded significantly.[166] Why this was done is not known. It could have been because of the decline of mining in the

---

159 - *Sydney Mail*, June 22, 1889, page 1331; *Riverine Gazette*, August 27, 1889, page 3.

160 - *Australian Town & Country Journal*, June 22, 1889, page 44; *Daily Telegraph*, June 19, 1889, page 7; *Sydney Morning Herald*, June 19, 1889, page 9; *Riverine Grazier* (Hay), August 27, 1889, page 3. *Sydney Mail*, June 15, 1889, page 1274.

161 - *Sydney Mail*, June 15, 1889, page 1274.

162 - *Maitland Mercury,* March 22, 1888, page 3; *Goulburn Evening Penny Post*, March 20, 1888, page 4; *Sydney Mail*, March 24, 1888, page 657.

163 - *The Argus*, Monday, May 21, 1888, page 8; *South Australian Register,* May 21, 1888, page 5; *Border Watch* (Mount Gambier), May 23, 1888, page 3; *Inquirer and Commercial News* (Perth), June 8, 1888, page 3; *Daily News* (Perth), June 8, 1888, page 3; *Albury Banner*, May 25, 1888, page 19.

164 - *South Australian Register*, November 21, 1887, page 6; February 28, 1889, page 4.

165 - *NSW Government Gazette*, 290, June 4, 1889, page 3911; *Sydney Morning Herald*, June 5, 1889, page 4.

166 - The Cobar Mining District was proclaimed in March 1878. *NSW Government Gazette,* 91, March 29, 1878, pages 1273-1274.

Milparinka area, and that he would move his base to Cobar, a more central location for the combined districts. Whatever the reason, just five months later, he retired and his work for the Colonial Government came to an end.[167]

Charles de Boos and his work

de Boos was a strong supporter of the 'the diggers'. At a presentation at the Braidwood Masonic Lodge in 1881 (see Chapter Ten), he gave expression to the way in which he carried out his work:

> *As some of you know, when I was in this district I considered it my duty always to give the digger my advice as to the best way for him to proceed in any difficulty, and not to send him to a lawyer to spend his money without perhaps getting any satisfaction after all. I consider a warden, as the name implies, should be the guide and protector of the digger. Any digger coming to me with a complaint was just in the same position to me, as a warden, as any man who comes to me with any complaint. As a magistrate I want to hear what he has to say before granting him a warrant. I am well aware that by following such a course I have greatly displeased the legal fraternity; but I cannot help that: I conscientiously regard it as in strict accordance with my duty, and I shall ever continue in it while I hold my present position.*[168]

Whilst he was at Temora, it was observed:

> *Mr. De Boos boldly stated in court some time back that he was here to protect the miner, and no one can doubt that the intention has been carried out to the letter. There is no unnecessary severity in fines or sentences as in the early days of the rush.*[169]

He endeavoured to undertake most of his duties 'on site', rather than in a court room, which was greatly appreciated. On occasions, he travelled on his own or with only one other person, which was cause for comment in the *Sydney Mail*. On a visit to Barmedman, "It may be remarked that Mr. De Boos was not attended by an orderly or any one connected with the police force".[170]

At times, de Boos was clearly frustrated with the Chinese miners. When it came to mining licence fees, "there is no scheme or trick they will not resort to, if by so doing they can escape payment".[171] He had problems in

---

167 - *Sydney Morning Herald*, November 23, 1889, page 14; *Government Gazette*, November 22, 1889.
168 - *Sydney Morning Herald*, June 30, 1881, page 5.
169 - *Cootamundra Herald*, June 4, 1881, page 2.
170 - *Sydney Mail*, January 28, 1882, page 136.
171 - *Annual Report of the Department of Mines, New South Wales, for the year 1875*. Government Printer, Sydney, page 45.

determining "the actual amount of gold mined at Delegate. The miners employed there are nearly all Chinese, who are particularly reticent in the matter of the gold obtained by them". Further, "large amounts have gone across the Border – smuggled, in fact – and have been taken into account as Victorian produce".[172] Nonetheless, he had a generally high regard for them:

> *Amongst other discouraging signs of the present droughty times is the fact that the number of Chinese working on the several gold-fields of the district has gradually dwindled down to a mere hand-full. As these hard-working, persevering men are satisfied with a very much smaller yield than would content a European, times must be very hard indeed when even they are driven out.*[173]

Apart from site inspections and writing reports, much of his work was done in meetings of the Wardens Courts, which were held in numerous locations, not just where de Boos was based. Much was routine: dealing with various applications relating to mining leases, suspension of labour conditions, settling disputes. Making decisions almost inevitably meant upsetting some people, as well as pleasing others. By no means were all of his rulings accepted. They were sometimes appealed; at times, his decisions were over-ruled. Nonetheless, he was generally highly regarded for his work. For example,

> *Whatever private vices we may have, let there be some public and political morality, and when in these degenerate times a government official shows a high sense of the duties of his office, he should be respected without reference to personal inconvenience. Your shifty dodger through the intricacies of the land law has no chance with Mr. De Boos, who has evidently mastered the meaning of the word warden, which is simply a guardian. Acting as a watchman over the interests of the miner, he invariably puts his foot down upon any outside pressure from interested and influential personages. The seat of justice has often been degraded in New South Wales; and something tells me that there is room for amendment on Temora, and that the stern attitude of Mr. De Boos, though it may be admired by honest men, excites the animus of many a greedy and unscrupulous land shark.*[174]

His contributions to the Annual Reports of the Department of Mines contain a wealth of detailed information about gold mining and related issues on the goldfields (Appendix 9.1). More than once, he was complimented for

---

172 - *Annual Report of the Department of Mines, New South Wales, for the year 1878.* Government Printer, Sydney, page 81.
173 - *Annual Report of the Department of Mines, New South Wales, for the year 1878.* Government Printer, Sydney, page 79.
174 - *Cootamundra Herald*, September 17, 1881, page 6.

the quality of his reports. For example, the Editor of the *Armidale Express* wrote: "As might be expected from the literary reputation of Mr. Warden De Boos, of Braidwood, his report on various gold fields in the Southern district is well worth reading".[175] He wrote numerous reports on specific topics and contributed material on the Southern Goldfields at Braidwood, The Valley (Araluen), Delegate, Kiandra, McLaughlin River, New Chum Hill, and Tumbarumba, and on tin at Kiandra for a major Department of Mines publication.[176]

In 1876, he provided samples of gold-bearing rocks from the Southern District for a New South Wales exhibit at the Centennial Exhibition held later in the year in Philadelphia.[177] They were exhibited in Sydney for a short period. In 1879, de Boos encouraged miners to visit the Sydney International Exhibition, advertisements telling them to apply for the "suspension of labour conditions on their several claims".[178]

Conclusion

But as indicated earlier in this chapter, there is more to Charles de Boos' time as a Colonial Government official.

---

175 - *Armidale Express*, October 20, 1876, page 4; *Freeman's Journal,* August 6, 1881, page 17.

176 - *Mines and Mineral Statistics of New South Wales, and Notes on the Geological Collection of the Department of Mines.* Compiled by direction of the Hon. John Lucas, M.P., Minister of Mines. Government Printer, Sydney, 1875; *Manaro Mercury*, November 20, 1875, page 4.

177 - *Sydney Mail,* January 1, 1876, page 11; *Australian Town and Country Journal,* January 1, 1876, pages 20-21.

178 - Advertisements appeared in numerous local papers, including the *Manaro Mercury,* July 30, 1879, page 2 and the *Telegraph and Shoalhaven Advertiser, July 31, 1879, page 3.*

Chapter Ten

The Temora Incidents: Setting the record straight

A short series of events during his time in Temora have been given far more prominence than they merit in the biographical and other writings about de Boos. They have inaccurately and unjustifiably portrayed much of his life and work. As a consequence, in order to set the record straight, this part of his story must be told in some considerable detail.

His entry in the *Australian Dictionary of Biography* states that "at Temora de Boos was accused of partiality, insobriety and improper language. Three times in the Legislative Assembly in 1882 William Forster asked questions about his conduct and was told by the Minister of Justice that he had been reprimanded, although some of the complaints had not been substantiated".[1] The observation in the 'Austlit' data base that "Some controversy clouded his tenure as a warden"[2] and the statement in *The Oxford Companion to Australian Literature* that "his appointment as mining warden and police magistrate [were] posts in which he was considerably criticised", are simply not correct.[3] Only with respect to Temora does the 'Austlit' comment have any validity. Holt is the only author who provides any sources for the comments, namely the *Votes and Proceedings* of the New South Wales Legislative Assembly. Whilst these are essential sources, they are limited and provide only part of the story. Now, however, with modern research aids making materials much more accessible, it is possible to provide a more complete and accurate account of the events in Temora in 1882.

As mentioned in Chapter Nine, when de Boos returned to Temora on February 22, 1881, he could not have received a warmer welcome. His work and actions were widely supported. When the member for Gundagai in the New South Wales Parliament, William Forster, suggested that matters

---

1 - Holt 1972.
2 - www.austlit.edu.au .
3 - Wilde, Hooton and Andrews 1994, 225.

relating to certain land dealings should be taken out of the hands of de Boos, it was immediately condemned by the Editor of the *Cootamundra Herald*: "If Mr. De Boos has the pluck to stand in the gap and prevent the aggression of the unscrupulous, he is worthy of honour".[4] Further, his high regard and popularity with the miners remained.

> WARDEN DE BOOS.
>
> *The Warden is very popular with the miners, and earns golden opinions by his courtesy and willingness to answer questions in cases where people cannot interpret the law. Whether this is acceptable to the legal fraternity is a problem not hard to solve. Mr. De Boos boldly stated in court some time back that he was here to protect the miner, and no one can doubt that the intention has been carried out to the letter.[5]*

However, with the expansion of gold mining and the increasing number of matters brought before the Warden's Court, it was inevitable that his judgements would not please everyone.[6] Further, it was hardly surprising that some of his decisions were appealed. In late 1881-early 1882, a number of his decisions were overturned in the Mining Appeal Court;[7] in mid-1882, five decisions of de Boos were reversed by Judge David Forbes at the Mining Appeal Court held in Cootamundra.[8] He had difficulties with the South Australian Puddling and Mining Company and its manager, Captain Thomas Matthews;[9] and at least one of the local district's solicitors claimed he had problems with de Boos.[10] An undoubted further complication was that, at least initially, his son William may have been the only solicitor resident in Temora. On the other hand, there were suggestions that the Temora miners were a particularly litigious lot: "Mr. Warden de Boos has it [the Temora goldfield] under complete control, and his urbane manners and active habits have done much to check litigation. It is well that it is so, for Temora miners have been, and in fact are, remarkably litigious. Mr. de Boos keeps as many cases as he possibly can out of court. He follows the system of going to the claims and settling trivial disputes promptly".[11]

---

4 - *Cootamundra Herald*, July 9, 1881, page 6; *Burrangong Argus*, July 16, 1881, page 4. The matter went on for some time: *Temora Star*, September 17, 1881, page 2.

5 - *Cootamundra Herald*, June 4, 1881, page 2; June 6, 1881, page 2; *Sydney Morning Herald*, September 24, 1881, page 10.

6 - For example, *Sydney Mail*, November 19, 1881, page 848.

7 - *Sydney Morning Herald*, August 31, 1881, page 5; *Gundagai Times*, November 29, 1881, page 2; *Australian Town & Country Journal*, January 28, 1882, page 154.

8 - *Evening News*, June 21, 1882, page 3.

9 - *Temora Star*, October 1, 1881, page 2; January 25, 1882, page 2.

10 - *Australian Town & Country Journal*, October 1, 1881, page 665; *Cootamundra Herald*, April 16, 1881, page 7.

11 - *Sydney Morning Herald*, September 24, 1881, page 10; *Sydney Mail*, October 1, 1881, page 593.

In his 1881 report for the Department of Mines, de Boos noted that at Barmedman, there "were more than the usual number of disputes, and in consequence the Warden's Court was for a time inundated with business".[12]

Over this period, there were two local newspapers in Temora, the *Star* and the *Herald*; in nearby Cootamundra, there was the *Cootamundra Herald*. Both the *Temora Star* and the *Temora Herald and Mining Journal* began publication in 1880, but the earliest surviving copy of the *Temora Herald* is for April 21, 1882. The *Cootamundra Herald* commenced publication in 1877.[13] Little affection existed between the *Temora Star* on the one hand and the *Temora Herald* and *Cootamundra Herald* on the other, with frequent critical comments of the *Star* and its editor.[14] As for the *Star*, not only did it attack its competitors, from August 1881,[15] it provided frequent and increasing criticism of de Boos and his work: for example, "… under the present Warden's administration the written law is not worth the paper it is written on. Precedents and practice of the court all go for nothing, and *SSic voleo sic jubeo* [roughly translated, 'Such as I wish, so do I order'] of the Warden is the only law of the land".[16] The *Star* also provided space for criticism of de Boos from Henry Margules.[17]

The *Star*'s criticism culminated in two editorials, on March 1 and 8, 1882. Whilst acknowledging his "uprightness and singleness of purpose", the writer described de Boos as "wrong-headed, perverse, and systematically erroneous in his actions as a public officer"; a series of criticisms culminated in the accusation of partiality towards people in court who were represented by his son William.[18]

> *We have pointed out from time to time, as occasion arose, that his habit of giving advice to suitors before they come before him in open Court was not conducive to raise the dignity of the Bench in public estimation. We have also not unfrequently drawn attention to serious errors in the administration of the goldfield which, in our opinion, have tended to retard the progress of the community. We have pointed out that the policy pursued by him as a Warden tended to drive away capital from the field, which*

---

12 - *Annual Report of the Department of Mines, New South Wales, for the year 1881*, page 54.
13 - There were also reports of a *Temora Leader*, first published in July 1880, but no copies have been located (*Sydney Morning Herald*, July 31, 1880, page 6). Also published in 1880 was the *Temora Telegraph and Mining Advocate*, but only the first issue dated July 29, 1880, has survived.
14 - *Cootamundra Herald*, September 10, 1881, page 2; September 21, 1881, page 1; January 18, 1882, page 2.
15 - *Temora Star*, August 20, 1881, page 2; September 10, 1881, page 2; December 24, 1881, page 2.
16 - *Temora Star*, December 24, 1881, page 2; *Temora Star*, September 10, 1881, page 2.
17 - *Temora Star*, November 23, 1881, page 2.
18 - *Temora Star*, March 1, 1882, page 2; March 8, 1882, page 2.

> *in a place like Temora, the future of which entirely depends upon the development of its quartz reefs, will be acknowledged to be a public calamity. Yet, while adversely criticising his actions, we gave Mr. De Boos credit for uprightness and singleness of purpose. We were still fondly believing that however warped his judgement might be, his actions as the administrator, or his decisions as the primary judge of this goldfield, sprang from pure, if mistaken, motives. We know that his sympathies are thoroughly communistic; and hence we had more than one instance to record where bona fide compliance with all that the Mining Act and Mining Regulations require did not prove efficient protection. We deprecated the feeling of insecurity which his judicial decisions had the tendency to develop in every holder of property. These, in the eyes of most people, would be considered very grave charges in themselves – and, if so inclined, we might have drawn up an indictment against the Warden of this goldfield which would have gone far to demonstrate that, whatever ornament to the Civil Service he might prove in another position, as a Warden he was a mistake; but we were ready to condone his shortcomings so long as we held the belief that his decisions on the Bench were based upon upright conviction. A Judge – like Caesar's wife – should be above suspicion. It is with no inconsiderable pain that we are compelled to give up that belief. We cannot blink the fact any longer that in his judicial capacity his conduct is biased to a very appreciable extent in favour of that party to a suit who has the acumen to employ his son to advocate his cause. It is already a public secret that with Mr. DeBoos, junior, as representative in Court a case is 'safe', because the father, on the Bench, looks kindly upon the client on the floor of the Court whose cause is pleaded by the son. Public opinion even goes further than this; and it is boldly asserted that cases for trial are discussed beforehand between judge and advocate. Whether this impression be right or wrong, the public backs its opinion; and nineteen out of twenty plaintiffs secure the services of Mr. DeBoos, the younger, as advocate to curry favour with Mr. DeBoos, the elder, on the Bench. We were at first inclined to look upon the association of father and son as respective positions on this goldfield as a matter of taste. But a close observance of the proceedings in the Warden's Court can only lead to one conclusion – and that conclusion, we regret, is not flattering to the presiding magistrate. We have there the spectacle of the judge browbeating the advocates opposed to the one favourite member of the profession, while pari passu giving every latitude to the latter. We see him lose his temper when the son is in danger of losing his case. If pointedly cross-examining 'adverse' witnesses in order to weaken their evidence; if putting leading questions to 'favourable' witnesses for the purposes of strengthening a case watched over with paternal care; and finally, if prompting the halting argument of his offspring every now and then with a timely 'cue', are signs from which to draw deductions, then we say these signs are extant. The public will coincide with us that this is a public scandal and should not be tolerated any longer.[19]*

There was widespread anger at the charges made against de Boos by the *Temora Star*.[20] Along with the charges, the subsequent major debate within the Temora community and the two large and rowdy public meetings held in support of de Boos (Figure 10.1), were widely reported, not only in the

---

19 - *Temora Star*, March 1, 1882, page 2.
20 - *Evening News*, March 2, 1882, page 3; *Temora Herald*, May 2, 1882, page 2.

local and Sydney papers, but also in the other colonies. At the same time, whilst most people supported de Boos, there was a significant minority that did not.[21]

de Boos took out a writ for £10,000 for libel against the *Temora Star* and its Editor over the statements.[22] At the second public meeting, a committee was formed to raise funds for his libel case; £200 was raised at the meeting and it soon reached £300.[23] This only led to even more controversy.

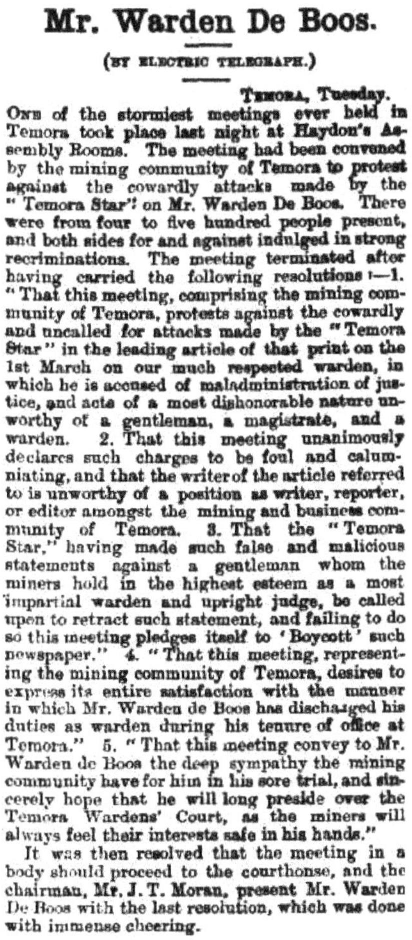

Mr. Warden De Boos.
(BY ELECTRIC TELEGRAPH.)

TEMORA, Tuesday.

ONE of the stormiest meetings ever held in Temora took place last night at Haydon's Assembly Rooms. The meeting had been convened by the mining community of Temora to protest against the cowardly attacks made by the "Temora Star" on Mr. Warden De Boos. There were from four to five hundred people present, and both sides for and against indulged in strong recriminations. The meeting terminated after having carried the following resolutions :—1. "That this meeting, comprising the mining community of Temora, protests against the cowardly and uncalled for attacks made by the "Temora Star" in the leading article of that print on the 1st March on our much respected warden, in which he is accused of maladministration of justice, and acts of a most dishonorable nature unworthy of a gentleman, a magistrate, and a warden. 2. That this meeting unanimously declares such charges to be foul and calumniating, and that the writer of the article referred to is unworthy of a position as writer, reporter, or editor amongst the mining and business community of Temora. 3. That the "Temora Star," having made such false and malicious statements against a gentleman whom the miners hold in the highest esteem as a most impartial warden and upright judge, be called upon to retract such statement, and failing to do so this meeting pledges itself to 'Boycott' such newspaper." 4. "That this meeting, representing the mining community of Temora, desires to express its entire satisfaction with the manner in which Mr. Warden de Boos has discharged his duties as warden during his tenure of office at Temora." 5. "That this meeting convey to Mr. Warden de Boos the deep sympathy the mining community have for him in his sore trial, and sincerely hope that he will long preside over the Temora Wardens' Court, as the miners will always feel their interests safe in his hands." It was then resolved that the meeting in a body should proceed to the courthouse, and the chairman, Mr. J. T. Moran, present Mr. Warden De Boos with the last resolution, which was done with immense cheering.

Figure 10.1. Evening News, March 21, 1882, page 3; Australian Town and Country Journal, March 25, 1882, page 540.

INSANITY AT TEMORA

Observers cannot but be struck with the fact, apparently, that a number of wild men have, as if by a peculiar direction of Satan, been brought together to blast the character of the Temora community. It is becoming famous for chiselling, moonlight-flitting, dogging, plundering, incendiarism, law-wrangling, slandering, libelling, lying, and hating; and it has been lately threatened with boycotting.[24]

In the meantime, the New South Wales Minister of Justice had established an inquiry into the accusations made against de Boos by the *Temora Star*.[25]

---

21 - *Temora Star*, March 22, 1882, page 2; March 25, 1882, page 2; March 29, 1882, page 2; *South Australian Register*, March 22, 1882, page 6; *Maitland Mercury*, March 23, 1882, page 2; April 11, 1882, page 2; *Australian Town & Country Journal*, March 25, 1882, page 540; *Cootamundra Herald*, March 25, 1882, page 6; *Wagga Wagga Advertiser*, March 25, 1882, page 2; *Southern Argus* (Goulburn), March 25, 1882, page 2; *Australian Town & Country Journal*, March 23, 1882, page 540; *Sydney Mail*, March 25, 1882, page 482.

22 - *Temora Star*, March 29, 1882, page 3; *Cootamundra Herald*, April 1, 1882, page 5.

23 - *Sydney Morning Herald*, March 27, 1882, page 5; *Australian Town & Country Journal*, April 8, 1882, page 635.

24 - Editorial in the *Cootamundra Herald*, April 15, 1882, page 4.

25 - *Australian Town & Country Journal*, March 11, 1882, page 443.

Shortly after the controversy generated by the *Temora Star* editorials, problems emerged for de Boos with the town's Progress Committee and the election of a new committee in April, 1882.[26] "Great excitement is being manifested over the forthcoming election of the Progress Committee, it having been determined to keep Warden Deboos's opponents from getting into power";[27] people were urged to "Cross out the enemies of the Warden" and were reminded that "Warden de Boos is your True Friend" (Figure 10.2);[28] "The issue between the factions is the enemies of Warden de Boos versus his friends, the latter being in a great majority".[29] In the election, William received the largest number of votes.[30]

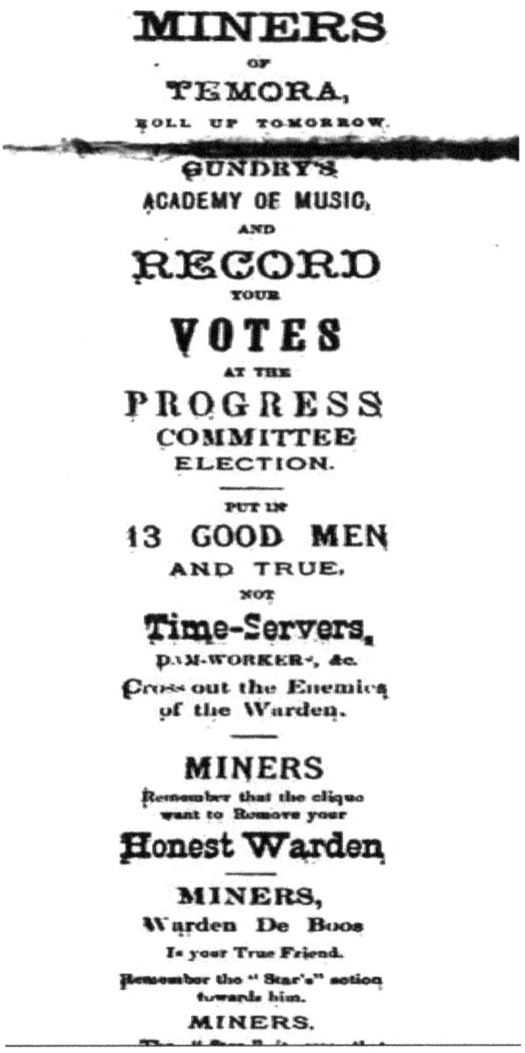

Comments on the election provided an opportunity for the Editor of the *Herald* to wax eloquent about the *Temora Star*.

Figure 10.2. Part of a full-column advertisement. Temora Herald, April 21, 1882, page 1.

The wily editor, of a local print, in his last effusion, preparatory to the declaration of the poll for the Progress Committee – with unprecedented artfulness, to prevent what might be disastrous to some of the dishonourably returned candidates to that body as representatives of the people of Temora – attempts, by side-winds, inuendoes, and 'foul

---

26 - *Temora Star*, April 19, 1882, page 2; October 22, 1881, page 2; April 12, 1882, page 2. William was a member and later Secretary, until he resigned in late 1882. *Temora Star*, November 4, 1882, page 2.
27 - *South Australian Register*, April 18, 1882, page 5.
28 - *Temora Herald*, April 21, 1882, pages 1 and 2.
29 - *Maitland Mercury*, April 25, 1882, page 3, from the *Evening News*, April 22; *Temora Star*, April 29, 1882, page 2; *Temora Herald*, April 21, 1882, page 2.
30 - *Temora Star*, April 26, 1882, page 2; *Cootamundra Herald*, April 29, 1882, page 3.

aspersions', on some of those concerned in bringing to light the shady transactions of certain people – to throw dust in the eyes of the 'body politic', in order to serve ends degrading, and may we say dishonest. With an effort worthy of a sorcerer, he compares the antagonists of a certain clique to Homer's 'Old Man of the Sea', Proteus, attributing all the 'chameleon' characteristics of this celebrated Homeric notability to the Temora 'Old Man' – whom no one who knows the person himself could but say 'Thou art the man'; for the writer of Saturday's article, by his 'vaticination' – and general all-round 'angelic' breathings – first to one and then to the other, in drawing a picture of Homer's Proteus, has, in an unguarded moment, drawn a life-like picture of himself, forgetting at the time Robert Burns' words – 'Oh! that the Gods the gift would gie us, to see oursels as others see us'. This Starry Proteus congratulates the community on the issue of the Progress elections being entirely foreign from the supposed one, viz., between the friends and foes of Mr Warden De Boos, but notwithstanding this haphazard congratulation, we contend that it was the real issue of the fight.[31]

Unfortunately, April 21, 1882, is the earliest issue of the *Temora Herald* available, so what the *Herald* had to say about earlier events in Temora and especially the charges made by the *Star* and its comments on the public meetings are not known. But there is no doubt that de Boos was given strong support by the *Herald*.[32]

Two months after the accusations were made, the *Herald* reported that it had learned "that the defendant, Mr Samuel Hawkins, has offered an abject apology to the plaintiff, of such a nature that the Department may allow it to be accepted by the plaintiff, such apology to have due publicity in the colonial newspapers".[33] But it was another two months before the matter was settled.[34] The *Temora Star* published a withdrawal of the charges and an apology, but being placed in the lower part of a page of advertisements, it was hardly given "due publicity" (Figure 10.3).[35] With "an apology" signed by Mr. Wehr, stating that he wrote the article without the knowledge or consent of Mr. Hawkins and all of the legal costs that had been incurred paid by the defendant, de Boos dropped the action.[36] The apology was "considered sufficient by the Minister of Justice".[37]

---

31 - *Temora Herald*, May 2, 1882, page 2.
32 - It can be noted that the offices of the *Temora Herald* were located in the premises of De Boos Brothers, Auctioneers: *Temora Herald*, October 27, 1882, page 3.
33 - *Temora Herald*, May 30, 1882, page 2.
34 - *Evening News*, July 4, 1882, page 3.
35 - *Temora Star*, July 12, 1882, page 3; see also *Australian Town and Country Journal*, July 8, 1882, page 14.
36 - *Australian Town & Country*, July 8, 1882, page 62.
37 - *Cootamundra Herald*, July 12, 1882, page 2; *Southern Argus*, July 6, 1882, page 2.

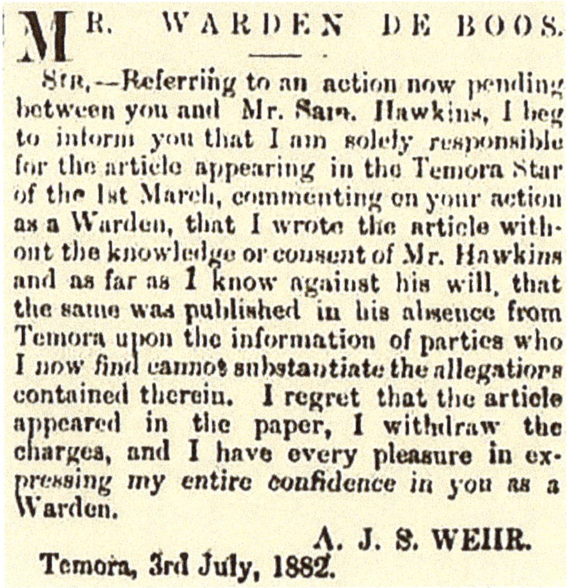

> MR. WARDEN DE BOOS.
>
> SIR,—Referring to an action now pending between you and Mr. Sam. Hawkins, I beg to inform you that I am solely responsible for the article appearing in the Temora Star of the 1st March, commenting on your action as a Warden, that I wrote the article without the knowledge or consent of Mr. Hawkins and as far as I know against his will, that the same was published in his absence from Temora upon the information of parties who I now find cannot substantiate the allegations contained therein. I regret that the article appeared in the paper, I withdraw the charges, and I have every pleasure in expressing my entire confidence in you as a Warden.
>
> A. J. S. WEIR.
> Temora, 3rd July, 1882.

Figure 10.3. Temora Star, July 12, 1882, page 3.

In the circumstances, given the many demands of his work, his involvement in so much else that was going on in Temora, as well as family issues, it is perhaps not surprising that he became unwell: "Mr. Warden de Boos is very ill, and with difficulty sat in the Warden's Court to-day [April 6]".[38] It was reported that "Mr. De Boos' health has recently given him cause of uneasiness, and that he has consequently applied to be relieved from his onerous duties for a time, and that the Government have granted his request".[39] He returned later in the month "much improved in health".[40] However, his return was short-lived, as in May, he left again, this time "for a fortnight's leave of absence".[41] The criticisms continued, over his work, a lack of decorum, the use of profane language, and "the general hubbub" in meetings of the Warden's Court.[42] The demands of his work continued to take their toll on his health.[43] He took leave of absence again in September,

---

38 - *Maitland Mercury*, April 11, 1882, page 4; *Evening News*, April 8, 1882, page 4; *Sydney Mail*, April 8, page 560; April 15, 1882, page 602; *Grenfell Record*, April 15, 1882, page 3; *Temora Star*, April 15, 1882, page 2.

39 - *Temora Star*, April 15, 1882, page 2.

40 - *Sydney Morning Herald*, April 26, 1882, page 6; *Temora Star*, April 26, 1882, page 2.

41 - *Temora Star*, April 29, 1882, page 2; May 10, 1882, page 2; *Temora Herald*, May 2, 1882, page 2; May 31, 1882, page 2

42 - *Temora Star*, July 22, 1882, page 2; July 29, 1882, page 2; August 9, 1882, page 2; *Temora Herald*, September 22, 1882, page 2.

43 - *Sydney Morning Herald*, August 30, 1880, page 6. His youngest daughters were with him around this time, there being a report of a buggy accident involving William "and his two sisters" (*Temora Herald*, July 4, 1882, page 2). *Evening News*, April 8, 1882, page 4; *Temora Star*, April 5, 1882, page 2.

though this was in connection with libel action -"a most damnable one" - de Boos had taken out against Margules (which was later discontinued), rather than his health.⁴⁴

At least as early as 1876, William Forster started asking questions in the Legislative Assembly about de Boos.⁴⁵ And he did not let up, as this was personal (see below and Chapter Twelve). He gave a Notice of Motion in the Legislative Assembly:

> *That an address be presented to the Governor, praying that his Excellency will be pleased to cause to be laid on the table of this House copies of all correspondence, minutes, reports, memorials, petitions, complaints, or appeals, giving reference to any alleged misconduct of Mr. Charles De Boos, Police Magistrate and Warden at Temora: also of all proceedings before any Court or Commission of Inquiry into any charges against the said Mr. Charles De Boos.*⁴⁶

In response to questions from him, William Foster, the Minister of Justice, stated that "There were complaints of his partiality, insobriety and improper language used by him. Several letters had been sent to the government on the subject. In some instances, the complaints were not substantiated. [One complainant, an Abel Trevethan, did not seem to exist.] Mr. de Boos had been reprimanded and threatened with removal in case of repetition of his misconduct" (Figure 10.4).⁴⁷

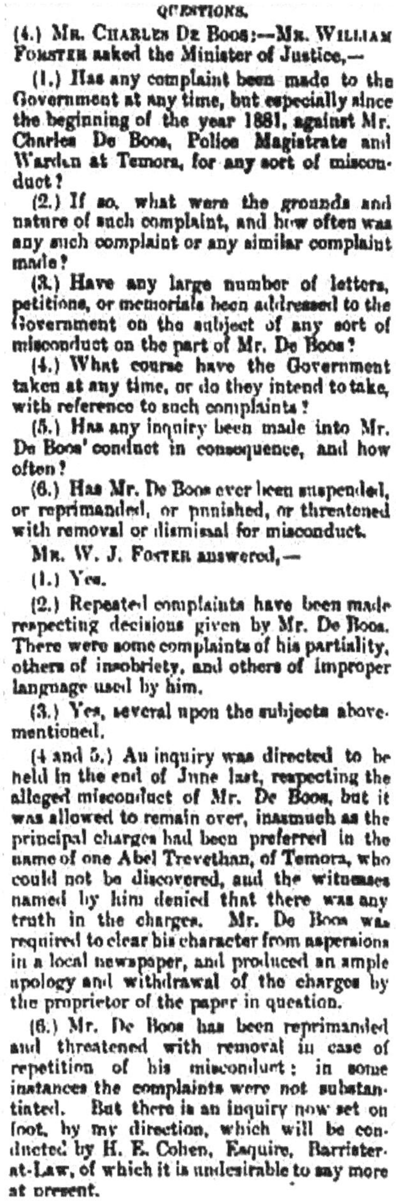

> QUESTIONS.
> (4.) Mr. CHARLES DE BOOS:—Mr. WILLIAM FORSTER asked the Minister of Justice,—
> (1.) Has any complaint been made to the Government at any time, but especially since the beginning of the year 1881, against Mr. Charles De Boos, Police Magistrate and Warden at Temora, for any sort of misconduct?
> (2.) If so, what were the grounds and nature of such complaint, and how often was any such complaint or any similar complaint made?
> (3.) Have any large number of letters, petitions, or memorials been addressed to the Government on the subject of any sort of misconduct on the part of Mr. De Boos?
> (4.) What course have the Government taken at any time, or do they intend to take, with reference to such complaints?
> (5.) Has any inquiry been made into Mr. De Boos' conduct in consequence, and how often?
> (6.) Has Mr. De Boos ever been suspended, or reprimanded, or punished, or threatened with removal or dismissal for misconduct.
> Mr. W. J. FOSTER answered,—
> (1.) Yes.
> (2.) Repeated complaints have been made respecting decisions given by Mr. De Boos. There were some complaints of his partiality, others of insobriety, and others of improper language used by him.
> (3.) Yes, several upon the subjects abovementioned.
> (4 and 5.) An inquiry was directed to be held in the end of June last, respecting the alleged misconduct of Mr. De Boos, but it was allowed to remain over, inasmuch as the principal charges had been preferred in the name of one Abel Trevethan, of Temora, who could not be discovered, and the witnesses named by him denied that there was any truth in the charges. Mr. De Boos was required to clear his character from aspersions in a local newspaper, and produced an ample apology and withdrawal of the charges by the proprietor of the paper in question.
> (6.) Mr. De Boos has been reprimanded and threatened with removal in case of repetition of his misconduct; in some instances the complaints were not substantiated. But there is an inquiry now set on foot, by my direction, which will be conducted by H. E. Cohen, Esquire, Barrister-at-Law, of which it is undesirable to say more at present.

Figure 10.4. Temora Star, October 4, 1882, page 2.

---

44 - *Temora Herald*, September 8, 1882, page 2; *Temora Star*, September 6, 1882, page 2; *Evening News*, September 6, 1882, page 4.
45 - *Evening News*, November 27, 1876, page 3.
46 - *Sydney Morning Herald*, September 21, 1882, page 5; *Temora Star*, October 4, 1882, page 2.
47 - *Sydney Daily Telegraph*, September 27, 1882, page 3; from *New South Wales Votes and Proceedings of the Legislative Assembly, No. 20,* September 26, 1882. Government Printer, Sydney, page 84; *Sydney Morning Herald*, September 27, 1882, page 6.

Charles de Boos had never made any secret of his support for miners. As to "insobriety", this is hard to believe. Throughout his career as a journalist, and particularly when reporting on the goldfields, he had been very critical of the excessive consumption of alcohol; he would also have had personal knowledge of the problems from being a publican in Sydney.

Despite de Boos being reprimanded, even though he was virtually cleared of the charges and the *Temora Star* had withdrawn all the accusations it had made, William Forster was not satisfied. Largely in response to questions from him, the government set up a further inquiry, seemingly into the same charges.[48] It was undertaken by Henry Cohen, a barrister-at-law.[49] On arriving in Temora, he stated that "the de Boos inquiry is purely departmental, and will be held with closed doors, and that the evidence is not to be published until after the conclusion of the case".[50] How serious an inquiry it was is difficult to judge, as the next day it was reported that "The de Boos inquiry is going on. The witnesses are not put on oath. Several witnesses are absent".[51] One person could not be found, while another, A.J.S. Wehr, who was reported as being on the list of witnesses, declined, stating that "as the enquiry is, according to the information at hand, chiefly directed at Mr. de Boos' private life, allow me to say that I have neither hand nor part in it".[52] Cohen left Temora after less than two days, with the general belief "that the Warden will be exonerated from the charges made against him".[53]

> *We understand that a most numerously signed memorial will be forwarded this week to the Minister of Justice, setting forth that Mr Warden De Boos has been subjected to an annoying persecution by malevolent parties on whose corns the Warden has trodden, and also expressing the deep sympathy of the miners for Mr De Boos in the invidious position in which he was placed.*[54]

Following the visit of Cohen, there was still little peace for de Boos in Temora.[55] Even with Cohen's inquiry still in progress, Forster asked further

---

48 - *New South Wales Votes and Proceedings of the Legislative Assembly,* No. 27, September 26, 1882, page 111-112.
49 - The Minister of Justice wanted the inquiry to be publicised, but wanted "the newspaper proprietors to insert a paragraph, but not an advt." This was regarded as "Departmental parsimony" (*Temora Herald,* October 3, 1882, page 2).
50 - *Sydney Morning Herald,* October 4, 1882, page 10.
51 - *Sydney Morning Herald,* October 5, 1882, page 9.
52 - *Temora Star,* October 4, 1882, page 2.
53 - *Sydney Morning Herald,* October 6, 1882, page 8; *Temora Herald,* October 6, 1882, page 2; October 10, 1882, page 2.
54 - *Temora Herald,* October 10, 1882, page 2.
55 - *Temora Herald,* October 20, 1882, page 2; November 14, 1882, page 2.

questions in the Legislative Assembly in early October 1882, most of them going over similar ground to before.[56] He seemed to take every opportunity to 'get at' de Boos. One of Forster's colleagues, Robert Levien (the Member for Tamworth), was also pursuing de Boos. In the Legislative Assembly on October 24, 1882, he moved a motion for all papers connected with a number of cases tried before Warden de Boos at Temora to be placed on the table of the House.[57]

Nonetheless, de Boos returned to Temora on September 28, 1882, and was back at work at the beginning of October, but for little more than three weeks, sitting for the last time in the Temora Court on October 25, 1882.[58] Though he was still officially the Mining Warden and Police Magistrate, reports indicated that he was suspended, Warden R.R. Morrisett from Sofala taking his place temporarily, much to the displeasure of many people, in Temora and Sofala.[59] A public meeting at Barmedman gave its full support to de Boos: "The Warden had enemies, but they were not the working miner but men who wanted to serve their own ends"; de Boos "had been a man who had tried to do all that he could for the working miner, and if he were suspended for any time it would be a serious loss. He had simply tried to do too much".[60]

Despite all that he had done through his work, the support of many people, and his community activities, de Boos left Temora at the end of October 1882 without any reported farewells. However, his departure was no doubt accompanied with at least some personal relief. Then, before any further questions were asked and before Cohen had presented the report of his inquiry, William Forster died suddenly on October 29, 1882.[61] And this seems to have relieved de Boos of any further difficulties.

But why did Forster take up such an attack on de Boos? He was the member for the nearby Legislative Assembly electorate of Gundagai (which included Cootamundra), but there is no indication that he had received

---

56 - *New South Wales Votes and Proceedings of the Legislative Assembly, No. 20*, September 26, 1882, page 84, No. 27, October 6, 1882, pages 111-112, and No. 29, October 11, 1882, page 122 (the latter was on a different matter).

57 - *New South Wales Votes and Proceedings of the Legislative Assembly, No. 36*, October 24, 1882, page 155; *Evening News*, October 25, 1882, page 8.

58 - *Temora Star*, September 30, 1882, page 2; October 4, 1882, page 2; October 28, 1882, page 2.

59 - *Evening News*, November 4, 1882, page 2.

60 - *Temora Herald*, November 10, 1882, page 2; November 14, 1882, page 2.

61 - *Gundagai Times*, October 31, 1882, page 2.

any representations about the matters from concerned voters. From the volumes of the Legislative Assembly's *Votes and Proceedings*, it seems that Forster had a habit of asking questions about matters from many parts of the colony. However, the most likely explanation in this instance is that by picking up the questionable allegations against de Boos, Forster was able to 'get his own back' for what happened many years earlier when de Boos was a reporter for the *Sydney Morning Herald*. As discussed in Chapter Twelve, "His satirical writings about Sydney politicians … did not make him many friends",[62] particularly the five series of articles entitled "The Collective Wisdom of New South Wales", published in the *Herald* and *The Sydney Mail* between 1867 and 1871. By the early 1880s, if not earlier, it was well known that de Boos had been the author, and given some of the statements, Forster clearly had grounds for being displeased with de Boos.[63] Interestingly, an editorial and series of reports in the *Cootamundra Herald* in July 1882, following a speech given by Forster, contained just as much criticism of him as the de Boos articles.[64] de Boos was by no means the only one to be justifiably very critical of him.[65] The entry in the Australian Dictionary of Biography describes Forster, in part, as "disagreeable", "dangerous", and "Never a friendly man".[66]

Whilst de Boos must have wondered what would happen following the allegations made against him, he did not lose his government positions. In early January 1883, he was returned to Copeland as Police Magistrate and Clerk of Petty Sessions,[67] and subsequently made "a Warden of the Hunter and Macleay Mining District".[68] Perhaps somewhat surprisingly, the initial appointment was made when Foster was Minister of Justice before the December 1882 election. With the new government of Alex Stuart, Cohen was appointed Minister of Justice.[69] de Boos retained his positions. Surely, if Cohen had found anything in Temora to justify further action against

---

62 - Crittenden 2004, 1-3.

63 - *Sydney Morning Herald*, July 22, 1867, page 5; August 8, 1867, page 5; August 19, 1867, page 5; November 11, 1867, page 5; November 18, 1867, page 5; December 2, 1867, page 5.

64 - "Mr. Forster's Unhappy Speech", an editorial in the *Cootamundra Herald*, July 1, 1882, page 4, followed by seven articles in subsequent issues through the month of July.

65 - Editorials in the *Temora Star*, July 5, 1882, page 2; August 9, 1882, page 2.

66 - Nairn 1972.

67 - *NSW Government Gazette*, 533, December 29, 1882, page 6859.

68 - *NSW Government Gazette*, 46, February 6, 1883, page 666. *Sydney Morning Herald*, December 30, 1882, page 6; from *Government Gazette*, December 29, 1882.

69 - *Sydney Morning Herald*, January 6, 1883, page 10.

de Boos, he would have taken it, rather than leaving him in his important judicial positions at Copeland.[70]

For the *Temora Star*, the changes of staff in the Temora court provided another opportunity to criticise de Boos. There was fulsome praise for Morrisett. But for de Boos, there was further critical comment (for example, "The 'free and easy' style that had disgraced our court proceedings"), and much displeasure that he had actually been given another appointment.[71] But the *Temora Herald* reminded the *Star* of the apology it had earlier made to de Boos: "Surely our Mephistophelian friend cannot so soon forget Mr De Boos' kindness in accepting from him a most abject apology instead of ruining him at law. But again, Temora gratitude".[72]

If the events outlined above did occur, certainly to the extent claimed, from what is known of de Boos, they would have been quite out of character. Clearly, he experienced some serious problems, but the nature of his work, his overall workload, his family situation, and the actions of William Forster are more likely to have been the reasons for the questions that, up to now, have continued to be raised about his time in Temora in 1881-82.

A truer picture of his work

The very nature of his work as a Colonial Government official and especially as a mining warden, meant that de Boos simply could not please everyone. Nonetheless, he was highly respected and had a high reputation for dealing fairly and justly with people over a period of nearly fifteen years until his retirement in 1889. He was complimented personally for his work in all of his appointments. As noted earlier, when he was moved from Braidwood, "Several public meetings [were] advertised to petition for his retention here. His decisions have never been appealed", while at Temora, "Great regret is expressed at the news that Mr. Warden de Boos is about to be removed".[73] In a telegram to the Minister of Mines just before he left Temora, de Boos stated: "The miners are all in good heart. There is no grumbling, and very few leaving the ground".[74] After just a few months in Copeland,

---

70 - No references have been found to the report by Cohen or to the consequences of the various papers being placed on the table of the House (if this was ever done).
71 - *Temora Star*, January 6, 1883, page 2; *Sydney Mail*, January 6, 1883, page 23.
72 - *Temora Herald*, January 19, 1883, page 2.
73 - *Sydney Morning Herald,* August 30, 1880, page 6; *Sydney Morning Herald*, July 31, 1880, page 6.
74 - *Australian Town and Country Journal*, August 14, 1880, page 310.

> *A complimentary banquet was given to Mr. Chas. De Boos, our late Warden and P.M. at [Williams' Royal Hotel] Copeland last night, on the eve of his departure for Temora. The event was of a more than usually enthusiastic nature: all classes of the community joined in expressing their appreciation to Mr. de Boos many sterling qualities. Mr. de Boos left Copeland universally regretted, and carries with him the best wishes of the public at large and of the mining community, particularly. Mr. J. Wadell, Manager of the Joint Stock Bank, was in the chair, and Mr. B. Benjamin in the vice-chair. Mr. Jas. Baker, our new warden attended, and paid Mr. de Boos the guest of the evening a very high tribute of respect, which was duly acknowledged.*[75]

As noted earlier, when he returned to Temora in January 1881, he was warmly welcomed by the local miners and the lawyers: "Great satisfaction is expressed by the miners at Mr. Charles de Boos' appointment as Warden here, as he is everywhere a great favourite with miners".[76] By the time of his departure from his second term in Copeland in 1887, it was very much a community in decline, as clearly indicated by the local correspondent for the *Maitland Mercury*:

> *The too evident wane of prosperity here is to be marked by the removal of our Police Magistrate. Government retrenchment is coming home to us with a vengeance when we are no longer to have such an official, combining as he does Warden, Mining Registrar, Commissioner for Affidavits, &c., &c.; certainly no end of inconvenience will be felt by the residents of Copeland, and by a wide area of squatting population and settlers, in losing Mr. de Boos. Personally, we are being deprived of a fair and impartial administrator of the law, as well as a gentleman both charitable and ready to assist in any movement having for its object the welfare of the public. Sincerely we trust that, whatever misfortune his removal may be to us, gain in every way may be the result to him and his respected and accomplished daughters.*[77]

Nothing better counters the negative views and statements about de Boos and his work than two very special presentations made to him in Braidwood in June 1881.[78] Firstly, on June 24, St. John's Day (a special day for Freemasons), he was presented with "a very handsome gold past-masters jewel from the members of the Lodge of Truth and other members of the Masonic order in the district" (Figure 10.5).[79] He had been Worshipful Master of the Lodge for three years, 1878-80, and as in the case of previous

---

75 - *Maitland Mercury*, February 19, 1881, page 4; see also *Australian Town & Country*, February 19, 1881, page 347; *Sydney Morning Herald*, February 17, 1881, page 5

76 - *Sydney Morning Herald*, January 22, 1881, page 5; *Cootamundra Herald*, June 4, 1881, page 2.

77 - *Maitland Mercury*, April 2, 1887, page 16S; *Australian Town and Country Journal*, January 3, 1885, page 24.

78 - For a full account, see Crabb 2015b.

79 - *Sydney Morning Herald*, 30 June 1881, p. 5 (from the *Braidwood Dispatch*). There were two other lodges in the Braidwood district, 'Lodge St John' at Araluen and 'Lodge Peabody' at Major's Creek. "Although there were many Chinese working on the goldfields, not one Chinese name has been found among the membership lists of the three Lodges" (Reynolds 1989).

recipients, the gift was "a token of esteem for his valuable services rendered to the Craft"; in response de Boos "returned thanks in an affectionate and feeling manner".[80] The gift was described as "a splendid work of art … of solid eighteen carat gold" made by W.A. Jeffs of Sydney.[81] The local paper added that the award also recognised "the great services he had rendered … in this district during his residence here". In Temora, "Great satisfaction [was] expressed amongst miners at Warden de Boos' speech as to a warden's duties, at the Braidwood banquet".[82]

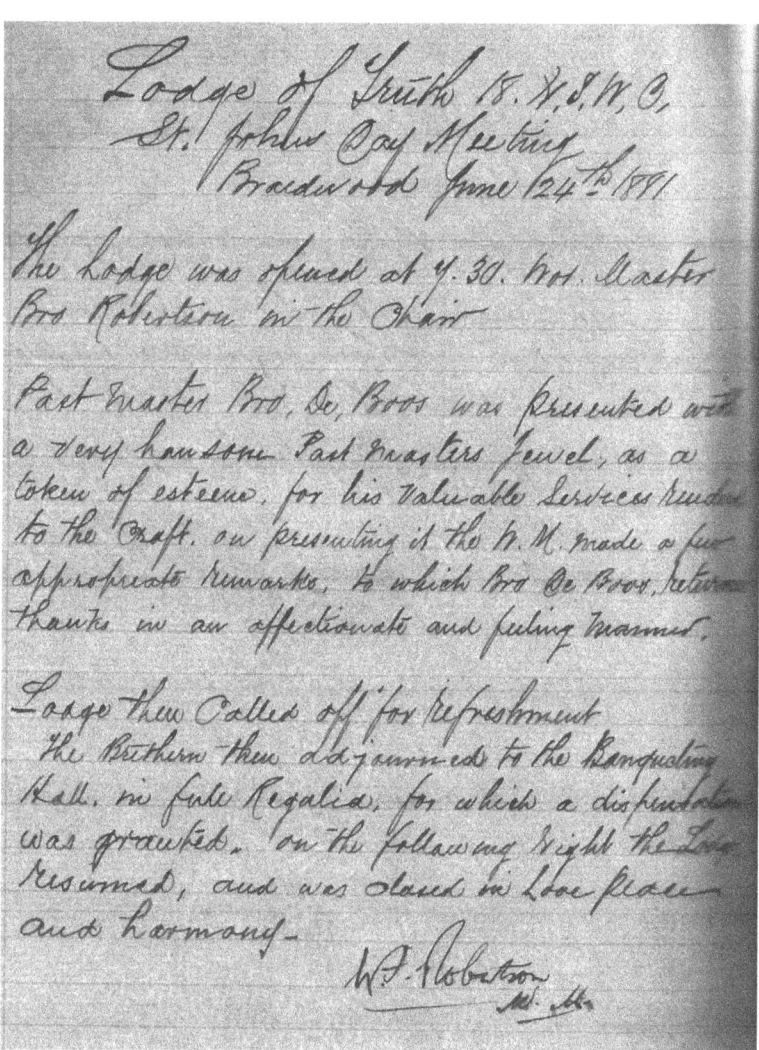

Figure 10.5. "Past Master Bro. De Boos was presented with a very hansom Past Masters Jewel, as a token of esteem, for his valuable services rendered to the Craft. On presenting it the H.M. made a few appropriate remarks, to which Bro De Boos returned thanks in an affectionate and feeling manner". Extract from the Minutes Book for the Meeting of the 'Lodge of Truth, Braidwood, on June 24, 1881, page 287. Courtesy Mr. Doug Edwards, Secretary of the Lodge of Truth, July 11, 2014.

---

80 - Lodge of Truth Minute Book, record of St. Johns Day Meeting, Braidwood, June 24, 1881. *History of the Lodge of Truth, No. 26, Braidwood, U.G.L. of N.S.W., March 1860, to December, 1935.* 10-12. The "Craft" is the whole of Freemasonry, from the local Lodge to the movement worldwide. Access to the records of the Lodge of Truth and other information on the Freemasons, courtesy Mr. Doug Edwards, Secretary of the Lodge of Truth, June 17, 2014, and July 11, 2014.

81 - *Goulburn Evening Penny Post*, June 21, 1881, page 3: from the *Braidwood Dispatch*.

82 - *Sydney Morning Herald*, July 1, 1881, page 6.

During the same visit to Braidwood, de Boos received an even more remarkable gift from the local Chinese community, a gold medal, "a token of their esteem for the very fair and impartial manner in which he always settled their mining disputes while he was warden of the Braidwood district".[83] "The medal is of virgin gold, procured in the locality, and is the work of a Chinese jeweller named Tommy Ah Chong. On one side it bears an inscription in Chinese characters, and on the other side … is English. The latter was engraved by Mr. Hardy of Sydney. The medal is contained in a neat case made of colonial wood, and lined with velvet, the work of Mr. A. Macdonald, of Braidwood" (Figures 10.6a and 10.6b).[84]

Figure 10.6a. The Chinese text on the medal presented to Charles de Boos. The script is read from right to left, and top to bottom: First line: Qing guan min le: [Since you are] such a "Qing guan" (honest and upright official) people are happy; Second line: Zai Buliehuo: in Braidwood; Third line: Tangren jingsong: Present to you by the Chinese with high respect.

The translation is by Dr Tana Li, Director of the Centre for the Study of the Chinese Southern Diaspora, School of Culture, History and Language, ANU, February 4, 2014. The 50 mm diameter medal is now in the collections of Mitchell Library in the State Library of New South Wales. It was donated to the Library in March 1928, by Mrs. Estelle Annie Iredale Holmes, the daughter of Charles Edward's oldest child, Mary Ann Agnes. I am indebted to Megan Atkins and her colleagues at the Library for a personal viewing of the medal and for the photographs, December 15, 2013.

---

83 - *Sydney Morning Herald*, 22 March 1881, p. 5. *Cootamundra Herald*, June 18, 1881, page 4.

84 - *Sydney Morning Herald*, April 23, 1881, page 5; *Sydney Mail*, March 26, 1881, pages 513-514.

Figure 10.6b. The English text on the reverse side of the medal presented to Charles de Boos.

Figure 10.7. Mei Quong Tart. Source: National Library of Australia, Canberra, PIC Box PIC/7193# PIC/7193.

The gift was organised by Mei Quong Tart, a leading member of the Chinese community in the Braidwood district (Figure 10.7).[85] It was made from small pieces of gold contributed by each of the Chinese gold miners in the district.[86] The presentation was made by Thomas Forsythe of Bell's Creek, as Quong Tart was visiting his family in China.[87] In a report of de Boos' funeral, the medal was described as "one of the old gentleman's most treasured possessions".[88]

Conclusion

There is a question that has to be asked. Why, when near the end of his working life, was Charles de Boos sent to Milparinka, probably further from Sydney than any other location for a Colonial Government appointment? Could someone, 'at long last', have achieved 'pay-back'? He had upset more than one politician in his days as a journalist. The far north-west corner of New South Wales was a hard area for gold miners, and it must also have been for the Mining Warden. Then, having the Cobar district added to his responsibilities may well have been just too much, as no more than a few months later, in November 1889, Charles de Boos left his position at Milparinka and ended his employment with the New South Wales Colonial Government.[89] Two official notices stated he had retired,[90] but a later one may have been more accurate as it stated he had resigned.[91]

Charles de Boos had a remarkable career in the service of the New South Wales Government and especially the people of the goldfields. As was very modestly stated in his obituary, "In the discharge of that work Mr. De Boos more than justified the appointment".[92] He may not have had any

---

85 - Lea-Scarlett 1974.

86 - Travers 1981; McGowan 2007; Ellis 1989, 86-89. Quong Tart was not a member of the 'Lodge of Truth'. It appears that he was considered for membership in 1871, but this was withdrawn because of his association with "the irregular Chinese Lodge" at the Chinese diggings at Jembaicumbene (Reynolds 1989). In 1885, Quong Tart was initiated into the 'Lodge of Tranquility' at Bondi, "one of the first people of Chinese descent in the world to be admitted into a Freemason order" (Fitzgerald 2002, 29, 93-97).

87 - In one obituary, it was stated that "Armed with this 'passport' it would have been possible for him to have travelled all over China without molestation" (*The Cumberland Argus and Fruitgrowers Advocate* (Parramatta), November 3, 1900, page 10). As yet, no corroboration has been found for this statement, or of the likelihood of it being correct. Also, this report seems to confuse the two presentations, referring to "a Chinese Masonic medal".

88 - *Sydney Morning Herald*, November 1, 1900, page 7.

89 - *Government Gazette* of November 22, reported in *Sydney Morning Herald*, November 23, 1889, page 14.

90 - *NSW Government Gazette*, 356, July 12, 1889, page 4752; *NSW Government Gazette*, 622, November 22, 1889, page 8327.

91 - *NSW Government Gazette*, 47, January 21, 1890, page 605.

92 - *Sydney Morning Herald*, October 31, 1900, page 7.

official recognition for his almost 15 years of service, but he had received the appreciation of the people on the goldfields, especially the diggers, and that would more than likely have been sufficient for him.

Chapter Eleven

His Family and Retirement

Charles and his wife Sarah had a total of twelve children. At the time of de Boos' retirement in 1889, only six were still alive. Regarding the others, Emily (1861) lived for ten weeks; Henry (1862-1863) for three months; Henrietta (1867) for less than an hour; an un-named daughter was still-born (1869); and Aimee (1871) survived for four weeks. His second daughter, Sarah Susannah (1851-1880), died aged 29 years.[1] His three sons each spent most of their lives beyond Sydney, and despite the difficulties that Charles experienced in Temora, each spent varying periods of time in the town. The three girls made their homes in Sydney. During his retirement, he was able to share in the successes and well-being of his children and their families.

Marie (Mary Ann) (1849-1913)

Being the eldest daughter, Marie (Mary Ann) almost certainly had considerable domestic responsibilities after the death of her mother in 1872. These may have continued after her father left Sydney for Braidwood, looking after her younger siblings.

She married James Woodburn Meikle, on May 8, 1877.[2] An employee of the Colonial Treasury, he died suddenly some twenty years later, collapsing at work from a believed cerebral haemorrhage.[3] Marie died suddenly on May 19, 1913, in North Sydney.[4]

---

1 - *Sydney Morning Herald*, December 28, 1880, page 1. It was not "the residence of her brother", but of her sister and brother-in-law, James Meikle, at 52 John Street, Woollahra. *Sands' Sydney and Suburban Directory for 1880*. J. Sands, Sydney.
2 - *Sydney Morning Herald*, June 7, 1877, page 1.
3 - *Evening News*, December 11, 1897, page 5.
4 - *Sydney Morning Herald*, June 4, 1913, page 12.

Charles Edward, Jr. (1853-1913)

Charles, Jr. moved to Temora with his father and remained there and prospered for some thirty years. He was a Licensed Auctioneer,[5] and from mid-1881, there were regular advertisements in the *Temora Herald*, as well as other newspapers, for auctions by the 'De Boos Brothers' at their rooms in Temora (Figure 11.1).[6] The brother was no doubt William, who likely played a very small role. The business expanded beyond that of share brokers, agents, and auctioneers to include newsagents, stationers, booksellers, and the sale of postage stamps (Figure 11.2).[7] At some date, a second store was established in Wyalong, about 60 km north-west of Temora. In 1894, Charles was joined in partnership by J.J. Peadon, a prominent businessman

DE BOOS BROTHERS,
Auctioneers,
STOCK AND SHARE-BROKERS,
Mining and General Agents,
HOSKINS STREET, TEMORA.

Outside Sales attended to. Returns promptly made. Cash advanced on Goods for absolute sale.

Offices of Shamrock and Eureka Gold-Mining Co., No Liability; and TEMORA HERALD Newspaper Co., Limited. 515

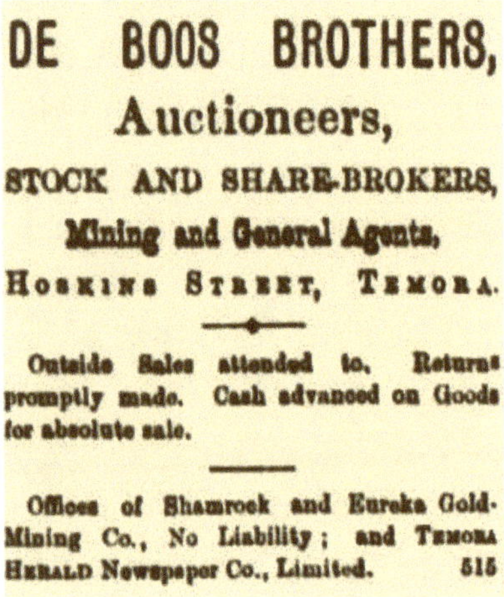

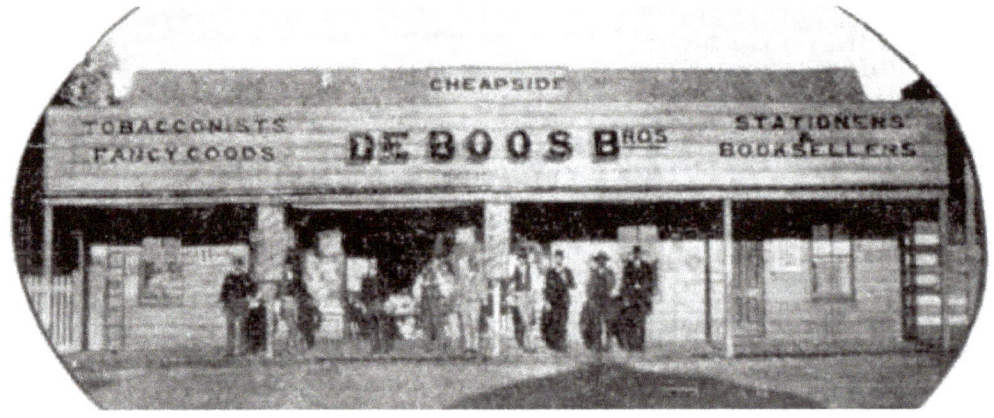

Figure 11.1. Temora Herald, October 27, 1882, page 3.

Figure 11.2. Australian Town and Country Journal, January 7, 1893, page 27.

5 - *NSW Government Gazette*, 187, May 5, 1881, page 2563. Charles de Boos, jnr., licensed auctioneer for the Young district. *Cootamundra Herald*, May 14, 1881, page 2.

6 - *Temora Star*, September 17, 1881, page 3; *Sydney Morning Herald*, March 4, 1882, page 15; *Temora Herald*, January 26, 1883, page 3, and January 30, 1882; January 9, 1883, page 2.

7 - *Referee* (Sydney), March 28, 1894, page 6; *NSW Government Gazette*, 150, March 6, 1888, page 1651; *NSW Government Gazette*, 286, May 8, 1894, page 3005.

in Wagga Wagga (Figure 11.3),⁸ but this lasted for only "a short time".⁹ Prior to early 1900, the business seems to have changed hands, and was soon in the name of another member of the de Boos family, 'M.A. DeBoos' or 'Mrs. DeBoos'. This was Matilda Ann (nee Tremewen), who Charles had married in 1886.

Figure 11.3. Wyalong, 1894: the premises of 'De Boos & Peadon' next to the 'Bank of New South Wales'. Source: Wales Staff News, 11 (4) (1977), page 5.

It is hardly surprising that Charles Jr. became further involved in gold mining, following on from his activities noted in Chapter Eight. He was the Legal Manager of the 'Shamrock & Eureka Tribute Gold Mining Company, No Liability, Temora', of which William was also a shareholder.¹⁰ In 1897, he was a Director of the Temora Deep Lead Gold Mining Co. NL; Francis was the Mine's Legal Manager.¹¹ The display of a large stone in the de

---

8 - *Wagga Wagga Express*, April 12, 1894, page 2; *Wagga Wagga Advertiser*, April 28, 1888, page 3; July 1, 1890, page 2. *Wyalong Star*, May 8, 1894, page 1.

9 - *Wagga Wagga Advertiser*, September 16, 1902, page 2; *Sydney Mail*, September 24, 1902, page 784. Formerly a well-respected man in Wagga Wagga and Wyalong, Peadon moved to Sydney and became a commercial traveler. In 1902, no doubt because of health problems, he attempted to murder his wife and six children; one child escaped, two were killed, his wife and other children were all injured; he committed suicide.

10 - *NSW Government Gazette*, 79, February 24, 1882, page 1070; 175, May 2, 1882, page 2445; 267, July 4, 1882, page 3555; *Temora Star*, July 1, 1882, page 3; *Temora Herald*, November 3, 1882, page 3; January 9, 1883, page 2.

11 - *Index to Surnames in the NSW Record of Mines, 1897*, compiled by John Berry, Woollamia, 2006, Record, page 185.

Boos Brothers store suggests that the business played an important part in Temora's gold mining industry, including placing on display the more than 300 oz. 'Mother Shipton' nugget.[12] He strongly believed there were gold deposits at Temora that could be exploited by deep mining.[13] He was involved in efforts to establish public crushing and cyanide plants,[14] and later in a syndicate to work the Deutscher's Golden Gate claim.[15] In 1908, he stood for election as an alderman on the local council, but was unsuccessful.[16]

Quite apart from his business activities, de Boos Jr. was extremely busy with a variety of activities in the Temora community. He was one of the signatories to a Petition for the establishment of the Municipality of Temora.[17] He was Secretary of the Temora Progress Committee and the Jockey Club, Vice-President of the Temora Cricket Club,[18] and President of the Temora Railway League.[19] In later years, he was appointed a J.P., Magistrate[20], a member and later chairman of the Licensing Court,[21] "coroner at Temora, and for the colony generally",[22] and a member of the Temora and Cootamundra Local Land Board.[23] He was a member of the School of Arts Committee,[24] captain of the Temora Rifle Club,[25] and cricket matches were played between Temora and Bute for the de Boos Cup.[26] He was a very active participant in musical events, being a member of the special choir that gave concerts to celebrate the consecration of the Roman Catholic Church in Temora,[27] and a soloist at a concert in aid of the

---

12 - 'The Mother Shipton' nugget, along with two other nuggets that were originally part of the large one, were found in 1885 in the reef claim of the same name. Reports vary as to the actual weight of the gold, but it was certainly over 300 oz. (www.temoraruralmuseum.com/local-history.php ; Webster 1950, 48-50; *Sydney Mail*, October 24, 1885, page 852; *Sydney Morning Herald*, November 26, 1885, page 9; *Cootamundra Herald*, August 13, 1887, page 4).

13 - 'Letter to the Editor: Testing deep leads': *Sydney Morning Herald*, November 2, 1898, page 4.

14 - *Temora Star*, July 12, 1899, page 2; *Temora Star*, May 27, 1899, page 2; *Wyalong Star*, December 22, 1894, page 3.

15 - *Wyalong Star*, December 19, 1902, page 2.

16 - *Albury Banner*, February 7, 1908, page 46; *Wagga Wagga Advertiser*, February 11, 1908, page 1.

17 - *NSW Government Gazette*, 247, April 20, 1891, page 2993.

18 - *Australian Town and Country Journal*, September 15, 1900, page 52.

19 - *Cootamundra Herald*, May 23, 1885, page 6; December 12, 1885, page 5; September 28, 1887, page 6; August 10, 1887, page 6; June 29, 1889, page 6; June 18, 1898, page 4.

20 - *Wagga Wagga Advertiser*, April 24, 1888, page 2.

21 - *NSW Government Gazette*, 77, February 1, 1895, page 708; *Temora Star*, October 7, 1905, page 4.

22 - *Sydney Morning Herald*, February 4, 1895, page 6.

23 - *NSW Government Gazette*, 585, July 23, 1897, page 5200; *Evening News*, September 10, 1896, page 4.

24 - *Temora Star*, August 3, 1883, page 2; July 30, 1904, page 2.

25 - *Temora Star*, October 27, 1906, page 2.

26 - *Cootamundra Herald*, January 27, 1900, page 3.

27 - *Freeman's Journal*, October 1, 1881, page 11.

Church of England Building Fund (along with his sister Lucille).[28] Like his father, he was a member of 'The Owl Club': of one show, the *Cootamundra Herald* wrote, "always a favourite with the Temora audiences, [he] made a great hit in his comic solo".[29] Following his father, he was a committed Freemason, being master of Lodge Temora.[30] In 1908, he was described as "one of the best known citizens in the town".[31]

Late in 1911, Charles sold his business in Temora, resigned from his numerous activities, was given numerous farewells, and moved to Sydney to live in Burwood.[32] He died on September 1, 1913, aged 59, leaving his wife, Matilda, and their adopted daughter Ethel Lilla Coupland (nee Engstrom).[33] They had no children of their own.

Francis George (1855-1906)

Francis George (Frank), the second son of Charles de Boos, was with him in Braidwood. In 1878, he became assistant postmaster in Tenterfield, where he spent five years.[34] After only a short period of time, he gained very wide publicity as a result of "the falling of the plaster ceiling of the miserable den that is made to do duty for a post office. Fortunately Mr. De Boos had left the office a few minutes before the whole of the ceiling fell down in a mess, causing, as may be imagined, great dirt and confusion".[35] In April 1883, he moved to Millie, a small settlement north of Narrabri, as Post and Telegraph Master.[36] In the same year, he married Mary Larracy of Bungulla, about 7 km south of Tenterfield, though just when and where are not known. They had at least nine children.

Information about Francis is very limited. His first child was born in Millie in 1884,[37] with others born at Narrabri, Tenterfield, and Emmaville (north

---

28 - *Temora Star*, December 31, 1881, page 3.
29 - *Cootamundra Herald*, October 15, 1881, page 3; *Temora Star*, September 24, 1881, page 3; April 7, 1900, page 2.
30 - *Evening News*, June 21, 1898, page 7.
31 - *Wagga Wagga Advertiser*, February 11, 1908, page 1.
32 - *Cootamundra Herald*, October 17, 1911, page 2; *Truth* (Sydney), October 22, 1911, page 10.
33 - *Sydney Morning Herald*, September 2, 1913, page 8; September 4, 1913, page 10; *Cootamundra Herald*, September 9, 1913, page 2; *Wyalong Advocate*, September 6, 1913, page 4.
34 - *Armidale Express*, May 25, 1883, page 3
35 - *Maitland Mercury*, December 5, 1878, page 7. From *Tenterfield Star*, November 30, 1878.
36 - *NSW Government Gazette*, 174, May 1, 1883, page 2290.
37 - *Sydney Morning Herald*, June 25, 1884, page 1.

north-west of Glen Innes) through to 1893. The next information about him is being Post and Telegraph Master at Deepwater (north of Glen Innes) in mid-1894.[38] He was also appointed a deputy registrar under the Electoral Act.[39] In 1895, it seems that he was to be transferred from Deepwater,[40] but less than three weeks later, he resigned from his position as Post and Telegraph Master there.[41] In 1897, his eighth child was born in Temora. In early 1899, he was appointed "Valuator of the rateable property" in the Borough of Temora.[42] He was Poll Clerk and Returning Officer for Municipal Elections.[43] He reportedly worked for a local solicitor for several years. He was appointed secretary of the Temora Masonic Lodge in 1899.[44] Frank died in Temora on January 19, 1906, after a long illness with lung problems.[45] No more than three months later, his eldest son died after a long illness.[46] In 1911, Mary married James Baker, then the Mining Warden in Temora. She died in West Wyalong in 1951.

William Peter (1858-1895)

William spent some time with his father in Braidwood before returning to Sydney to become a solicitor's articled clerk. In September 1881, he applied for and was granted admission as an Attorney, Solicitor and Proctor of the Supreme of Court of New South Wales.[47] He then moved to Temora where he set up his own legal practice. He spent much of his time dealing with cases before the Mining Warden's Court, which often caused controversy (see Chapter Ten). He was the solicitor for a number of local mining and other companies, such as the Temora Quartz Crushing Company.[48]

---

38 - *NSW Government Gazette*, 301, May 14, 1894, page 3150.

39 - *Australasian Star*, May 15, 1894, page 3.

40 - *NSW Government Gazette*, 486, July 20, 1895, page 4733.

41 - *NSW Government Gazette*, 531, August 9, 1895, page 5084; *Daily Telegraph*, August 10, 1895, page 11.

42 - *NSW Government Gazette*, 231, March 21, 1899, page 2325; *Temora Star*, March 22, 1899, page 2.

43 - *Temora Star*, February 10, 1900, page 2.

44 - *Sydney Morning Herald*, June 22, 1899, page 5; *Evening News*, May 21, 1900, page 7; *Evening News*, October 19, 1901, page 7.

45 - "Obituary". *Temora Star*, January 24, 1906, page 3; see also January 27, 1906, page 1 and page 5; *Tenterfield Intercolonial Courier*, February 6, 1906, page 2; *Temora Independent*, January 21, 1906, page 2.

46 - *Temora Star*, April 14, 1906, page 2.

47 - *Maitland Mercury*, September 29, 1881, page 4.

48 - *Temora Star*, February 8, 1882, page 2; May 31, 1882, page 3; September 20, 1882, page 3; July 27, 1883, page 3; *Wagga Wagga Advertiser*, May 12, 1888, page 3.

William married Elizabeth Margaret Williams at Little Billabong, north of Holbrook, on June 28, 1882. She was the daughter of a squatter, and it was a "high life" wedding.[49] Their daughter Maude was born in Temora on July 6, 1883. He participated in the community, being a soloist at a 'Grand Concert in aid of the Church of England Parsonage Funds',[50] and was a complimented gardener.[51] Around August 1884, William left Temora "owing to the failing state of his health", moving to Corowa "where the milder climate [was] more congenial to his constitution".[52] There he set up a legal practice (Figure 11.4). He was elected to the Corowa Progress Committee in late 1884 and became Chairman of Corowa Public School at the beginning of 1885.[53] During this time, their second daughter Lucille was born in Albury in 1885.

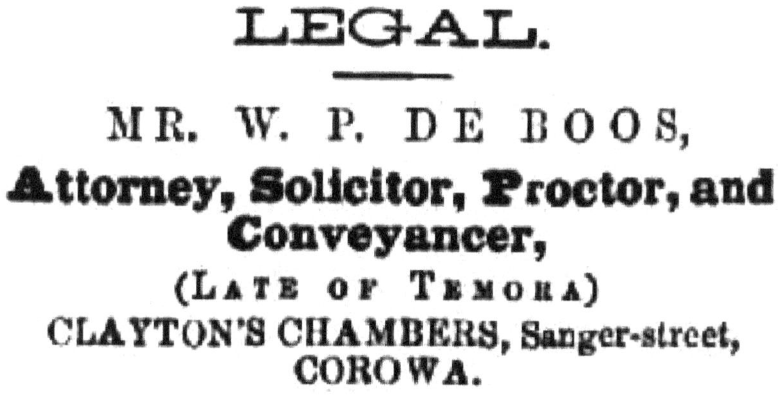

LEGAL.

MR. W. P. DE BOOS,
Attorney, Solicitor, Proctor, and Conveyancer,
(LATE OF TEMORA)
CLAYTON'S CHAMBERS, Sanger-street, COROWA.

Figure 11.4. Albury Banner, August 29, 1884, page 24; Corowa Free Press, April 17, 1885, page 1.

By mid-1886, he was back in Sydney for what seems to have been a limited period, with offices at Stephen Court, 99 Elizabeth Street. Why he returned to Sydney is not known. He was involved in several legal cases, including a bigamy case before the Metropolitan Court and then the Supreme Court.[54] But not everything went well. A case against him for obtaining money and

---

49 - *Evening News*, June 30, 1882, page 2; *Temora Herald*, July 4, 1882, page 2; *Albury Banner*, July 7, 1882, page 22.
50 - *Temora Star*, January 20, 1883, page 3.
51 - *Temora Star*, December 8, 1882, page 2.
52 - *Burrangong Argus*, October 1, 1884, page 2; *Australian Town & Country Journal*, August 16, 1884, page 353.
53 - *Corowa Free Press*, October 3, 1884, page 2; *Sydney Mail*, January 3, 1885, page 21.
54 - *Sydney Morning Herald*, August 6, 1886, page 5; August 28, 1886, page 8; *Sydney Morning Herald*, December 18, 1886, page 10.

goods by false pretences was discharged.[55] In late 1886, he was declared insolvent and his "Household furniture and effects" put up for auction.[56] In the Insolvency Court his liabilities were assessed at £576 12s. 11d., his assets £22 10s.[57]

What happened after that is unknown, but in March-April 1887, a number of advertisements in the *Cootamundra Herald* stated that he would "commence practising in Cootamundra in a few days".[58] However, he did not move to Cootamundra, but to Narrandera.[59] There he continued in business as a very successful solicitor (apart from being charged and acquitted of embezzlement).[60] Among other things, he defended striking shearers in a number of controversial cases in 1890.[61] At some stage, he contracted phthisis (tuberculosis) and became too ill to continue working. He died on July 15, 1895. An obituary stated that "as a lawyer, he displayed a good deal of acumen, and was recognised by members of his profession as a gentleman of undoubted ability, and sound judgement".[62]

Lucille Grace (1864-1938)

Considerable musical abilities made Lucille perhaps the most well-known of Charles' children. These talents had been recognised early, with her performances in Temora and Copeland.

In Sydney, she was taught by W.G. Broadhurst,[63] who was an extremely active and well-known musician, organist, conductor, and teacher, in both church and secular circles.[64] (He was occasionally termed a 'Professor of Music'.) Lucille became a singing and music teacher (Figure 11.5), and an increasingly well-known vocalist. She was clearly in much demand as a

---

55 - *Evening News*, July 12, 1886, page 3.
56 - *NSW Government Gazette*, 683, November 30, 1886, page 8249; *NSW Government Gazette*, 710, December 14, 1886, page 8563.
57 - *Sydney Daily Telegraph*, November 19, 1886, page 3.
58 - *Cootamundra Herald*, March 16, 1887, page 5.
59 - *Wagga Wagga Advertiser*, March 17, 1888, page 2; *Narrandera Argus*, July 16, 1895, page 2.
60 - *Wagga Wagga Express*, January 19, 1895, page 4; January 24, 1895, page 2; *Narrandera Argus*, January 29, 1895, page 2.
61 - *Wagga Wagga Express*, September 30, 1890, page 3; *Wagga Wagga Advertiser*, October 4, 1890, page 4; *Daily Telegraph*, September 30, 1890, page 5; October 4, 1890, page 6.
62 - *Narrandera Argus*, July 16, 1895, page 2.
63 - *Wagga Wagga Advertiser*, October 1, 1887, page 2.
64 - *Sydney Morning Herald*, January 4, 1879, page 11.

soloist, taking part in many kinds of concerts in various parts of Sydney, as reported in the City's papers from 1884 through to 1892.[65] She must have spent some time in Narrandera with William and his family, as she sang at a few functions there.[66] At one of the concerts, her performance was described as "the gem of the evening".[67]

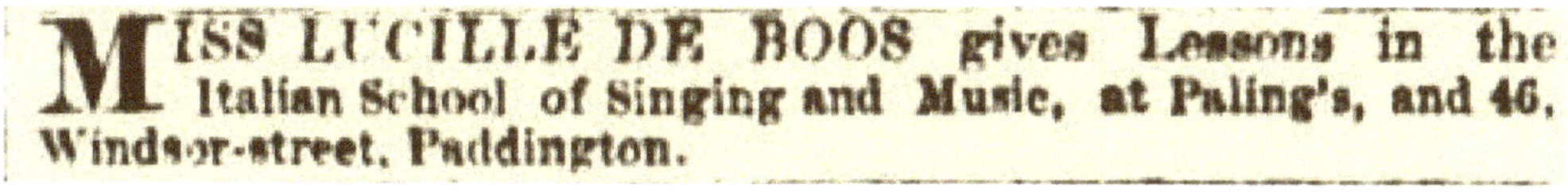

> MISS LUCILLE DE BOOS gives Lessons in the Italian School of Singing and Music, at Paling's, and 46, Windsor-street, Paddington.

Figure 11.5. Sydney Morning Herald, September 12, 1885, page 3.

Of particular interest was her participation in concerts in Wagga Wagga in September 1887 in connection with the opening of the new St. Michael's Church, along with its new organ.[68] The organist was W.G. Broadhurst, who had moved to Wagga Wagga in early 1881, initially as organist at St John's Church.[69] Lucille returned in January 1888 to sing at the farewell concert for Broadhurst marking his move to Melbourne.[70] She went to Wagga Wagga again in late 1889 to sing at a concert in aid of St Michael's Church building funds.[71]

On March 21, 1892, Lucille married Edward Henry Oxnard Smith, jun., son of E.H.O. Smith, of Sunderland, England, at Holy Trinity Church, Dulwich Hill.[72] Unfortunately, following her marriage, she seems to have done very little singing.

---

65 - For example, *Sydney Morning Herald*, September 4, 1884, page 9; *Cumberland Mercury* (Parramatta), October 4, 1884, page 5; *Evening News*, May 25, 1885, page 6; July 2, 1885, page 5; *Sydney Mail*, July 11, 1885, page 9; *Australian Town and Country Journal*, July 25, 1885, page 186; *Cumberland Mercury*, August 1, 1885, page 3; August 24, 1885, page 7; September 3, 1885, page 7; *Sydney Morning Herald*, September 12, 1885, page 3; *Daily Telegraph*, September 29, 1885, page 6; *Australian Town & Country Journal*, October 3, 1885, page 706; *Sydney Morning Herald*, January 23, 1889, page 7; *Sydney Morning Herald*, August 16, 1889, page 8; *Sydney Morning Herald*, March 26, 1890, page 5; *Daily Telegraph*, November 29, 1890, page 6; *Evening News*, June 27, 1891, page 6.

66 - For example, *Australian Town and Country Journal*, March 28, 1891, page 16; April 11, 1891, page 16; May 23, 1891, page 16; August 8, 1891, page 17.

67 - *Evening News*, March 26, 1891, page 5.

68 - *Wagga Wagga Advertiser*, September 27, 1887, page 3; October 1, 1887, page 2; October 6, 1887, page 3; October 8, 1887, page 2; *Freeman's Journal*, October 8, 1887, page 15; *Sydney Morning Herald*, September 30, 1887, page 8; *Australian Town & Country Journal*, August 8, 1887, page 276.

69 - *Australian Town & Country Journal*, February 26, 1881, pages 397 and 423.

70 - *Wagga Wagga Advertiser*, January 5, 1888, page 3; January 7, 1888, page 3.

71 - *Wagga Wagga Advertiser*, November 12, 1889, page 3; *Sydney Mail*, November 23, 1889, page 1177.

72 - *Sydney Morning Herald*, April 7, 1892, page 1.

Estelle Evangeline (1866-1939)

Estelle was Charles' youngest daughter. On August 22, 1894, she married Charles Watson, at Nethermains, Bronte, the residence of her sister, Mary Ann, and brother-in-law, James Meikle.[73] Prior to her marriage, she worked in the Government Sheriff's Office. Living in the northern Sydney suburb of Ryde, in a house no doubt appropriately named "Congewoi" (after some of Charles' satirical writings, see Chapter Twelve), she and her husband provided a home for her father during the last years of his life. She died on February 21, 1939. At the time of her death, she and her husband were living in Epping.[74]

Retirement

At the end of 1889, de Boos returned to Sydney, where he spent the rest of his life. Initially, he lived at 65 Paddington Street, Paddington, and from 1891 through to at least 1893, he lived in his own house, named 'Gartz', in Eltham Street, Petersham, no doubt with his youngest daughters, Lucille and Estelle.[75]

For a short time at least, he turned his attention to politics. He was listed as a 'Ministerialist' ('free-trader') candidate for the electorate of Gloucester at the 1891 New South Wales elections, along with three other candidates, W.M. Rue, R.A. Price and J.S. Hart.[76] However, only Price and Hart were nominated, and the seat was won by Hart.[77]

de Boos continued to be actively involved in the Freemasons (Figure 11.6). His name is one of over 900 included in a 'List of Notable and Famous Australian Freemasons' compiled by Lodge Devotion 723 in Melbourne.[78] In earlier years, he had been a member of the Cambrian Lodge in Sydney, the Lodge of Truth in Braidwood, the Temora Lodge, and in retirement,

---

73 - *Evening News,* August 24, 1894, page 3; *Daily Telegraph.* September 1. 1894, page 10.
74 - *Sydney Morning Herald,* February 22, 1939, pages 14 and 13.
75 - *Sand's Sydney and New South Wales Directory 1890.* Sands & Co., Sydney; 1891, page 345; 1892, page 375; 1893, page 395. There is no record of him in the 1894 issue.
76 - *Daily Telegraph,* June 6, 1891, page 6; June 10, 1891, page 6; *Sydney Mail,* June 13, 1891, page 1316; *Sydney Morning Herald,* June 22, 1891, page 6; June 25, 1891, page 6.
77 - *Sydney Morning Herald,* June 29, 1891, page 6.
78 - www.lodgedevotion.net/devotionnews/famous-australian-freemasons/large-list-of-notable-and -famous-freemasons, accessed June 9, 2017.

a member of the New Brunswick Lodge in Ryde, with the designation of P.G.S.W. (Past Grand Senior Warden). On February 3, 1892, he was one of a number of masons from Sydney at "The ceremony of consecration and dedication of the Masonic Lodge Jersey, No. 204, and the installation of officers" at Peak Hill, south-west of Dubbo.[79] Later in the year, he was present at the laying of the Foundation Stone of Christ Church Cathedral in Newcastle, also participating in a special Masonic ceremony that preceded the Cathedral ceremony.[80] In the same month, he represented the New Brunswick Lodge at a large Masonic gathering for the installation of the Governor, the Earl of Jersey, as a Grand Master.[81]

Figure 11.6. Charles de Boos in his Freemason's regalia. Source: The Sydney Mail, November 10, 1900, page 1108.

Charles de Boos died on October 30, 1900, from "senile decay" and "cardiac failure" after being unwell for over a year (Figure 11.7). At the time of his

---

79 - *Sydney Morning Herald*, February 6, 1892, page 10; *Sydney Mail*, February 13, 1892, page 385.
80 - *Sydney Morning Herald*, June 3, 1892, page 5; *Daily Telegraph*, June 3, 1892, page 5.
81 - *Evening News*, June 29, 1892, page 3; *Evening News*, June 29, 1892, page 3.

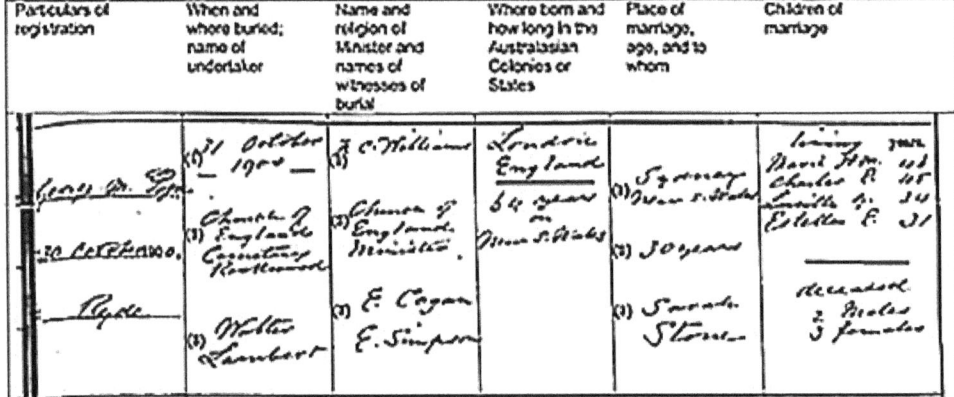

Figure 11.7. Death Certificate for Charles de Boos. His father was not a "wholesale jeweller", though his stepfather was.

death, he was the senior member of the press in Sydney.[82] There was a long obituary in the *Sydney Morning Herald*,[83] and shorter ones appeared in many other newspapers.[84] He was buried in the Anglican section of the Rookwood Cemetery, in a plot next to where his wife Sarah and daughter Sarah Susannah were buried (Figure 11.8).[85] Of the "Many old friends [who] forwarded letters and telegrams of sympathy", Quong Tart was the only person mentioned by name.[86]

Figure 11.8. Grave Plots of Charles and Sarah de Boos at Rookwood Cemetery, Sydney. Nothing remains of the headstone on Charles' grave. Photograph by Shirley Drury, c. mid-1990s. Care of the headstones is a family responsibility and Sarah's has deteriorated significantly. Personal communication, Leona Robinson, Client Services Manager, Rookwood Cemetery, April 3, 2022; personal visit April 18, 2022.

---

82 - *Albury Banner*, January 25, 1901, page 29.

83 - *Sydney Morning Herald*, October 31, 1900, page 7.

84 - *Evening News*, October 31, 1900, page 4; *Temora Star*, October 31, 1900, page 2; *Daily Telegraph*, October 31, 1900, page 6; *Australian Star*, November 1, 1900, page 6; *Grafton Argus*, November 2, 1900, page 2; *Glen Innes Examiner*, November 2, 1900, page 2; *Temora Star*, November 3, 1900, page 2; *Queanbeyan Age*, November 3, 1900, page 2; *Cumberland Argus* (Parramatta), November 3, 1900, page 10; *Australian Town and Country Journal*, November 10, 1900, page 41; The reports of his death and funeral in the *Sydney Morning Herald* were reprinted in the *Euroa Advertiser* (November 23, 1900, page 3), but there was no indication that he was related to the de Boos family in Euroa (see Appendix 3.1).

85 - *Sydney Morning Herald*, October 31, 1900, page 1 and 12; November 1, 1900, page 7.

86 - *Sydney Morning Herald*, November 1, 1900, page 7.

Chapter Twelve

The Writings of Charles de Boos

Mid-nineteenth century colonial Australia was a much more literate society than many would imagine today. "Indeed, colonial Australians – including, remarkably, those who arrived as convicts – had significantly higher literacy rates than the general British population".[1] Contemporary newspapers provide clear evidence of this, not just papers such as *The Argus* in Melbourne and the *Sydney Morning Herald*, but also many of the country ones, some of which "attained a 'literary-ness' and quality unimaginable today".[2] They were more than the major sources of news. Through their advertisements, they were important means of communication. They were also the major source of recreational reading of all kinds, including fiction, satire, humour, and poetry.

The readership for recreational writing was large, and for most people the newspapers were their only source. They were less expensive than books, more readily available and there were few lending libraries, certainly beyond the major cities. Some eighty per cent of Australian colonial newspapers contained some kind of Australian and overseas fiction. There was clear demand for Australian stories. Much was syndicated nationally, individual stories being printed in large numbers of papers, especially the non-metropolitan ones.[3] "Writing in 1882, Richard Twopenny described Australia as 'the land of Newspapers' and estimated the colonial per capita purchase of newspapers to be five times that in Britain".[4] Until relatively recently, much of this was unknown, essentially due to the massive size of the newspapers archive. However, the continued growth of the National Library of Australia's 'Australian Newspaper Digitisation Program' and the availability of the digitised newspapers through the Library's 'Trove' website has made exploration of the archive possible.[5]

---

1 - Bode 2018.
2 - Stewart 1988.
3 - Bode 2017; Webby 2003; Webby 2009a.
4 - Bode 2018, 63.
5 - nla.gov.au/australian-newspaper-plan ; nla.gov.au/Australian-newspaper-digitization-program/ . The work is by no means complete, but its continued existence and development is at the mercy of inadequate federal government funding.

With the creation of this massive resource, a major project initiated by Bode is investigating the fiction content of this archive. 'To be continued … The Australian Newspaper Fiction Database', has estimated that between 1865 and 1914, more than 21,000 forgotten novels, novellas and short stories were published in Australian newspapers.[6]

Much of the material was unattributed, even when the newspaper owners and editors knew the authors' names. This was certainly true of journalists, who were important contributors to the recreational reading contained in newspapers. In the view of Stewart, "literary Australia was largely journalists' Australia".[7] Journalism provided the writers with an income, and in the absence of any significant local book publishing, the newspapers were the outlets for their other work. The weeklies that were gradually added to the 'dailies', contained much larger literary sections, providing a place for the longer serialised stories. These included the *Australian Town and Country Journal* (companion to Sydney's *The Evening News*), the *Australasian* (companion to the Melbourne *Argus*), and *The Leader* (companion to *The Age*). To these were added the periodicals, such as *The Australian Journal*.[8]

From the time de Boos joined John Fairfax & Sons in 1856 through to the mid 1870s, his output of written work was prodigious. Beyond his reporting, it was a remarkably productive period, in which he made use of his experiences as a reporter and the material he collected. His primary outlet was the *Sydney Morning Herald* and, from July 7, 1860, *The Sydney Mail*, the weekly publication of the Fairfax company (much of it condensed from the *Herald*), and much later *The Echo*.[9] As with other writers, very few of de Boos' writings had his name on them. He used several pseudonyms: John Smith, Pleeseman A., Redde Pepper, Peter Pick, and Theodore Aurelius Midge.[10] And these may not be all of them. His literary writings that can be clearly identified are discussed in this chapter. Those that may be his work will have to await further study and textual analysis for clear determination

---

6 - Bode 2018; 2017; 2016; 2012; Bode and Hetherington 2014. For the results of Bode's ongoing research, see cdhrdatasys.anu.edu.au/tobecontinued/

7 - Stewart 1988; numerous journalists are mentioned, but not de Boos.

8 - Webby 1981.

9 - Walker 1976, 71.

10 - Crittenden 1996a. There may be others.

(see 'Other Possible Works' at the end of the chapter). Then there are no doubt still other writings that have yet to be found.

Satire

In the 1860s, political satire became an important contributor to the newspapers of New South Wales, from conservative, liberal and radical viewpoints. For de Boos, reporting debates in the New South Wales Parliament provided him with the material for two long-running satirical columns, the writings of 'Mr. John Smith, of Congewoi Farm' and 'The Collective Wisdom of New South Wales'.

John Smith and Congewoi (1862-1870)

The first of the satirical columns appeared in the *Sydney Morning Herald* in 1862. Based on the activities of the Legislative Assembly, they were written under the pseudonym of 'Mr. John Smith of Congewoi Farm', or Congewoi, on the Lower Hawkesbury. They "described the doings of parliament and the politicians in a primitive form of 'Strine' [Australian slang]" and were a popular form of 'Hansard'.[11] 'Mr. John Smith' was a not-so-young farmer, who had spent his whole life on a farm, which in his younger days, more often than not took priority over school.

> *Look here, Mr. Editor, I sint much of a hand at writing, and it comes more natural to me to use a hoe than a pen, but when I've got anything to say perhaps I can say it as well as another. I'm no chicken now, and when I was a youngster there wasn't so much learning and that sort of thing knocking about then as there is now. All I learnt was picked up at a sixpenny school by bits at a time, and then I had to walk seven miles into Windsor to get even that. Well, it aint the same now, I reckon; but in them days every soul on a farm had to earn his tucker, and no mistake, and if too young to handle the hoe, or drive bullocks we had to herd pigs. The old man, that's my old man, had a pretty tidyish lot of grunters, and thought a deal more about them than he did of his kids, as he used to call us, and so long as his pigs had their bellies full it didn't matter much to him how empty our heads were left. But, law, what fun we used to have. That's Jem and me – Jem's me brother. We were only little bits of chaps- about so high – and it used to take two of us to manage the unruly varmints. They hadn't much of a chance with us, for me and Jem could both use a stockwhip or a bullockwhip then just as well as we can now, and I am open to make a bet that I will kill a fly on a bullock, with a sixteen-foot lash at the first offer.[12]*

---

11 - Holt 1972.
12 - *Sydney Mail*, February 15, 1862, page 1.

As John Hirst commented, at this time there was little respect for the Colonial Parliament and its members; it was no longer "a place that [people] should be able to respect. ... Rich and educated people now regarded politicians as a bunch of incompetents".[13] They became the butt of satirical writing, not least from de Boos. The first series, entitled 'Men who *Have* been Raised', was published in *The Sydney Mail* and the *Sydney Morning Herald* in 1862 (Appendix 12.1). Others followed: a short series of 'Letters from Congewoi' later in 1862 (Appendix 12.2) and occasional individual letters, such as an address to the 'Congewoi Young Men's Association'.[14] A series of letters from Congewoi started in *The Sydney Mail* in 1865, under the heading 'The Congewoi Chesterfield; or Letters to Young Men on First Hanging Out on their Own Hook, by Mr. John Smith' (Appendix 12.3). Numerous other letters, as short series and individually, appeared in the *Herald* and the *Mail* in 1868 through to late 1870 (Appendices 12.4, 12.5 and 12.6). Some of the articles were reprinted in other newspapers, such as the *Queanbeyan Age* and the *Launceston Examiner*.

Mr. John Smith's columns were a frequently unflattering commentary on the government, politicians, and public life of the day. Much of their humour derived from "Smith's uneducated dialect and comic misspellings" (Figure 12.1).[15] They got the 'anonymous' writer and the *Herald* into trouble more than once, not least because virtually all parliamentary members received a mention, usually by name. In one Assembly debate, the writer was described, among other things, as a 'downright liar', a 'hireling", and a 'ruffian'.[16] "There was a legend that Sir John Robertson once attended at the office of the 'Herald' with a huge horse-whip to flog 'John Smith' if he could find him".[17] Not surprisingly, the identity of 'Mr. John Smith' was a matter of much speculation, with comments as to whether or not it was Charles de Boos or one of several other possible writers.[18] By late 1866, the author's identity was known, and as one newspaper observed, the Congewoi letters were "a species of composition in which his [de Boos] *forte* lies".[19]

---

13 - Hirst 2002.

14 - *The Sydney Mail*, April 19, 1862, page 5; *Sydney Morning Herald*, April 22, 1862, page 3; *Sydney Morning Herald*, November 20, 1863, page 5; November 23, 1863, page 3.

15 - Wilde, Hooton and Andrews 1994, page 182.

16 - *Sydney Morning Herald*, August 28,1867, page 2; September 2, 1867, page 5.

17 - "Notes and Notions" by Quilp. *National Advocate* (Bathurst), November 1, 1900, page 2; *Daily Telegraph*, October 31, 1900, page 6.

18 - *Maitland Mercury*, December 11, 1862, page 3; *Bell's Life of Sydney*, September 29, 1866, page 4.

19 - *Maitland Mercury*, September 18, 1866, page 2.

> Now we've got a new Parliment and a hole loter new men in it, and so, thinks I, peeple 'll like to know sumthing about 'em; specially them as havn't showed up much in public afore. I've left the Parliment chaps alone a long while now: ever since I pulled 'em up a bit about being raised up like mushrooms on the free selection scot. That doj is pretty well worked out now, and the hon. Jack has pretty well used up all his free selection credit with the people by this time. But, my word, it was a stunning good cry in its time; and what staggers me is that the hon. Jack actually went to the country—that's what they call the general election, but why, I can't make out, seeing as the hon. Jack didn't go to the country at all, but was elected in town—Charley Cowper went to the country, but then that was only because they wouldn't have him in town—but the hon. Jack went to the country without some free something or other to sing out about, and to bamboozle the electors over. I fancy, if I'd been in his plase I'der had a free something as doz put the comether on some of 'em. There's ony two trees as he's used up—that's free selection and free trade, and there must be a deal more on 'em if they was only looked up a bit. Praps the poor chap was bothered a bit about other things, and hadn't time to hunt up the other frees, or else you'der been sure to have had him pitching one on'em forward to blow about.

Figure 12.1. 'Mr. John Smith visits the Assembly'. Sydney Mail, February 5, 1870, page 9.

Figure 12.2. Sydney Morning Herald, August 27, 1874, page 6.

> IN THE PRESS,
> and will be published about the 30th August,
> THE CONGEWOI CORRESPONDENCE,
> being the Letters of
> Mr. JOHN SMITH
> on various subjects—political and otherwise; edited by
> CHAS. DE BOOS.
> Price 10s.   As only a limited number of copies has been printed early application will be necessary.
> E. R. COLE, Publisher, King and George streets.

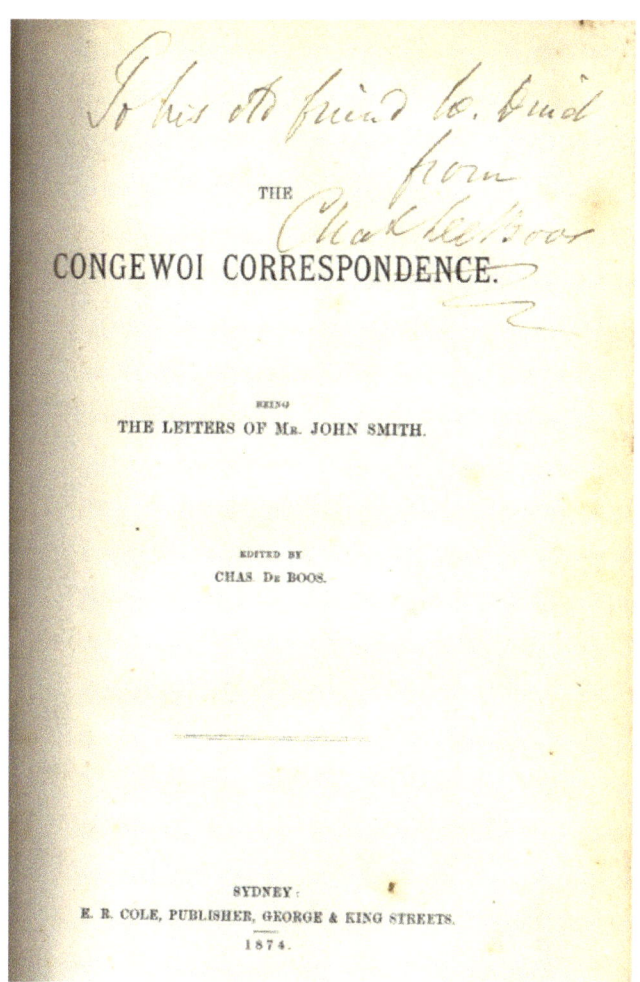

Figure 12.3. The title page of The Congewoi Correspondence, with the author' signature. Copy courtesy Paul Waite, whose late wife Kay was a descendant of Charles de Boos.

In 1874, a selection 'John Smith's' letters was published in book form, *The Congewoi Correspondence*, edited by Charles de Boos (Figures 12.2 and 12.3). The publication attracted numerous reviews.[20] They were more than favourable! de Boos

> *was just the man to take stock of this lot, and he did it with a keen, cutting, truthful force and humour, which at once secured him the ear of the public, and the intense hatred of his 'subjects'. There is no denying the striking likeness of most of Mr. Smith's Parliamentary portraits to the illustrious originals, and just as little the skill with which, having cut out the particular beast "spotted" for the occasion, the sturdy old bushman handled his stockwhip.*
>
> *Though much of the individual interest of these graphic sketches may have faded with the mushroom celebrities whom they helped to fame, yet their literary colour and strong honest sense are as sound as ever. In our political mob there will always, we are afraid, be a certain proportion of "scrubbers" and "crawlers", "runts" and "warrigals"; and so long as this unfortunate state of things exists, so long may this clever little volume be safely recommended as an admirable manual for constituencies.*[21]

There was a long review in the *Sydney Morning Herald*.[22]

> *The Congewoi letters were some years ago published periodically in this journal, and then attracted considerable attention. The writer, having now collected and added some little finish to them, which, in the hurry of their previous composition was probably wanting, presents the whole to the public in a book-form as a compilation. ...*

The review concluded,

> *Mr. Smith is an intelligent and sarcastic observer of human nature as developed in the arena of politic; but although his letters are, as has been seen, devoted to a pretty unshrinking exposé of the weaknesses of public men, there is interwoven with them such a genial flow of gossip about country life, illustrated by characteristic stories, that this book must be interesting to all.*

It has been suggested that possible 'models' for Smith are Sam Slick, a Nova Scotian character created in 1835 by the Canadian writer Thomas Haliburton (1796-1865), and the 1860s American frontier humorist-philosopher 'Artemus Ward', an "illiterate rube with Yankee common sense" created by the American stand-up comedian Charles Farrer Browne (1834-1867).[23] But did de Boos need a 'model'? He clearly had more than

---

20 - *Sydney Morning Herald*, November 5, 1874, page 6; *Illustrated Sydney News*, October 17, 1874, page 19.
21 - *Australian Town and Country Journal*, October 17, 1874, page 608.
22 - *Sydney Morning Herald*, November 11, 1874, page 6.
23 - Wilde, Hooton and Andrews 1994, 182; Cogswell 1976; Haliburton 1836; Browne 1862, 1865; https://en.wikipedia.org/wiki/Charles_Farrer_Browne .

enough inspiration from his subject matter and ample time to hear and observe their activities. The situation was surely ready-made for him.

Before the above series were written, several articles were published in 1861 and 1862 that may well be the work of de Boos. All have the colonial parliament and its members as their subject matter.[24] One was written under the pseudonym, 'Auditor',[25] as well as two poems by 'Pleeseman A'.[26] Another pseudonym appeared in 1864 with a series of letters to the Editor of *The Sydney Mail* with the title **"The Midge Correspondence"** (1863-64). They provided a satirical look at government through the eyes of Theodore Aurelius Midge, a clerk in the 'Circumlocution Office'. As the titles of the individual letters indicate, they cover a variety of topics and grievances (Appendix 12.7). At the end of 1863-early 1864, letters to the *Sydney Morning Herald* by 'Lexilogus' (another pseudonym) provided a prospectus of his forthcoming book, 'The Manual of Parliamentary Slang; or, Vituperative Vade-mecum'. It was "dedicated (without permission) to the Honorable Slang-wangers of the Legislative Assembly".[27]

The Collective Wisdom of New South Wales: I see a Stranger in the House (1867-1871)

If Mr John Smith and the Congewoi correspondence caused de Boos problems with the politicians of the day, 'The Collective Wisdom of New South Wales: I see a stranger in the House', created even more. There were five series, published in the *Herald* and *Mail* (Appendix 12.8). Based on the proceedings of the NSW Parliament, they spared few members of the House, individually and collectively. He was often unimpressed with the proceedings as a whole:

> *If the House continues to move on the same dosey, dreamy kind of way as that in which it has been going for the last fortnight, I shall be driven in sheer desperation to throw down my pen, for my subjects threaten to die out from absolute inanition, having already become fearfully attenuated from the continued absence of mental pabulum.*[28]

---

24 - "Mr. John Lucas out of his calmer moments. A scene in the Assembly, April 5th", *The Sydney Mail*, April 13, 1861, page 3; "A Specimen of the Legislative Assembly Reports", *The Sydney Mail*, February 8, 1862, page 3; *Sydney Morning Herald*, February 6, 1862, page 4.

25 - "Random Recollections of a Debate" by "Auditor", *Sydney Morning Herald*, April 16, 1861, page 2.

26 - "The Opening of Parliament": *The Sydney Mail*, May 31, 1862, page 5; "The Opening of Parliament" by Pleeseman A 99, Poet Laureate to the N.S.W.G.F.F. *Sydney Morning Herald*, June 3, 1862, page 3. "The Volunteer Review": *The Sydney Mail*, July 5, 1862, page 5; *Sydney Morning Herald*, July 7, 1862, page 2.

27 - *Sydney Morning Herald*, December 12, 1863, page 8; December 29, 1863, page 8; December 31, 1863, page 8; January 4, 1864, page 5; January 15, 1864, page 5; *The Sydney Mail*, January 9, 1864, page 7; *Goulburn Herald*, January 6, 1864, page 3.

28 - *Sydney Morning Herald*, August 19, 1867, page 5.

If such collective comment was not enough, individuals were identified by name. By way of illustration, the following are some of his observations about William Forster.

> Mr. Forster, who never lets slip a chance of saying something sarcastic or damaging whenever the chance is given him and who is utterly careless as to which side of the House his allusion injures.
>
> Mr. Forster has established for himself a reputation for wordy pugnacity, and is now beginning to gather the fruits that are sure to be borne by so dangerous a character. He is so persistently and so universally captious, that there is hardly a member of the House to whom he has not administered a verbal dig in the ribs. None are too high, as none are too low, to be secure from this gentleman's sarcasm, rendered all the more pungent and striking, and all the more forcible from the peculiarly quiet and innocent manner in which the words are uttered. He has now come to be generally regarded as the Ishmael of the House, whose tongue is against every man in the House, as every man's tongue is against him.
>
> Forster has snarled and snapped, but then he does this so regularly, that it may almost be regarded as his chronic state.
>
> Mr. Forster, in his usual cynical manner ...
>
> Mr. Forster... lost his temper... that innate spirit of opposition that forms part of his idiosyncrasy.
>
> Mr. Forster will say all the most excruciatingly bitter things which an imagination rich in sarcasm can furnish.[29]

As observed in Chapter Ten, it is perhaps no wonder that fifteen years on, such comments came back to bite de Boos.

But Forster was not the only member with complaints about the articles and their writer. Some of these resulted in an Adjournment debate in the Legislative Assembly on August 27, 1867, moved by James Hart. He claimed to have been misrepresented, and there were scathing comments about de Boos: "Absolute falsehoods were told"; "this hireling"; "The lies of this ruffian were so palpable"; and "the writer of the article ... was so contemptable". However, not everyone was uncharitable. For John Stewart, "As far as his recollection served him the circumstance took place as the writer represented it". In the opinion of Daniel Egan, "the whole conduct of the Press with regard to the House during the last fourteen years had

---

29 - *Sydney Morning Herald*, July 22, 1867, page 5; August 5, 1867, page 5; August 19, 1867, page 5; December 9, 1867, page 5; November 18, 1867, page 5; December 2, 1867, page 5.

been most charitable. The question was put and negatived".[30] de Boos responded, in part:

> *I ought to feel exceedingly proud, for I have had the honour of a special debate devoted to me exclusively. I must, however, admit that the procedure was not so much a debate, as an opportunity that was given to hon. gentlemen who had grievances against me to abuse a luckless wight [sic] who had no chance of answering them. It must be confessed that I have somewhat nettled certain honourable members by telling the truth of them, thereby stinging them all the more. Truth, we know, is always harder to bear than aught else, so that a travestie [sic] of tenfold virulence would pass without remark, whilst the plain, unvarnished fact would enrage beyond measure.*[31]

But there was more criticism later.[32]

The satirical writings of de Boos are of more than passing interest. The writer of his Obituary observed:

> *A striking tribute to his writings is that even those of them which were written on ephemeral subjects, and which had politicians now forgotten as their heroes, may now be read with interest. The men are dead, and the writer is now dead, and the subjects, then of absorbing moment, have fallen into the waters of oblivion; but the humour of the sketches survives, and the good workmanship appreciated by the Herald readers of years ago will appeal to all judges of style in literature today".*[33]

Much later, a biographer commented,

> *After a century his weekly column, 'The Collective Wisdom of New South Wales' in 1867-71, still brings to life a host of politicians and well-known figures, for his quick ear caught many exchanges omitted in the official reports.*[34]

Social and political commentary

'Random Notes from a Wandering Reporter' (see Chapter Seven) contained much social and political commentary, particularly in relation to the goldfields. de Boos wrote of the living and social conditions, especially for women and children; alcohol abuse and violence; Aborigines; Chinese miners; and bushrangers. As indicated earlier, with respect to the treatment of women, Aborigines, and the Chinese, his views were ahead of the times.

---

30 - *Sydney Morning Herald*, August 28, 1867, page 2.
31 - *Sydney Morning Herald*, September 2, 1867, page 5.
32 - Critical letters relating to the above series to the Editor of the *Sydney Morning Herald*: February 23, 1870, page 5; March 26, 1870, page 7.
33 - *Sydney Morning Herald,* October 31, 1900, page 7.
34 - Holt 1972.

The Poor Man (1864)

The major work of social commentary by de Boos was *The Poor Man*, or to give it its full title, *The Poor Man: being some account of the extraordinary Adventures met with, of the Strange Sights seen, and of the curious Things Heard, by Mr. Redde Pepper, in his Search after that much injured Individual*, was written under the pseudonym, Redde Pepper.[35] It was serialised in *The Sydney Mail* and the *Sydney Morning Herald* (Appendix 12.9). Central to the story is 'free selection'. As discussed in Chapter Seven, the Lands Acts and their outcomes gave rise to significant controversies; '*The Poor Man*' complements what de Boos wrote in some of his 'Random Notes'.

The story is told by the fictitious Mr. Redde Pepper, "a wealthy Sydney landowner who, because he sympathises with the poor man, supports the liberals' arguments that the poor man should own and cultivate land".[36] He travelled widely in New South Wales in search of 'the poor man', "to take him in situ, and to show him to the world as he really is. I would visit him in his home ... and would narrate his wrongs, his grievances, and his doleful position, in terms that should draw tears even from the hard-hearted citizens of Sydney".[37] He went as far as to say, that he was "determined" to find "this poor man", or he "would perish in the attempt".[38] But he could find no support for his sympathies.

> *The satire ridicules Mr Pepper's liberal sentiments as naïve. Indeed, even the free selectors whom Pepper meets dismiss the liberals' arguments as foolish errors. As a result, the satire purports to reflect the free selectors' agreement with the conservatives' position on the land law. The satire contributed to conservative political discourse, which asserted that the working classes not only were harmed by legislative attempts to turn them into property owners but also would benefit if their property was repossessed.*[39]
>
> *At the end of some eighteen instalments, that had taken Mr Pepper from country lanes, to free settlers' cottages, to the back streets of Sydney, and finally to Darlinghurst gaol, the poor man remained ultimately elusive or rather, as the satire was intended to highlight illusory.*[40]

---

35 - This work has been the subject of considerable analysis by two academic lawyers, Nancy Wright and Anthony Buck (Buck 1996; Wright 2005a, 2005b; Wright and Buck 1998, 2001), including a full reprint with an extended introduction (much of it repetition of material from their earlier publications) (Buck and Wright 2005). There is no mention of de Boos on the cover or title page, and it is not until page twelve of the 24-page introduction that his name is mentioned. See also Atkinson 2006.

36 - Buck and Wright 2005, 13.

37 - *The Sydney Mail*, March 19, 1864, page 3.

38 - *The Sydney Mail*, March 12, 1864, page 9.

39 - Buck and Wright 2005, 13-14.

40 - Buck and Wright 2005, 11.

As well as its concern for the land issue, property and property law, *The Poor Man* covered other contemporary issues: "His descriptions of rural and city life, his encounters with the working classes and embattled settlers provide … insight into the values and shared assumptions of mid-nineteenth century colonial society".[41] Further, *The Poor Man* has been described as "a marvellous exposition of conservative attitudes to the social transformation brought about by the gold rush and manhood suffrage".[42] The "social transformation" of New South Wales and Victoria was more than well known to de Boos.[43]

> *His descriptions of rural and city life, his encounters with the working classes and embattled settlers provide not only insight into the values and shared assumptions of mid-nineteenth century colonial society but also an exposition of conservative attitudes to the social transformation caused by manhood suffrage.*[44]

Twenty-five years later, in a short article about Sir John Hay, de Boos continued his attack on the Robertson Land Acts. He wrote that Hay

> *advocated Free Selection after Survey, and carried it against the Free Selection before Survey, of the Robertson Land Bill, and the bill was thrown out, the result being a dissolution of Parliament, a new election in a fit of Free Selection madness – and the passing of the Robertson Land law as soon as the House met – almost without discussion. Since then the Land law of the colony has been nothing but a source of heart-burning and strife. Amendment after amendment has been made, only driving matters from bad to worse, until now both selectors and squatters are discontented and almost defiant.*[45]

In 1865, two short series of articles, under two more pseudonyms, appeared in *The Sydney Mail*. The first was **"The Corncobs: a History of a Colonial Family, gathered from their own Correspondence"** (1865) (Appendix 12.10). The articles were letters written by 'Julia Corncob', 'John Corncob', 'Robert Corncob', 'William Corncob', and others in response to their letters. Though in many respects fiction, the series gave expression to various social issues, including women's property and other rights.[46] In

---

41 - Buck and Wright 2005, 11-12.

42 - Publisher's publicity note, Australian Scholarly Publishing. www.scholarly.info/book/193 , accessed March 10, 2016.

43 - A favourable review of de Boos' *Fifty Years Ago* (see Chapter 13) was not so complimentary about some of his other writings and stated that "*The Poor Man* did not interest its readers" (*Bell's Life in Sydney*, September 29, 1866, page 4). This was not entirely true, as the letter to the Editor by 'Cayenne' titled 'The Veritable Poor Man' makes clear (*Sydney Morning Herald*, June 25, 1864, page 6).

44 - Buck and Wright 2005, 11-12; Gollan 1960, 32.

45 - de Boos 1889.

46 - Wright (2005b) suggests that "Circumstances similar to those involved in *Davis v. Crispe* are the basis of the plot of *The Corncobs*" (*Sydney Morning Herald*, June 8, 1835, page 2).

1871, an advertisement appeared for a new 'Sensation Drama' at the Prince of Wales Opera House in Sydney called "Foiled: or, Australia Twenty Years Ago" by Walter H. Cooper. It stated that part of the drama was "suggested to the author by the story entitled 'The Corncobs', written by Mr. Charles de Boos, and published in the Sydney Mail".[47] The other series was **"Mr. Shortsight's Journeyings. (Showing many extraordinary things which may happen to a man in the bush.)"** (1865). The introduction is about the *Herald* and himself, Jonas Shortsight, as he sets out in support of 'Free Selection' and in opposition to the views of the *Herald*. He writes of his travels, his accommodation, and recounts stories told to him by the people he met in central west New South Wales (Appendix 12.11).

Fiction: in the Bush and on the Goldfields

Up to the mid-1860s, the fictional writings of de Boos were set in the bush of pre-gold rush New South Wales. For these, he drew on his personal knowledge and experiences of the country and country people. His major work, *Fifty Years Ago* (1866), set primarily in the lower Hunter Valley, merits separate consideration (see Chapter Thirteen). After this, almost all of his writings were set in the goldfields of Victoria and especially New South Wales.

The Stockman's Daughter (1856)

The Stockman's Daughter tells of a property owner, his son, bushrangers (one with no redeeming features, the other a 'gentleman'), an Aborigine, the stockman (with a mysterious background), and the stockman's daughter (a young lady who was determined to clear her father's name). The story is set in the Bungendore-Lake George area (near present-day Canberra); other places are fictional. As for the hotel in Bungendore, the present Lake George Hotel was originally called the Harp Inn when it opened in 1838 and is one of the oldest continuously licenced pubs in NSW.[48] Knowledge of the novel's setting had obviously been acquired some years earlier during his travels through the area in the 1840s. The relatively short novel may also

---

47 - *Sydney Morning Herald*, April 24, 1871, page 8.
48 - Davenport et al. 1990.

have owed something to the story of the bushranger Jacky Jacky's activities in the Bungendore area in the early 1840s.[49]

"*The Stockman's Daughter* is a bushranging story which anticipates many of the later themes and stock situations and characters in colonial fiction".[50] Henry Kingsley's *The Fortunes of Geoffrey Hamlyn* is sometimes "regarded as the beginning of Australian literature",[51] but *The Stockman's Daughter* was much earlier, certainly the early chapters de Boos published in his Melbourne newspaper, *The Telegraph* in 1855 (see Chapter Six), while Boldrewood's *Robbery Under Arms* did not appear in *The Sydney Mail* until 1882-83. For Crittenden, "In many ways *The Stockman's Daughter* is a more interesting tale than *Geoffrey Hamlyn* and truer to life in the outback of Australia".[52] The full serialisation of *The Stockman's Daughter* appeared in *The People's Advocate and New South Wales Vindicator* between September 6 and November 1, 1856 (Appendix 12.12).[53] There was not much in the way of literary work in the *Advocate*, and the serialisation of the story was something of an exception.[54] The story was in effect 'lost' until its chance rediscovery by Victor Crittenden, well before the digitization of newspapers, and republished by him in 2009.

Mr. Pick, the Gold Miner (1867)

'Mr. Pick, the Gold Miner' was the first of de Boos' fictional writings to be set in the goldfields of NSW and Victoria. The stories of gold mining and gold miners are told by an old digger, Peter Pick, and written as "Letters" serialised in *The Sydney Mail* and the *Sydney Morning Herald* (Appendix 12.13). There is a significant autobiographical element to the stories (Figure 12.4).

---

49 - Two reports of the same event are very different: *Australasian Chronicle*, January 19, 1841, page 3; *Sydney Herald*, January 20, 1841, page 2.
50 - Wilde, Hooton and Andrews 1994, page 226; Watson 2012, 144-145.
51 - Crittenden 2009a; Crittenden 2009b.
52 - Crittenden 2009a; Kingsley 1859.
53 - In the Fisher Rare Book Collection of the University of Sydney Library, there is a very old paste-up of the *Advocate* article, with some hand-written corrections. Unfortunately, the provenance of this item is not known and the same applies to the person who made the corrections (personal communication, Sarah Hilder, Fisher Rare Book Collection, May 30, 2013).
54 - There was some poetry in almost every issue, including the twenty-part serialisation of Charles Harpur's extended work, 'Songs, Epigrams, Notes, and Opinions, & c.'. *The People's Advocate*, April 4, 1856, to December 20, 1856.

> That's one of my experiences, and I'll give you some more of 'em as I go on, besides telling you a bit or two of what I've seen at different places, and describing some of the coves I've met with. Rare rum characters I have come across at times, people of all sorts, miners, squatters, squatters' men and officials, swagmen and bagmen, loafers, cross coves, and highwaymen, I've seen a little of all of 'em, and if I can only keep myself at it, as I mean to do at present, though there's no knowing how long I may continue in the same humour, I'll see if I can't hit out a few sketches for you, to let the people of Sydney know what the life of a digger really is, and that it's a deal besides gold that he gets, and that when he makes a haul he generally has to pay pretty dear for it.
> Your obedient servant,
> PETER PICK.

Figure 12.4. The conclusion to Peter Pick's first letter. Sydney Mail, May 11, 1867, page 3.

Mark Brown's Wife: a tale of the goldfields (1871)

Mark Brown's Wife: a tale of the goldfields was serialised in *The Sydney Mail* (Appendix 12.14) and republished as a "new Story" in *The Echo* in 1887.[55] In 1892, it appeared again, serialised in six instalments in *The Australian Journal*, under the title, *In the Early Fifties: a story of Australian life*.[56] It was stated to have been "Published by special arrangement with the Author", though there was no indication as to just what that meant. It was republished in book form in 1992.[57]

Set in 1854, de Boos portrays gold-rush Melbourne and the shanty Canvas Town (see Chapter Six) and the brutality of life on the early Victorian goldfields, with the story ending in Forbes and the Lachlan diggings in NSW.[58] The following account of the story is taken from Kate Watson's *Women Writing Crime Fiction*.

> This is a very violent story and the criminal impetus and content arises from Ruggy Dick, the villain, and his actions. Mark Brown's wife, [the beautiful] Ciceley Drake, is made a fallen woman as a consequence of Dick's deliberate miscommunication of information. Dick intercepts Mark's letters to Cicely, and then anonymously and deceptively informs Cicely that her husband, Mark, is dead. This information leads her

---

55 - The *Echo* was a Fairfax evening paper, published from May 1, 1875, to July 22, 1893 (Walker 1976, 76-77; Souter 1981, 591-594).

56 - *The Australian Journal*, Vol. XXVII, 321 (February), 291-296; 322 (March), 349-355; 323 (April), 407-413; 324 (May), 465-472; 325 (June), 523-528; 326 (July), 581-588.

57 - de Boos 1992.

58 - The Victorian goldfields also provided the setting for another early Australian novel, *The Queen of the South*, by George Isaacs under the pen-name, 'A. Pendragon' (1858). Isaacs was on the Victorian goldfields in the early 1850s. It is not known if he ever met Charles de Boos, but before he left London, Isaacs knew Charles' younger brother, the solicitor Thomas de Boos. Based on a letter from Harry Rogers to George Isaacs, dated July 25, 1848, in the State Library of South Australia. The two were friends with Thomas in London. Information kindly provided by Anne Black, University of Adelaide, July 19, 2013.

> to be seduced by and bear the illegitimate child of 'the Master' in whose house she was working. To add to this list of insults and unfortunate incidents imposed upon Cicely, she is then murdered by Dick. A similar fate awaits Mark: Dick shoots Mark through the shoulder, breaks his jaw, then strips his body and places it on top of an ant bed. ...
>
> *Mark Brown's Wife* features a detective figure – a miner and friend of Mark Brown, who is called Tom Drewe, and who for the most part retrospectively narrates the tale. ... Tom sounds authentically Australian in his use of colloquial language, but he also instils the values of 'mateship'. ... Tom's painstaking detective work is contrasted to the corrupt and incompetent police. He mixes detecting modes by employing the methods of an indigenous tracker at the diggings to find Job Hicks and his dog. Tom's final confrontation with Dick is indicative of the retributive capacity of the Australian land itself; in attempting to escape, Dick falls down a shaft concealed by dry bushes. ... As Dick's death is not instantaneous, the land punishes and tortures him for his crimes.[59]

Wright and Buck suggest that *Mark Brown's Wife* was based on the 1870 New South Wales Gold Fields Royal Commission.[60] This is unlikely for at least two reasons. Firstly, de Boos knew enough about Melbourne and the Victorian and New South Wales goldfields from his own experience; secondly, it seems unlikely that Wright and Buck were aware of de Boos' earlier and extensive work on the goldfields at the time of their publication.

With a background in law, Wright brings her own interpretations to the writings of de Boos. But can she be so sure that various legal issues were the prime focus of some of his writings? She rightly points out that de Boos was more than just a storyteller, stating that he was "unique among writers of popular literature in colonial Australia because he wrote about property law in a wide variety of fiction and nonfiction genres". de Boos "incorporates in the novel two topical issues about property law: married women's property and goldfield regulations. Rather than writing a conventional narrative about men's adventures on the goldfields, de Boos divides the novel between the life experiences of a husband and wife".[61] Wright also notes that he emphasised the fact that wives and widows "shared with indigenous people one characteristic: they were citizens without enforceable property rights". *Mark Brown's Wife* "realistically represents the poverty and dislocation suffered by wives during the gold rush. In the novel, de Boos also allegorically signifies the erosion of married women's legal rights, the loss of which repeatedly makes Cicely 'vanish' from the sight of officers of the law, both judges and the police".[62]

---

59 - Watson 2012, 145-146; Wright 2005b; Crittenden 1992.
60 - Wright and Buck 1999; Gold Fields Royal Commission of Inquiry 1871.
61 - Wright 2005b.
62 - Wright 2005b.

The Secret of the Old Shaft (1889)

Not long before he retired, advertisements appeared in the *Sydney Morning Herald* for a new story, *The Secret of the Old Shaft*, that was serialised in *The Echo*. It was described as 'A New Sensational Australian Tale' (Appendix 12.15).[63] It appeared again in *The Australian Journal* in 1893, this time under the title *The Mystery of Big Oakey*.[64] The *Journal* stated: "The proprietors of the Australian Journal take pleasure in announcing that they have purchased the rights of publication of an Original Serial Story of Australian Life and Character, entitled 'The Mystery of Big Oakey' by Chas. De Boos".

Set in the Turon Valley in the early 1850s, Tom Brown finds a murdered digger at the bottom of an old mine shaft. The inquest determines it was accident, but Tom and his mate discover otherwise when they bury the person. In a complicated story, Tom helps determine that the victim was Reginald Dollington. His identity had been taken by his cousin, 'The Count', who was subsequently charged with the murder, only to commit suicide in gaol. Tom returns to England having gained a large estate and marries his long-time sweetheart.[65]

Me and My Horse (1889)

Me and my Horse; showing How I got Him, How I kept Him, and all about Him was published in *The Echo* in 1889, after de Boos had retired (Appendix 12.16). In several advertisements, it was described as 'A Story for Christmas Week'.[66] Written in colloquial language, it is a sketch about life on the Peel River goldfields in northern NSW. Crittenden describes it as "a comic novelette very much in the later *Bulletin* style. It tells the story of how the narrator, a young gold miner, acquires the horse [which had fallen down a mine shaft]. The first part is a funny story in itself. It continues with the various situations in which his horse involves him. ... It has stories on how the horse lost him a sweetheart and how he gained a wife and concludes with how he lost the horse and how he found him again".[67]

---

63 - *Sydney Morning Herald*, September 3, 1889, page 6.
64 - *The Australian Journal*, 1893. Vol. XXVIII, Part 333 (February), 291-296; Part 334 (March), 349-354; 335 (April), 407-412; 336 (May), 465-470; 337 (June), 523-529; 338 (July), 613-617; 339 (August), 657-662; Vol. XXIX, 340 (September), 31-33.
65 - www-austlit-edu-au.rp.nla.au/page/C487777
66 - For example, *Sydney Morning Herald*, December 12, 1889, page 10; *The Echo*, December 14, 1889, 23, 28. It was published in book form in 2004 (de Boos 2004).
67 - Crittenden 2004.

Other writings

In the early 1860s, several serialised stories were published in *The Sydney Mail* and the *Herald* that had nothing to do with his work for the Fairfax company. They covered a variety of topics. The first was **"My Holiday" (1861)** (Appendix 12.17).[68] The story told of a walk de Boos did with two friends, Nat and Tom, and 'Spanker' the dog, from Manly to Palm Beach and Barrenjoey. It gave him a welcome break from the Colony's Parliament and politics. The articles provide a descriptive account of the areas through which they walked, now suburban Sydney that is now vastly different.

He wrote a few Aboriginal legends. Though published not long after "My Holiday", at least parts of **"The Yo-Yo: a legend of the Lachlan district" (1861-62)** were written much earlier (see Chapter Five), making them some of de Boos' earliest writings, and before *The Stockman's Daughter* (Appendix 12.18). In an 'Author's Preface' to the story, he wrote:

> *The first four chapters of this sketch, - for it is but little more, - were written some fifteen years ago, and were intended, as then plotted, for a romance of a much more pretentious character than the one now completed. It was based upon one of the most interesting of the aboriginal legends, - one very generally pervading the native tribes of the Lachlan district; and also upon the then very prevalent belief existing amongst the old government hands of the colony, that gold had been found, and was to be found in some parts of the interior. When the gold discovery did take place, the author mentioned the tale he had plotted to several friends, at whose request it was then finished, but in a less extensive form than at first projected. Though somewhat crude and incomplete, such as it is, it is submitted to the reader, with a full trust in his forbearance and indulgence.*[69]

Another Aboriginal story was **"Moruya, the Black Eagle of Colo" (1862)**. According to de Boos, this was to be the first of a series of "Tales" or "the wild legends of Barranjuee" (Appendix 12.19), but no others have been found. In a short Preface, de Boos wrote,

> *A few weeks of rest enable me to redeem the promise I made to the readers of 'My Holiday' that at some future date I would relate to them some of the wild legends of Barranjuee. How far it may be interesting it is not of course for its author to say; but I trust the same indulgence that was shown to my previous writings will be extended to the one I now present to the readers of the Sydney Mail.*[70]

---

68 - It was republished in book form in 1991 as *My Holiday and other Early Travels from Manly to Palm Beach 1861* (Jennings 1991). It was also reprinted in the *Pittwater Online News*, Issue 144, 5-11 January 2014: www.pittwateronlinenews.com/my-holiday-by-charles-de-boos-1861.php .
69 - *Sydney Morning Herald*, November 29, 1861, page 8.
70 - *The Sydney Mail*, May 17, 1862, page 2.

However, he did write another 'legend' in 1871. At the end of his third series of 'Random Notes' (see Chapter Seven), de Boos recounts a visit to the Blue Mountains near Blackheath. His descriptions of the scenery and vegetation are superb, and what he sees has a real impact on him. With a guide, he makes his way to Govett's Leap. He wonders about the name, and in response his guide tells him **"The Legend of Govett's Leap" (1871)** (Appendix 7.6). At the end, de Boos confessed that the story was just fiction: "the plain matter of fact [is that] truth was kept back, in order that your readers might better enjoy the fiction".[71]

In December 1865, there were advertisements in the *Sydney Morning Herald* for the Christmas Supplement in *The Sydney Mail* of December 23, 1865 (Figure 12.5).[72] Heaton indicated that some or all of the **"Christmas Stories"** were the work of de Boos.[73] Nine of the stories appear to have been reprinted in one of the *Mail*'s Christmas Supplements in 1866 (Appendix 12.20). Three were reprinted much later in *The Albury Banner*. In response to a reader's enquiry, the Editor stated that they were the work of de Boos.[74]

As noted above, shortly before his departure from the New South Wales public service in 1889 and for a few years into his retirement, de Boos returned to his writing.[75] Two other stories are known. **"A reminiscence" (1891)**, set in the Lake George-Gundaroo area is about a bushranger named Charlie Curran, some of his unlawful activities, and his arrest.[76] In 1892, **"The Squatter's Dream"** was published in the *Manaro Mercury*.[77] It is the story of a young Englishman, Gerard Temple, set up on a station in south-west Queensland by his wealthy grandfather. After seven years on the station, his health restored, he has a strange dream. A sudden call to return to England, provides a real life and death story that parallels the dream, ending with the death of a very unpleasant usurper.

---

71 - *Sydney Morning Herald,* March 25, 1871, pages 5 and 6.

72 - Unfortunately, the Supplement and other pages from this issue are missing. They are not included in the microfilm copy held by the National Library of Australia or the digital copy on the Library's website.

73 - Heaton 1879; *Windsor & Richmond Gazette*, July 20, 1889, page 1.

74 - *Albury Banner*, March 18, 1881, page 23; April 1. 1881, page 20; April 8, 1881, page 20; April 15, 1881, page 20; May 6, 1881, page 13.

75 - de Boos 1889; "The portrait is rather a better one than usual", *Sydney Morning Herald*, March 29, 1889, page 5.

76 - *Australasian Pastoralists' Review*, September 15, 1891, pp. 242-243; *Goulburn Herald*, October 16, 1891, page 3; *The Hay Standard*, October 28, 1891, page 2

77 - *Manaro Mercury*, April 16, 1892, page 2.

> THE SYDNEY MAIL of THIS DAY (Saturday)
> CONTAINS:
> AN EXTRA CHRISTMAS SUPPLEMENT,
> Comprising Original and Selected Articles of Entertaining and Instructive Literature, as follows:—
> Christmas
> Christmas in the Bush
> Australian Ghosts
> The Spectre on the Stairs
> Fisher's Ghost
> The Australian Banshee
> The Lady with the Lantern
> Treated as one of the Family
> Rambles for Christmas Flowers
> Christmas in Sydney and the Suburbs
> Story of Reynard the Fox
> The White Silk Bonnet.

Figure 12.5. Sydney Morning Herald, December 23, 1865, page 12.

Other possible work

It is impossible to be certain that all of Charles de Boos' writings for the Fairfax company, as well as other publications, have been identified. There are numerous writings that may or may not be his work; some of those that may be his are listed in Appendix 12.21, but none can be confirmed. To positively identify any that are his work would require considerable detailed textual analysis.

Conclusion

All of the writings outlined above were in addition to the main work de Boos was employed to do, namely reporting on the NSW Colonial Parliament and undertaking his numerous travels to report for the *Herald*. They constitute a remarkable achievement and library.

Chapter Thirteen

A Special Publication: Fifty Years Ago: an Australian tale

1866 marked a major publishing event in the life of de Boos. In August of that year, the first of numerous advertisements appeared in the *Sydney Morning Herald* and other newspapers for his novel, *Fifty Years Ago, an Australian tale*. It was also an advertisement that named him as the author of several well-known but previously anonymous writings (Figure 13.1).

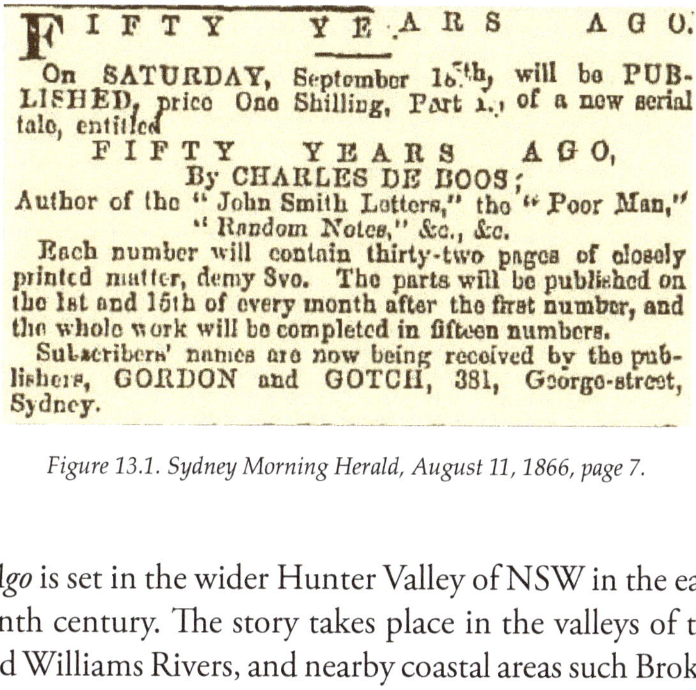

FIFTY YEARS AGO.

On SATURDAY, September 15th, will be PUBLISHED, price One Shilling, Part 1., of a new serial tale, entitled

FIFTY YEARS AGO,
By CHARLES DE BOOS;
Author of the "John Smith Letters," the "Poor Man," "Random Notes," &c., &c.

Each number will contain thirty-two pages of closely printed matter, demy 8vo. The parts will be published on the 1st and 15th of every month after the first number, and the whole work will be completed in fifteen numbers.

Subscribers' names are now being received by the publishers, GORDON and GOTCH, 381, George-street, Sydney.

Figure 13.1. Sydney Morning Herald, August 11, 1866, page 7.

Fifty Years Ago is set in the wider Hunter Valley of NSW in the early years of the nineteenth century. The story takes place in the valleys of the Hunter, Paterson and Williams Rivers, and nearby coastal areas such Broken Bay and Port Stephens; there is also mention of Newcastle, Sydney, and Wallis Plains (Figure 13.2). The "small settlement on the southern bank of the Hunter, a little below its confluence with the Williams", with "a public house, a small store, and a blacksmith's shed, beside one or two huts in close proximity", and "a constable" (page 176), is no doubt what is now Raymond Terrace.[1] Other locations, for example, Myrtle Creek (page 66), Bald Rock (page

1 - Page numbers are taken from the 1999 Mulini Press edition of *Fifty Years Ago* (see below).

81), Mt Pleasant Homestead (page 239), Blue Gum Flat (page 282), and Big Swamp (page 300), are almost certainly fictitious.[2] The same is true of the names of the Aboriginal tribes, Gurrubull, Turrubull, Port Stephens and Manning River (page 220), and Colo (page 278). On the other hand, the general descriptions of the rivers and the natural vegetation, such as the cedar forests somewhere on the banks of the Williams River (pages 148-149) and areas of coastal scrub (page 145) and swamplands (page 300), could not be more vivid.

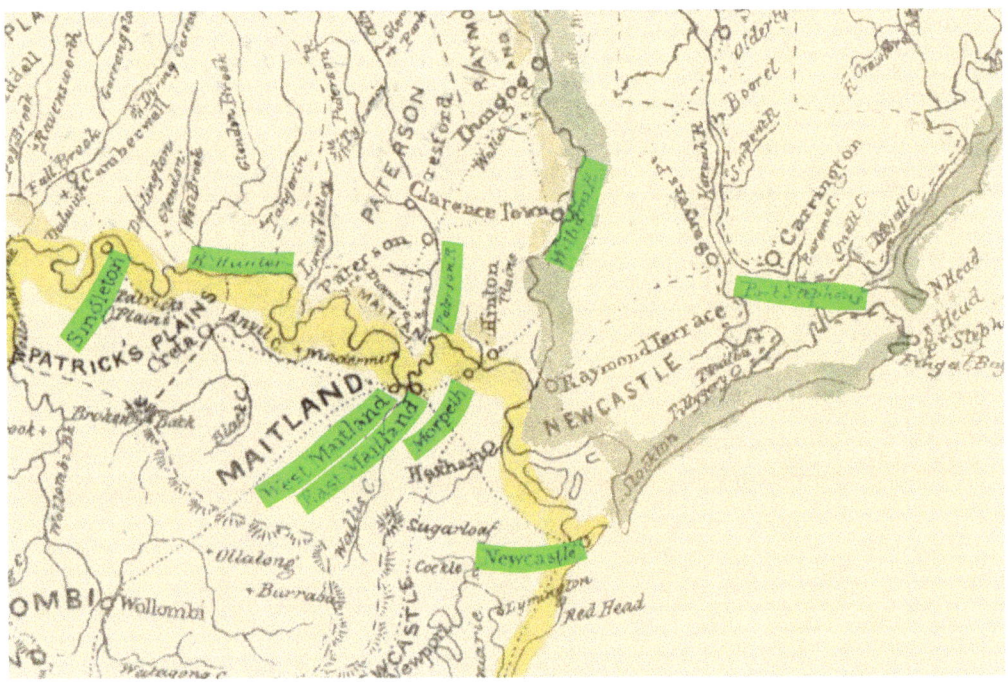

Figure 13.2. Combined excerpts from contemporary maps of the Counties of Durham, Gloucester, and Northumberland. Source: Wells 1848, between pages 158-159, 182-183, and 324-325. Original maps by J. Allan, Lithographer, 2 Hunter Street, Sydney.

The story

Fifty Years Ago is a story of early settlers and Aborigines, of murder, revenge, retribution and finally redemption. It is divided into four parts or books, each with a story of its own, but the main story and the characters involved are developed throughout all four parts.[3]

---

2 - In spite of extensive searches, real places with these names have not been found.

3 - Healy 1972.

Book 1, The Oath. While George Maxwell, the settler and central character of the story, is away looking after his sheep, his wife and two daughters are massacred, and his son left for dead by a group of Aborigines from the Maroo tribe, the chieftains, Macomo, Atara and Opara. On finding his family dead and rescuing his half-buried but still alive son Jamie, George and his brain-injured son swear vengeance on the killers and determine to hunt them down. On the anniversary of the killing, they would kill one of the three Aborigines, cut off his hand and nail it to a tree. They become Aboriginal haters. Early in the search, aided by their "miraculously-gifted dog, Blucher",[4] they are joined by Eumerella, most of whose tribe, including her brother, had been wiped out by the Maroo, after which Opara made her his wife. She was also seeking revenge. With her help, George finds the three Aborigines, warns them of their fate, and then lets them go.

Book 2, The First Black Hand. The location of much of Book 2 is Alexander Morrison's flour mill at Myrtle Creek, near its confluence with the Paterson River. With the help of George and Jamie, Eumerella plots the death of the Maroo tribe in their abortive attack on the mill. At the time of the second anniversary, almost the entire Maroo tribe was massacred, but the three sought by George and Jamie survive. Subsequently, Opara is found and killed on the first anniversary. At his lonely grave, "nailed to the rude cross that formed its headpiece, [was] a black right hand yet dripping blood" (page 147).

Book 3, The Second Black Hand. Set in the forests on the banks of the Williams River, Book 3 tells the story of the murder of a Negro cedar-cutter, Black Harry, by his then mate Ironbark Jack, and Jack's attempt to pin the blame on Atare. However, with the help of George and Jamie, the authorities release Atare and Jack is found guilty. But then they go after Atare, track him down and kill him, and Jamie cuts off his right hand and nails it to a tree. George, however, is beginning to seek forgiveness (page 232).

---

4 - *The Age*, September 21, 1867, page 5.

Book 4, The Third Black Hand. The search for the third victim, Macomo, the last of the Maroo, continues, but in the longest of the four books, the story does not go to plan. There is much activity. Numerous characters are introduced, including a so-called 'Pleasant Party' of bushrangers, led by Lanty, with an escaped convict and Gentleman Jack (who tells George of the unholy vow that destroyed his life), and a squatter and his family (at Mount Pleasant on the edge of Wallis Plains), with whom Macomo seeks refuge and warns them of the nearby bushrangers. By way of another sub-story, Macomo had met Coolamie from another tribe, and she became his devoted wife. She helps Gentleman Jack escape, but is killed by a bushranger's bullet meant for Jamie. By then Jamie had developed what Healy describes as a "maniacal obsession", but was eventually speared, mutilated, and killed by another Aboriginal tribe. George, however, near despair, comes to regret his oath and hatred in the face of Macomo's suffering, and the humanity and nobility that gradually emerge. He comes to a new understanding of the Aborigines. At the same time, through his contact with the white squatter and his family and his relationship with Coolamie, Macomo comes

> to appreciate the full measure of suffering involved for George in the original massacre. Macomo and George are eventually reconciled over the grave of the victims and a pact of humanity is performed between black and white. It is both shattered and consummated, however, at the same moment when Macomo is killed by a bushranger's bullet meant for George.[5]

What had initially been a rational decision for vengeance, could no longer be sustained. Macomo twice saved George's life, and Aborigines helped George bring the bushrangers to justice. "George recognises Macomo's deep regret for his original crime as repentance, and, he says, 'repentance should be crowned with forgiveness'".[6]

> The reconciliation between the two of them is symbolised, appropriately enough, by a handshake, rather than the severed hands of the earlier sections, and by the tears that George is finally able to shed. For Macomo's part, his loss of Coolamie has finally enabled him to arrive at the one element of humanity in which he was still lacking, to understand the pain that his original outrage had inflicted on George.[7]

Alone in his old age, George eventually finds redemption (Figure 13.3).

---

5 - Healy 1972.
6 - Hamer 1989.
7 - Clancy 1999a.

Figure 13.3. One of A.J. Fisher's drawings: The Reconciliation at the Grave, Jamie, George, and Macomo. Source: de Boos 1999, last page.

This is the briefest of summaries.[8] There are many sub-plots and numerous other characters, white, Aboriginal, and even an American Negro. There are stories of changing relationships, between black and white, between different white groups, between different Aboriginal tribes, between coloured and white, and coloured and Aboriginal. They are stories of changing societies and their interactions in very early colonial New South Wales, set among the cleared lands of the settlers, the timber cutters, and the natural bush and forested lands.

Its publication

Unusually for the time, *Fifty Years Ago* did not appear first as a newspaper serial, but as a series of fifteen pamphlets, or rather signatures, from September 15, 1866, to July 29, 1867 (Appendix 13.1). The cover was the same for each issue, an illustration by F.C. Terry that included some of the story's main events and characters (Figure 13.4). The back cover contained advertisements, one for the Australian Mutual Provident Society and another for *The Letters of Mr John Smith of Congewoi*, which "Shortly will be Published" (Figure 13.5). The last issue included the title page and table of contents. Each issue was of a set number of pages, regardless of what stage

---
8 - The most extended summary is to be found in Clancy 1999a, 1999b.

the story was at. Another unusual feature was praise for the production of the story: "It is printed by Mr. Cunningham, which is a sufficient guarantee that in general appearance it will bear favourable comparison with the best productions of the English press".[9] On the other hand, at one shilling for each part, the *Wagga Wagga Express* commented that it was "perhaps, in these days of cheap literature, a trifle too dear".[10] By November 1867, it was "on sale in one volume" at a cost ten shillings, reduced to five shillings by the following year.[11] The book was widely publicised, both within and beyond New South Wales. The complete book was published in Sydney, not in London, yet another unusual feature for the time. If it had been published in London, it and the author may well have been much better known. The book's dedication provides an interesting comment on the nature of publishing at the time, and the importance of newspapers in the emergence of Australian literature (and makes it even more unusual that it was not serialised in the *Sydney Morning Herald*).

Figure 13.4. The cover of the signatures of Fifty Years Ago, designed by F.C. Terry. It shows George Maxwell in the centre, with the flour mill, the squatter's cottage, the three Aborigines, and a bush party.

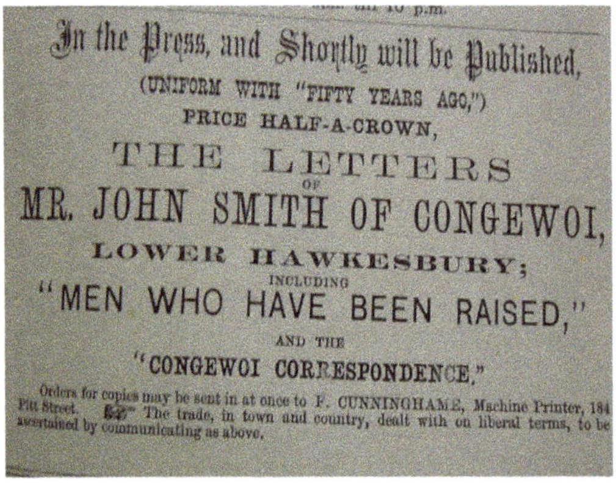

Figure 13.5. Advertisement inside the back cover.

---

9 - *Empire*, September 25, 1866, page 4.
10 - *Wagga Wagga Express*, September 22, 1866, page 2.
11 - *Sydney Morning Herald*, November 21, 1867, page 1; de Boos 1867, 471 + vi pp, Gordon & Gotch, 281, George Street, Sydney. Some years ago, Berkelouw's of Berrima had a copy of the original edition listed for sale in their 'Latest Acquisitions Catalogue 358' (n.d.). It was inscribed by the author, 'To Mr. John Tighe from his sincere friend & brother in law, The Author, … Charles de Boos'. It was described as 'scarce' and priced at $650.

To JOHN FAIRFAX, ESQ., whose helping hand has been the mainstay of the early footsteps of the

infant literature of Australia, THIS WORK IS INSCRIBED, with every feeling of respect,

by his faithful servant and friend, CHARLES DE BOOS.

A court case relating to the publication provides an interesting insight into book publishing at the time.[12] de Boos sued the printer of *Fifty Years Ago*, Frances Cunninghame, former editor and publisher of *The People's Advocate*, for proceeds from the sale of his book. Though Gordon & Gotch was the publisher, it was de Boos who was in dispute with the printer over payments he claimed he should have received, a view shared by the court verdict. At the time, few authors made any money from their writing.[13]

In 1869-70, two years after its first publication, the story appeared again, this time serialised in *The Australian Journal*, with the addition of numerous line drawings by A.J. Fisher (Appendix 13.2). In 1900-01, a further thirty years on, the story appeared again in *The Australian Journal*, but this time without illustrations and with a new title, *Retribution, or Eighty Years Ago* (Appendix 13.3). It is not known if de Boos gave permission for the re-publication or, more especially, the change of title. Publication was continued and concluded after his death, but there was no mention of his passing in the *Journal*.

In 1999, the 1869-70 version from *The Australian Journal*, including the illustrations, was republished in one volume by Victor Crittenden's Mulini Press, making it available to a whole new readership.[14] More recently, the book was re-published by Cambridge Scholars Publishing in 2009 and by General Books LLC of Memphis, Tennessee, in 2009 and 2012 (Figure 13.6). In the latter version, the only 'extra' is a one column generic explanatory note from the publisher, including the warning "that the book may have numerous typos, missing text, images and indexes", but also the claim that "our software is 99 percent accurate if the book [that is copied] is in good condition". Different covers to the book have been shown in

---

12 - *Sydney Morning Herald*, October 29, 1867, page 2; cf. Bode 2012.

13 - Barton 1889 and introductory comments by Crittenden in the 1993 re-issue of *Publishing Literature in N.S.W.: the Status of Literature in 1889*.

14 - de Boos 1999.

online advertisements, but they all appear to have the same ISBN, 978-0217213400. The 2012 copy has 253 pages of small text, printed in three columns per page, without a break.[15]

Figure 13.6. Cover of General Books edition, 2012.

Settler and Savage in Australia One Hundred Years Ago

An abridged, or rather an emasculated version, or even a "gutted" one in the view of Healy, was published in 1906.[16] Once again, the story was given a new title, *Settler and Savage in Australia One Hundred Years*

---

15 - www.ebay.com.au/itm/Fifty-Years-Ago-An-Australian-Tale-9780217213400-by-Charles-De-Boos-Paperback-/ Accessed July 17, 2013. www.holisticpage.com.au/fifty-years-ago-charles-de-boos/9780217213400, accessed July 17, 2013.

16 - Healy 1989, xvi. There were numerous notices regarding the publication of the book: for example, *Sydney Morning Herald*, November 17, 1906, page 4; *Australian Town and Country Journal*, November 21, 1906, page 43; *The Advertiser*, Adelaide, November 24, 1906, page 13; *The Register* (Adelaide), November 24, 1906, page 9; *The Mercury* (Hobart), November 29, 1906, page 6; *Examiner* (Launceston), December 14, 1906, page 3.

Ago. It was published by the New South Wales Bookstall (Figure 13.7).[17] Rowlandson stated he had purchased the copyright from the heirs of de Boos, though there was no indication they had given their permission for changes to be made. After being "carefully revised and illustrated", it was the publisher's hope, that "in its new dress, the book may prove as attractive as it did forty years ago, and thereby justify the present edition".[18] It was generally well received.[19]

> **SETTLER AND SAVAGE**
> IN AUSTRALIA ONE HUNDRED YEARS AGO.
> By CHARLES DE BOOS.
> Cloth, 3s 6d ; Paper, 2s 6d (postage 5d.)
>
> This is a reprint of a book (published in 1867) entitled "Fifty Years Ago," which for graphic description of the relationships existing between the blacks and the whites in the early days of Australian settlement is unrivalled. The interest starts in the first chapter with the massacre of a white settler's family, and never flags throughout the entire book. The terrible oath of vengeance taken against the murderers, and the fulfilment of the oath, make up one of the most thrilling stories ever written. Running side by side with the scheme of revenge, and incidental to it, are various phases of early colonial life, depicted in language that is tense and strong in every line. Few of the books of to-day can equal this in vivid coloring, adventure, and dramatic situations. It holds the reader spellbound to the end.
>
> **N.S.W. BOOKSTALL COMPANY,**
> 476 GEORGE-ST., SYDNEY, AND ALL BRANCHES.

Figure 13.7. Sunday Times, November 18, 1906, page 2. See also Sydney Morning Herald, November 17, 1906, page 4; Newcastle Morning Herald, November 17, 1906, page 3.

In some respects, a new title and an abridgement may seem to have been a good idea, but it left out much that was essential to making the characters and events true to life. Not everyone approved of the new title, though it was acknowledged that the edition made the work of de Boos available to a new generation of readers.[20] The characters, both white and black, were not from the 'wild west', and never thought of themselves as being so, no matter how much Rowlandson and many of his reading public would have liked them to be.[21] Further, "the very strong historical sense of the novel, the sense that it is firmly rooted in time and place" was lost in the abridgement.[22] Interestingly, in concluding a review of *Settler and Savage* published in *The Bulletin*, A.G. Stephen stated: "De Boos, despite

---

17 - New South Wales Bookstall Company, Sydney, 1906. It sold for 3/6d, and 2/6d for the paperback version (Mills 1991).
18 - From the book.
19 - For example, *Sydney Mail*, December 5, 1906, page 1432; *Australasian Town and Country Journal*, November 21, 1906, page 43; *The Advertiser* (Adelaide), November 24, 1906, page 13; *The Mercury* (Hobart), November 29, 1906, page 6; *Examiner* (Launceston), December 14, 1906, page 3; *Newcastle Morning Herald*, November 17, 1906, page 10; *Australian Star*, November 24, 1906, page 9; *Freeman's Journal*, December 1, 1906, page 33.
20 - *Sydney Morning Herald*, November 17, 1906, page 4.
21 - Durack 1962; Healy 1972; Clancy 1999a, 1999b.
22 - Clancy 1999b.

his environment and his period, manfully cleared the way for the writers of this more hopeful period".[23] *Settler and Savage: one hundred years ago in Australia* was re-issued in 2012, and advertised on-line, with a rather inappropriate cover very similar to that of the 2012 re-issue of *Fifty Years Ago* (Figure 13.8).[24]

Figure 13.8. Cover of General Books edition / RareBooksClub.com, 2012.

The addition of the line drawings to the 1869-70 version, the change of title in 1890, and especially the *Settlers and Savages* version, are examples of changing the nature of stories to suit the times, a practice that was then

---

23 - Stephens 1906.
24 - Rare Books Club, Nashville. 94 pages. ISBN-13: 978-1236311320; ISBN-10: 1236311329.

not uncommon.[25] However, 're-making' novels in this way took them out of the historical context in which they had been written.[26]

Fifty Years Ago: Contemporary Commentary

Fifty Years Ago aroused much interest from the publication of the first chapters through to the complete volume. A summary of the first seven chapters, along with the first extract, appeared in the *Sydney Morning Herald*.[27] With publication of further parts, many newspapers (not just in NSW) contained advertisements, extracts, summaries, and reviews.[28] Reviews and commentaries, however, were limited and the commentators unknown (Appendix 13.4).[29] In the *Ballarat Star*, one said "The writing is not wanting in descriptive power, and is far superior to most of the essays which have recently been made in the same direction by colonial authors".[30] In one of the more detailed early reviews, *Bell's Life of Sydney* provided a mixed comment on the first parts of the story. "His characters stand distinct from the canvas", no "miserable washy style of portraiture we meet with in the common run of novels"; "his descriptions of bush life are perfectly accurate;" "The blacks, perhaps, may have a trifle too much of Fenimore Cooper's Red Indians about them; but that is all that can be objected to them. Otherwise, they are so true to nature that we almost fancy we can smell them". Finding "a perceptible flavour of Dickens" in the book, the reviewer wondered what right de Boos had to make use of his ideas. The main "error of judgement", however, was the portrayal of Jamie, "the idiot boy", as a person with a "deranged intellect" could not possibly have maintained his rage against the blacks. However, readers "one and all", were advised "to procure a copy from their booksellers, and judge for themselves".[31] A short review in the *Sydney Punch* was followed by an unusual one in verse (Figure 13.9).[32]

---

25 - See for example, Eggert 2013, 2005.
26 - Personal communication, Professor Paul Eggert, May 23, 2014.
27 - September 9, 1866, page 5; September 12, 1866. page 6.
28 - For example: *Sydney Morning Herald*, October 3, 1866, page 3; October 15, 1866, page 3; November 26, 1866, page 2; *The Empire*, September 4, 1867, page 5.
29 - *Bell's Life in Sydney and Sporting Chronicle*, September 29, 1866, page 4; *Mercury* [Hobart], September 26, 1866, page 3; October 10, 1866, page 3.
30 - *Ballarat Star*, September 27, 1866, page 2.
31 - *Bell's Life of Sydney*, September 29, 1866, page 4.
32 - *Sydney Punch*, September 22, 1866, page 8; October 27, 1866, page 179.

A long review, with extended quotations, in the *Sydney Morning Herald* was generally very favourable, except for de Boos' depictions of the Aborigines. It is "the main defect of this story", while "the character of the Great Chief of the Maroo is certainly more that of the Red Man of J. Fenimore Cooper than that of the Black Man of Australia". Nonetheless, "We have great pleasure in recommending it to our readers".[33]

FIFTY YEARS AGO.
REVIEW OF PART I.

Mr. CHARLES DE BOOS,
Inspired by the Muse,
Has written a work which all folks should peruse :
'Twill instruct and amuse
By original views,
Intermingled with truths which none can refuse :
And this great piece of fiction
And elegant diction,
PUNCH hereby, whilst humbly admiring, reviews ;
That's to say, he'll endeavour,
From Part One of this clever
Production, to give you a sketch of the plot ;
And he trusts by so doing
To lead "not a few" in-
To giving their names as "subs." on the spot.

CHAPTER I.

TIME ! ! ! (*Tom Sayers.*)

Fifty years ago !
Things were looking very slow ;
And our "glorious" institutions hadn't burst into full blow.
Fifty years ago !
Sydney town was but so-so ;
And Sydney Cove and Cockle Bay had ne'er a wharf to show.
Fifty years ago !
Martial law ruled high and low ;
And a naughty man or woman got a heavy "*quid pro quo.*"
Fifty years ago !
All was not quite "*comme il faut ;*"
And Free Selection, blessed boon, was but "*in embryo.*"

Figure 13.9. The first two sections of an unusual review. Sydney Punch, October 27, 1866, page 179.

---

33 - *Sydney Morning Herald*, September 20, 1867, page 6.

An extended review also appeared in *The Argus*.[34] It began with a double-edged statement: "Amid the numerous publications that profess to give some description of Australian life and scenery, it is gratifying to find one that is not absolutely incorrect in all its details". The writer then launched into an extended tirade about the poor quality and the total inaccuracy of just about everything written about Australia, due to "the gross ignorance" of both Australian and English writers. So, it was "gratifying to discover that a book has at last been written which is both accurate and amusing". "Fifty Years Ago is very far below the standard that ought to be reached, but it is an infinite improvement upon the usual trash that is palmed upon the public as descriptions of colonial life. Above all, it has the merit of being accurate … Mr. De Boos' descriptions of bush scenery are extremely vivid, and are marked by an accuracy of details which is as rare as it is pleasant". However, the book still had "many defects". One was that though well drawn, there were "too many characters and incidents that are not relevant to the main story"; "Cooper has evidently been Mr. De Boos' model. George Maxwell is copied from the Silent Hunter, and is a colonial edition of *Nick of the Woods*. Moreover, the black-fellows talk a little too much like Red Indians". However, "The chief fault of his book is due to his own ambition. He has introduced so many characters that the reader gets tired of them, but his descriptions are uncommonly vivid and accurate, and the "sensation" episodes of the story, though repeated somewhat too frequently, seldom overstep the bounds of probability. We can fairly congratulate Mr. De Boos upon the production of a very readable volume, and hope to hear more of him".[35]

Fifty Years Ago: Recent Commentary

Fifty Years Ago has received very little consideration in writings about Australian literature. Further, what has been written has been largely divorced from the total corpus of writings by de Boos and even more so from his overall life and work. The discussions have been largely without context. Consequently, many are misleading and inaccurate, though some have made worthwhile and perceptive observations. However, it must be acknowledged that those who contributed to the earlier commentaries

---

34 - *The Argus*, September 21, 1867, pages 5-6.
35 - *The Argus*, September 21, 1867, pages 5-6.

had limited research resources, and certainly not the opportunities now provided through the National Library of Australia's 'Trove' website. It is this resource more than anything else that has made this biography possible.

The key commentators have been Clive Hamer,[36] John Healy,[37] Victor Crittenden, Laurie Clancy,[38] William Wilde and David Headon,[39] and Nancy Wright and Anthony Buck.[40] The following discussion, much of which is based on their work, is primarily concerned with four issues. Firstly, to what the book may be owed; secondly, de Boos' knowledge of the location and its environment; thirdly, for the time, his unusual presentation of Aborigines; and fourthly, the quality of his writing and the place of the book in early Australian literature.

To what did de Boos owe his story and its characters?

As indicated above, there were contemporary references to the contribution that Fenimore Cooper's (1789-1851) 'Leatherstocking Tales' and especially his 'Red Indians' may have made to *Fifty Years Ago*.[41] It may be "a tale of adventure in the manner of Fenimore Cooper",[42] but the influence of Cooper's American Indians on de Boos' Australian Aborigines is surely exaggerated. Regardless of how much use he may have made of Cooper's work, de Boos had had more than enough experience of and with Aborigines long before he wrote *Fifty Years Ago*, as evident, for example, in 'The Yo-Yo', 'Morouya, the Black Eagle of Colo', and *The Stockman's Daughter*. He certainly did not need Cooper's characters to the extent imagined by Richard Pascal, who described de Boos' Aborigines as "unquestionably modelled on Cooper's Indians". Pascal was clearly unaware of de Boos' other writings, or anything of the story of his life. Pascal does not tell us from his reading of *Fifty Years Ago*, what he meant by de Boos coming "near to adding the crime of plagiarism to his various other misdeeds".[43] Healy also states that

---

36 - Hamer 1957a; 1957b; 1965; 1989. The last reference is to one of a series of seven articles in which Hamer considers the writings of Charles Harpur, Henry Kendall, Adam Lindsay Gordon, Charles de Boos, and Marcus Clarke.
37 - Healy 1972; 1978, 47; 1989.
38 - Clancy 1999a; 1999b.
39 - Wilde and Headon 1994.
40 - Wright and Buck 1999; Wright 2001.
41 - Decker 2015.
42 - Hamer 1989; see Cooper 1823; 1841.
43 - Pascal 1989.

for de Boos, Cooper was "a major influence", but like Pascal, he also was unaware of other works by de Boos.[44] Further, de Boos did not need the 1857 Hornet Bank Massacre (the killing of the Fraser family and others at Hornet Bank Station, on the upper Dawson River) to form the basis for his story, as suggested by Patricia Clarke.[45]

If the story has a debt to anything, it is to the crimes and trials of the infamous Joseph Wilkes in 1857, and it is one that de Boos acknowledged.[46] Nearly ten years later, de Boos was searching through an old volume of the *Votes and Proceedings* of the NSW Legislative Assembly and "accidentally" found the *Second Progress Report from The Select Committee on 'Administration of Justice and Conduct of Official Business in Country Districts', with reference to the petitions of Joseph Wilkes, Cornelius Delohery, and Thomas Abbott*:[47]

> *In turning over the leaves, a passage in print accidentally caught my eye. I read that passage as well as several others which followed. I became interested, and read on and on until I made myself acquainted with the whole circumstances of the case detailed. The whole thing seemed to me so extraordinary that I could not rest satisfied until I had followed the matter up to its ending. This took me beyond the Blue-book, which may be said to have concluded the third Act of a Five Act Tragedy. I think the story will be found interesting. I am sure it has a moral, which I would wish to be better recognised than it is.*[48]

The Committee "heard the petition of one Joseph Wilkes relating to an accusation of judicial incompetence. Wilkes filed this petition in order, he claimed, to secure redress of specific grievances resulting from the investigation of the death of his wife and two of his children. His testimony and other evidence, in due course, made the Select Committee suspect Wilkes of the crimes. The Select Committee learned that mysterious and unresolved murder cases had occurred previously where Wilkes had lived. In fact, as the Committee discovered, Wilkes was implicated in the deaths of two men in the 1830s and the death by poisoning of his two daughters in 1853. The Select Committee in their Report recommended further investigation of Wilkes, which resulted in his conviction for murder".[49]

---

44 - Healy 1972.

45 - Clarke 2005. The Massacre occurred at a station near where seven years old Rosa and her family were living. She used it in Praed 1885 and 1902.

46 - The crimes and trials are summarised briefly in Wright 2001.

47 - *Second Progress Report from The Select Committee on 'Administration of Justice and Conduct of Official Business in Country Districts', with reference to the petitions of Joseph Wilkes, Cornelius Delohery, and Thomas Abbott.* New South Wales Votes and Proceedings of the Legislative Assembly, 1856-57. Government Printer, Sydney, 1857. pp. 979-1025.

48 - *The Sydney Mail*, May 30, 1868, page 12.

49 - Wright and Buck 1999; *Sydney Morning Herald*, April 23, 1858, page 5.

de Boos clearly realised the potential of the material he had found. The words quoted above are part of his introduction to "The Romance of the Blue Books (Collected, Collated, and put into presentable Literary Form, specially for *the Sydney Mail*)", which he called "Pursued by Fate" (Appendix 13.5).[50] This was the first way he used the material, "a true crime serial" that was published in seven parts in *The Sydney Mail*. The story was told devoid of the sensationalism of the government report and of much crime fiction of the period, where it was almost a requirement.[51] He also used the material "to address the subjects of frontier justice and the need to reform the law of evidence – subjects that concerned legislators in NSW from 1839 to 1849", including the admissibility of evidence presented by Aborigines.[52] The other work, *Fifty Years Ago*, de Boos wrote as a historical novel, but again, it was perhaps not just a story. For Nancy Wright,

> The theme that binds the four books of Fifty Years Ago together is the need to renounce a code of revenge that had been used to rectify wrongs in the colony around the first decade of the nineteenth century. The narrative showed how the developing role of the colonial police and the law made it necessary to foreswear vengeance in order to secure justice.[53]

But, as we have seen, this is only one reading, for de Boos tells many stories within his story. Just how 'dependent' de Boos was on other stories is yet another story, and by no means a simple one. The other writers claiming to know the 'sources' for *Fifty Years Ago* clearly had very limited knowledge of de Boos, his work and his other writing.

The setting and its environment

Fifty Years Ago is set in the wider Hunter Valley of New South Wales. As discussed in Chapter Five, it was long believed that de Boos knew the area from his initial settlement in New South Wales as a farmer, but this was not the case. The source of his knowledge was much more likely to have come from his time in Maitland and his travels through the area as a reporter for the *Sydney Morning Herald*.

---

50 - Wright and Buck 1999; *The Sydney Mail*, May-August, 1868. In the Rare Books Room of the Fisher Library, University of Sydney, there is a paste-up of the newspaper articles of Chapters I to VI, with Chapter VII in hand-written form (RB 1580.55). The latter extends over 19 small pages, many of them torn, and all in a fragile condition (as at August 8, 2013). The provenance of the material is unknown. Comparison with some known handwriting of Charles de Boos suggests that this item was not hand-written by him (cf. Crittenden 2004, 1).

51 - Wright and Buck 1999.

52 - Wright 2001.

53 - Wright (2001) is highly complementary of de Boos' work.

de Boos was a reporter, with excellent powers of observation and description. He writes of the squatter, his house and farming, of the flour mill and the water source that provided the power. He recounts with some praise the work of the timber sawyers and splitters, who, despite the destruction their work entails, he describes as the real pioneers, including the American Negro, Black Harry. But then, there is a sudden change. The sawyer's

> *occupation then as now, was equivalent to nothing more nor less than the destruction of everything in the shape of native growth upon the land taken up. ... No matter how magnificent may be the trees he has thrown down, they are ruthlessly consigned to the flames as the speediest means of getting them out of the way.*
>
> *In this way nothing is left for a future day, and the woodman who follows after must go for trees suitable for his purpose past where the hand of man has denuded the ground of the beauteous growth with which nature had covered it (page 148).*

In Clancy's view, "There are some magnificent descriptions of natural landscape".[54] This is hardly surprising, as de Boos had "a thorough knowledge of the Australian bush"; Hamer suggests he was in "awe" of it. "The novel successfully captures both the physical environment and the psychological ambience of colonial times".[55] "There are no loving descriptions of the Australian bush, such as characterise *The Recollections of Geoffrey Hamlyn*, for instance; but there is also none of that patronising attitude that Australia is a fascinating oddity". de Boos describes the bush, "not as a place of beauty, but as a sombre, cruel, teeming tangle of luxurious growth – a description of a coastal rain forest of a quality uncaptured by any other pen".[56] It is an area of cedar brush on the banks of the Williams River and merits full quotation.

> *The heavy brushes and especially those dense jungley forests in which the cedar luxuriates have always been noted for being dank, damp and unhealthy. The lofty trees running up from one hundred to one hundred and fifty feet in the air, interlace their boughs until they exclude the burning heat of the sun, and under this shelter a dense undergrowth of vegetation flourishes, so rankly, that no ray of light still less of heat ever penetrates to the soil. Mosses and lichens abound, the former hanging often in long pendant streamers from the boughs of the timber of lower growth, or spreading over and devouring the dead wood that cumbers the ground in all directions and forms by its decay food for a future generation of its species. Fungoidal and parasitical growths of most rare and strange descriptions, flourish upon the decay of the vegetable matter around and in the miasmatic emanations exhaled from the constant moisture, attaching*

---

54 - Clancy 1999a.
55 - Wilde, Hooton and Andrews 1994, 178.
56 - Hamer 1957a.

themselves sometimes to the trees, sometimes to the decaying branches that lay around, and sometimes springing up luxuriantly from between the vast masses of roots that only half buried in the soil, twine and twist along the surface of the earth in every direction in search of an unoccupied piece of ground into which to plunge to procure nourishment for the giant mass for which they have to provide support. In these brushes the trees are of enormous size, the trunk often running up to a height of a hundred and twenty feet before a bough protrudes from it and straight as an arrow. But huge as are these trees, the cedars are giants even amongst these vegetable monsters. Rearing up their heads far above their lofty fellows of the forest, and spreading out their branches far and wide in spite of all opposition, these monarchs of the bush might, from their towering height, be often seen and marked from a great distance, and when one of these fathers of the bush fell under the persevering attacks of the sawyers, the light of day has been let in upon an area of nearly a rood, upon which for long ages previously the sun had never shone. The undergrowth was also close and tangled, the shrubs, and creeping and climbing plants binding together and matting so closely as to make it a work of great difficulty and labour to penetrate through the vast vegetable barrier that was presented at every step. The wild vine threw out its long cable like shoots, now twining up some lofty branch, now hanging in fanciful festoons as it pushed across from tree to tree, and anon laying out along some bough like a vast boa lying in wait for its prey. Other minor creepers availed themselves of its support to climb upwards in their search after light and air, rewarding it for its aid by decorating its dark rugged bark with their gorgeous flowers. These flowers, often of the most brilliant hues, were scattered amongst the branches of the larger trees into which the plants had mounted, and amongst which they twisted and twined (page 149).

Another quotation:

The moon is riding high in the heavens, occasionally shining out brightly, the heavy rain drops that hang upon the foliage of the trees and bedew the grass, sending back her rays as if from a polished surface; and then, some heavy cloud comes sweeping on and overshadows her, and all is covered with a black pall of darkness, creeping along the earth like a sombre mantle, throwing the farther hills into deep shade, approaching nearer and nearer till hill and gully are merged in one in the overwhelming darkness, crossing the water-courses, and making their thick and sombre timber look blacker still, till every trace of light is shut out, then obscuring the hills on the other side, and going on and on till all is deep impenetrable shade. The ground is dank and wet, saturated with moisture, and the foot sinks into the sloppy yielding soil at every step. With every gust that sweeps over, showers of rain drops are scattered down from the trees above, rattling on the ground so forcibly and continuously that it is doubtful for a time whether or not another shower has fallen from the skies (page 77).

The Aborigines in *Fifty Years Ago*

The Aborigines, and Macomo in particular, are central to the story of *Fifty Years Ago*. They are portrayed in many and often contradictory ways. In the early chapters, the descriptions are the conventional ones; they are savages, vindictive and brutal. But this changes, and the book moves "a long way from the smug generalisations about blacks in the earlier sections".[57] Healy notes that de Boos "has a sympathy and compassion for them which suggests contact, knowledge and understanding of their ways". He states that "*Fifty Years Ago* used aboriginal material more seriously and extensively than any preceding novel".[58] Such comments support de Boos' knowledge of the Aboriginals, rather than any "major influence" of Cooper. Just as he knew the bush, so he knew Aborigines and their tribal lives. He had observed and had contact with them over many years and in many locations. Hamer extends such an assessment, noting that de Boos recognises that the Aboriginals have their own skills (such as tracking), their own moral code, and their own religious beliefs "that are just as valid as the Christian doctrines".[59] There is a respect for them in de Boos' writing in the way "a century later they were viewed by Xavier Herbert in *Capricornia* and *Poor Fellow My Country*. de Boos

> understands their natural resentment of the ruthless way the whites have dispossessed them. One of his black protagonists, Opara, says: 'The whites have taken away our hunting grounds, destroyed our forests, driven off the animals that provided us with food. They have slaughtered our warriors in the bush, or made them as helpless gins with their burning water in the settlements. They have debauched our women and made our children a useless mongrel breed unworthy to tread in the footsteps of our fathers'. This is a fairly discerning attitude for 1866.[60]

So, too, was de Boos' "almost unconscious recognition of the shared humanity of blacks and whites", and that, in words he gave to Coolamie, 'The white man and his law has done but little good for the black'".[61] "De Boos' sympathetic observations, coupled with his imaginative and sensitive analysis, produced an interpretation of Aboriginality highly unusual for the time".[62] His "somewhat revolutionary conclusion in favour of the Aborigines contrasts greatly … with their disparagement in other colonial literature".[63] And there is George Maxwell's "slow realisation of the futility of his quest for vengeance".[64]

---

57 - Clancy 1999a.

58 - Healy 1972. In this paper, Healy gave considerable attention to *Fifty Years Ago*, but in his 1978 book, *Literature and the Aborigine in Australia, 1770-1975*, de Boos gets only a footnote (page 47). There are no real changes to the second edition (1989), except for a new, extended introduction. In it, among other things, he comments on why he left out de Boos and *Fifty Years Ago*: on the basis of what he says, it is difficult to see why he did so (page xv-xvi). Clancy (1999b) also observed that "oddly enough it does not appear in [Healy's] pioneering work".

59 - Hamer 1989.

60 - Hamer 1989.

61 - Clancy 1999a, quotation from page 361.

62 - Wilde and Headon 1994.

63 - Anon. 1994.

64 - Clancy 2004, 99.

Clancy wrote that *Fifty Years Ago* "is one of the few nineteenth century novels to treat the Aboriginal people with some insight and respect, however inadvertent or unconscious. Almost despite itself, it eventually transcends the prejudices that were endemic in colonial literature". Given what we now know about de Boos, there was surely nothing "inadvertent or unconscious" about what he wrote, and it should be no surprise that the book "eventually transcends the prejudices that were endemic in colonial literature" and society at large.[65]

Wright picks out other concerns of de Boos in *Fifty Years Ago*, as well as in *Pursued by Fate*, namely the then inadmissible testimony of Aborigines, a situation that did not change until 1867. She noted that this had nothing to do with "their knowledge, reliability or competence", but because they were regarded as unable to give evidence under oath.[66] In Part 3 of the book, "the murder of a sawyer, Black Harry, by a white man, Ironbark Jack, fails to be resolved by the authorities because they cannot accept the testimony of aborigines who can give circumstantial evidence about the crime".[67] Wright goes on to say, "De Boos encourages his readers to appreciate that religious belief did not prevent Wilkes from attempting to deceive the Select Committee and for that reason, by analogy, religious belief should not be the criterion of a witness's competence". For Wright, de Boos was not only a novelist but also an advocate of law reform, who "through the power of narrative, contributed to the legislative reform which was finally achieved in 1867".[68]

> *De Boos was one of the first of our writers to look sympathetically at the Aborigine. ... While he presents them initially as blood-thirsty murderers who slaughter a family of white settlers, he shows that they were acting in defence of their land, that violence was their instinctive reaction to a threat posed by the white invaders, that they didn't know any better. During the course of the novel he brings them to an awareness of right and wrong, and while his overall tone remains patronising he suggests towards the end that, through the processes of education and civilisation, harmony between whites and blacks might eventually be achieved.[69]*

---

65 - Clancy 1999a.
66 - Wright 2001.
67 - Wright and Buck 1999.
68 - Wright 2001.
69 - D'Ath 1993.

Fifty Years Ago in early Australian literature

Fifty Year Ago is an historical novel set in the early years of the nineteenth century and of colonial New South Wales. de Boos had no limitations in terms of observation, description, and reporting, and he uses these to the full, as his depiction of the cedar brush quoted above indicates. He had a thorough knowledge of the topics about which he wrote. As a good journalist, his writing was "factual, realistic and sternly truthful, providing sufficient motives for all actions, noble and unworthy, whether done by blacks or whites".[70] He could tell a good story, even though in terms of fiction, his style may have been "unadorned and often plebeian".[71] He certainly had little skill in "recording conversation or the normal intercourse between human beings".[72] Even worse was "the highly stylised, literary language of the blacks" and "the execrable Irish and Scottish and black American".[73]

Clancy describes it as "a powerful and complex novel".[74] There may be too many characters and sub-stories, ones that appear and disappear, but they contribute to the picture of Australia at the time. In Clancy's view, it is "a long, over-plotted and yet absorbing novel".[75] At times, de Boos is certainly long-winded.

> Yet the sluggishness of the movement of the book, in which de Boos is prepared to freeze any moment for an extrinsic commentary, gives it an authority and depth of significance that Rowlandson's abridgement does not have. He examines the phenomenon of the Indian hater as seriously as Robert Montgomery Bird.[76] His character drawing of George and the multitude of white characters has a vigour which surpasses that of Rowcroft[77] and Haydon,[78] and an honesty which approaches that of Dickens.[79]

---

70 - Healy 1972.
71 - Hamer 1957a.
72 - Hamer 1989.
73 - Clancy 1999a.
74 - Clancy 2004, 99.
75 - Clancy 1992, 18.
76 - Bird 1837.
77 - Rowcroft 1851.
78 - Haydon 1854.
79 - Healy 1972.

Clancy adds two views on de Boos' prose. It is

> *often florid and repetitive, his attention to detail often seems tedious and obsessive and his didacticism frequently and distractingly intrudes into the narrative. And yet, the abbreviated version does not work. Especially in its heavy excisions from the final and most extended section, it distorts motivation and destroys the dense circumstantiality of the world that de Boos has painstakingly built up.*

Of the book as a whole,

> *It is easy to point to the weaknesses in Fifty Years Ago and yet the failure of the abbreviated version (which removed most of them) suggests that they are very bound up with its many felicities. The excision of the digressive opening chapters involves the loss of the very strong historical sense of the novel, the sense that it is firmly rooted in time and place. It was a country and a time de Boos knew very well and the book has an authenticity that is rare in colonial fiction. There are some magnificent descriptions of natural landscape and detailed accounts of what he has observed, from the Aboriginal weapons to the process of milling and timber clearing. He understands too the historical processes of squatting and of clearing the land.*[80]

A short assessment

In Clancy's words, *Fifty Years Ago* is "one of the most powerful and neglected of all colonial fictions".[81] Hamer regards it as "one of the best books written in the infancy of Australian literature".[82] The period 1859 to 1889 marked "the beginnings of the Australian novel" and "there was no novel written in the period which is more Australian".[83] Suggestions that it was the first genuinely Australian novel are perhaps more debateable, as they would seem to ignore *The Stockman's Daughter*.

> *de Boos wrote a novel that is as Australian as those of Joseph Furphy. And it, 'Fifty Years Ago' appeared as early as 1866. His faith in Australia is implicit rather than avowed. His book so exuded the sap of the gumtree and takes so much for granted the strength of Australian manhood that there is no need for him to boast extravagantly about the future greatness of this promising land. He simply describes the Australian background as it is, and against it sets a true-to-life, exciting novel of human passions. Unlike Furphy he sees no need to be aggressively Australian, defensive, sensitive of criticism, nor constantly comparing Australia with England. Not living in an age of rising nationalism, he is not even interested in such a comparison.*[84]

---

80 - Clancy 1999a.
81 - Clancy 1993.
82 - Hamer 1957a.
83 - Hamer 1965.
84 - Hamer 1957b.

Fifty Years Ago, like *The Stockman's Daughter*, was an Australian novel well ahead of the time that is generally seen as "the emergence of the distinctly Australian novel".[85]

---

85 - Hamer 1965.

Chapter Fourteen

Charles de Boos the Writer

de Boos was one of the more important professional writers in nineteenth century New South Wales and Victoria. His writing, as a journalist, government employee, and writer of fiction, extended over a period of close to fifty years, from the mid-1840s to the early 1890s. His output was remarkable, especially during the time he was with John Fairfax & Company.

The journalist

He likely started his career as a journalist with the *Sydney Gazette*, for which he was noted as a "significant contributor".[1] Given that he returned thanks to a toast for "The *Maitland Mercury*, and the liberty of the press" at a dinner in Singleton for the visit of the Governor, he may also have worked for the *Maitland Mercury*, but that is speculation.[2]

The first reporter employed in Australia with a knowledge of shorthand, he worked as a general reporter for *The Argus* and the *Sydney Morning Herald*. He covered parliamentary proceedings in the days before 'Hansard'. For both newspapers, he was a valued investigative reporter and a respected commentator. In the words of the Editor of *The Argus*, he was "a man of intelligence and integrity, we can pledge ourselves to the truthfulness of his statements". Some years later, the Editor of the *Herald* credited him with the same qualities.[3] And as early as 1855, the *Geelong Advertiser* described him as "a skilful veteran of the press in Victoria, and perhaps the most clever reporter in the colony".[4] His writings provide eye-witness accounts and a consistent view on many issues over important periods in the colonial histories of Victoria and especially New South Wales. Published primarily

---

1 - Wilde, Hooton and Andrews 1994, 734.
2 - *Maitland Mercury*, February 10, 1847, page 2; *Sydney Morning Herald*, February 12, 1847, page 3.
3 - *The Argus*, March 16, 1852, page 2; *Sydney Morning Herald*, July 23, 1857, page 4.
4 - *Geelong Advertiser*, July 11, 1855, page 2.

in the *Sydney Morning Herald* and *The Argus*, his accounts of all aspects of the goldfields are without equal, constituting an historical source that is essentially untapped.

On two occasions, he started his own papers, *The Metropolitan* in Sydney and *The Telegraph and Sporting Times* in Melbourne. Initially well-received, they were very short-lived, like so many others from this period. Regrettably, no copies of either paper exist.

As observed earlier, the parliamentary work, much of it in the evenings and at night, was not good for his eyesight or his mental well-being.[5] Nonetheless, his work and experiences as a general reporter, a goldfields reporter, and a parliamentary reporter gave de Boos the material for much of his other writing. In particular, "His role as the Herald's parliamentary reporter provided him with exact knowledge of legislation about property debated in the Assembly and the Council – knowledge that informed not only his political columns and special reports from the goldfields but also the plots of his novels".[6]

The Government reporter and recorder

As far as can be gathered, de Boos' writing more or less stopped when he left John Fairfax & Sons in 1872. To begin with, his time was taken up with other activities and more especially caring for his family following the death of his wife. From 1875, his writing skills were transferred to the preparation of public documents. Along with many reports on specific issues, his contributions to the Annual Reports for the Department of Mines (from Braidwood, Temora, Copeland, and Milparinka) contain a wealth of information. And as noted in Chapter Nine, he was complemented more than once on the quality of his reports. These were largely concerned with matters of mining and processing gold and other minerals, though by no means limited to them. For example, whilst at Braidwood, he more than once expressed concern for the miners and other residents of the Araluen Valley after flooding. His concern over domestic water supplies was frequently expressed. Even during this period of his life, it is unlikely that

---

5 - *Sydney Morning Herald*, April 23, 1866, page 3; May 16, 1857, page 7.
6 - Wright 2005b.

all the stories about him were true. He certainly never mentioned being shot by bushrangers.

> *His official life had not been at all humdrum. In 1874 the bushrangers were still abroad in Australia, and as a magistrate Mr. de Boos had almost as stirring times as when campaigning in Iberia, or stirring the ire of politicians in Sydney. Once he was shot by bushrangers, but not severely wounded, and, following a very distinguished precedent, de Boos did not rest satisfied until he had hunted down his assailants and handed them over to justice.*[7]

As a Police Magistrate, he made referrals to higher courts and wrote reports on specific matters. However, records for the Department of Justice and Public Instruction[8] in the 1870s and the Department of Justice from May 1880 are limited and patchy in many ways.[9] It is not known if de Boos provided any annual reports as a Police Magistrate comparable to those he wrote as a Mining Warden.

A Writer of Fiction

Had de Boos not joined the NSW Colonial Government public service, there is little doubt that he would have continued his writing, but his new employment did not permit him to take on any other paid work (not that he would have received much if anything for his stories). He observed this rule, though others did not, including Marcus Clarke and Thomas Browne (alias Rolf Boldrewood).[10] But as Crittenden commented, they had friends "to encourage [their] superiors to blink at any 'misconduct' such as writing";[11] and Browne "saw his writings as a [necessary] supplement to his official income".[12]

His fiction covered a variety of genres, as discussed in Chapter Twelve. In particular, his satirical writings provide an alternative record of the activities of the Colonial Parliament and its members, whilst much of his other fiction contained significant social commentary.

---

7 - From an obituary: 'Death of Charles de Boos. A Pioneer Pressman'. *Daily Telegraph*, October 31, 1900, Page 6. Nothing has been found to substantiate these 'stories'.
8 - *New South Wales Government Gazette*, 291 (Supplement), December 9, 1873, page 3447.
9 - Hamilton 2015, 161.
10 - Boldrewood 1888, 1890.
11 - Crittenden 1996; Eggert and Webby 2006, xxiv-xxvii.
12 - Eggert and Webby 2006; Hamilton 2015, 139-159; Inglis Moore 1969; Baldwin and Boyd-Davis 2001.

His Contribution to Australian literature

de Boos wrote Australian stories for Australian readers. His work was published in Australia, and he was one of the few to be published here in book form.[13] Over the same period, most authors living in Australia wrote "for an English audience or at least for an audience of Englishmen transported to this new country", and "they portrayed that part of Australian society that was closest to English",[14] with all the deficiencies noted in Chapter Thirteen by a reviewer in *The Argus*.[15]

During his lifetime, de Boos was known and complimented for many of his writings,[16] as indicated by reviews of *Fifty Years Ago* and references in these to his other work. *The Congewoi Correspondence* was frequently the subject of favourable comment. In an 1896 review of "Australian Literature", 'F.M.' commented: "Charles de Boos, also, good journalist and true, and writer of several good Australian works".[17] His name was included favourably in lists of authors of the time. He was among those present at a 'Complimentary Banquet' for W.H. Hicks, to mark his retirement from the proprietorship of *Sydney Punch*.[18] Of course, opinions varied then as now, but at the beginning of 1884, in a very critical review of the second number of the *Sydney Quarterly Magazine*, the poor quality of contemporary writing resulted in a lament for earlier writers.

> *Of this we are quite certain, that the Bob Lowes, Peter Possums, Deniehys, Martins, de Boos, Fosters, Bartons, Dalleys, Mortons, & c., of by-gone days have not donated their talents to the newer men. If those of that brilliant galaxy who have passed away had left their mantles, and their survivors felt disposed to aid in promoting Australian literary efforts, we might predict a future for the Quarterly; and it deserves to have one.*[19]

Through the mid and latter parts of the nineteenth century, whilst numerous writers had their work serialised in colonial newspapers, publication in England was the norm for Australian writers. They included Catherine Spence, Thomas Browne (alias 'Rolf Boldrewood'), Henry Kingsley

---

13 - It is unlikely that he made any money from his fiction over and above his Fairfax pay, as "local publication usually meant publication at the author's expense" (Webby 2000).
14 - Hamer 1965.
15 - *The Argus*, September 21, 1867, pages 5-6.
16 - For example, "The Excursion Train". *Cootamundra Herald*, September 13, 1893, page 4.
17 - *Australian Star*, November 7, 1896, page 7.
18 - *Daily Telegraph*, June 23, 1881, page 3; *Evening News*, June 23, 1881, page 2.
19 - *Illustrated Sydney News*, January 19, 1884, page 11.

(brother of Charles), Ada Cambridge, John Boyle O'Reilly, Marcus Clarke, Jessie Couvreur (alias 'Tasma'), and Rosa Praed.[20] de Boos was a significant exception, as none of his work was published overseas.[21] Further, almost all his work was published in newspapers, which had very limited physical lives. Combined, these facts no doubt contributed to him being less known than the writers mentioned above; to having a more limited readership; and a consequent 'slipping from view'.

But why has de Boos and his work continued to be so little known? Most surveys and reviews of Australian literature make no mention of him, editors and contributors seemingly unaware of his work, and while some who are aware are not accurate. There is no mention of de Boos in the very early work by Turner and Sutherland[22] or in Miller's *Australian Literature from its Beginnings to 1935*, not even in a list of fiction writers of 'The Colonial Period'.[23] The same is true of Green's large two volume *A History of Australian Literature*, including the later revised edition;[24] Kramer's *Oxford History of Australian Literature*;[25] and Stewart's study of early Australian literature and journalism.[26] No mention is to be found in Pierce, Hunter and Stewart's *The Oxford Literary Guide to Australia*;[27] Arnold, Nieuwenhuizen and Spearritt's *Who's Who of Australian Writers*, in spite of it being a listing "thousands of authors";[28] or Morrison's essay on "Serial fiction in Australian colonial newspapers".[29] Elizabeth Webby rightly observes in *The Cambridge Companion to Australian Literature*:

> *The construction by later nationalist literary critics and historians of the 1890s as the decade when Australian literature first 'came of age' has had many unfortunate consequences for the work of earlier writers, relegating them to the status of the immature or merely imitative.*[30]

But there is no mention of de Boos in any of her writings. The same is

---

20 - Clancy 1992; Clarke 1874; Cambridge 1890; 1883/1891; Couvreur 1889; O'Reilly 1879; Praed 1887; Spence 1854.
21 - Another exception was George Isaacs (alias A. Pendragon), whose 1858 novel *The Queen of the South* was published in South Australia (Black 2020).
22 - Turner and Sutherland 1898.
23 - Miller 1940, 1956, 10.
24 - Green 1961; 1984-85.
25 - Kramer 1981.
26 - Stewart 1988.
27 - Pierce, Hunter and Stewart 1993.
28 - Arnold, Nieuwenhuizen and Spearritt 1995.
29 - Morrison 1995.
30 - Webby 2000; 1981; 2003; 2009a; 2009b.

true of *The Oxford Literary History of Australia*, edited by Bennett, Strauss and Wallace-Crabbe.[31] A small exception, de Boos is found in *The ALS Guide to Australian Writers*, but only *Fifty Years Ago* is mentioned.[32] A few others have been kinder, such as contributors to *The Oxford Companion to Australian Literature*,[33] Healy[34] and Wright,[35] and especially Hamer, Clancy, and Crittenden.[36]

The absence of de Boos in more recent volumes is harder to understand: *The Cambridge History of Australian Literature*;[37] the *Macquarie Pen Anthology of Australian Literature*;[38] *The Burning Library*;[39] and *Colonial Australian Fiction: Character Types, Social Formations, and the Colonial Economy*.[40] He is included in Arnold and Hay's huge bibliography, but only six of his works are listed.[41]

'Trove' and the digitisation of newspapers and other documents are relatively recent, and this biography could not have achieved its results without such research tools, which have made materials so much more accessible. But the groundwork was laid without such tools, both in this study and in the earlier work of a small number of people, particularly Clive Hamer, working in the late 1950s to the mid-1960s.[42] There can no longer be any excuses for the lack of consideration of the writings of Charles de Boos.

What are some of the consequences? de Boos has not been recognised as he deserves to be, nor given his rightful place in the history of Australian literature. Writing early in the twentieth century, A.G. Stephen in a review of *Settler and Savage* published in *The Bulletin*, stated: "It is the Australian novel in the making, the Australian novel with difficulty acclimatising itself

---

31 - Bennett, Strauss and Wallace-Crabbe 1998.
32 - Duwell, Ehrhardt and Hetherington 1997.
33 - Wilde, Hooton and Andrews 1994.
34 - Healy 1972.
35 - Wright 2001; 2005b.
36 - Hamer 1957a, 1965; Clancy 1992, 2004; Crittenden 1996b.
37 - Pierce 2009.
38 - Webby 2009b; Jose 2009.
39 - Williamson 2012. The author describes his book as "an attempt to reconstitute a lost back-story of our literature. It is braided from the lives and works of authors who have been underestimated or discredited by ways of thinking about literature reinstituted in recent decades". Yet all but one of his selected writers are from the twentieth century, the exception being from the 1890s.
40 - Gelder and Weaver 2017.
41 - Arnold and Hay 2001, 447-448.
42 - Hamer 1957a, 1957b, 1965.

upon Australian soil, tardily shaking off the influences of over-seas. ... De Boos, despite his environment and his period, manfully cleared the way for the writers of this more hopeful time".[43] *Fifty Years Ago*, like *The Stockman's Daughter*, was an Australian novel well ahead of the time that is generally seen as "the beginnings of maturity for the Australian novel", with writers such as Joseph Furphy, Miles Franklin, Mrs Gunn and William Hay writing in the eighteen nineties and shortly after the turn of the century. "[B]ut de Boos had forestalled them by a generation".[44] Hamer's earlier comment that "Joseph Furphy's *Such is Life* is usually regarded as the first Australian novel that is truly Australian in spirit" is clearly in need of revision.[45]

Without de Boos, there are deficiencies in current work on Australia's early colonial literary history. Morrison made the incorrect statement relating to serial fiction that "The Melbourne *Age* led the way in 1872 while most of the other dailies that featured serial fiction began to do so in the 1880s".[46] Bode has shown it was much earlier. The *Advocate*, *Herald*, and *Mail* were well ahead of this: for example, de Boos' 'The Stockman's Daughter', 'Mr Pick the Miner', and 'Mark Brown's Wife'; John Hux's 'Emma Westan: a Tale of Australia, Founded on Fact' published in *The Sydney Mail*.[47] In the *Macquarie Pen Anthology of Australian Literature*, Webby was incorrect in saying that "Boldrewood was the first to make an Australian working-class man the narrator of a novel,"[48] as 'Mark Brown's Wife' is essentially 'told' by Tom Drewe, a gold miner.

The huge corpus of writings of Charles de Boos is his legacy. Neglected for too long, it merits an accurate and detailed examination and assessment. Without this, the history of Australia's early colonial literature is incomplete.

---

43 - Stephens 1906.
44 - Hamer 1965; Franklin 1901; Gunn 1908; Hay 1907.
45 - Hamer 1957a. Given the comments by some writers regarding the supposed dependence of de Boos on other writers, it is interesting to note Hamer's suggestion that Furphy may have drawn on *Fifty Years Ago* for his novel *Such is Life* (written in 1897, published 1903).
46 - Morrison 1995.
47 - Crabb 2020.
48 - Webby 2009b; Jose 2009.

Chapter Fifteen

Charles de Boos

Figure 15.1. Charles de Boos, from an Obituary. Daily Telegraph, October 31, 1900, page 6.

A life of so many strands has made for a complex narrative. So, in endeavouring to say something about Charles de Boos himself, are there any common threads that can help to bring this complex narrative together?

There can be little doubt that the most compelling aspect of his life must have been his Huguenot origins. He was a descendent and member of a remarkable people who survived unbelievable experiences over hundreds of years but who maintained their collective identity.

His travels were remarkable, and they occupy much of this biography. Then again, perhaps they were not so remarkable in the context of the

Huguenot diaspora. The documentation of his travels and experiences, in his newspaper columns and his fiction, tell us as much about de Boos himself as they do of the topics about which he wrote. In the absence of any personal or family papers, we must glean what we can about him from his own writings and what others wrote about him. Early on in his working life, the Hobart *Mercury* wrote of him in a somewhat exaggerated yet very kindly form:

> *A literary man, living the life of the rover, with a love of adventure, and a kindly and ingenious disposition, Mr. de Boos has laid up stores of information and experiences of the most valuable kind, of which he is now delivering himself in a pleasing and instructive manner for the benefit of the rising youth of Australia. The most observant of travellers and the most accurate of chroniclers, the author is just the man to write the early history of colonisation in the great Southern Continent. Familiarly acquainted with every mile of the country in New South Wales, Queensland, and Victoria, he has an extensive field before him.*[1]

As has been indicated, he frequently expressed his concerns for the natural environment and the damage being done to it, especially by gold mining and land clearing. He was critical of the problems created by bad governments, bad governance, and bad government regulations. On such matters, even as a government official, he did not fear making his views known.

But if there is any one over-riding aspect of his life, it was his concern for people, those he lived with and those he met, and the societies in which they lived. His concerns were for those in the multi-cultural, multi-class societies of Sydney and Melbourne and even more so those of the goldfields. He wrote of those disadvantaged in so many ways, the less fortunate members of society, especially women, children, Aborigines, Chinese, and other minority groups. Yes, he was a person of his times, as in the vocabulary he sometimes used, but in so many ways he was also ahead of his time.

The social conditions of women and children were a particular concern, not least in the way they were affected by the crime, violence, and lawlessness on some of the diggings. He frequently attributed problems to excessive alcohol consumption from so many hotels and especially the illegal 'sly grog shops', many of which operated with impunity. He may have been a publican at times, but that did not stop him condemning the abuse of

---

1 - *The Mercury* (Hobart), October 10, 1866, page 3.

alcohol and the consequences. At the same time, he was full of praise for the communities that lived peacefully, especially those where there were no law enforcement officials.

de Boos showed respect for people who frequently were shown none and often abused. His compassion for others was nowhere more evident than in his response to the body in the Fitzroy River. His concerns for women have already been mentioned. He did not see why a woman could not hold a mining licence. In his respect for the Aborigines, he was way ahead of his time. In his view, there should be equal justice for all. The less fortunate should not be further disadvantaged, regardless of race, 'class' or money; the 'diggers' always had his support. He was as critical of white settlers when they massacred Aboriginals at Myall Creek, especially defenceless women and children, as he was of the Aborigines who murdered white people. He believed that Aborigines should be allowed to give evidence in court cases, especially where they could provide eye-witness accounts. He had the same respect for migrants of other races, especially the Chinese. He condemned the treatment of the Chinese at Lambing Flat in the strongest terms, along with John Hux and John West. He praised "the way that the men of Tambaroora act[ed] towards a man like themselves, though he chances to be born in China".[2] The respect of the Chinese for de Boos was evident in the presentation of the medal at Braidwood and the message from Quong Tart at his funeral.

Everywhere he lived and worked, he made significant contributions to the local communities, being involved in the establishment and support of hospitals, jockey clubs, schools, Anglican and other churches, art and music societies. This was done as an individual, through groups, as a local councillor, and as member of the Masonic order. Small acknowledgements of his local work can be found in streets named after him in Temora, Barmedman, and Wyalong.

His contribution to the Colony of New South Wales and to the Colonial Public Service demonstrate his obvious love of Australia; only rarely did his thoughts go back to the country of his birth. In the *Herald*'s obituary, the writer stated (more accurately this time) that de Boos "in the course

---

2 - *Sydney Morning Herald*, September 30, 1865, page 4.

of his long life did much to benefit the country of his adoption and … incidentally made existence happier and smoother for his contemporaries".[3]

His work as a journalist and as a government official meant a lot of time was spent away from home, quite apart from the evening work in the Colonial Parliament. It is little wonder that there were periods when he and his wife needed domestic help. There would have been hard times, especially following the deaths of children and then the illness and death of his wife. But given his own happy childhood, his own home must surely have been a happy home. At the end of his series 'My Holiday', he wrote of "the wild Indian yell with which I was greeted by my youngsters on entering my own door".[4] And the musical activities of Charles and family members, especially Lucille, must surely be further indications of a good family life.

> *If we may take a metaphor from Mr. De Boos' journalistic profession we may say that the last word of his life has been written, the last proof has been pulled, the paper has gone to press, and, no doubt, with human errors, but with an overwhelming proportion of good work and sterling merit, lies an open page of which the author has no need to be ashamed.*[5]

In de Boos' obituary in the *Sydney Morning Herald*, the writer stated that "his life history may be told in a few words".[6] As this book has shown, nothing could be further from the truth. As early as 1852 he wrote, in a somewhat self-deprecating manner, that he had had "a somewhat motley existence".[7] That was true of his life both before and after 1852. He was most definitely a "not-so-ordinary individual".[8]

---

3 - *Sydney Morning Herald*, October 31, 1900, page 7.
4 - *Sydney Mail*, September 14, 1861, page 2.
5 - *The Sydney Mail*, November 10, 1900, page 1096.
6 - *Sydney Morning Herald*, October 31, 1900, page 7.
7 - His own words, *The Argus*, May 8, 1852, page 4.
8 - Curthoys and McGrath 2009, 187.

Appendices

Appendix 3.1

Relatives of Charles de Boos who also migrated to Australia in the 19th Century

Henry Woodcock de Boos

Henry Woodcock followed his older brother to Australia, arriving in Sydney on January 17, 1849.[1] In 1854, he was appointed an Attaché of His Hawaiian Majesty's Commission to the Independent States and Tribes of Polynesia, sailing to Tahiti in October 1854.[2] He married Mariah Singleton (1847-1909) in Newcastle in 1865; they had nine children. He worked for many years as a Colonial Government public servant, occupying numerous positions, in particular being appointed "warden's clerk and mining registrar at Gulgong", which he held from 1878 to 1892.[3] From June 1885, he was also clerk of petty sessions.[4] He retired in 1892 due to ill-health. (He went missing for some weeks following Christmas, 1892.[5]) Two years later, on September 25, 1894, Henry was charged at the Water Police Court in Sydney with three instances of embezzlement in 1892.[6] At the subsequent trial in Gulgong, he was "fined £20, in default six months' imprisonment. Fine paid".[7] He was much involved in the Gulgong community, being a church warden at St. Luke's Church of England, a member and 'Worshipful Master of the Abbotsford Masonic Lodge in Mudgee, and a member of the

---

1 - *Sydney Morning Herald*, January 18, 1849, page 2; Trinder and Fearnley 2005.
2 - *Empire*, October 17, 1854, page 1; *Sydney Morning Herald*, October 17, 1854, page 1; *Empire*, October 31, 1854, page 4; Tate 1961.
3 - From *Government Gazette*, March 8, 1878, *Sydney Morning Herald*, March 9, 1878, page 8; *Evening News*, April 30, 1875, page 2. See his reports in the Department of Mines Annual Reports.
4 - *Sydney Morning Herald*, June 6, 1885, page 9.
5 - *Australian Star*, January 19, 1893, page 5.
6 - *Evening News*, September 26, 1894, page 5; *Australian Town and Country Journal*, October 6, 1894, page 5; Australian Star, October 2, 1894, page 5.
7 - *New South Wales Police Gazette and Weekly Record of Crime*, October 24, 1894, page 361.

Public School Board.[8] He died in Leichhardt, Sydney, on July 18, 1908, aged 81.[9]

de Boos' first two years at Gulgong coincided with the last two years of Thomas Browne's time there as Mining Warden and Police Magistrate. Certainly initially, Browne was a very inexperienced public servant. Further, "unlike most Gold Fields Commissioners, he was substantially at odds with his community".[10] He was constantly criticised, especially by the *Gulgong Guardian* (1871-1873) and its editor, Thomas Frederick DeCourcy Browne (no relation). Among other things, he was criticised for spending time writing rather than doing his job. Browne, as Rolf Boldrewood, made use of his Gulgong experiences in some of his writing, such as *Robbery Under Arms* (1888) and *The Miner's Right: a tale of the Australian goldfields* (1890). Was Henry the mining registrar that Browne did not get on well with, and who figured in *The Miner's Right*?[11]

John de Boos

John and Mary (nee Lane) de Boos and their three children, Mary Ann, Charles Lane, and Frederick John, were already in Melbourne when Charles and family arrived. They had been married in Christ Church Spitalfields in 1842. They sailed to Australia on the 506-ton barque *Asiatic*, which left London and Plymouth in late August-early September, 1849, arriving in Port Adelaide on December 26, 1849, with 152 passengers.[12] It was scheduled to continue to Port Phillip, but it did not do so. Passengers for Port Phillip completed their journey on the *Glen Huntly*, arriving there on January 4, 1850.[13] After a period in Melbourne, and then joining the gold diggers at Forest Creek, John de Boos moved to Euroa. At later dates, he was joined by three of his siblings, Charlotte Mary and Henry,[14] and Matilda; precise dates of arrival have not been found. Henry died at Euroa, aged 28 years, on August 8, 1855.[15]

---

8 - *Sydney Mail*, May 15, 1886, page 1033; *Sydney Morning Herald*, April 10, 1890, page 4; *Sydney Mail*, June 26, 1886, page 1344; *Sydney Morning Herald*, August 17, 1878, page 3.

9 - *Sydney Morning Herald*, July 21, 1908, page 6; *Evening News*, August 20, 1908, page 3.

10 - Hamilton 2015, 139-159.

11 - Jinks 2005b.

12 - *South Australian Register*, December 29, 1849, page 2.

13 - *Sydney Morning Herald*, January 19, 1850, page 4.

14 - *The Argus*, May 21, 1853, page 1.

15 - *The Argus*, August 18, 1855, page 4; Corfield 2003, 123-124; Toohill 2015, 93-95.

Of particular interest is the fact that John spent some of his early time in Melbourne working for *The Argus*. In August 1851, the paper "despatched a reporter" to the Anderson's Creek gold field; it was John de Boos. His first report was headed "The Victoria Gold Field"; others followed, headed 'Victoria Diggings', attributed to "a correspondent" and "our special correspondent".[16] That they were the work of John de Boos is indicated by an article in *The Argus* entitled "The First Gold-Field in Victoria. How I discovered it", written many years later by Louis John Michel who had made the find. He stated that his party included "Mr. de Boos, from The Argus office, whose report on the trip and success of every one of the party in finding gold may be found in *The Argus* for July, 1851".[17] It seems, however, that digging for gold became more attractive than reporting about it, as John's obituary noted that "On the breaking out of the gold fever he went with a party to the Forest Creek rush, but although they got on good gold they could not continue mining on account of bad water and the prevalence of sickness among the party".[18] Some confirmation of this is provided by the fact that in early 1852, there was unclaimed mail for him at the Mount Alexander Diggings.[19]

John and his family then moved to Euroa and were among the town's pioneering citizens. They and their descendants played a major role in the town's development.[20]

Vernon C. de Boos

A nephew of Charles de Boos, Vernon arrived in Sydney on the 1172 tons *Lady Octavia* on February 22, 1875. Having left Start Point in England on December 1, 1874, it had been a rough trip.[21] His time in Australia was very short, as after just over four months, he was the victim of a shooting accident near Murrurundi, in the upper Hunter Valley. At the end of a shooting trip, "while lifting the gun off the vehicle without sufficient

---

16 - *The Argus*, August 16, page 2; August 18, page 2; August 22, 1851, page 2.
17 - *The Argus*, December 28, 1895, page 9. The report was published in *The Argus* on August 7, 1851, page 2.
The work of John de Boos for *The Argus* was also covered in his obituary in *The Euroa Advertiser*, March 11, 1898, page 2.
18 - *The Euroa Gazette*, March 11, 1898, page 2.
19 - *Victoria Government Gazette*, January 14, 1852, page 19.
20 - DeBoos 1934.
21 - *Sydney Morning Herald, February 24, 1987, page 4*.

care, the weapon exploded", shooting him in the face.[22] He died shortly afterwards in Newcastle on June 9, 1875, from "fearful injuries".[23] He was 22 years of age. It is not known what occupation he had taken up or what had taken him to the Hunter Valley.

Appendix 6.1

Reports in *The Argus* 'From Our Special Commissioner' (Charles de Boos), 1852.

Title	Number	Date	Page
The Diggings		March 16	2
Mount Alexander		March 19	2
Mount Alexander	III	March 22	2
Mount Alexander		March 26	2
Mount Alexander		March 30	2
Mount Alexander		April 5	2
Mount Alexander		April 21	4
Mount Alexander	VIII	April 26	4
Mount Alexander	IX	April 29	4
Mount Alexander	X	May 1	4
Mount Alexander	XI	May 6	4
Mount Alexander	XII	May 8	4
Mount Alexander	XIII	May 19	4

Appendix 6.2

Clunes, by 'Our Special Correspondent', *The Argus*, 1851.

Title	Date	Page	Writer
The Clune Diggings	August 5	2	OSC
The Victoria Gold Field	August 7	2	About Anderson's Creek; no attribution
Clune's Diggings	August 9	2	OSC, from Carpenter's Inn
The Victoria Gold Diggings. Anderson's Creek	August 11	2	"we dispatched a reporter"
The Clunes Diggings, on the Deep Creek	August 11	2	G.H. Wathen
The Clunes Diggings	August 13	2	OSC
The Clunes Diggings	August 16	2	OSC

---

22 - *Maitland Mercury*, May 20, 1875, page 5.
23 - *Maitland Mercury*, June 24, 1875, page 4.

| Victoria Diggings (Anderson's Creek) | August 18 | 2 | A.C. |
| Victoria Diggings | August 22 | 2 | OSC |

Appendix 6.3

'The Diggings' by 'Our Special Commissioner', *The Argus*, April-July 1853.

Number	Date	Page	Written from
	April 27	4	Creswick's Creek
II	May 7	4	Ballarat
III	May 13	6	Ballarat
	May 31	5	Creswick's Creek
V	June 6	9	Creswick's Creek
	June 10	6	Creswick's Creek
	June 14	6	Birch's Creek
	June 22	7	Ballarat
IX	June 28	4	
X	June 30	2	Ballarat
XI	July 5	4-5	Ballarat

Appendix 7.1

'The Goldfields of New South Wales', *Sydney Morning Herald*, 1857.

Number	Date	Page	Places visited
1	April 20	2	"The Steamer": steamer *Williams* to Newcastle, then to Morpeth, road to Maitland, horse to Lochinvar, Black Creek, Singleton, Glennies Creek, Muswellbrook, Aberdeen, Scone, Page Valley.
2	April 23	5	Valley of the Page, Murrurundi, Tamworth, the Moonbies.
3	May 1	2	Bendemeer, Carlisle's Gully, Armidale.
4	May 4	2	'From Armidale to Oban', on Good Friday, April 10, 1857.
5	May 8	2	'Oban' diggings.
6	May 11	2-3	'From Oban to Rocky River': Oban, Armidale, Rocky River, Uralla.
7	May 12	3	'The Rocky River': Rocky River / Uralla.
8	May 16	4	'From the Rocky River to the Hanging Rock': Uralla / Rocky River, Nundle / Hanging Rock.
9	May 16	4 & 7	'The Hanging Rock', about 25 km south of Tamworth.
10	June 26	4	'Back to Sydney': Hanging Rock, Gunnoo Gunnoo, Breeza (42 km south-east of Gunnedah), Maitland, Sydney. Far too wet to go directly to Mudgee. 'Sydney to Mudgee': Penrith, Mount Victoria, Hartley, Bowenfels, Barnaby's Inn at Round Swamp. Includes comment that he saw Penrith "ten years back".
11	June 27	6	Barnaby's Inn, Mudgee.

12	July 1	3	'Mudgee', 'Mudgee to Murrendi': Gratti Creek, 'Murrendi'
13	July 2	2	'Murrendi to Burrandong': got lost; 'Burrandong'.
14	July 3	5	'Burrandong to Muckrawa', 'Muckrawa', 'The Ironbark'.
15	July 6	3	'The Wellington Road': Ironbark, 'Stoney Creek', 'Back to Burrendong'.
16	July 7	3	'From Burrendong to Louisa Creek': Louisa Creek.
17	July 9	8	'Avisford', 'The Meroo'.
18	July 15	2	'From Louisa to Tambaroora': Tambaroora and district; Opossum Creek.
19	July 20	2	'From Tambaroora to Sofala'.
20	July 21	8	Sofala, Turon, Big and Little Oakey Creeks.
	July 23	4	Editorial commenting on reports.
21	July 29	2	'Sofala to Bathurst': Bathurst and Kelso.
22	August 3	2	'Bathurst': 'Bathurst to Tuena': Coolooloo Creek, Moolgonia.
23	August 5	5	'Bathurst to Tuena': comment about Trunkey Creek, Tuena
24	August 18	4	'Tuena to Goulburn': Binda, Goulburn

Much of these reports were summarised (though at some length) in the special '*Sydney Overland Mail*' supplements written especially for overseas readers.[24]

Appendix 7.2

The Journeys to and from Canoona, 1858.

Month	Date	Day	Event
September	16	Thursday	Sailed from Sydney on the *Yarra Yarra* (*Sydney Morning Herald*, September 17, 1858, page 4).
	17	Friday	Newcastle: taking on coal
	21	Tuesday	Moreton Island
	22	Wednesday	Curtis Island
	23	Thursday	Keppel Bay
	24	Friday	Rockhampton
	27	Monday	Left for Canoona
	29	Wednesday	Reached Canoona
October	1	Friday	Started on trip back to Rockhampton
	4	Monday	Reached Rockhampton
	8	Friday	Sailed for Sydney on the *Wonga Wonga*
	12	Tuesday	Back in Sydney (*Sydney Morning Herald*, October 13, 1858, page 4).
	14	Thursday	Left Sydney at 3.00 p.m. on the *Wonga Wonga* (*Sydney Morning Herald*, October 15, 1858, page 4).
	18	Monday	Keppel Bay
	19	Tuesday	Rockhampton

24 - *Sydney Morning Herald*, May 23, 1857, pages 5-6, July 18, 1857, page 5, September 10, 1857, page 11.

	25	Monday	In Rockhampton
	29	Friday	In Rockhampton
November	6	Saturday	Returned from Canoona at midnight
	7	Sunday	Aborted trip north
	9	Tuesday	Back in Rockhampton
	20	Saturday	In Rockhampton
	26	Friday	Left Rockhampton on the *Corio*.
	27	Saturday	Left Keppel Bay
	28	Sunday	Left Port Curtis
December	4	Sunday	Reached Sydney (*Sydney Morning Herald*, December 6, 1858, page 4). Corio S.N. Co., a 125 tons steamship. Captain Brown, own agent. Had 61 passengers.

Appendix 7.3

'Fitzroy Diggings', *Sydney Morning Herald*, 1858.

Number	Date	Page	Title
I	October 5	4	'Fitzroy Gold-Fields'. A voyage "of more than ordinary pleasure" on the *Yarra Yarra* from Sydney by way of Newcastle and a very difficult channel through Moreton Bay to Rockhampton.
II	October 13	5	'Fitzroy Diggings'. The forty miles from Rockhampton to Canoona on foot, a two-day journey. Canoona and its failure. Four days later he was back in Rockhampton, and along with hundreds of others trying to get a boat to Sydney.
III	October 16	5	'Fitzroy Diggings'. Aspects of the Canoona district: squatters, "savage and hostile" Aborigines, alligators.
IV	October 27	2	'Fitzroy Diggings'. Concerns for the hundreds of people stranded along the Fitzroy and what they might do. But he was back in Rockhampton, having sailed on the *Wonga Wonga*.
V	October 30	4	'Fitzroy Diggings'. "Nothing doing; ... all at the very last point of hopelessness".
VI	November 6	5	'Fitzroy Diggings'. Conditions in Rockhampton. People keep arriving.
	November 17	5	'Fitzroy Diggings'. A further account of conditions; no hope of any gold at Canoona. Information on passenger arrivals and departures.
	November 23		'Fitzroy Diggings'.
	November 27	5	'Fitzroy Diggings'. News from Rockhampton and a detailed account of a two-day trip in a small boat 'Up the Fitzroy'. Much information about the flora and fauna.
	December 7	4	'Fitzroy Diggings'. An eight-day return trip to Sydney. The "collapse" of Rockhampton.

Not all of the articles were numbered. A summary of his writings appeared under the heading, "Postscript to the Summary for England: the Fitzroy Diggings". *Sydney Morning Herald*, December 11, 1858, page 5.

Appendix 7.4

'Random Notes from a Wandering Reporter', Series One, 1865*

No.	Sydney Morning Herald	Page	The Sydney Mail**	Page	Places Visited
I	July 5	5	July 15	6 & 3	Wingecarribee Swamp, Kangaloon, Robertson.
II	July 6	8	July 15	6 & 3	Kangaloon, Berrima.
III	July 13	2	July 15	6 & 3	Berrima, Wingello, Marulan, Goulburn.
IV					
V	July 17	5	July 22	8	Araluen.
VI	July 19	5	July 22	3	Araluen, Majors Creek, Jembaicumbene, Shoalhaven Diggings.
VII					
VIII	July 24	2	July 29	5	Mongarlowe, Braidwood.
IX	July 25	2	July 29	5	Braidwood, Boro, Lake Bathurst, Lake George, Currawang, Collector, Wollogorang, Mummel, Grabben Gullen.
X	July 26	8	August 5	5-6	On farming and the Land Act in the area.
XI	August 11	2	August 19	8	Upper Murrumbidgee (not clear just where), Yass Plains.
XII	August 14	8	August 19	8	Burrangong goldfields, including Wombat and Tipperary, Lambing Flat.
XIII	August 16	5	August 26	5	Lambing Flat / Young, Lake George, Collector, Gunning.
XIV	August 18	2	August 26	5	Yass, Bowning, Binalong, Lambing Flat / Young.
XV	August 22	2	August 26	5-6	Young, Weddin Mountains, Bogolong, The Pinnacle, Currajong / Billibong (the Lachlan goldfields), Forbes.
XVI	August 23	2	September 2	7	Forbes, Murga, Orange.
XVII	September 6	8	September 9	6	Orange district, Lucknow.
XVIII	September 11	2	September 16	5	Orange district: gold mining.
XIX	September 12	2	September 16	10	Orange district: copper mining.
XX	September 14	2	September 16	11	Orange district: agriculture. "I visited Orange some two years ago …" ***
XXI	September 15	2	September 23	5	Orange.****
XXII	September 26	2	September 30	5-6	Orange, Ophir, Tambaroora.
XXIII	September 28	2	October 7	3	Tambaroora. (Lengthy discussion of land policies.)
XXIV	September 30	4	October 7	3	Tambaroora, Upper Turon Valley, Wattle Flat, Sofala. (Suicides and leprosy among Chinese miners.)

XXV	October 4	2	October 14	5	Peel, Bathurst.
	October 7	7	October 14	5	Bathurst, Glanmire.
	October 12	2	October 14	3	Bathurst, Bowenfels, Hartley. Concluding note of thanks to people he had met.

*A comment in the last article indicated there had been a problem with the numbering of his articles, which would account for there being no articles numbered IV and VII. However, whilst there is no apparent gap in the record between articles VI and VIII, the gap between III and V takes the reader directly from Goulburn to Araluen. The absence of any comment on his journey from Goulburn to Araluen really does suggest that article IV was not published. He just could not have gone such a distance without having anything to say about the journey.

** They were not numbered in *The Sydney Mail*.

*** This and other references in the series to visits about two years ago, are to the series 'Pen and Ink Sketches' of late 1863-early 1864.

**** "I am not a lawyer, and I may say that I have never done thanking Providence for it".

Appendix 7.5

'Random Notes from a Wandering Reporter', Series Two, 1866.

No.	Sydney Morning Herald	Page	The Sydney Mail	Page	Places Visited
I	April 23	3	April 28	5	By sea to Newcastle (last there 8-9 years ago), train to Singleton.
II	April 25	2	April 28	5	Singleton / Patrick's Plains ('selectors' and farming; disputes between different types of settlers).
III	May 3	2	May 5	3	Singleton (description of town), Great Northern Road, on horseback: Glennies Creek, Muswellbrook (agriculture).
IV	May 4	5	May 5	9	Muswellbrook (description of town and district), Aberdeen (one of two stores "kept by a Chinaman"), Scone.
V	May 9	2	May 12	6	Scone, Bellevue, Belltrees, Denison
VI	May 11	5	May 12	9	Denison, Monan Creek (isolated free selectors; comments about 'Captain Thunderbolt' and his mistress), Glenrock.
VII	May 21	2	May 26	6	Nundle, Hanging Rock, Peel River.
VIII	May 23	3	May 26	9	Nundle: relations between Europeans and Chinese. Happy Valley, Dry Creek, Foley's Creek, Swamp Oak Creek, Bowling Alley Point, Monroe's Creek (mainly Chinese).
IX	May 24	3	June 2	5-6	Nundle, Peel River, Tamworth, Dongwon Creek, Liverpool Plains (drought), Moonbi, Bendemeer (exchanges with an Aboriginal who spoke very good English).

X	May 28	2	June 2	6	Bendemeer, crossed Macdonald River (had been here before), Carlisle's Gully, Kentucky Station (drought ridden), Uralla / Rocky River ("a long straggling township of one street").
XI	May 30	5	June 2	6	Rocky River, Kentucky Creek (Fulcrum Mining Co.); problems with regulations. Nundle: what will happen when the Commissioners are removed; total inadequacy of court / legal system.
XII	June 2	8	June 9	5	Rocky River, Bellala Station, Stony Batter (most miserable country – no feed for his horse), Mt. Lowry (or Lousy), Ironbark (or Woods Reef), after a very difficult journey: "not by any means an important gold field".
XIII	June 6	2	June 9	5	Ironbark, Kelly's Reef, Addisons Reef: reef mining.
XIV	June 13	2	June 16	5	Ironbark, Barraba (on the Manilla River), Lower Bingara (once flourishing diggings in a miserable state).
XV	June 14	2	June 16	3	Bingara, Bull, Myall Creek, Inverell.
XVI	June 18	8	June 23	7	Inverell, planned to go to Tenterfield, but bad weather caused him to head for Armidale.
XVII	June 21	5	June 23	9	Paradise Creek Station, Limestone, Armidale area (agriculture, more criticism of Land Acts).
XVIII	June 27	2	June 30	5	Armidale. New England district (agriculture, sheep farming, shepherds, property boundaries, problems of free selection).
XIX	June 29	2	July 7	7	Armidale and New England (stations and their residences, agricultural and pastoral activities, Uralla, Salisbury Plains, Terrible Vale Station, in sight of Bergen-op-Zoom Station).
XX	July 3	5	July 7	7	Graveyard – unknown? Walcha (had a miserable night in an inn), issues of free selectors, cattle stealing, etc.
XXI	July 10	2	July 14	6	Walcha, Branga Park Station, Branga Plains Station (more heavy rain, wet and cold, saved by New England hospitality), Great Port Stephens Trail, Shaking Bog, a guide through the bush.
XXII	July 30	2	Not published in *Mail*.		Virtually no roads or tracks, very difficult, partly along a creek: old sheep station of A.A. Company, Newindock, "enormous mountain range", Hungry Hill, Geera Flat Station, Gloucester, after another hard journey on a road that was "toilsome and dreary".
XXIII	August 3	3	August 11	5	Gloucester (AA Company town), Stroud ("fenced-in township"), Raymond Terrace and Hunter Valley.
XXIV	August 6	2	August 11	5	Coal mining in the Lower Hunter Valley.
XXV	August 10	5	August 18	6	Coal mining in the Lower Hunter Valley.
XXVI	August 13	2	August 18	6	Coal mining in the Lower Hunter Valley.
XXVII	August 20	6	August 25	5	Waratah, Newcastle.

Appendix 7.6

'Random Notes from a Wandering Reporter', Series Three, 1870-1871.

No.	Sydney Morning Herald	Page	The Sydney Mail	Page	Title and Places Visited
I	July 5	5	July 9	10	'The Rail and the Road': by train through the Blue Mountains to Wallerawang, then road to Cudgegong (50 miles in 12 hours, most at night).
II	July 9	5	July 23	6	Cudgegong, the Cinnabar Mines.
III	July 14	5	July 30	7	'The Gulgong Rush': Gulgong.
IV	August 8	5	August 13	10	Tambaroora.
V	August 11	5	August 20	6	The Bald Hills.
VI	August 15	5	August 27	6	Hill End; the Bathurst to Trunkey road.
					Break.
VII	October 20	5	October 22	15	The Bowenfels coalfield.
VIII	October 28	5	November 12	7	The Turon.
					Presumably, he then returned to Sydney.
IX	January 20	5	January 28	11	To Goulburn: "The trip to Goulburn is a very different thing now to what it used to be when I first travelled that road, at the end of 1839".
X	January 28	7	February 4	6	Goulburn and the return to Sydney.
XI	February 25	6	March 4	15	Blue Mountains. "I have given you more than one sketch of the trip across the Blue Mountains in different series of my random notes, - sketches of what was to be met with on horseback, and what was to be seen by rail". Blackheath, Govett's Leap.
XII	March 7	2	March 11	40	Legend of Govett's Leap, Part I.
XIII	March 16	6	March 18	87	Legend of Govett's Leap, Part II.
XIV	March 25	5	April 1	156	Legend of Govett's Leap, Part III. It was a fictional story.

Some of the articles in the *Mail* were headed "The Tourist: Wandering Notes by a Random Reporter".

Appendix 7.7

'Random Notes from a Wandering Reporter', Series Four, 1871.

No.	Sydney Morning Herald	Page	The Sydney Mail	Page	Places Visited
I	July 13	5	July 15	622-623	'Gulgong'

II	July 19	5	July 22	654-655	'Gulgong'
III	July 24	2	July 29	686-687	'Gulgong', 'Mudgee'
IV	July 26	5	July 29	687	'Tambaroora': also Hill End and Hawkin's Hill ("I have, upon more than one occasion during the last fourteen years that you have commissioned me to visit and report upon the gold-fields of New South Wales, …").
V	August 1	5	August 5	726-727	'Hawkin's Hill' [or Hawkins' Hill]
VI	August 4	5	August 12	750-751	'Hawkin's Hill'
VII	August 7	2	August 12	751	'Hawkin's Hill'
VIII	August 11	5	August 19	782-783	'Hawkin's Hill'

Appendix 7.8

'Random Notes by a Wandering Reporter', Series Five, 1872.

Sydney Morning Herald	Page	The Sydney Mail	Page	Places Visited
January 17	5	January 20	73-74	'Hill End' and Tambaroora. This was a specific trip to Hill End.
March 6	7	March 9	299	'The Shale and Oil Company' I (near Mt Victoria)
March 7	5	March 16	317	'The Shale and Oil Company' II
March 8	5	March 30	411	'The Oil and Shale Oil Company' III
June 28	3	June 29	815	'Wattle Flat'
July 4	3	July 6	20	'Wattle Flat (continued)'

Appendix 7.9

'Pen and Ink Sketches', 1863-64.

No.	Sydney Morning Herald	Page	The Sydney Mail	Page	Title
I	November 26	5	November 28	3	'The Eugowra Rocks' (site of "the great Escort robbery"); Eugowra Creek; Orange; Wentworth Mines (about 1,200 people); Pretty Plains (agriculture); two copper mines.
II	December 14	8	December 19	6	A somewhat contradictory account of 'Forbes'

III	December 25	2	December 26	12	'The Frontage System'
IV	December 29	2	January 2	5	'The Pine Forest', on the journey from Forbes to Young; The Pinnacle, Bogalong
V	January 7	2	January 9	3	'Young'
VI	January 14	2	January 16	3	'The Burrangong Gold-Field'; Chinese miners.

Appendix 7.10

The frontage system

The 'frontage claim system' was originated in Ballarat to solve, in a measure, certain local difficulties which presented themselves. As the auriferous bearing channels deepened and passed beneath flows of basalt great difficulty was experienced in following them, and to save useless expenditure the plan was devised authorizing claims of a definite length along the supposed course of the 'gutter', but of indefinite width. Beginning at the last known point of discovery on the 'gutter' arcs of circles were described, so as to include any possible course of the 'lead', and with such radii as would give to each portion between two adjacent arcs a width equal to that allowed for a claim. These rainbow-shaped claims were designated frontage claims, and were held without the usual development requirement until the course of the 'lead' was determined. As soon as this was fixed the claims were limited laterally between the bounding arcs. This plan resulted in a stimulating of development for a time, but as work progressed the system became so complicated (for the leads branches, cross leads were encountered, and one set of frontage claims overlapped another) that it led to apparently interminable litigation. The system was therefore abandoned in Ballarat on September 7, 1866. R. Brough Smyth, in summing up the results of this system in 1869, says:

> The rights acquired under this system remain, but the mining companies are striving earnestly to procure large areas under lease from the Crown; and it is not too much to say that, wealthy as Ballarat is, it would have been immensely more prosperous if, instead of the frontage claims, the local bodies had in the first instance granted sufficiently large areas, with well-defined boundaries, to persons willing to incur and able to fulfill reasonable obligations as to the employment of labor and the investment of capital.

In 1862 New South Wales adopted in a modified form the frontage system. ... the regulations were repeatedly amended, and the system became operative only when deemed desirable by the resident gold commissioner. In practice it was not utilized to any great degree and has now been abandoned.[25]

Appendix 8.1

'Random Notes by a Wandering Reporter', 1874-1875.

No.	Sydney Morning Herald	Page	The Sydney Mail	Page	Places visited
	November 2	2			Nine hours by 'The Mail' train to Raglan, then a 15-20 passenger coach to Bathurst.
II	November 5	6	November 7	591	Bathurst.
III	November 16	5	November 21	647	Bathurst: continued.
IV	November 23	3	November 28	683	Orange.
V	December 1	6	December 12	759	The Western Copper Country: Orange, Wellington
6	December 3	3			The Western Copper Country (continued): Bathurst district.
7	December 7	6			The Western Copper Country: The Bowenfels Coal Field; Lithgow Valley.
VIII	December 11	2	December 19	776	The Lithgow Valley Coal Mining Company: The Bowenfels Coal Mining Company; The Esk Bank Colliery; Vale of Clwydd Copper Mining Company.
IX	December 12	7			Esk Bank Copper Smelting Works: Mort's Slaughtering Establishment; The Milburn Creek Copper Mine.
IX (sic)	January 2	7	January 9	53	The Lithgow Valley Iron Working Company.

Appendix 9.1

Contributions to the Annual Reports of the Department of Mines, New South Wales.

Year	Location	District	Pages
1875	Braidwood	Southern District	43-49
1876	Braidwood	Southern District	63-65
1877	Braidwood	Southern District	89-97

---

25 - Extracts from Veitch 1911, 111-112, 136.

1878	Braidwood	Southern District	79-83
1879	Braidwood	Southern District	107-115
1880	Copeland	Hunter and Macleay	171-174
1881	Temora	Lachlan	52-54
1882	Temora	Lachlan	55-57
1883	Copeland	Hunter and Macleay	97-99
1884	Copeland	Hunter and Macleay	93-95
1885	Copeland	Hunter and Macleay	87-89
1886	Copeland	Hunter and Macleay	87
1887	Milparinka	Albert	105-107
1888	Milparinka	Albert	120-121

Appendix 12.1

'Men who *Have* been Raised', 1862.

The Sydney Mail	Page	Sydney Morning Herald	Page	Title
February 15	1	February 20	3	
February 22	2	February 22	6	"Mr. Dalgleish"
March 1	2	March 4	3	"Mr. Love"
March 8	2	March 10	3	"Caldwell and Stewart"
March 15	2	March 19	2	"Mr. W.B. Allen"
March 22	8	March 24	3	"Mr. Buchanan"
March 29	8	March 31	3	"Mr. Dangar"
April 5	5	April 7	3	
April 12	5	April 14	2	
April 26	8	April 28	2	
May 3	4	May 5	2	
May 10	8	May 12	3	

Appendix 12.2

'Letters from Congewoi', 1862.

The Sydney Mail	Page	Sydney Morning Herald	Page	Title
August 30	5	September 2	3	Mr. John Smith, on Government
September 6	5	September 8	3	Mr. John Smith, on Honesty
September 20	5	September 20	3	Mr. John Smith, on Finance
September 27	2	September 29	3	Mr. John Smith, on Tracking
November 1	8	November 3	2	Mr. John Smith, on Dodging

Appendix 12.3

'The Congewoi Chesterfield', *The Sydney Mail*, 1865.

Date	Page	Title
April 15	8	
April 22	3	On Deportment Generally
April 29	3	On Deportment in Partic'lar
May 20	3	On Deportment in Partic'lar (continued)
June 10	8	On Deportment in Partic'lar (continued)
July 1	6	

Appendix 12.4

'Mr John Smith's Visit to Sydney', *The Sydney Mail*, 1868.

Date	Page	Title
February 8	12	Letter the First. Shows how Mrs. John Smith contrived to get her own way, and how Mr. John Smith had his Revenge
February 15	12	Letter Two. He Discourseth upon the South Head Rush
February 22	12	Letter III. He goes to see all the sights, and suggests a new Style of Illumination
February 29	12	Letter Four. Looks at the demonstration patriotically and regards the Illumination from a new point of view
March 7	12	Letter V. Narrates the Adventures at the Levee [for the Duke of Edinburgh].

Appendix 12.5

'Mr. John Smith Visits the Assembly: the new members', 1870.

Number	The Sydney Mail	Page	Sydney Morning Herald	Page
I	February 5	9	February 7	3
II	February 12	9	February 14	3
III	February 19	12	February 21	6
IV	February 26	8-9	February 28	6
V	March 5	9	March 7	3
VI	March 12	9	March 14	2
VII	March 19	8	March 22	6

VIII	March 26	9	March 28	6
IX	April 2	9	April 4	6
X	April 16	9	April 18	6

Appendix 12.6

Other letters by Mr John Smith.

The Sydney Mail	Page	Sydney Morning Herald	Page	Title
		November 20, 1863	5	The New Fish, by John Smith, jun.
		January 8, 1870	10	Mr. John Smith, of Congewoi, Again
October 22, 1870	7	October 18, 1870	5	The State of Public Business. Mr. John Smith gives his Opinions upon the Parliament and its Doings
		November 1, 1870	3	The Assembly and the Stranger. Mr. Smith Appeals to the Herald
December 10, 1870	11	December 6, 1870	5	Mr. John Smith on the Crisis. Mr. Smith asks for Information. Written from the Haystack Inn, George-street South.

Appendix 12.7

'The Midge Correspondence', 1863-64.

No.	The Sydney Mail	Page	Sydney Morning Herald	Page	Title of Letter
I	September 5	11	September 7	3	Mr. Midge has a grievance, but does not tell it – though he tells us who he is
II	September 12	10	September 18	2	Mr. Midge lectures upon natural history, and at last states his grievance
III	September 19	9	September 22	3	Mr. Midge enters into particulars and tells some official secrets
IV	October 3	3	October 5	3	Mr. Midge tells us nothing that we did not know before
V	October 10	3	October 12	2	Mr. Midge gets back to his grievances, and becomes tiresome
VI	October 17	3	October 20	2	Mr. Midge gives his idea of the crisis

VII	October 24	9	October 27	3	Mr. Midge tries his hand at description, and puts his foot in it
VIII	October 31	9	November 2	2	Mr. Midge gives his idea of a recent dinner at which he was not present, and continues his portrait painting
IX	November 28	9	November 30	3	Mr. Midge has more grievances, and escapes a great danger
X	December 5	3	December 8	3	Mr. Midge relates some more facts physiological and piscatorial and then dives into abstruse political matters
XI	December 12	3	December 15	3	Mr. Midge relates an affecting incident, and then has a go in at the dignities
XII	December 19	3	December 26	3	Mr. Midge discourses upon late hours, and relates a reminiscence
XIII	December 26	9	December 28	2	Mr. Midge discourses upon marital duties generally, but more particularly with reference to a late celebrated occasion
XIV	January 9	10	January 9		Mr. Midge manifests evident dyspeptic symptoms and apologises for his loss of amiability
XV	January 16	3	January 11	3	Mr. Midge makes a new application of an old term, and discourses seriously on morality
XVI	January 23	3	January 25	2	Mr. Midge is forced into the ranks of the unemployed, and continues his new application of the old term
XVII	February 6	11	February 8	2	Mr. Midge goes to the picnic
XVIII	February 13	9	February 15	2	Mrs. Midge expresses her intention to appeal to Caesar [Mrs. Amelia Midge, nee Hopkins].
XIX	February 20	11	February 22	2	Mr. M. looks enviously upon one Department of the Government and informs us of an important society about to be formed
XX	March 5	3	March 7	2	Mr. Midge finds comfort, and explores some little dodges

Appendix 12.8

"The Collective Wisdom of New South Wales".
Series One, 1867-68.

Number	Sydney Morning Herald	Page	The Sydney Mail	Page
I	July 8	5	July 13	8
II	July 15	5	July 20	5
III	July 22	5	July 27	5

IV	July 29	5	August 3	5
V	August 5	5	August 10	5
VI	August 12	5	August 17	8
VII	August 19	5	August 24	8
VIII	August 26	5	August 31	8
IX	September 2	5	September 7	8
X	September 9	2	September 14	8
XI	September 17	5	September 21	8
XII	September 23	5	September 28	5
XIII	September 30	5	October 5	8
XIV	October 7	5	October 12	8
XV	October 14	2	October 19	8
XVI	October 21	5	October 26	8
XVII	October 28	5	November 2	8
XVIII	November 4	5	November 9	8
XIX	November 11	5	November 16	8
XX	November 18	5	November 23	8
XXI	November 25	5	November 30	8
XXII	December 2	5	December 7	8
XXIII	December 9	5	December 14	8
XXIV	December 16	5	December 21	3
XXV	December 23	5	December 28	8
XXVI	January 13	2	January 18	8
XXVII	January 20	5	January 25	5
XXVIII	March 2	5	March 7	5
XXIX	March 16	5	March 21	10
XXX	March 23	5	March 28	10
XXXI	March 30	5	April 4	11
XXXII	April 6	5	April 11	7
XXXIII	April 13	5	April 18	6
XXXIV	April 20	5	April 25	11
XXXV	April 27	5	May 2	12

Series Two, 1868-69.

Number	Sydney Morning Herald	Page	The Sydney Mail	Page
I	October 17	5	October 24	6
II	December 14	5	December 19	11

III	December 21	5	December 26	10
IV	December 28	2	January 2	11
V	January 11	5	January 16	6
VI	January 18	5	January 23	6
VII	January 25	4	January 30	10
VIII	February 1	5	February 6	6
IX	February 8	5	February 13	6
X	February 15	5	February 20	7
XI	February 22	5	February 27	10
XII	March 1	5	March 6	6
XIII	March 8	5	March 13	6
XIV	March 15	5	March 20	7
XV	March 22	5	March 27	10
XVI	March 29	5	April 3	6
XVII	April 5	5	April 10	6

Series Three, 1869.

Number	Sydney Morning Herald	Page	The Sydney Mail	Page
I	October 4	5	October 9	11
II	October 11	5	October 16	6
III	October 18	5	October 23	7
IV	October 25	5	October 30	6
V	November 1	5	November 6	10
VI	November 8	2	November 13	7
VII	November 15	3	November 20	7
VIII	November 19	5	November 20	13

Series Four, 1870.

Number	Sydney Morning Herald	Page	The Sydney Mail	
	February 7	5	February 12	6
II	February 14	5	February 19	7
III	February 21	7	February 26	10
IV	February 28	5	March 5	6
V	March 7	5	March 12	6
VI	March 14	5	March 19	7
VII	March 21	5	March 26	7
VIII	March 28	5	April 2	6
IX	April 4	5	April 9	6
X	April 11	5	April 16	6

XI	April 18	2	April 23	10
XII	April 25	5	April 30	6
XIII	May 2	5	May 7	10
XIV	May 9	11	May 14	10

Series Five, 1871.

Number	Sydney Morning Herald	Page	The Sydney Mail	Page
	January 30	5	February 4	6
II	February 6	5	February 11	6
III	February 13	7	February 18	6
IV	February 20	5	February 25	10
V	February 27	5	March 4	27
VI	March 6	5	March 11	60
VII	March 13	5	March 18	90
VIII	March 20	5	March 25	103
IX	March 27	5	April 1	152
X	April 3	5	April 8	194
XI	April 10	5	April 15	219-22
XII	April 17	5	April 22	252
XIII	April 24	5	April 29	284
XIV	May 1	5	May 6	314
XV	May 8	5	May 13	344
XVI	May 15	5	May 20	359
XVII	May 22	5	May 27	405
XVIII	May 29	5	June 3	424
XIX	June 5	5	June 10	455
XX	June 12	5	June 17	490
XXI	June 19	5	June 24	519-52
XXII	June 26	5	July 1	557

Appendix 12.9

'The Poor Man', 1864.

No.	The Sydney Mail	Page	Sydney Morning Herald	Page	Title
1	March 12	9	March 14	2	Shows who Mr. Pepper is, and what he projected
2	March 19	3	March 22	2	Shows how Mr. Pepper set out on his Travels, and what success he met with

3	March 26	9	March 29	2	Discourseth upon Virtue, and showeth how Mr. Pepper fell into difficulty
4	April 2	9	April 4	3	Introduces a Character to whom the Attention of the Reader is particularly invited
5	April 9	12	April 11	2	Gives some idea of the Residence of a well-to-do Australian Settler
6	April 16	11	April 22	2	Narrates the abrupt departure of Mr. Pepper, and a conversation that occurred on the road
7	May 7	3	May 9	2	Describes the Home of a Poor Settler
8	May 14	9	May 19	3	Introduces the Reader to the Interior of the Poor Settler's Home, as well as to the Individual Himself
9	May 28	9	May 30	3	Takes Mr. Pepper further into the Country
10	June 4	9	June 6	3	Introduces the Reader to a Stringy-Barker
11	June 18	2	June 20	2	Enters into Particulars Concerning the Stringy Barker
12	June 25	9	June 27	3	Shows the little Game of the Stringy Barker and Foreshadows a Tragedy
13	July 2	3	July 4	2	Is Serious, and of course Uninteresting
14	July 9	12	July 9	8	Describes the reasons for Mr. Pepper's return to Sydney
15	July 23	9	July 25	3	At Last Gives Promise of Success
16	August 13	3	August 17	3	Tells how Mr. Pepper follows up his Adventure
17	September 3	9	September 5	3	Takes Mr. Pepper to the Police Court, and gives him a fore-shortened glimpse of the object of his Search
18	September 17	3	September 19	2	Shows how Mr. Pepper went to gaol, what the consequences were, and how he and his search were knocked on the head

Appendix 12.10

'The Corncobs', *The Sydney Mail*, 1865.

Date	Page	Letter Number	Title
January 14	3		How we got our Information
		I	A Mystery
		II	A Little Game
January 21	3	III	A Family in Difficulties
		IV	A Struggling Genius
February 4	11	V	Doubts
		VI	A Bushman

		VII	Another Victim
February 11	8	VIII	Matters of Opinion
		IX	Matters of Fact
		X	Ominous
February 25	8	XI	Evidence
		XII	Ideas
March 4	8	XIII	An Attack
		XIV	Tracks
March 11	8	XV	Fingers
		XVI	Boots
		XVII	Parallels
March 18	7	XVIII	Bowled Out
		XIX	The Last
March 25	11	XX	Something More: Enclosure No. 1: A False Step
April 1	8		Enclosure No. 2: All Right

Appendix 12.11

'Mr. Shortsight's Journeyings', *The Sydney Mail*, 1865.

Date	Page	
October 28	3	Introductory Epistle, Jonas Shortsight: To the Editor of the Mail; No. I
November 4	11	II
November 11	11	III
November 18	6-7	IV
November 25	2	V
December 2	3	(VI)
December 9	6	VII
December 16	8	VIII

Appendix 12.12

'The Stockman's Daughter', *The People's Advocate*, 1856.

Date	Page	Chapter	Title
September 6	6	I	A Knight of the Road
		II	The Traps
		III	The Robbery "Put Up'
September 13	6	IV	The Home Station
		V	The Lovers

September 20	6	VI	Father and Son
		VII	Robbery and Murder
September 27	6	VIII	Father and Daughter
		IX	The Letter
October 4	6	X	The Letter
		XI	The Daughter's Vow
October 11	6	XII	The Flight
October 18	6	XIII	The Fellowship of Crime
		XIV	A Maiden's Courage
October 25	6	XV	Too Late
		XVI	The Devil's Hole
		XVIII*	The Capture
November 1	5	XIX	Conclusion

* There was no chapter numbered XVII.

Appendix 12.13

'Mr Pick, the Gold Miner', 1867.

No.	The Sydney Mail	Page	Sydney Morning Herald	Page	Title
I	May 11	3	May 13	2	Mr. Pick opens his Subject
II	May 18	3	May 20	3	Mr. Pick describes a new Rush and Narrates an Incident
III	May 25	3	May 27	3	Mr. Pick concludes the Narrative of the Incident and Discourses thereupon
IV	June 1	3	June 5	2	Mr. Pick's Speculation in Shares
V	June 8	3	June 11	3	Mr. Pick upon Mates
VI	June 15	3	June 17	2	Another of Mr. Pick's Mates
VII	June 22	3	June 16	3	Upon Gold-Fields' Agitators
VIII	June 29	3	July 5	3	On Fees
IX	July 6	3	July 8	6	On Official Demeanour
X	July 13	3	July 19	6	Old Nugget
XI	July 20	3	July 22	9	Old Nugget (continued)
XII	July 27	3	July 29	2	Local Courts
XIII	August 3	3	August 5	6	The Punch and Judy Man
XIV	August 10	3	August 12	6	How Mr. Pick was Robbed
XV	August 17	3	August 21	3	How he Found the Thief
XVI	August 24	11	August 26	6	Diggings Preachers
XVII	August 31	3	September 2	3	Charity
XVIII	September 7	3	September 9	6	Mr. Pick as an Amateur Detective
XIX	September 14	3	September 19	6	Mr. Pick as an Amateur Detective

XX	September 21	3	September 23	6	Prospecting
XXI	September 28	3	September 30	6	The Lonely Prospector
XXII	October 5	3	October 7	6	The Placer
XXIII	October 12	3	October 14	3	On the Road
XXIV	October 26	5	October 28	2	Worked Out

Appendix 12.14

'Mark Brown's Wife', *The Sydney Mail*, 1871.

Date	Pages	Parts	Chapters
May 20	378-379	I	I – II
May 27	410		III - IV
June 3	441-442		V - VI
June 10	475-476		VII - VIII
June 17	505-506		IX - X
June 24	538-539		XI - XII
July 1	570		XIII - XIV
July 8	602-603	II	I - II
July 15	635		III - IV
July 22	666-667		V – VI
July 29	698-699		VII – VIII
August 5	730-731		IX
August 12	762-763		X - XI
August 19	794-795	III	I - II
August 26	826-827		III
September 2	857-858		IV - V
September 9	890-891		VI
September 23	955		VII - VIII
September 30	986		IX – X - XI

Appendix 12.15

'The Secret of the Old Shaft', *The Echo*, 1889.

Date	Page	Part	Chapter
September 7	3	I Found Dead	1 The Old Shaft
September 9	2		2 The Count
September 10	2		3 Brought to the Surface

Date	Page		Chapter
September 11	2		4 The Inquest
September 12	2		5 Further Evidence
September 13	2	II Tom Brown	1 Tom Brown Tells His Story
September 14	3		2 Tom Brown Sketches His History
September 16	2		3 Tom Brown's History Concluded
September 17	2		4 Searching
September 18	2		5 Found
September 19	2		5 Continued
September 20	2		6 Aimee
September 21	4	III On the Track	1 The First Move
September 23	2		2 Reginald Dollington
September 24	2		2 Continued; 3 The Boots
September 25	2		3 Continued
			4 Aimee Astonishes Tom
September 26	2		4 Continued
September 27	2		5 Drawing Closer
September 28	3		5 Continued
		IV The Dollington Family	1 The First of the Dollingtons
September 30	2		1 Continued
			2 The Dollingtons of the Past
October 1	2		2 Continued
			3 The Dollingtons of the Present
October 2			3 Continued
October 3	2		4 Some Letters
October 4	2		5 Some More Letters
October 5	4	V Hunted Down	1 The Rubbish Heap
October 7	2		2 Mr. Sharp Makes a Move
October 8	2		3 Searching for Evidence
October 9	2		3 Continued; 4 The Dentist
October 10	2		4 Continued
October 11	2		5 Face to Face

Appendix 12.16

'Me and My Horse', The Echo, 1889.

Date	Page	Chapter
December 23	2	1
December 24	2	2
December 25*		3

December 26	2	4
December 27	2	5
December 28	4	6

*This issue of the paper is missing from the bound volume in the National Library of Australia.

Appendix 12.17

'My Holiday', 1861.

The Sydney Mail	Page	Sydney Morning Herald	Page
June 22	2	June 24	2
June 29	2	July 1	2
July 6	2	July 8	3
July 13	2	July 15	2
July 20	6	July 22	3
July 27	2	July 29	3
August 3	2	August 5	2
August 10	2	August 12	2
August 17	8	August 19	6
August 24	2	August 26	3
August 31	2	September 2	3
September 7	2	September 9	3
September 14	2	September 16	3

Appendix 12.18

'The Yo-Yo: a Legend of the Lachlan District', 1861-62.

The Sydney Mail	Page	Sydney Morning Herald	Page	Title
November 30	2	November 29	8	Author's Preface; Chapter I: The Old Black
December 7	2	December 6	6	Chapter II: Dick Williams
December 14	2	December 25	6	Chapter III: The Sawyer's Home
December 21	2	December 25	6	Chapter IV: The Men's Hut
December 28	2	December 30	2	Chapter V: The Bush Fiend

Date	Page	Date	Page	Chapter
January 4	2	January 10	2	Chapter VI: A Doubtful Repast
January 11	2	January 10	2	Chapter VII: The Black Water Hole
January 18	2	January 22	3	Chapter VIII: The Compact
January 25	2	January 27	3	Chapter IX: The Forfeit

Appendix 12.19

'Tales of Barranjuee. No. I. Morouya, the Black Eagle of Colo', *The Sydney Mail*, 1862.

Date	Page	Chapter	Title
May 17	2	I	Preface / The Warning
May 24	2	II	Playing Possum
May 31	2	III	The Out Scout
June 7	2	IV	Trapped
June 14	2	V	The Traitor
June 21	2	VI	The Rescue
June 28	2	VII	The Attack
July 5	2	VIII	On the Trail
July 12	2	IX	The Captive
July 19	2	X	The Ambush
July 26	2	XI	The Trial Found
August 2	2	XII	Planning
August 9	2	XIII	The Rescue
August 16	2	XIV	Conclusion

Appendix 12.20

'Christmas Stories', 1866.

Christmas Tales. The Overlanders. Where they camped on Christmas Eve, and the Yarns they Spun. The Old Squatter's Story; The Young Super's Story; The Doctor's Story; The Governess's Story; The Camp-Keeper's Story. *The Christmas Supplement to The Sydney Mail*, December 22, 1866, pages 5-7.

Christmas. Christmas in the Bush; Australian Ghosts; The Spectre on the Stairs; Fisher's Ghost; The Australian Banshee; The Lady with the Lantern;

Treated as One of the Family; and Rambles for Christmas Flowers. *The Christmas Supplement to The Sydney Mail*, December 29, 1866, pages 5-7.

Appendix 12.21

Some writings that may be the work of de Boos, but not confirmed as such.

'To the working men of New South Wales: Letter I' by 'A Working Man'. *Sydney Mail*, December 1, 1860, page 8; Letter II, December 8, page 8.

1863

'Bushrangers and Bushranging', from Our Special Reporter. *Sydney Morning Herald*, November 21, 1863, page 13.

1864

'Rambles through Sydney, Part I: In the Streets and Lanes'.

Sydney Morning Herald	Page	The Sydney Mail	Page	No.	Title
May 12	2	May 14	3	I	The Rocks
May 19	5	May 28	5	I	The Rocks (continued)
May 26	2	June 4	5	II	Woollomooloo
May 30	3			II	Woollomooloo (continued)
June 3	2	June 11	5	III	Sussex-street and Darling Harbour
June 15	3	June 18	7	III	Sussex-street and Darling Harbour (continued)
July 1	2	July 2	12	IV	Upper Watershed of Darling Harbour
July 15	2	July 16	11	IV	Upper Watershed of Darling Harbour (continued)

Note 'Editorial' in the *Sydney Morning Herald*, July 12, 1864, page 4.

1867

'Sketches in the City. No. 1. The Police Courts'. *The Sydney Mail*, October 5, 1867, page 3; 'No. 2. The District Court'. *The Sydney Mail*, October 26, 1867, page 3.

'Hartley Kerosene Works'. *The Sydney Mail*, October 19, 1867, pages 5-6.

'Locked Up by a Jury of Twelve who could not agree upon a verdict, and passed the night in manufacturing Christmas Stories: 1. The Actor in the Bush; 2. Lawyers and Clients; 3. Running away from the Runaway; 4. Won and Lost; 5. The Story of a Moonbeam; 6. The Judge and the Reporter; 7. How I became a Shot; 8. My First Spec; 9. Commercial Morality; 10. Mexican Vengeance; 11. Who Won't tell a Tale; Foreman. A Bold Client'. *The Sydney Mail*, December 21, 1867, Christmas Supplement, pages 5-9.

1868

'Saved from the Flames: being stories saved from the waste paper basket'. *The Sydney Mail*, December 26, 1868, Christmas Supplement, pages 5-8.

1870

'Sydney by Night', 1870.

No.	Sydney Morning Herald	Page	The Sydney Mail	Page	Title
1	July 1	5	July 9	7	A Visit to the Rocks
2	July 8	5	July 16	3	Donovan's Lane, the Pigeon-house and Cohen's-court
3	July 15	5	July 23	6	Sixpenny Lodging-Houses
4	July 20	5	July 30	7	Druitt-street and Wallace-lane
5	July 30	7	August 6	6	Elizabeth-street and its Vicinity
6	August 6	7	August 13	10	The Soup Kitchen – a nice Quartette
7	August 23	8	August 20	6	Exeter Place
8	August 23	5	August 27	6	Exeter-place, The Dog-catcher, Mother Lymner's

1873

'The Northern Coast', from 'Our Special Reporter', 1873.

Sydney Morning Herald	Page	The Sydney Mail	Page	Title
October 6	3	October 11	470	A Trip to the Manning River: by sea to Newcastle and up the Manning River to Cundle ("a private township"), Taree
October 9	6	October 11	470	Manning River district
October 13	3	October 18	497	Manning River to Port Macquarie (by road)

October 15	7	October 22	529	Port Macquarie II
October 21	3	November 8	589-590	Port Macquarie III district and agriculture
		November 8*	590	Macleay District
October 30	6			Macleay District II, Kempsey
November 3	3			Macleay district, Kempsey
November 10	2	November 15*	621-622	Macleay District III, Nambucca and Bellinger Rivers, Grafton
November 11	2-3	November 15*	621-622	Sugar growing on the Clarence River: a trip in a drogher
November 19	4-5	November 29*	708	Richmond River and district, Casino, Lismore, Ballina, Sydney

* Edited versions of what appeared in the *Sydney Morning Herald*.

Appendix 13.1

Fifty Years Ago: signature version, 1856-1857

I, September 15; II, October 1; III, October 15; IV, November 1; V, November 15; VI, December 1; VII, December 15; VIII, ; IX, February 1; X, March 1; XI, March 15; XII, April 1; XIII, April 15; XIV, July 15; 15; XV, July.

Appendix 13.2

Fifty Years Ago. *The Australian Journal*, 1869-1870

Vol. IV, 47 (April), 449-458; 48 (May), 513-522; 49 (June), 577-590; 50 (July), 641-655; 51 (August), 705-720; Vol. V, 52 (September), 1-15; 53 (October), 65-78; 54 (November), 129-145; 55 (December), 193-207; 56 (January), 253-269; 57 (February), 312-322.

Appendix 13.3

Retribution, or Eighty Years Ago in *The Australian Journal*, 1900-1901

Vol. XXXV, 416 (January), 1-10; 417 (February), 79-85; 418 (March), 125-131; 419 (April), 187-198; 420 (May), 249-258; 421 (June), 327-336; 422 (July), 389-400; 423 (August), 451-461; 424 (September), 497-507; 425 (October), 591-601; 426 (November), 621-631; 427 (December),

707-715; Vol. XXXVI, 428 (January), 17-27; 429 (February), 95-102; 430 (March), 125-132; 431 (April), 185-194; 432 (May), 265-273; 433 (June), 347-355; 434 (July), 389-393.

Appendix 13.4

Contemporary reviews of *Fifty Years Ago*.

Paper	Date	Page	Content
Sydney Morning Herald	September 13, 1866		Review and commentary on the first part
Sydney Morning Herald	September 20, 1866	6	Review
The Argus	September 21, 1866	5	Review
Sydney Morning Herald	September 22, 1866	5	Brief notice
Freeman's Journal	September 22, 1866	594	Review, extract
Empire	September 25, 1866	4	Review
Hobart Mercury	September 26, 1866	3	Review
Ballarat Star	September 27, 1866	2	Review
Bell's Life	September 29, 1866	4	Review, extracts
Hobart Mercury	October 10, 1866	3	Review, extracts
Empire	September 4, 1867	5	Summary of whole book
Sydney Morning Herald	September 20, 1867	6	Review
Argus	September 21, 1867	5-6	Summary, whole book
Sydney Morning Herald	March 21, 1868	8	Advertisement, one volume. 10/-

Appendix 13.5

'The Romance of the Blue Books', *The Sydney Mail*, 1868

May 30, page 12; June 6, page 9; June 13, page 9; June 20, page 9; June 27, page 8; July 4, page 9; August 1, page 9.

References

Allbrook, Malcolm and Melanie Nolan (2018): "Australian biography amid the recent biographical turn". *Australian Journal of Biography and History*, 1, 3-21.

Annear, Robyn (1999): *Nothing but Gold: the diggers of 1852*. Text Publishing, Melbourne.

Anon. (1836): *British Auxiliary Legion of Spain. Army List, corrected to 4th June, 1836 (for October 1836)*. London. 24 pp. The British Library, London.

Anon. (1859): "A fit of the gold-fever". *Chamber's Journal of Popular Literature, Science and Arts*, No. 279, May 7, 289-292.

Anon. (1994): "Fifty Years Ago: an Australian tale". pp. 277-278 in *The Oxford Companion to Australian Literature*, edited by William H. Wilde, Joy Hooton, and Barry Andrews. Oxford University Press, Melbourne.

Armand, Élodie (2017): "Les clos-masures au patrimoine mondial l'UNESCO? La Seine-Maritime lance un grand inventure", https://actu.fr/societe/les-clos-masures-patrimoine-mondial-lunesco-seine-martitime-lance-grand-inventaire_855995.html.

Armstrong, Henry J. (1901): *A Treatise on the Law of Gold Mining in Australia and New Zealand*. Second edition. Charles F. Maxwell, Melbourne, 32-35.

Arnold, John and John Hay (Editors) (2001): *The Bibliography of Australian Literature: A-E*. Australian Scholarly Publishing, Kew.

Arnold, John, John Nieuwenhuizen and Peter Spearritt (Editors) (1995): *Who's Who of Australian Writers*. D.W. Thorpe, Melbourne.

Atkinson, Alan (2006): "One in the eye for the PC brigade". *Sydney Morning Herald / Spectrum*, January 14-15, 21.

Baker, D.W.A. (1958): "The origins of Robertson's Land Acts". *Historical Studies: Australia and New Zealand*, 8(30), 166-182.

Baldwin, Barry and Ruth Boyd-Davis (2001): *Diary of a Goldfield*. Ruth Boyd-Davis and Barry Baldwin, Gulgong.

Barton, George B. (1889): "The status of literature in New South Wales. I. How the Government looks at it; II. How the publishers look at it; III. How the newspaper proprietors look at it". *The Centennial Magazine*, 2(1), 71-73; 2(2), 89-92; 2(3), 238-240. Re-issued 1993 as *Publishing Literature in N.S.W.: the Status of Literature in 1889*, with an introduction by V. Crittenden. Mulini Press, Canberra.

Bate, Weston (1988): *Victorian Gold Rushes*. McPhee Gribble Publishers / Penguin Books Australia, Melbourne.

Bate, Weston (2001): "Gold: social energizer and definer". *Victorian Historical Journal*, 72, 7-27.

Baxter, Carol (2011): *Captain Thunderbolt and his Lady*. Allen & Unwin, Sydney.

Benedict, Philip (1975): "Catholics and Huguenots in Sixteenth-century Rouen: the demographic effects of the religious wars". *French Historical Studies*, 9, 209-234.

Benedict, Philip (1978): "The Saint Bartholomew's Massacres in the Provinces". *The Historical Journal*, 21(2), 205-225.

Benedict, Philip (1985): "Civil war and natural disaster in Northern France". pp. 84-105 in *The European Crisis of the 1590s: essays in comparative history*, edited by Peer Clark. George Allen & Unwin, London.

Benedict, Philip (1991): "The Huguenot population of France, 1600-1685: the demographic fate and customs of a religious minority". *Transactions of the American Philosophical Society*, 81(5), i-ix + 1-164.

Benedict, Philip J. (2004): *Rouen During the Wars of Religion*. Cambridge University Press, Cambridge.

Bennett, Bruce, Jennifer Strauss and Chris Wallace-Crabbe (Editors) (1998): *The Oxford Literary History of Australia*. Oxford University Press, Melbourne.

Bernard, Gildas (1981): *Guide des Recherches sur l'Histoire des Families*. Archives Nationales, Paris.

Bernard, Gildas (1987): *Les Families Protestantes en France, XVIe siècle – 1792: Guide des Recherches Biographiques et Généalogiques*. Archives Nationales, Paris.

Bird, Robert Montgomery (1837): *Nick of the Woods, or The Jibbenainosay. A Tale of Kentucky*. Two volumes. Carey, Lea & Blanchard, Philadelphia.

Black, Anne (2020): *Pendragon: the life of George Isaacs, colonial wordsmith*. Wakefield Press, Adelaide.

Blainey, Geoffrey (2006): *A History of Victoria*. Cambridge University Press, Melbourne.

Bode, Katherine (2012): "'Sidelines' and Trade lines: publishing the Australian novel, 1860-1899". *Book History*, 15, 93-122.

Bode, Katherine (2016): "Thousands of titles without authors: digitized newspapers, serial fiction, and the challenges of anonymity". *Book History*, 19, 284-316.

Bode, Katherine (2017): "Fictional systems: mass-digitization, network analysis, and Nineteenth-Century Australian newspapers". *Victorian Periodicals Review*, 50(1), 100-138.

Bode, Katherine (2018): *A World of Fiction: digital collections and the future of literary history*. University of Michigan Press, Ann Arbor.

Bode, Katherine and Hetherington, Carol (2014): "Retrieving a world of fiction: building an index – and an Archive – of serialized novels in Australian newspapers, 1850-1914". *Script & Pen*, 38(3), 197-211. Variation in *The Indexer*, 33(2) (2015), 57-65.

Bois, Guy (1984): *The Crisis of Feudalism: Economy and Society in Eastern Normandy c. 1300-1550*. Cambridge University Press, Cambridge / Editions de la Maison des Sciences de l'Homme, Paris.

Boldrewood, Rolf (1888): *Robbery Under Arms*. Three volumes. Remington & Co., London. Abridged one volume version, Macmillan, London, 1889.

Boldrewood, Rolf (1890): *The Miner's Right: a tale of the Australian goldfields*. Macmillan, London.

Bost, Charles Marc (1984): *Familles Protestantes du Pays de Caux: Levesque, Besselièvre, Lemai(s)tre, Fauquest et autres*. Volume 1. Charles Bost, Lillebonne.

Bourne, J.M. (1979): "The East India Company's Military Seminary, Addiscombe, 1805-1858". *Journal of the Society for Army Historical Research*, 57, 206-222.

Braudel, Fernand (1988): *The Identity of France, Volume I, History and Environment*. Translated by Siân Reynolds. William Collins, London.

Brett, Edward M. (2005): *The British Auxiliary Legion in the First Carlist War*. Four Courts Press, Dublin.

Brodie, Nicholas Dean (2015): *Kin: a Real People's History of our Nation*. Hardie Grant, Melbourne.

Broome, Richard et al. (2016): *Remembering Melbourne, 1850-1960*. Royal Historical Society of Victoria, Melbourne.

Browne, Charles Farrer (1862): *Artemus Ward His Book*. Carleton, Publisher, New York.

Browne, Charles Farrer (1865): *Artemus Ward; his travels*. Carleton, Publisher, New York.

Buck, A.R. (1996): "'The Poor Man': rhetoric and political culture in mid-nineteenth century New South Wales". *Australian Journal of Politics and History*, 42, 203-219.

Buck, A.R. and Nancy E. Wright (Editors) (2005): *The Poor Man: law and satire in 19th Century New South Wales*. Australian Scholarly Publishing, Melbourne.

Butterfield, John J. (1854): *The Melbourne Commercial, Squatters and Official Directory*. James J. Blundell & Co., Melbourne, 1854.

Cambridge, Ada (1890): *A Marked Man: some episodes in his life*. Heinemann, London.

Cambridge, Ada (1883/1891): *The Three Miss Kings*. Melville, Mullen & Slade, Melbourne.

Cameron, Marcia (2019): "Charles Joseph La Trobe 1801-1875: first Lt-Governor of Victoria". *Huguenot Times*, 33, 1-10.

Canning & Clyde Road Residents Association (2000): *The Book of Addiscombe*. Halsgrove Publishing, Tiverton, 25.

Chater, Kathy (2012): *Tracing your Huguenot Ancestors: a guide for family historians*. Pen & Sword Books, Ltd., Barnsley.

Clancy, Laurie (1992): *A Reader's Guide to Australian Fiction*. Oxford University Press, Melbourne.

Clancy, Laurie (1993): "Colonial books that are made to order". *Weekend Australian Review*, March 20, 6.

Clancy, Laurie (1999a): "Introduction: A Neglected Novel: Charles de Boos' Fifty Years Ago". pp. 2-9 in *Fifty Years Ago: an Australian tale*. Mulini Press, Canberra.

Clancy, Laurie (1999b): "A Neglected Novel: Fifty Years Ago by Charles de Boos". *Margin*, 48(July-August), 2-16.

Clancy, Laurie (2004): *Culture and Customs of Australia*. Greenwood Press, Westport, Connecticut.

Clarke, Marcus (1874): *His Natural Life / For the Term of His Natural Life*. G. Robertson, Melbourne / R. Betley, London, 1875.

Clarke, Patricia (2005): "Turning fact into fiction: the 1857 Hornet Bank Massacre". *Margin*, 65, 8-17.

Clarke, Rev. W.B. (1871): "On the Progress of Gold Discovery in Australasia, from 1860 to 1871". pp. 533-555 in *The Industrial Progress of New South Wales: being a Report of the Intercolonial Exhibition of 1870, at Sydney; together with a variety of papers illustrative of the Industrial Resources of the Colony*. Government Printer, Sydney.

Clayton, Peter (2015): "Obituary: Victor Crittenden 1925-2014". *Australian Academic & Research Libraries*, 46, 56-57.

Coertzen, Pieter (2013): "The Bible and the broken chain: the Huguenots and freedom of religion". pp. 28-35 in *The Huguenots: France, exile & diaspora*, edited by Jane McKee and Randolph Vigne. Sussex Academic Press, Brighton.

Cogswell, Fred (1976): "Haliburton, Thomas Chandler". *Dictionary of Canadian Biography*, Vol. 9. University of Toronto Press, Toronto / Université Laval, 2003. www.biographi.ca/en/bio/haliburton_thomas_chandler_9E.html

Colyer-Fergusson, T.C. (Editor) (1906): *The Registers of the French Church of Threadneedle Street, London, Part III, 1685-1714*. Quarto Series, Volume XVI. Huguenot Society of London, London.

Colyer-Fergusson, T.C. (Editor) (1916): *The Registers of the French Church of Threadneedle Street, London, Part IV, 1707-1840*. Quarto Series, Volume XXIII. Huguenot Society of London, London.

Cooper, J.F. (1823): *The Pioneers, or, The sources of the Susquehanna: a descriptive tale*. Carey & Lea, Philadelphia.

Cooper, J.F. (1841): *The Deerslayer, or, The first war-path, a tale*. Lea & Blanchard, Philadelphia.

Corfield, Justin (2003): *The Ned Kelly Encyclopedia*. Lothian Press, South Melbourne.

Corvisier, André (1974): "Les religionnaires employés dans les manufactures de la généralité de Rouen en 1700". *Bulletin de la Société de l' Histoire du Protestantisme Français*, 120 (avril-mai-juin), 282-296.

Cottret, Bernard (1991): *The Huguenots in England: Immigration and settlement c.1550-1700*. Translated by P. and A. Stevenson. Cambridge University Press, Cambridge, and Editions de la Maison des Sciences de l'Home, Paris.

Couvreur, Jessie ('Tasma') (1889): *Uncle Piper of Piper's Hill: an Australian novel*. Trubner, London.

Coverdale, John F. (1984): *The Basque Phase of Spain's First Carlist War*. Princeton University Press, Princeton.

Crabb, Peter (2010): "The Canoona Gold Rush through the eyes of Charles de Boos". *Margin: life and letters of Early Australia*, 80, 33-42.

Crabb, Peter (2014): "Charles de Boos and Hill End-Tambaroora, 1857-1872". *Hill End & Tambaroora Gathering Group Newsletter*, 14 (January), 4-5, and 15 (September), 7-8.

Crabb, Peter (2015a): "A Visit to the Western Goldfields". *Hill End & Tambaroora Gathering Group Newsletter*, 16 (January), 7-8.

Crabb, Peter (2015b): "A unique event: Charles de Boos and the Braidwood Chinese gold miners". *Chinese Southern Diaspora Studies*, 7 (2014-15), 142-148. Chl-old.anu.edu.au/publications/csds/csds2014/csds2014_12.pdf

Crabb, Peter (2020): "John Augustus Hux (1826-1864): a colonial goldfields' reporter". *Australian Journal of History and Biography*, 3, 79-102.

Crabb, Peter, Alexis Antonia and Hugh Craig (2014): "Who Wrote 'A Visit to the Western Goldfields'? Using Computers to Analyse Language in Historical Research. *History Australia*, 11(3), 177-193.

Crabb, Peter, Brendan Dalton, Hugh Craig and Alexis Antonia (2019): "The enigmatic Bartholomew Lloyd alias Frederick Dalton: identity and mobility during the gold rush era in New South Wales". *History Australia*, 16(2), 358-374.

Crittenden, Victor (1992): "Introduction". pp. i-iii in *Mark Brown's Wife: a tale of the gold-fields* by Charles de Boos. Mulini Press, Canberra.

Crittenden, Victor (1996a): *Pseudonyms used by Australian Writers: Nineteenth Century*. Mulini Press, Canberra.

Crittenden, Victor (1996b): "The writings of Charles de Boos". *Margin: life and letters of early Australians*, 38, 6-10.

Crittenden, Victor (2004): "Introductory note". pp. 1-3 in *Me and My Horse: Showing how I got him, How I kept him, and All about him. Being sketches of life on the Peel River diggings* by Charles de Boos. Mulini Press, Canberra, Canberra.

Crittenden, Victor. (2009a): "Introduction", pp. v-ix, to *The Stockman's Daughter: a Bushranger Novel of 1856* by Charles de Boos. Mulini Press, Canberra.

Crittenden, Victor (2009b): "The Stockman's Daughter: Charles de Boos' bushranger novel of 1856". *Margin*, 77, 5-9.

Curthoys, Ann and John Docker (2006): *Is History Fiction?* UNSW Press, Sydney.

Curthoys, Ann and Ann McGrath (2009): *How to Write History that People Want to Read*. UNSW Press, Sydney.

Dalton, Brendan, Alexis Antonia, Peter Crabb and Hugh Craig (2016): "Identifying another goldfields reporter: Frederick Dalton (1815-1880)". *History Australia*, 13(4), 557-574.

Darragh, Thomas A. (1997): *Printer and Newspaper Registration in Victoria, 1838-1924*. Elibank Press, North Perth.

D'Ath, Justin (1993): "White on black". *Australian Book Review*, 154, 35-39.

Davenport, John et al. (1990): *A Walk Around Historic Bungendore Village*. Bungendore and District Historical Society, Bungendore.

Davies, Alan (2013): *The Greatest Wonder of the World*. State Library of New South Wales, Sydney.

Davies, Horton, and Marie-Hélène Davies (2000): *French Huguenots in English-Speaking Lands*. Peter Lang Publishing, New York.

Davison, Graeme (2016): "Gold-Rush Melbourne". pp.52-66 in Richard Broome: *Remembering Melbourne 1850-1960*. Royal Historical Society of Victoria, Melbourne.

de Boos, Charles (1867): *Fifty Years Ago: an Australian tale*. Gordon & Gotch, Sydney. Republished Muilini Press, Canberra, 1999.

de Boos, Charles (1889): "Eminent Men of New South Wales: The Honorable Sir John Hay". *The Sydney Quarterly Magazine*, March, 2-5.

de Boos, Charles (1992): *Mark Brown's Wife: a Tale of the Gold-fields*. Mulini Press, Canberra.

de Boos, Charles (2004): *Me and my Horse; showing How I got Him, How I kept Him, and all about Him*. Mulini Press, Canberra.

de Boos, Charles (2009): *The Stockman's Daughter: a tale of the new country*. Mulini Press, Canberra.

DeBoos, C.L. (1934): *A Brief History of the Early Days of Euroa*. Euroa Gazette Print, Euroa.

Decker, George (2015): "Cooper, James Fenimore". *Encyclopaedia Britannica Ultimate Reference Suite*. Encyclopaedia Britannica, Chicago.

Delbridge, Arthur et al. (Editors): *The Macquarie Dictionary*. The Macquarie Library, Macquarie University, Sydney.

Dunstan, David (2003): "The Argus: the life, death and remembering of a great Australian newspaper". pp. 9-42 in *The Argus: the life and death of a great Melbourne newspaper, 1846-1957*, edited by Muriel Porter. RMIT University, Melbourne.

Durack, Mary (1962): "In search of an Australian frontier". *The Texas Quarterly*, 5(2), 10-15.

Duwell, Martin, Marianne Ehrhardt and Carol Hetherington (Editors) (1997): *The ALS Guide to Australian Writers: a bibliography*. University of Queensland Press, Brisbane.

Dyster, Barrie (1988): "The discrete interest of the Bourgeoisie, before the Age of Gold". pp. 1-11 in *Nineteenth-Century Sydney: essays in urban history*, edited by Max Kelly. Sydney University Press, Sydney

Eggert, Paul (2005): "The bibliographic life of an Australian classic: *Robbery Under Arms*". *Script and Print*, 29, 73-92

Eggert, Paul (2013): *Biography of a Book: Henry Lawson's While the Billy Boils.* Sydney University Press, Sydney.

Eggert, Paul and Elizabeth Webby (Editors) (2006): *Rolf Boldrewood: Robbery Under Arms.* University of Queensland Press, Brisbane.

Ellis, Netta (1989): *Braidwood, Dear Braidwood.* N.N. and N.M. Ellis, Braidwood.

Evans, E.E. (1959): *France: a geographical introduction.* Chatto and Windus Ltd., London.

Fagette, P. (1975): *British Participation in the First Carlist War 1833-40.* M.A. thesis, California State University, Fullerton, California. University Microfilms International, Ann Arbor.

Farrington, Anthony (Editor) (1976): *The Records of the East India College, Haileybury, and other Institutions.* H.M.S.O., London.

Ferguson, Audrey (1972): "Dalgleish, Daniel Cameron (1827-1870)". *Australian Dictionary of Biography*, at https://adb.anu.edu.au/biography/dalgleish-daniel-cameron-3354/text5053 , accessed May 16,2021.

Fitzgerald, John (2002): *Big White Lie: Chinese Australians in White Australia.* UNSW Press, Sydney.

Franklin, Miles (1901): *My Brilliant Career.* William Blackwood & Sons, Edinburgh.

Frémont, Armand (1977): *Atlas et Géographie de la Normandie.* Flammarion et Editions Famot, Paris

Frémont, Armand (1981): *Paysans de Normandie.* Flammarion, Paris.

Fritsch, R.S. et al. (1992): *Temora Yesterday and Today 1880-1980: includes History Update to 1992.* Temora Historical Society Inc., Temora.

Fuller, Tony (2001): "Huguenots at the HEIC College at Addiscombe, Surrey". *Huguenot Families*, No. 4, 15-17.

Furphy, Joseph (1903): *Such is Life: being certain extracts from the diary of Tom Collins.* The Bulletin Newspaper Co. Ltd., Sydney.

Gardiner, Lyndsay (1967): "Kerr, William (1812-1859)". *Australian Dictionary of Biography*, at http://ADB.anu.edu.au/biography/kerr-william-2304 , accessed May 20, 2015.

Gelder, Ken and Rachael Weaver (2017): *Colonial Australian Fiction: Character Types, Social Formations, and the Colonial Economy*. Sydney University Press, Sydney.

Gibson, Jeremy and Mervyn Medlycott (2001): *Militia Lists and Musters 1757-1876: a Directory of Holdings in the British Isles*. Genealogical Publishing Company, Baltimore.

Gill, S.T. (1855): *The Diggers and Diggings as They Were in 1852*. Lithographed by Campbell & Ferguson. James J. Blundell & Co., Melbourne.

Gittins, Jean (1981): *The Diggers from China: the story of the Chinese on the Goldfields*. Quartet Books, Melbourne.

Gold Fields Royal Commission (1871): *Gold Fields Royal Commission of Inquiry. Report of the Royal Commission appointed to Inquire into the working of the present Gold Fields Act and Regulations of New South Wales, and into the best means of securing a permanent water supply for the gold fields of the Colony*. Report, Appendix, Minutes of Evidence. Government Printer Sydney, 1871. In *New South Wales Votes and Proceedings of the Legislative Assembly, during session 1871-2*, Volume II. Government Printer, Sydney, 1872; pages 135-372. Evidence by de Boos, pages 151-154.

Golder, Hilary (1991): *High and Responsible Office: a history of the New South Wales magistracy*. Sydney University Press / Oxford University Press, Melbourne.

Gollan, Robin (1960): *Radical and Working Class Politics: a study of Eastern Australia, 1850-1910*. Melbourne University Press, Melbourne.

Goodman, David (1994): *Gold Seeking: Victoria and California in the 1850s*. Allen & Unwin, Sydney.

Goodman, David (2018): "Gold and the Public in the Nineteenth Century gold rushes". pp. 65-87 in Benjamin Mountford and Stephen Tuffnell (Editors) (2018): *A History of Gold Rushes*. University of California Press, Oakland.

Grant, James and Geoffrey Serle (1957): *The Melbourne Scene, 1803-1956*. Melbourne University Press, Melbourne.

Green, H.M. (1961): *A History of Australian Literature: pure and applied*. Volumes 1 and 2. Angus & Robertson, Sydney. Revised edition by Dorothy Green, 1984-85.

Griffiths, Tom (1987): *Beechworth: an Australian country town and its past*. Greenhouse Publications, Richmond.

Griffiths, Tom (2016): *The Art of Time Travel: historians and their craft*. Blanc Inc., Melbourne.

Grishin, Sasha (2015): *S.T. Gill & his Audiences*. National Library of Australia, Canberra.

Grishin, Sasha (2016): "Different strokes". *Panorama: Canberra Times*, June 18, pages 6-7.

Gunn, Mrs Aeneas (1908): *We of the Never-Never*. Hutchinson, London.

Gwynn, Robin (1983): "The number of Huguenot immigrants in England in the late seventeenth Century". *Journal of Historical Geography*, 9(4), 384-395.

Gwynn, Robin (1998): *The Huguenots of London*. The Alpha Press, Brighton.

Gwynn, Robin (2006): "The Huguenot dilemma: Anglicanism or non-conformity?" *Huguenot Times*, 8, 1-5.

Gwynn, R.D. (2011): *Huguenot Heritage: the history and contribution of the Huguenots in Britain*. Second revised edition. Sussex Academic Press, Brighton.

Haliburton, Thomas C. (1836): *The Clockmaker; or, the sayings and doings of Samuel Slick, of Slickville*. The Novascotian, 1835; Joseph Howe, Halifax, 1836; Richard Bentley, London, 1838.

Hamer, Clive (1957a): "*Fifty Years Ago* – an overlooked novel". *Southerly*, 18(1), 41-44.

Hamer, Clive (1957b): "Critical notes on the Australian novel, 1859-1889". *Biblionews: Book Collectors' Circle of Australia*, 10(11), 35-37.

Hamer, Clive (1965): "The surrender to truth in the early Australian novel". *Australian Literary Studies*, 2(2), 103-116.

Hamer, Clive (1989): "The redemptive theme in Australian literature (5) Charles de Boos (1819-1900)." *Western Impact* (West Australian Uniting Church, Perth), 9 (11), 10.

Hamilton, G. James and Barry Sinclair (2009): *Thunderbolt: scourge of the ranges*. Phoenix, Hyland Park, N.S.W.

Hamilton, John P. (2015): *Adjudication on the Gold Fields in New South Wales and Victoria in the 19th Century*. Federation Press, Sydney.

Hardy, J.R. (1855): *Squatters and Gold-diggers, Their Claims and Rights*. W.R. Paddington, Sydney.

Hauser, Henri (1899): "The French Reformation and the French People in the Sixteenth Century". *American Historical Review*, 4(2), 217-227.

Hay, William (1907): *Herridge of Reality Swamp*. T. Fisher Unwin, London.

Haydon, G.H. (1854): *The Australian Emigrant: a rambling story, containing as much fact as fiction*. Arthur Hall, Virtue & Co., London.

Healy, J.J. (1972): "The treatment of the Aborigine in early Australian fiction, 1840-1870". *Australian Literary Studies,* 5 (3), 233-253.

Healy. J.J. (1978): *Literature and the Aborigine in Australia, 1770-1975.* University of Queensland Press, St. Lucia.

Healy. J.J. (1989): *Literature and the Aborigine in Australia.* Second edition. University of Queensland Press, St. Lucia.

Heaton, J.H. (1879): *Australian Dictionary of Dates and Men of the Time: containing the History of Australasia from 1542 to May 1879.* George Robertson, Sydney.

Henty, George A. (1902): *With the British Legion: a story of the Carlist Wars.* Charles Scribner's Sons, New York / Blackie & Son Ltd., London.

Higgins, Matthew (1990): *Gold and Water: a history of Sofala and the Turon goldfield.* Robstar Pty Ltd., Bathurst.

Hirst, John (2002): "The distinctiveness of Australian Democracy". *Quadrant,* 308, 19-27.

Hirst, John (2003): "Edward Wilson, journalist and editor". pp. 61-76 in Muriel Porter (Editor) (2003): *The Argus: the life and death of a great Melbourne newspaper, 1846-1957.* RMIT University, Melbourne.

Hoare, M. and J.T. Radford (1976): "Smith, John (1821-1885)". *Australian Dictionary of Biography, Volume 6.* Melbourne University Press, Melbourne.

Hocking, Geoff (1994): *Castlemaine: from camp to city 1835-1900.* Five Mile Press, Knoxville, Victoria.

Hodge, Brian (2009): *Golden Hill End.* Tambaroora Star Publications, Penshurst, Sydney.

Holmes. John H. (2000): "Pastoral lease tenures as policy instruments 1847-1997". pp. 212-242 in S. Dovers (Editor): *Environmental History and Policy: still settling Australia.* Oxford University Press, Melbourne.

Holt, Edgar (1967): *The Carlist Wars in Spain.* Putnam & Co. Ltd., London.

Holt, L.V. (1972): "De Boos, Charles Edward Augustus (1819-1900)". pp. 38-39 in *Australian Dictionary of Biography,* Volume 4. Melbourne University Press, Melbourne.

Holt, Mack P. (1995): *The French Wars of Religion, 1562-1629.* Cambridge University Press, Cambridge.

Inglis Moore, T. (1969): "Browne, Thomas Alexander (Rolph Boldrewood) (1826-1915)". pp. 267-269 in *Australian Dictionary of Biography,* Volume 3 Melbourne University Press, Melbourne.

Isaacs, George (A. Pendragon) (1858): *The Queen of the South: a Colonial Romance: being pictures of life in Victoria in the early days of the diggings.* W. Barnet Printers, Gawler, South Australia.

Isaacs, V. and R. Kirkpatrick (2003): *Two Hundred Years of Sydney Newspapers: a short history.* Rural Press Ltd., North Richmond.

Jennings, Guy (Editor/Compiler) (1991): *My Holiday and other Early Travels from Manly to Palm Beach 1861.* Aramo Pty Ltd., Newport Beach.

Jinks, Brian (2005a): *Goldfields Life in the photographs of Beaufoy Merlin and Charles Bayliss.* Brian Jinks, Gulgong.

Jinks, Brian (2005b): *Gold and Browne: a goldfields tale with a happy ending.* Brian Jinks, Gulgong.

Johnson, J.C.F. (1881): *To Mount Browne and Back or Moses and Me.* Advertiser Print, Adelaide.

Jose, Nicholas (Editor) (2009): *The Macquarie Pen Anthology of Australian Literature.* Allen & Unwin, Sydney.

Keay, John (2010): *The Honorable Company: a history of the English East India Company.* Harper Collins, London.

Keesing, Nancy (Editor) (1967): *Gold Fever: the Australian Goldfields 1851 to the 1890s.* Angus & Robertson Ltd., Sydney.

Kelly, William (1859): *Life in Victoria or Victoria in 1853 and Victoria in 1858.* Chapman & Hall, London / Historical Reprints Series No. 6. Lowden Publishing Co., Kilmore.

Kingsley, Henry (1859): *The Recollections of Geoffry Hamlyn.* Macmillan, Cambridge.

Kirkpatrick, Rod (2000): *Country Conscience: a history of the New South Wales provincial press, 1841-1995.* Infinite Harvest Publishing, Canberra.

Kirkpatrick, Rod (2016): *Dailies in the Colonial Capitals: a short history.* R. Kirkpatrick, 22 Thurlow Street, Newmarket, Queensland.

Kramer, Leonie (Editor) (1981): *The Oxford History of Australian Literature.* Oxford University Press, Melbourne.

Labrousse, Elisabeth (1987): "Great Britain as envisaged by Huguenots of the Seventeenth Century". pp. 143-157 in *Huguenots in Britain and their French Background, 1550-1800*, edited by Irene Scouloudi. Macmillan Press, London.

Lardner, William (1837): "Account of the epidemic which attacked the British Auxiliary Legion in the winter of 1835-36, at Vittoria in Spain". *The Lancet*, 28(725), 622-625.

Lawrence, Susan and Peter Davies (2019): *Sludge: disaster on Victoria's goldfields*. La Trobe University Press / Black Inc., Melbourne.

Lawrence, Susan, Peter Davies and Jodi Turnbull (2016a): "The archaeology of Anthropocene rivers: water management and landscape change in 'Gold Rush' Australia". *Antiquity*, 90 (353), 1348-1362.

Lawrence, Susan, Peter Davies and Jodi Turnbull (2016b): "The archaeology of water on the Victorian goldfields". *International Journal of Historical Archaeology*, 21, 49-65.

Lea-Scarlett, E.J. (1974): "Mei Quong Tart (1850-1903)". *Australian Dictionary of Biography*, at https://adb.anu.edu.au/biography/mei-quong-tart-4181/text6719 , accessed May 19, 2021.

Lee, Hermione (2009): *Biography: A Very Short Introduction*. Oxford University Press, Oxford.

Littleton, Charles (2003): "Acculturation and the French Church of London, 1600-circa 1640". pp. 90-109 in *Memory and Identity: the Huguenots in France and the Atlantic Diaspora*, edited by Bertrand Van Ruymbeke and Randy J. Sparks. The University of South Carolina Press, Columbia.

Loveday, P. and A.W. Martin (1966): *Parliament, Factions and Parties: the first thirty years of responsible government in New South Wales, 1856-1889*. Melbourne University Press, Melbourne.

Loveday, P. and A.W. Martin (1977): "Colonial politics before 1890", in *The Emergence of the Australian Party System*, edited by P. Loveday, A.W. Martin, & R.S. Parker. Hale & Iremonger, Sydney, 5-43.

Low, F. (1844): *The City of Sydney Directory for MDCCCXLIV-V*. E. Alcock, City Printing Office, Sydney.

Mackay, Angus (1853): *The Great Gold Field: a pedestrian tour through the first discovered gold district of New South Wales in the months of October and November, 1852*. W.R. Piddington, Sydney.

McCalman, Iain, Alexander Cook and Andrew Reeves (Editors) (2001): *Gold: forgotten histories and lost objects of Australia*. Cambridge University Press, Cambridge.

McCalman, Janet (2021): *Vandemonians: the Repressed History of Colonial Victoria*. The Miegunyah Press, Melbourne.

McGowan, Barry (1996a): *Bungonia to Braidwood: an historical and archaeological account of the Shoalhaven and Mongarlowe goldfields*. Barry McGowan, Canberra.

McGowan, Barry (1996b): *Lost Mines Revisited: historic mining communities of the Monaro, Southern Tablelands and South West Slopes districts*. Barry McGowan, Canberra.

McGowan, Barry (2000): *The Golden South: a history of the Araluen, Bell's Creek and Major's Creek gold fields*. Barry McGowan, Canberra.

McGowan, Barry (2007): "The making of a legend: Quong Tart on the Braidwood Goldfields". *Journal of Australian Colonial History*, 9, 69-98.

McGowan, Barry (2008): "From fraternities to families: the evolution of Chinese life in the Braidwood District of New South Wales, 1850s-1890s". *Chinese Southern Diaspora Studies*, 2, 4-33.

McGowan, Barry (2010): *Dust and Dreams: mining communities in south-east New South Wales*. UNSW Press, Sydney.

McHugh, Evan (2011): *Bushrangers: Australia's greatest self-made heroes*. Viking, Melbourne.

McKee, Jane and Randolph Vigne (Editors) (2013): *The Huguenots: France, exile & diaspora*. Sussex Academic Press, Brighton.

McLaren, Beth (Editor) (1974): *Trials and Triumphs: Barmedman, 1874-1974*. Barmedman Centenary Executive Committee, Barmedman.

McQueen, Ken (2007): "A thirsty and confusing diggings: The Albert Goldfield, Milparinka-Tibooburra, north-western NSW". *Journal of Australasian Mining History*, 5, 67-96.

McQueen, Ken (2008): "Abandoned hopes: reef mining on the Albert Goldfield, north-western NSW". *Journal of Australasian Mining History*, 6, 111-135.

MacTaggart, Claire (2014): "Corner Country, NSW: edge of the map". *Country Style*, October, 90-96.

Madelaine, Victor (1906): *Le Protestantisme dans le Pays de Caux (Ancien Colloque de Caux Havre et Dieppe Exceptés) d'après les Documents Rassemblés et les Notes Recueille par feu M. Émile Lesens; classes, cordonnés & complétés*. Henri Yvon, Bolbec. Reprinted by HardPress Publishing, Miami.

Manneville, Phillippe (1987): "Le temple protestant de Bolbec (Seine-Maritime), 1790-1877". *Revue d'histoire de l'Église de France*, 73(190), 61-64.

Marr, David (2016): "The art of biography: three personal rules of writing". *The Monthly*, December, 64-68.

Martin. E.A. (1884): *The Life and Speeches of Daniel Henry Deniehy*. George Robertson & Co. Ltd, Melbourne and Sydney, and McNeil and Coffee, Sydney, 140-142. purl.library.usyd.edu.au/setis/id/p00030

Mayne, Alan (2003): *Hill End: an historic Australian goldfields landscape*. Melbourne University Press, Melbourne.

Meister, Daniel R. (2018): "The Biographical Turn and the case for Historical Biography". *History Compass*, 16(1). doi.org/10.1111/hic3.12436.

Mentzer, Raymond A. and Andrew Spicer (2002): *Society and Culture in the Huguenot World, 1559-1685*. Cambridge University Press, Cambridge.

Mentzer, Raymond A. and Bertrand Van Ruymbeke (Editors) (2016): *A Companion to the Huguenots*. Brill's Companions to the Christian Tradition, Volume 68. Koninklijke Brill NV, Boston.

Meuvret, J. (1965): "Demographic crisis in France from the Sixteenth to the Eighteenth Century". pp. 507-522 in *Population in History: essays in historical demography*, edited by D.V. Glass and D.E.C. Eversley. Edward Arnold, London.

Miller, E. Morris (1940): *Australian Literature from its Beginnings to 1935*. Volumes I and II. Sydney University Press /Oxford University Press, Melbourne.

Miller, E. Morris (1956): *Australian Literature: a bibliography to 1938, extended to 1950*. Edited with a historical outline and descriptive commentaries by Frederick T. Macartney. Angus and Robertson, Sydney.

Mills, Carol (1991): *The New South Wales Bookstall Company as a Publisher*. Mulini Press, Canberra.

Minet, William and William Chapman Waller (Editors) (1898): *Register of the French Church of La Patente, Spitalfields, London, 1689-1785*. Quarto Series No. XI. Huguenot Society of London, London.

Mitchell, Norman (1989): *Copeland Gold*. Norman Mitchell, Edgeworth, NSW.

Moens, William J.C. (1896): *The Registers of the French Church, Threadneedle Street, London*. Volume 1. Quarto Series No. IX. Huguenot Society of London, London.

Mollat, Michel (Editor) (1979): *Histoire de Rouen*. Edouard Privat, Toulouse.

Morris, Augustus and George Rankin (1883): 'Report of Inquiry into the State of Public Lands and the Operation of the Land Laws'. *Journal of the Legislative Council of New South Wales*, Vol. 34 (1), 271-448

Morrison, Elizabeth (1995): "Serial fiction in Australian colonial newspapers". pp. 306-324 in *Literature in the Marketplace: nineteenth-century British publishing and reading practices*, edited by John O. Jordan and Robert L. Patten. Cambridge University Pres, Cambridge.

Moye, D.G. (1959/2005): *Historic Kiandra: a guide to the history of the district*. Cooma-Monaro Historical Society, Cooma.

Nairn, Bede (1972): "Forster, William (1818-1882)". pp. 199-201 in *Australian Dictionary of Biography*, Volume 4. Melbourne University Press, Melbourne.

Nairn, Bede (1976): "Robertson, Sir John (1816-1891)". *Australian Dictionary of Biography*, National Centre of Biography, Australian National University, http://adb.anu.edu.au/biography/robertson-sir-john-4490/text7337

Nash, Robert (2005): "The silk weavers of Spitalfields". *Huguenot Times*, 6, 1-5.

Nash, Robert (2007): "The Pays de Caux in Upper Normandy: a Huguenot heartland". *Huguenot Times*, 9, 2-3.

Nash, Robert (2009): *The Hidden Thread: Huguenot families in Australia*. Huguenot Society of Australia, Sydney.

Nash, Robert (2021): "Huguenots of Soho and the West End". *Huguenot Times*, 37, 1-5.

Normand, Mathieu (2021): 'Seine-Maritime. Les clos-masures à l'Unesco: une nouvelle étape franchie pour la candidature'. https://actu.fr/societe/seine-maritime-les-clos-masure-a-l-unesco-etape-franchie-pour-la-candidature_41964706.html

O'Reilly, John Boyle (1879): *Moondyne: a story from the under-world*. The Pilot Publishing Co., Boston; *Moondyne: an Australian story*. George Robertson, Melbourne, 1880.

O'Shaughnessy, E.W. (1835): *Australian Almanac and General Directory*. John Innes, Sydney.

Ormsby, H. (1950): *France: a regional and economic geography*. Methuen & Co. Ltd., London.

Page, William (Editor) (1911): "Industries: silk-weaving" pp. 132-137 in *A History of Middlesex*, Volume 2. London. British History Online, www.britishhistory.ac.uk/vch/middx/vol2/pp132137 .

Pascal, Richard (1989): "Hawkeye and Chingachgook in the Outback: James Fenimore Cooper in Australian literature". pp. 67-77 in *James Fenimore Cooper: his country and his art. Papers from the Bicentennial Conference, July 1989*, edited by George A. Test. State University of New York College at Oneonta, New York.

Pearson, Leonard (1858): *The Emigrants' Guide to Port Curtis and the Canoona Gold Rush regions on the Fitzroy River, N.S.W.* Shaw, Hartnett & Co., Printers, Melbourne.

Pierce, Peter (Editor) (2009): *The Cambridge History of Australian Literature*. Cambridge University Press, Melbourne.

Pierce, Peter, Rosemary Hunter and Ken Stewart (Editors) (1993): *The Oxford Literary Guide to Australia*. Oxford University Press, Melbourne.

Porter, Muriel (Editor) (2003): *The Argus: the life and death of a great Melbourne newspaper, 1846-1957*. RMIT University, Melbourne.

Praed, Rosa (1885): *Australian Life Black and White: sketches of Australian life*. Chapman & Hall, London, 67-70.

Praed, Rosa (1887): *The Bond of Wedlock*. White, London.

Praed, Rosa (1902): *My Australian Girlhood: sketches and impressions of bush life*. T. Fisher Unwin, London.

Renders, Hans, Binne de Haan and Jonne Harmsma (Editors) (2017): *The Biographical Turn: lives in history*. Routledge, Abingdon.

Renout, Francis (2018): 'Les clos-masures, fermes typiques du Pays de Clos'. www.geneacaux.net/spip/spip.php?article425 .

Reynolds, E.A. (1989): "Lodges in the Braidwood District during the Gold Rush". *The NSW Freemason*, 21 (5), 11-12

Reynolds, John (1967): "West, John (1809-1873)". *Australian Dictionary of Biography*, Volume 2. Melbourne University Press, Melbourne. http://adb.anu.edu.au/bibliography/west-john-2784/text/3965

Robinson, M.E. (1974): "The Robertson Land Acts in New South Wales, 1861-84. *Transactions of the Institute of British Geographers*, 61, 17-33.

Rockhampton & District Historical Society (1961): *Canoona*. Rockhampton & District Historical Society, Rockhampton.

Rothstein, Natalie (1987): "Huguenots in the English Silk Industry in the Eighteenth Century" pp. 15-140 in *Huguenots in Britain and their French Background, 1550-1800*, edited by Irene Scouloudi. Macmillan Press, London.

Rowcroft, Charles (1851): *George Myford: an emigrant in search of a colony*. Simms & McIntyre, London.

Sangster, Richard (2020): 'Romantic London'. www.romanticlondon.com accessed November 7, 2020.

Schamberger, Karen (2015): 'Exclusion and a call for justice: the Lambing Flat banner'. Humanities Department Seminar Series, Museum Victoria, Melbourne, March 11

Scouloudi, I. (Editor) (1987): *Huguenots in Britain and their French Background, 1550-1800: contributions to the Historical Conference of the Huguenot Society of London, 24-25 September 1985*. Macmillan Press Ltd., Basingstoke.

Serle, Geoffrey (1963): *The Golden Age: a history of the Colony of Victoria, 1851-1861*. Melbourne University Press, Melbourne.

Serle, Geoffrey (1976): "Wilson, Edward (1813-1878)". p. 412 in *Australian Dictionary of Biography*, Volume 6. Melbourne University Press, Melbourne. http://adb.anu.edu.au/biography/wilson-edward-4866/text8131.

Sinnett, Frederick (1859): *An Account of the "Rush" to Port Curtis, including letters to the "Argus" as special correspondent from the Fitzroy River*. Roy & Richter, Printer, Geelong.

Smith, Peter C. (2015): *The Clarke Gang: Outlawed, Outcast and Forgotten*. Rosenberg Publishing, Dural, NSW.

Somerville, Alexander (1839): *History of the British Legion and War in Spain*. James Pattie, London.

Souter, Gavin (1981): *Company of Heralds: a century and a half of Australian publishing by John Fairfax Limited and its predecessors 1831-1981*. Melbourne University Press, Melbourne.

Spence, Catherine (1854): *Clara Morison: a Tale of South Australia during the Gold Fever*. John W. Parker & Son, London.

Spencer, William (1997): *Records of the Militia and Volunteer Forces 1757-1945*. Public Record Office, London.

Stanley, Peter (2014): "Not only, but also: a short history of Honest History". *History Australia*, 11(1), 219-224.

Steele, Allen (2009): "The Luneray Church celebrates 200 years!" *Huguenot Times*, 9, 3-4.

Stephens, A.G. (1906): "The Australian novel". *The Bulletin*, 27 (1399), December 6, 2.

Stewart, Ken (1988): "Journalism and the world of the writer: the production of Australian literature, 1855-1915". pp. 174-193 in *The Penguin New Literary History of Australia*, edited by Laurie Hergenhan et al. Penguin Books, Melbourne.

Stone, Douglas (2011): *Doug Stone's Gold Atlas of Victoria*. Outdoor Press, Euroa.

Stone, Douglas (2014): *Doug Stone's Gold Atlas of New South Wales*. Outdoor Press, Euroa.

Sutherland, N.M. (1987): "The Huguenots and the Edict of Nantes 1598-1629". pp. 158-172 in *Huguenots in Britain and their French Background, 1550-1800*, edited by Irene Scouloudi. Macmillan Press, London.

Swan, Keith (1971): *The Goldfields Society at Temora in 1880*. Riverina Conference Papers, No. 3. Institute of Riverina Studies, Wagga Wagga Teachers College, Wagga Wagga.

Tate, Merze (1961): "Hawaii"s early interest in Polynesia". *Australian Journal of Politics and History*, 7, 232-244.

Tedeschi, Mark (2016): *Murder at Myell Creek: the trial that defined a nation*. Simon & Schuster, Sydney.

Toohill, Trudy (2015): *The Reporting of Ned Kelly and the Kelly Gang.* Bollarong Press, Salisbury, Queensland.

Travers, Robert (1981): *Australian Mandarin: the life and times of Quong Tart.* Kangaroo Press, Kenthurst. Reprinted Rosenberg Publishing, Kenthurst, 2004

Treasure, Geoffrey (2013): *The Huguenots.* Yale University Press, New Haven and London.

Trinder, Aileen and Pat Fearnley (2005): *Unassisted Arrivals to NSW: index 1842-1855.* Pastkeys, Rockdale.

Turner, Henry G. and Alexander Sutherland (1898): *The Development of Australian Literature.* George Robertson & Co., Melbourne.

Van Ruymbeke, Bertrand (2003): "Minority Survival: the Huguenot Paradigm in France and the Diaspora". pp. 1-25 in *Memory and Identity: the Huguenots in France and the Atlantic Diaspora*, edited by Bertrand Van Ruymbeke and Randy J. Sparks. University of South Carolina Press, Columbia.

Van Ruymbeke, Bertrand and Randy J. Sparks (Editors) (2003): *Memory and Identity: the Huguenots in France and the Atlantic Diaspora.* University of South Carolina Press, Columbia.

Vatinel, Denis (1989): "Les protestants en Normandie et la Révolution française. I. Les protestants en Normandie à la veille de la Révolution". *Bulletin de la Société de l'Histoire du Protestantisme Français*, 135, 545-567.

Veitch, Arthur C. (1911): *Mining Laws of Australia and New Zealand.* Bulletin 505. United States Geological Survey, Washington.

Vernon, Alexandre (2014): "Clos-masures du Pays de Caux. La nécessité de planter des arbres et des brise-vent". *Patrimoine Normand*, 69 (février).

Vibart, H.M. (1894): *Addiscombe: its heroes and men of note.* Archibald Constable & Co., Westminster.

Vidal de la Blache, Paul (1903): *Tableau de la géographie de la France.* Hachette, Paris. Re-issued 2009 as part of *Histoire de France* series, edited by Ernest Lavisse. Éditions des Équateurs, Paris.

Waddington, M. Francis (1862): *Le Protestantisme en Normandie depuis la Révocation de l'Édit de Nantes jusqu'a la fin du dix-huitieme siecle (1685-1797).* J.-B. Dumoulin, Paris, and Chez Lebrument, Rouen.

Walker, R.B. (1976): *The Newspaper Press in New South Wales, 1803-1920.* Sydney University Press, Sydney.

Ward, John M. (1969): "Cowper, Sir Charles (1807-1875)". *Australian Dictionary of Biography.* https://adb.anu.edu.au/biography/cowper-sir-charles-3275/text4967.

Watson, Don (2014): *The Bush: travels in the heart of Australia*. Hamish Hamilton Penguin Group, Melbourne.

Watson, Kate (2012): *Women Writing Crime Fiction, 1860-1880: fourteen American, British and Australian authors*. McFarland & Co. Inc., Jefferson, North Carolina.

Webby, Elizabeth (1981) "Before the *Bulletin*: Nineteenth Century literary journalism". pp. 3-34 in *Cross Currents: magazines and newspapers in Australian literature*, edited by Bruce Bennett. Longman Cheshire, Melbourne.

Webby, Elizabeth (2000): "Colonial writers and readers". pp. 50-73 in *The Cambridge Companion to Australian Literature*, edited by Elizabeth Webby. Cambridge University Press, Melbourne.

Webby, Elizabeth (2003): "More than just the news: the literary content of early Australian newspapers". pp. 51-62 in *The Australian Press: a Bicentennial retrospect*, edited by Victor Isaacs and Rod Kirkpatrick. Australian Newspaper History Group, Middle Park, Queensland.

Webby, Elizabeth (2009a): "The beginnings of literature in colonial Australia". pp. 34-51 in *The Cambridge History of Australian Literature*, edited by Peter Pierce. Cambridge University Press, Melbourne.

Webby, Elizabeth (2009b): "Literature to 1900". pp. 15-21 in *Macquarie Pen Anthology of Australian Literature*, edited by Nicholas Jose. Allen & Unwin, Sydney.

Webster, R. (1950): *The First Fifty Years of Temora*. J.A. Bradley & Sons, Printers, Temora.

Wells, William Henry (1848): *A Geographical Dictionary; or Gazetteer of the Australian Colonies: their physical and political geography*. W. & F. Ford, Publisher, Sydney.

Wilde, W.H. and David Headon (1994): "Aborigine in white Australian literature". pp. 2-10 in *The Oxford Companion to Australian Literature*, edited by William H. Wilde, Joy Hooton, and Barry Andrews. Oxford University Press, Melbourne.

Wilde, William H., Joy Hooton, and Barry Andrews (Editors) (1994): *The Oxford Companion to Australian Literature*. Oxford University Press, Melbourne.

Williamson, Geordie (2012): *The Burning Library: our great novelists lost and found*. Text Publishing, Melbourne.

Wilton, Janis (2004): *Golden Threads: the Chinese in Regional New South Wales 1850-1950*. New England Art Museum, Armidale.

Winter, James (1993): *London's Teeming Streets, 1830-1914*. Routledge, London.

Woods, Carole (1985): *Beechworth: a titan's field*. United Shire of Beechworth / Hargreen Publishing Co., Melbourne.

Wright, N.E. (2001): "The problem of Aboriginal evidence in early colonial New South Wales". pp. 140-155 in *Law, History, Colonialism: the reach of Empire*, edited by Diane Kirkby and Catherine Coleborne. Manchester University Press, Manchester.

Wright, N.E. (2005a): "Reading the past: the dispossession of the poor and the Aboriginals in colonial New South Wales". pp. 103-124 in *The River of History" trans-national and trans-disciplinary perspectives on the immanence of the past*, edited by Peter Farrrugia. University of Calgary Press, Calgary.

Wright, N.E. (2005b): "'The Lady Vanishes': women and property rights in Nineteenth-Century New South Wales". pp. 190-206 in *Despotic Dominion: property rights in British settler societies*, edited by John McLaren, A.R. Buck, and Nancy E. Wright. UBC Press, Vancouver.

Wright, N.E. and Buck, A.R. (1998): "Tropes of dispossession: the political unconscious of 'The Land Question' in Colonial Australian literature". pp. 13-18 in *Land and Identity: proceedings of the 1997 Conference*, edited by Jennifer McDonnell and Michael Deves. Association for the Study of Australian Literature, *Armidale*.

Wright, N.E. and Buck, A.R. (1999): "'The Romance of the Blue Books': government publications and popular literature in colonial New South Wales". *Bulletin: Bibliographic Society of Australia and New Zealand*, 23(1), 27-35.

Wright, N.E. and Buck, A.R. (2001): "Property rights and the discourse of improvement in Nineteenth-Century New South Wales". pp. 103-116 in *Land and Freedom: law, property rights and the British diaspora*, edited by A.R. Buck, John McLaren and Nancy E. Wright. Ashgate Publishing Ltd., Aldershot.

Wright, Ray (2001): *A Blended House: the Legislative Council of Victoria 1851-1856*. Department of the Legislative Council, Melbourne. Also in *Victoria: Papers Presented to Parliament, Session 1999-2001*, Volume 17, No. 6. Government Printer, Melbourne.

www.ingramcontent.com/pod-product-compliance
Lightning Source LLC
Chambersburg PA
CBHW051329110526
44590CB00032B/4465